The Roman Republic and the Hellenistic Mediterranean

The Roman Republic and the Hellenistic Mediterranean

From Alexander to Caesar

Joel Allen

This edition first published 2020
© 2020 John Wiley & Sons, Inc.

All rights reserved. No part of this publication may be reproduced, stored in a retrieval system, or transmitted, in any form or by any means, electronic, mechanical, photocopying, recording or otherwise, except as permitted by law. Advice on how to obtain permission to reuse material from this title is available at http://www.wiley.com/go/permissions.

The right of Joel Allen to be identified as the author of this work has been asserted in accordance with law.

Registered Office(s)
John Wiley & Sons, Inc., 111 River Street, Hoboken, NJ 07030, USA

Editorial Office
101 Station Landing, Medford, MA 02155, USA

For details of our global editorial offices, customer services, and more information about Wiley products visit us at www.wiley.com.

Wiley also publishes its books in a variety of electronic formats and by print-on-demand. Some content that appears in standard print versions of this book may not be available in other formats.

Limit of Liability/Disclaimer of Warranty
While the publisher and authors have used their best efforts in preparing this work, they make no representations or warranties with respect to the accuracy or completeness of the contents of this work and specifically disclaim all warranties, including without limitation any implied warranties of merchantability or fitness for a particular purpose. No warranty may be created or extended by sales representatives, written sales materials or promotional statements for this work. The fact that an organization, website, or product is referred to in this work as a citation and/or potential source of further information does not mean that the publisher and authors endorse the information or services the organization, website, or product may provide or recommendations it may make. This work is sold with the understanding that the publisher is not engaged in rendering professional services. The advice and strategies contained herein may not be suitable for your situation. You should consult with a specialist where appropriate. Further, readers should be aware that websites listed in this work may have changed or disappeared between when this work was written and when it is read. Neither the publisher nor authors shall be liable for any loss of profit or any other commercial damages, including but not limited to special, incidental, consequential, or other damages.

Library of Congress Cataloging-in-Publication Data

Names: Allen, Joel, 1970– author.
Title: The Roman Republic and the Hellenistic Mediterranean : from Alexander to Caesar / Joel Allen.
Description: 1st edition. | New York, USA : Wiley-Blackwell, [2019] | Includes bibliographical references and index. |
Identifiers: LCCN 2019001986 (print) | LCCN 2019006263 (ebook) | ISBN 9781118959350 (Adobe PDF) | ISBN 9781118959367 (ePub) | ISBN 9781118959336 (hardcover) | ISBN 9781118959343 (paperback)
Subjects: LCSH: Rome–History–Republic, 265-30 B.C. | Mediterranean Region–History–To 476. | Civilization, Greco-Roman. | Rome–Relations–Mediterranean Region. | Mediterranean Region–Relations–Rome.
Classification: LCC DG241 (ebook) | LCC DG241 .A45 2019 (print) | DDC 938–dc23
LC record available at https://lccn.loc.gov/2019001986

Cover Design: Wiley
Cover Image: © salajean/iStock.com

Set in 10/12pt Warnock by SPi Global, Pondicherry, India

Printed in Singapore by C.O.S. Printers Pte Ltd

10 9 8 7 6 5 4 3 2 1

For Andy

Contents

Preface and Acknowledgments *xiii*
List of Credits *xv*

1   To 336: Four Peninsulas and a Delta *1*
       Timeline *1*
       Principal Themes *1*
1.1   Introduction *2*
1.2   Bronze Age Connections and Dark Age Divisions *4*
1.3   Resurgences of the Early Archaic Age *7*
1.4   Political Innovations of the Archaic Age *8*
1.5   Greeks vs. "Barbarians" *11*
1.6   Athenian Prosperity and its Discontents *12*
1.7   The Rise of Macedonia *15*
1.8   Conclusions *16*
       Further Reading *17*

2   To 336: Roman Origins and Institutions *19*
       Timeline *19*
       Principal Themes *19*
2.1   Introduction *20*
2.2   Italy in the Bronze and Dark Ages *20*
2.3   The Roman Monarchy *21*
2.4   The so-called Struggle of the Orders *25*
2.5   Roman Diplomacy and Empire in the Early Republic *28*
2.6   Early Roman Society *31*
2.7   Conclusion *33*
       Further Reading *33*

3   To 321: Alexanders in Asia and Italy *35*
       Timeline *35*
       Principal Themes *35*
3.1   Introduction *36*
3.2   The Ascent of Olympias and her Family *36*
3.3   One Alexander, in Asia *37*
3.4   Another Alexander, in Italy *41*
3.5   In Egypt and Mesopotamia *43*
3.6   Absolute Power *45*

3.7	The Second Samnite War	48
3.8	Imperial Styles: Persia, Rome, and Macedonia	49
3.9	Conclusions	50
	Further Reading	50

4 To 295: An Elusive Equilibrium 51

Timeline 51
Principal Themes 51

4.1	Introduction	52
4.2	The Limits of Alexander's Mystique	52
4.3	The Infrastructure of Conquest in Roman Italy	56
4.4	Athens under Demetrius of Phaleron	57
4.5	Other Western Powers: Syracuse and Carthage	59
4.6	Political Epiphanies	60
4.7	New Philosophies of Politics and Participation	63
4.8	The Battle of Ipsus and its Aftermath	64
4.9	Rome vs. Italy at the Battle of Sentinum	65
4.10	Conclusions	67
	Further Reading	67

5 To 264: The Path of Pyrrhus 69

Timeline 69
Principal Themes 69

5.1	Introduction	70
5.2	The Education of Pyrrhus	70
5.3	The Collapse of Demetrius Poliorketes	71
5.4	Pyrrhus and Rome	74
5.5	Pyrrhus and Sicily	79
5.6	Celtic Migrations to Asia Minor	79
5.7	Alexandrian Erudition	80
5.8	The Mediterranean Without Pyrrhus	81
5.9	Conclusions	83
	Further Reading	84

6 To 238: The Three Corners of Sicily 85

Timeline 85
Principal Themes 85

6.1	Introduction	86
6.2	The Origins of the First Punic War	87
6.3	The New Roman Navy	89
6.4	The Emergence of Minor Kingdoms in the Hellenistic East	90
6.5	Romans in North Africa	93
6.6	Boxing Matches, Part 1: The Ptolemies and the Antigonids	94
6.7	Boxing Matches, Part 2: Rome and Carthage	94
6.8	Boxing Matches, Part 3: The Ptolemies and the Seleucids	96
6.9	No Peace	97
6.10	Rome's Cultural Mélange	98
6.11	Conclusions	100
	Further Reading	100

7	**To 201: The Expanding Roman Horizon** *101*
	Timeline *101*
	Principal Themes *101*
7.1	Introduction *102*
7.2	Historicism in Literature: Naevius and Apollonius of Rhodes *102*
7.3	Rome's New Neighbors *104*
7.4	Successors to the Successors *105*
7.5	The Origins of the Second Punic War *107*
7.6	Rome's Initial Failures *109*
7.7	Adolescent Kings in Syria and Egypt *110*
7.8	The Five Fronts of the Second Punic War *111*
7.9	Rome, Triumphant and Transformed *113*
7.10	An Imperial Culture *116*
7.11	The End of the Second Punic War *117*
7.12	Antiochus III Becomes "Great" *117*
7.13	Conclusions *118*
	Further Reading *118*

8	**To 186: Hercules and the Muses** *119*
	Timeline *119*
	Principal Themes *119*
8.1	Introduction *120*
8.2	Philip V Faces East, Then West *120*
8.3	"Freedom of the Greeks" *122*
8.4	Romans in Spain *124*
8.5	The Roman Wars with Antiochus III and Aetolia *124*
8.6	Rome and the Other: Embrace and Rejection *129*
8.7	Conclusions *131*
	Further Reading *131*

9	**To 164: Hostages of Diplomacy** *133*
	Timeline *133*
	Principal Themes *133*
9.1	Introduction *134*
9.2	Rome as Referee *134*
9.3	The Power of Pergamon *135*
9.4	A New Balance of Power in the East *137*
9.5	Spain as the Laboratory of Empire *138*
9.6	The Plight of Perseus *138*
9.7	The Sixth Syrian War and the "Day of Eleusis" *140*
9.8	The Year 167 *141*
9.9	Three Celebrations *143*
9.10	Outsiders Regarding Rome *146*
9.11	Conclusions *148*
	Further Reading *148*

10	**To 133: The Price of Empire** *149*
	Timeline *149*
	Principal Themes *149*

10.1	Introduction	*150*
10.2	Internationalized Family Networks in Rome	*150*
10.3	Royal Pretenders	*154*
10.4	The Morality of Empire	*156*
10.5	The Carthage-Corinth Coincidence	*157*
10.6	The Roman Reorganization of Egypt, 145–139	*159*
10.7	Economic Crisis and the Rise of the Tribunate	*161*
10.8	The Reforms of Tiberius Gracchus	*163*
10.9	Conclusions	*164*
	Further Reading	*165*

11	**To 101: The "New Men" of Rome and the Mediterranean**	*167*
	Timeline	*167*
	Principal Themes	*167*
11.1	Introduction	*168*
11.2	Aristonicus and the People of Pergamon	*168*
11.3	Paos, Harsiese, and the People of Egypt	*169*
11.4	Gaius Gracchus and the People of Italy	*171*
11.5	Adherbal vs. Jurgurtha, in Numidia and in the Roman Senate	*173*
11.6	Marius and the People of Rome	*175*
11.7	A Celtic Resurgence	*176*
11.8	Shifts Among the Ptolemo-Seleucids	*176*
11.9	Mithridates VI	*177*
11.10	So-called Pirates and Bandits	*179*
11.11	Conclusions	*179*
	Further Reading	*180*

12	**To 79: Boundless Violence**	*181*
	Timeline	*181*
	Principal Themes	*181*
12.1	Introduction	*182*
12.2	Marius and Saturninus, Cornered by/in the Senate	*182*
12.3	The Cappadocian Throne: Mithridates VI vs. Rome	*183*
12.4	The Origins of the Social War	*184*
12.5	Attempts to Recover Asia Minor	*186*
12.6	The Conclusion of the Social War	*186*
12.7	The Resurgence of Mithridates	*187*
12.8	Sulla Seizes Command	*188*
12.9	Genocide, of a Form, in Asia Minor	*189*
12.10	The Sack of Athens	*190*
12.11	Sulla's Dictatorship	*192*
12.12	Conclusions	*196*
	Further Reading	*196*

13	**To 63: Extraordinary Commands**	*199*
	Timeline	*199*
	Principal Themes	*199*
13.1	Introduction	*200*
13.2	Sertorius, Mithridates, and the "Pirates"	*200*

13.3	Spartacus *202*
13.4	Rome Steadily Consolidates *204*
13.5	The Consulship of Crassus and Pompey *205*
13.6	Lucullus and the Origins of the Third Mithridatic War *206*
13.7	Tribunes and Imperial Commands *207*
13.8	Pompey Becomes "Great" *209*
13.9	Rome in the Absence of Pompey *211*
13.10	The Conspiracies of Catiline and Cicero *213*
13.11	Conclusions *214*
	Further Reading *215*

14 To 52: The World According to Pompey *217*
Timeline *217*
Principal Themes *217*
- 14.1 Introduction *218*
- 14.2 Pompey's *Pompa* *218*
- 14.3 The so-called "First" Triumvirate *220*
- 14.4 Clodius's Imperial Tribunate *222*
- 14.5 Poets and Politicians *224*
- 14.6 The Scandal of the Alexandrian Embassy *226*
- 14.7 Caesar in Gaul *226*
- 14.8 The Return of Cicero *227*
- 14.9 Displaying the "Exotic" *229*
- 14.10 Challenges to the Triumvirate *231*
- 14.11 Conclusions *232*
Further Reading *233*

15 To 44: Roman Alexanders *235*
Timeline *235*
Principal Themes *235*
- 15.1 Introduction *236*
- 15.2 Pompey's Sole Consulship *236*
- 15.3 A Planned Eastern Mission, Divisive and Unrealized *238*
- 15.4 The Start of a New Civil War *239*
- 15.5 Siege and Sojourn in Alexandria *241*
- 15.6 Caesar in Asia, Then Africa *242*
- 15.7 A Month-Long Triumph *244*
- 15.8 Caesar's Hellenistic Capital *246*
- 15.9 Conclusion: Caesar Exits a World *248*
Further Reading *248*

Epilogue: Not the End *249*
Ep.1. New "Funeral Games" *249*
Ep.2. The Second Triumvirate *251*
Ep.3. The Return of Cleopatra and the Ptolemies *252*
Ep.4. The End of the Roman Republic, but Not of the Hellenistic Mediterranean *254*

Index *257*

Preface and Acknowledgments

This book endeavors to put the historical narratives of various regions of the Mediterranean in tandem with each other for the course of the Hellenistic period – the Roman Republic, for certain, but also Greece, Asia Minor, Egypt, North Africa, and western Europe. With a task this enormous, one is reminded of the apocryphal Michelangelo and his thoughts on how to sculpt: what matters about the work is not what remains but what is chipped away. Limited space makes it impossible to go into detail about every aspect of a single civilization or culture. Rather I have favored episodes or trends that, in one way or another, brought one realm into contact with the next, or had a bearing on multiple regional contexts. Political and diplomatic histories tend to receive emphasis, although issues of social and cultural experience are present in every case, especially as they relate to the cosmopolitanism of this world.

In selecting texts to feature, I have eschewed ancient evidence that does not come from the time period covered by the chapter in which it appears. Thus for example, no primary source sidebar includes paragraphs by Livy, even though many influential stories of, say, the Roman monarchy were recounted by him, because he was writing hundreds of years later. While Polybius's researches are referenced on occasion, his own words do not appear until the chapter in which he himself was active. One fortuitous result has been the inclusion of a range of literary genres, including lyric poetry, comedy, epic, and personal letters. I have also made an attempt to incorporate several different modes of evidence, such as epigraphy and papyrology, to introduce the student to a variety of sources of information about antiquity. Unless otherwise noted, all translations are my own. Artifacts, too, date to the period of their chapter. This makes for perhaps strange but ultimately useful placements, such as the portrait of Demosthenes, which occurs in Chapter 5 even though the man himself was dead by Chapter 4, for the likeness was said to have been created and promulgated generations later as an act of political memory. Nevertheless, no standard is absolute: on some occasions, especially in sculpture, we see Roman copies of Greek originals, which recent scholarship has problematized as imperfect evidence for Hellenic art. Similarly, the best we can do for Callisthenes, contemporary historian of Alexander the Great, is a paraphrase – albeit a close and extensive one – by a later Roman author.

Partial funding for this project was generously provided by the Mellon Foundation as part of a grant secured by Michael Wolfe, Dean of Social Sciences at Queens College, the City University of New York. Two New York City institutions were critical for the compilation of images – the American Numismatic Society and the Metropolitan Museum of Art. The professional staff of the former, led by Peter van Alfen and including David Hill and Elena Stoyarik, gave indispensible assistance with the coins that appear herein, and the Metropolitan Museum's policies of open access have rendered its resources and treasures accessible to all. Wizard-like logistical support for acquiring the pictures, maps, and their rights was provided by Kitty Bocking, and the whole project was shepherded ably by Janani Govindankutty, Vimali Joseph, and Haze Humbert of Wiley-Blackwell, including enlisting the aid of two expertly critical anonymous reviewers. I am grateful, too, to colleagues whose conversations have illuminated several points (even if at times I myself remain in the dark, and through no fault of theirs) – Sulochana Asirvatham, Dee Clayman, Nick Cross, Penelope Davies, Josh Kinlaw, Myles McDonnell, Kat Moore, Josiah Osgood, Jennifer Roberts, Mark Wilson, and Liv Yarrow. The book is dedicated to Andrew Rich, who may not know the past of the Mediterranean Sea but certainly appreciates its present.

List of Credits

Map 1.1	*Source*: https://commons.wikimedia.org/wiki/User:Cplakidas#/media/File:The_Roman_Empire_ca_400_AD.png. Public Domain. *3*
Map 1.2	*Source:* Bibi Saint-Pol, https://commons.wikimedia.org/wiki/File:Map_Greco-Persian_Wars-en.svg. Licensed under CC BY-SA 3.0. *12*
Map 2.1	*Source:* © 2013. From *History of the Roman People* by Allen Ward et al. Reproduced by permission of Taylor and Francis Group, LLC, a division of Informa plc. *22*
Map 2.2	*Source:* © 2013. From *History of the Roman People* by Allen Ward et al. Reproduced by permission of Taylor and Francis Group, LLC, a division of Informa plc. *23*
Map 3.1	*Source:* Fig 11.2 *Alexander's Campaigns from Ancient Greece: A Political, Social and Cultural History* by Sarah Pomeroy et al © 2018, 2012, 2008, 1999, pages 440–441. *38*
Map 3.2	*Source:* d-maps.com. *43*
Map 6.1	*Source:* Peter Green "Alexander to Actium" University of California Press, 1990 map 15 p.218. *86*
Map 6.2	*Source:* Based on a map from "The Heritage of Hellenism" by John Ferguson, Thames & Hudson Ltd, London, 1973. *87*
Map 7.1	*Source:* Hoyos, D. ed. (2011). *A Companion to the Punic Wars.* Chichester, UK: Wiley Blackwell. *108*
Map 12.1	*Source:* Rosenstein, N. and Morstein-Marx, R. (eds.) (2011). *A Companion to the Roman Republic.* Chichester, UK: Wiley Blackwell. *193*
Map 13.1	*Source:* From: Cook, S.A., Adcock, F.E., Charlesworth, M.P. (eds.) (1932). *The Cambridge Ancient History, Volume 9: The Roman Republic*, 133–144. Cambridge University Press. *210*
Figure 1.1	*Source:* Prisma/Album/Superstock. *6*
Figure 1.2	*Source:* Reproduced with permission from AKG. *6*
Figure 1.3	*Source:* https://commons.wikimedia.org/wiki/File:Bisotun_Iran_Relief_Achamenid_Period.JPG. Public Domain. *10*
Figure 1.4	*Source:* Photo By DEA/G. NIMATALLAH/De Agostini/Getty Images. *13*
Figure 2.1	*Source:* © TopFoto/The Image Works. *21*
Figure 2.2	*Source:* © fototeca gilardi/Marka/Superstock. *30*
Figure 4.1	*Source:* (a) Greenshed, https://commons.wikimedia.org/wiki/File:Choragic_Monument_of_Lysicrates.jpg. Public Domain; (b) Courtesy of the Smithsonian Libraries, Washington, DC. *58*
Figure 4.2	*Source:* Historic Collection/Alamy Stock Photo. *62*

xvi | List of Credits

Figure 4.3   *Source:* (a) The Metropolitan Museum of Art, New York. Rogers Fund, 1913. Accession number 13.227.8; (b) The Metropolitan Museum of Art, New York. Marguerite and Frank A. Cosgrove Jr. Fund, 2012. Accession number 2012.385.   *64*
Figure 4.4   *Source:* Photo By DEA PICTURE LIBRARY/De Agostini/Getty Images.   *67*
Figure 5.1   *Source:* Photo by: PHAS/UIG via Getty Images.   *73*
Figure 5.2   *Source:* (a) and (b) courtesy of the American Numismatic Society, (c) © The Trustees of the British Museum.   *75*
Figure 5.3   *Source:* The Metropolitan Museum of Art, New York. Gift of Abby Aldrich Rockefeller, 1938. Accession number 38.10.   *78*
Figure 5.4   *Source:* The Metropolitan Museum of Art, New York. The Cesnola Collection. Purchased by subscription, 1874-76. Accession number 74.51.2370.   *81*
Figure 6.1   *Source:* Mhss, https://commons.wikimedia.org/wiki/File:Ashoka_edict_khalsi2.png. Public Domain.   *92*
Figure 6.2   *Source:* Photo courtesy © Archaeological Park of Paestum. Photographer: Francesco Valletta.   *98*
Figure 7.1   *Source:* Photo by CM Dixon/Print Collector/Getty Images.   *105*
Figure 7.2   *Source:* Heritage Image Partnership Ltd / Alamy Stock Photo.   *116*
Figure 8.1   *Source:* (a) Oronoz/Album/Superstock (b) akg-images/Album/Oronoz.   *122*
Figure 8.2   *Source:* Granger Historical Picture Archive/Alamy Stock Photo.   *126*
Figure 9.1   *Source:* Photo by: PHAS/UIG via Getty Images.   *136*
Figure 9.2   *Source:* École française d'Athènes.   *143*
Figure 10.1 *Source:* Author's work.   *151*
Figure 10.2 *Source:* Courtesy of the American Numanistic Society.   *155*
Figure 10.3 *Source:* akg-images/Peter Connolly.   *158*
Figure 11.1 *Source:* Photo by Leemage/Corbis via Getty Images.   *173*
Figure 11.2 *Source:* © Hervé Lewandowski, RMN-Grand Palais/Art Resource, NY.   *178*
Figure 12.1 *Source:* Yale University Art Gallery 2001.87.2744.   *186*
Figure 12.2 *Source:* Adapted from Schazmann and Herzog 1932, pl. 40.   *194*
             Source: De Agostini Picture Library/Bridgeman Images.   *194*
             Source: © Beaux-Arts de Paris, Dist. RMN-Grand Palais/Art Resource, NY.   *195*
Figure 13.1 *Source:* The Metropolitan Museum of Art, New York. Rogers Fund, 1972. Accession number 1972.11.1.   *203*
Figure 13.2 *Source:* Author's photo.   *211*
Figure 14.1 *Source:* akg-images.   *219*
Figure 14.2 *Source:* Bobak Ha'Eri, https://commons.wikimedia.org/wiki/File:060807-002-GettyVilla001.jpgLicensedunderCCBY-SA3.0.   *222*
Figure 14.3 *Source:* Marie-Lan Nguyen, https://commons.wikimedia.org/wiki/File:Frieze_Basilica_Aemilia_Massimo_n2.jpgLicensedunderCCBY2.5.   *223*
Figure 15.1 *Source:* Oltau, https://commons.wikimedia.org/wiki/File:Dendera_Tempel_Kleopatra_Cäsarion_04.jpg.LicensedunderCCBY3.0.   *243*
Figure 15.2 *Source:* The Metropolitan Museum of Art, New York. Edith Perry Chapman Fund, 1949. Accession number 49.11.3.   *247*

1

To 336: Four Peninsulas and a Delta

Timeline

814: Legendary date for the foundation of Carthage
776: First Olympic Games in Greece
Mid-eighth century: Earliest Greek colony in Italy, on Pithecusae in the Bay of Naples. Writing down of Hellenic epics.
734: Legendary date for the foundation of Syracuse
664–609: Assyrian domination of Egypt
c. 600: Approximate date for the foundation of Massilia
c. 561–527: Tyranny of Peisistratus in Athens
550–530: Reign of Cyrus the Great of Persia; conquest of Lydia and Babylon; liberation of Judaea
525: Persian conquest of Egypt
510–508: Overthrow of Hippias and foundation of democracy in Athens
490, 480–479: Wars between Persia and the Greeks
480: Battle of Salamis: Athens defeats the Persian navy; Battle of Himera: Syracuse defeats the Carthaginians
478: Foundation of the Delian League/Athenian Empire
472: Aeschylus, *The Persians*
447–438: Construction of the Parthenon in Athens
431–404: The Peloponnesian war between Athens and Sparta and their allies
359–336: Reign of Philip II in Macedonia
338: Battle of Chaeronea: Philip II defeats Athens and Thebes; death of Artaxerxes III of Persia

Principal Themes

- Cultures and civilizations along the Mediterranean littoral were interconnected in ways both productive and conflicting.
- General prosperity in the Bronze Age (c. 3100–1100) was followed by a period of inactivity in the so-called Dark Age (c. 1100–750) across the Mediterranean, from which complex societies reemerged in the Archaic Age (c. 750–500), a time when major cities like Carthage, Syracuse, and Rome took shape.
- Political innovations of the Archaic period include democracy in Athens, an inclusive imperial system among Persian dominions, and republics in Carthage and Rome.

The Roman Republic and the Hellenistic Mediterranean: From Alexander to Caesar, First Edition. Joel Allen.
© 2020 John Wiley & Sons, Inc. Published 2020 by John Wiley & Sons, Inc.

- During the Classical Age in Greece (c. 500–336), the Peloponnesian War (432–404) pitted Athenian and Spartan networks of allies against each other and grew to encompass theaters overseas, including in Sicily, Egypt, and the Persian Empire. Carthage and Syracuse simultaneously engaged in a long war for Sicily.
- Macedonia and Epirus, in the course of the fourth century, took advantage of privations resulting from the Peloponnesian War to expand their territory and influence, ultimately to prosecute a new war against Persia and the East.

1.1 Introduction

The Mediterranean Sea is locked by land on all sides, and is about as wide from west to east as the continental United States: the distance from Gibraltar to Alexandria is about the same as from San Francisco to New York, and Athens in the middle could be their Chicago in terms of relative positions against the compass. Unlike the United States, it should go without saying, water is everywhere, but it is a sea that is chopped up by a multitude of protruding and receding land masses, islands, coves, promontories, and bays. From most shorelines, it is not uncommon to see more land somewhere on the horizon, a day's boat ride away if wind and current should cooperate (see Map 1.1). The four peninsulas of this chapter title reach toward and twist away from each other. The combination of Italy and Sicily, as one goes southward, pushes at first from west to east, then curls back from east to west like a fisherman's hook. At its tip, it comes within a hundred miles of touching a second peninsula extending north and east from Africa: Cap Bon is modern Tunisia and in antiquity was the stronghold of Carthage. The Balkan Peninsula, culminating in Greece and the Peloponnese, like Italy, also sweeps west to east as one moves south. Its momentum disintegrates into a scattering of islands that skips nearly all the way to the broad west coast of Asia Minor, which is itself surrounded on three sides by the Black, Aegean, and eastern Mediterranean Seas, a fourth peninsula, albeit a massive one whose coasts are far from each other.

These four landmasses came to dominate affairs in the Mediterranean as homes to powerful civilizations, but it is possible to overstate their significance to the exclusion of others. For example, the model overlooks the protruding bump of North Africa that was the heartland of Cyrene, a powerful city-state throughout the Hellenistic period, and it sets aside certain large islands – the Balearics, Sardinia, Corsica, Malta, Crete, Rhodes, and Cyprus – which, with self-sustaining economies of agriculture, fishing, and production in their own right, offered more than just stopping points for seafarers. In the far southeast, or "lower right," corner, the Nile Delta, with its alluvial interpenetration of water and land, constitutes a kind of reverse peninsula, providing both entrance-in as well as security-out.

Depending on one's perspective or inclination, an option of metaphors is available for the student of Mediterranean topography, as it relates to history: are these realms engaged in boxing matches, or conspiring in team huddles? That is, one could emphasize the frequent conflict that flared among the various populations of the Mediterranean over millennia, or one could focus on the enormous abundance that came with communication and trade, which were relatively easy, especially by preindustrial standards. Today the term Mediterranean is used collectively: for travel brochures it might describe a salubrious climate of warm summers and mild winters; on menus, it marks a type of robust but healthy cuisine stocked with peppers, dates, olives, and grapes, and fortified with fish and with the products of sheep and goats, from meat to milk. A certain sameness characterizes the physical world of the coastal Mediterranean even as inland tracts vary widely from hot, dry deserts to well-watered mountain ranges. The entire vast "basin," if it may be called that, has been host to vastly different political regimes, societies, religions, and

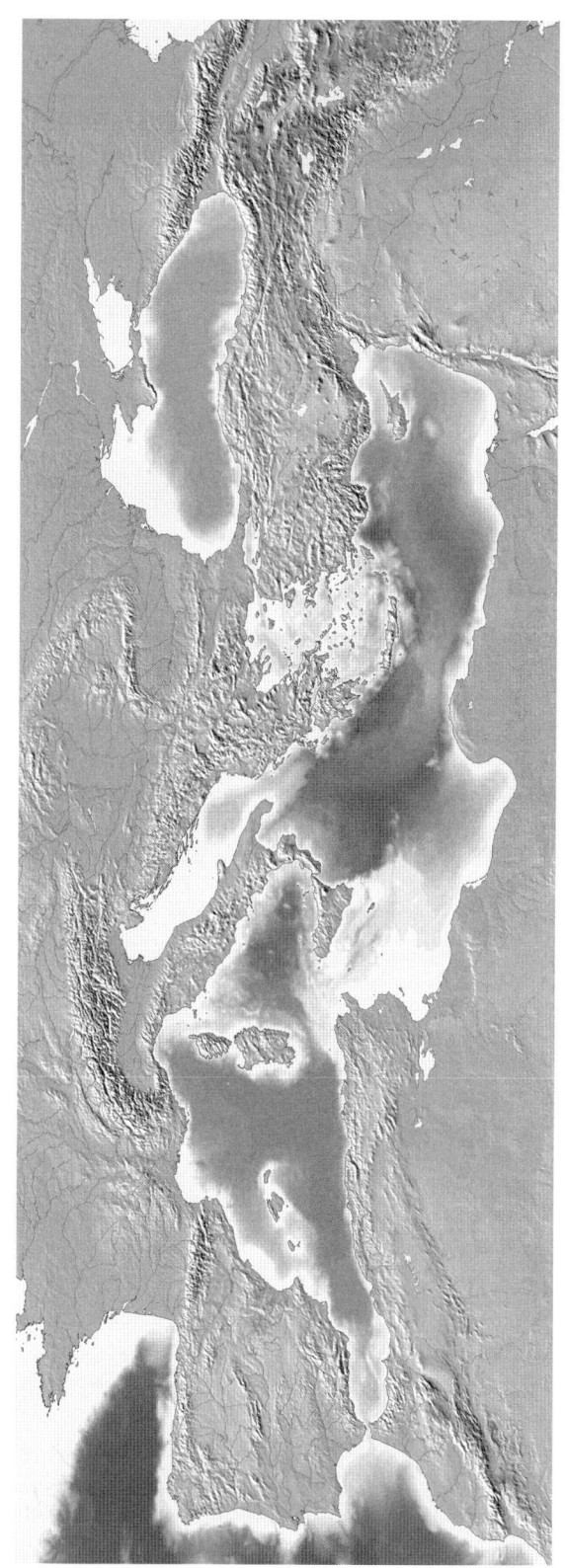

Map 1.1 Topographical map of the Mediterranean world.

empires, and yet in antiquity, any peoples near the sea might be seen as related somehow, with all being members of an *oikoumene*, a Greek term for the part of the world that was "inhabited." Herodotus saw the Etruscans in Italy as the descendants of wanderers from Asia Minor, and the Roman writer Sallust believed the Numidians of North Africa had as their ancestors displaced Persians who settled there and intermarried with indigenous tribes. In the 1940s, the French scholar Fernand Braudel pioneered a historical approach to the Mediterranean that encompassed all its regions as part of single world regardless of language, culture, and nation, a method that was advanced and updated by Peregrine Horden and Nicholas Purcell in 2000. This book is influenced by them, and also by Peter Green's magisterial *Alexander to Actium: The Historical Evolution of the Hellenistic Age* (1990), in its investigation of the interactions of Mediterranean cultures that coexisted in ways both productive (trade, pilgrimage, discovery) and not (warfare, slavery, forced migration), concentrating on a 300 year span of momentous change and volatility.

Our period is framed by the careers of two phenomenal leaders, not owing to any kind of inherent excellence on their part but because of the far-ranging changes that were wrought by their policies and campaigns. Alexander the Great moved Greek culture in a new direction when he led troops out of the Balkans and into Asia Minor, the Levant, Egypt, Mesopotamia, and the Hindu Kush in the 330–320s bce; nearly three centuries later, Julius Caesar did much the same thing for Italy, only this time moving west into Gaul, Britain, and Spain, before his own sojourn in Egypt and the rest of the East. Almost all dates in this study fall "before the common era," and so the abbreviation bce is hereafter generally left out except where context requires it. Two introductory chapters, which form the backdrop for developments in the ensuing sections, review major events and trends up to the launch of the two Alexanders' invasions in 336 (Chapter 3). The current chapter focuses on the East, principally the foundational histories of the Greeks, Phoenicians (which at this point may include the Carthaginians), and other residents of the Persian Empire as found in Egypt, Asia Minor, and further inland. Chapter 2 introduces the contemporaneous rise of Rome in Italy, which, while not disconnected from the rest of the Mediterranean, is treated separately given the prominence achieved by the Republic in later chapters. Historical evidence becomes more nuanced and plentiful as the period progresses, and so the coverage of material becomes denser with each chapter: Chapter 5 examines a 30 years span, while Chapter 15 is devoted to just six. Chapter titles include benchmark dates covered by each, though these temporal borders are porous and nonexclusive, and details that fall within one chapter's formal timeline may appear earlier or later, in keeping with thematic organizations.

1.2   Bronze Age Connections and Dark Age Divisions

The civilizations of the Mediterranean were interconnected from the earliest prehistory. The city-states of Sumer in Mesopotamia and the Nile regime of the Old Kingdom in Egypt both emerged around 3100, the start of the Bronze Age. These predate the Hellenistic world by nearly a full millennium more than the Hellenistic world predates this book's readership, and for our purposes it is sufficient to trace only broadly the relationships that existed among them and others, and the social, political, and geopolitical trends that came about as a result. International ties can be readily demonstrated through a number of evidential strands. A traffic in material goods is clear, as artifacts in Egyptian style and manufacture are found in Bronze Age graves in the islands, the Balkans, Asia Minor, and Mesopotamia, and vice versa. Written records, be they in Sumerian cuneiform, Egyptian hieroglyphics, or the primitive syllabic alphabet of early Greek from the mid-second millennium, record the movements of diplomatic embassies, military regiments, and merchant ships. Vestiges of Bronze Age writings also reveal several other hallmarks of complex societies and economies, such as business contracts, real estate transactions, marriage negotiations, legal codes, personal correspondence, and religious poetry. Mythologies of various regions show that ideas were circulating as easily as artifacts and travelers: a flood story exists in similar dimensions among the Sumerians, the Israelites, and the Greeks, for example. The creation myth recounted by Hesiod in the *Theogony* (c. 700), where younger generations of gods battle their elders, overlaps in significant ways with that of the earlier Hittites. Hittite tablets of the city of Hattusas from the thirteenth century speak of "Ahhiyawa" and "Denyen," almost certainly the same words as "Achaeans" and "Danaans," which Homer used in reference to the Greeks. Linguistic evidence among Indo-European languages also suggests either common roots for different cultures or a thorough trade in loanwords among them.

Powerful monarchies characterize most political systems of the Bronze Age, with the most significant variation being the size of the ruled community. In Mesopotamia, empires rose and fell in the course of the Bronze Age, and in between the imperial successes of a Sargon of Akkad or a Hammurabi of Babylon, city-states governed the territory immediately in their vicinity. By contrast, during the contemporaneous Middle Kingdom of Egypt (c. 2050–1780), the kings in question, called pharaohs, held sway over the entire Nile Basin. Monarchs in these cultures had different kinds of foundations in religion, whether they had exclusive rights to communicate with a deity, or, as in the case of Egyptian pharaohs, they *were* the deity in its earthly manifestation. The pharaoh – or rather, the timeline of the pharaohs, going both backward to those who were deceased and forward to those yet to be – represented an eternal cycle of power passing from Osiris, a god over the dead, to Horus, his son who inhabited the world of the living: any recently deceased pharaoh was playing the role of Osiris, whom the new pharaoh had only succeeded as Horus. As Egyptian society evolved, competing power structures placed limits on the pharaoh's absolute authority. In the course of New Kingdom Egypt (c. 1550–1100), coincident with the last phases of the Bronze Age, a priestly elite took on a greater role in local and regional governance, and when the Egyptian army ventured beyond the Delta into the Levant, the resultant empire required extra levels of administration, which further empowered nonpharaonic officials. Nevertheless, the nexus of Osiris and Horus remained deeply felt, a belief that Alexander the Great, Julius Caesar, and other leaders of the Hellenistic period would take advantage of.

The fusion of religion and politics was less existential in the Greek world of the Bronze Age. Among the Minoans of Crete, whose civilization was at its height from 1650 to 1400, no massive temples are in evidence, at least not on the scale of those in Egypt and Mesopotamia. The Minoans constructed large complexes of rooms, courtyards, and workshops that have reminded some of palaces in the Near East, while others have viewed them similarly to much earlier proto-urban settlements such as at Çatal Höyuk in Anatolia. Contemporary with the Minoans on mainland Greece were the so-called Mycenaeans, named after the earliest discovered and largest of their settlements, Mycenae, the mythic home of Agamemnon. Artistic styles and religious images show that the Minoans and Mycenaeans were in close contact and had affinities with each other, but several key differences existed between them. Living in highly fortified cities atop defensible hills, the Mycenaeans revered military life to a greater extent than in evidence among the Minoans, where the so-called palaces had no large walls and were often plotted in low, flat terrain; the miles of open ocean, and their skill at navigating them, apparently constituted the Minoans' principal line of defense (see Figure 1.1). The Mycenaeans also devoted more resources to the disposal of the dead than did the Minoans, as their enormous subterranean "bee-hive" tombs attest, in contrast with the comparatively paltry funerary remains found from Bronze Age Crete.

Perhaps the biggest difference between the two was in their technologies of writing: whereas hardly more than 100 clay tablets survive from the Minoans, in a pictographic script that is

Figure 1.1 Fresco of Akrotiri on the island of Thera (modern Santorini), c. 1650–1600 BCE. Ships powered by oars sail near an island and harbor, observed by spectators lining the walls. Scholars have been divided over whether the scene depicts a religious procession, a festival, or a naval battle.

poorly understood today (Linear A), the Mycenaeans have left thousands of tablets, whose syllabic alphabet (Linear B) – a technology borrowed from Phoenician writing systems – has been deciphered and translated as a primitive form of Greek. These texts describe a hierarchy of officials among the Mycenaeans, atop which governed a single ruler called the *wanax* with lesser titles beneath him, such as the *lawagetas*, evidently a kind of general, and the *pasireu* (linguistically the same as *basileus* in later Greek, plural *basileis*), seemingly large landowners. In time, the Mycenaeans eclipsed the Minoans: evidence at Knossos, the largest Minoan site on Crete, suggests it was occupied by Mycenaeans after 1400, who entered into a period of ascendancy as the Minoans declined.

Around 1200, much of the eastern Mediterranean experienced extreme pressures, and some cultures, such as the Hittites in Asia Minor, collapsed entirely. The causes of the strains are mysterious. Inscriptions and reliefs in Egypt refer to victories against marauders from the sea (see Figure 1.2). A contemporaneous Linear B tablet from the coastal city of Pylos in Greece intriguingly describes the stationing of troops along the shore to watch for invaders. Both of

Figure 1.2 Drawing from a relief of a mortuary temple of Ramses III at Medinet Habu, Egypt, c. 1150 BCE. Depicting a battle by land and sea, the scene has been associated with the invasion of the Sea Peoples.

these texts have collaborated in the naming of the theory of the "Sea Peoples," a tribe of unclear origins that was in motion either because they were the aggressors in a campaign of pillaging, or because they themselves were in flight from some unknown calamity. Whatever the case, the Egyptian empire shrank back to the bounds of its reliable delta, and the Mycenaean system of the *wanax*, *basileis*, and others, and even the knowledge of writing that allowed it to be documented, ceased to be. Many scholars associate the mythic kidnapping of Helen from Greece by Paris of Troy, and the vengeful fleet of Greeks sent into Asia Minor to get her back, with the crises of this period. Others conflate the arrival of the Philistines beyond Gaza in Israel with the Sea Peoples, as deflected from Egypt, although this is debated.

The ensuing time period, roughly 1100–750, has been called the Dark Ages, because our source material falls away precipitously, and little evidence survives to illuminate the various sorts of activities that we know of for the Bronze Age. Archeological evidence for Greece in the Dark Ages, such as at Lefkandi and Zagora, suggests that society disintegrated into hardscrabble family farms that operated independently and precariously with few of the benefits of trade or urban settlements. At Lefkandi, the cremated remains of a man were found next to the interred remains of a woman in a monumental structure that also included the grave of horses, evidently sacrificial victims. The couple clearly had some kind of elevated status, which suggests that an aristocracy persisted in some form; perhaps these dominant families were the remnants of the landowning *basileis* of the Mycenaean period.

The Nile domain of Egyptian pharaohs also fragmented into smaller, separate kingdoms in the Dark Ages. The so-called Third Intermediate Period, beginning around 1070 with the demise of the New Kingdom, was characterized by divisions among indigenous Egyptians and, eventually, conquest by outsiders such as the Nubians from the inland South. Seafaring of the kind depicted in Bronze Age frescoes was greatly reduced, in tandem with a slowing down of the economy.

1.3 Resurgences of the Early Archaic Age

Beginning in the eighth century, the doldrums gave way to faster movement of both people and ideas across the Mediterranean once again. The evidence for Greece has been especially prominent in modern academic studies, and many innovations of the so-called Archaic Age, approximately 750–500, have come to light there. Agriculture picked back up in its variety and complexity, according to the data of cooking spaces and trash heaps uncovered by archeologists. Landholders, whether owners or tenants, coalesced into regional *poleis* (singular, *polis*), city-states characterized by urban cores surrounded by supportive hinterland. Craftsmen came to specialize in specific skills, and technological advances, especially in metalworking, facilitated yet more efficient use of farmland. Military technology in the Greek world also underwent a revolution at this time, as the hoplite phalanx appears to have taken shape in the eighth century. Closely ordered rows of heavily armored infantry – the fundamental definition of the phalanx – now marched cooperatively on battlefields, with their shields lined up like a moving wall. Enemy phalanxes pressed each other in a great din of clanging weapons to disrupt the opposing side's cohesion and achieve a rupture that would put the losing army to flight. Politics at the time tended to be dominated by an oligarchic elite, perhaps in keeping with the ability of citizens to afford the bronze armor necessary to become a hoplite soldier, yet the *polis* still required a measure of political involvement from *all* of its residents, on a scale that Aristotle later saw as unique to the region. Each *polis* thus developed its own identity and sense of patriotism, yet the common language and religion in Greece allowed for degrees of association in certain facets of life. Mostly notably, Panhellenic (meaning, "all Greek") institutions took shape in the eighth century, such as the Delphic Oracle and the games at Olympia, whose first competition reportedly occurred in 776. The written form of Greek was also honed and practiced in common ways at this time, and literary historians usually assign the first recorded drafts of Homer's epics to the eighth century. The roles played by individual *poleis* in Homer's mytho-history were distinguished by their representative champions, Odysseus for Ithaca, Menelaus for Sparta, Agamemnon for Mycenae, and so on; the catalog of ships sailing for Troy in Book 2 of the *Iliad* thus lists prominent, independent members of a broadly shared culture.

Seafaring staged a comeback in the eighth century, and the Phoenicians led the way. By 800, they were exploring far afield in the West, where they founded a colony to control Cap Bon called Carthage, meaning "New City" in Punic. Greeks took to the colonization trend a couple of generations later. Their burst of activity in the eighth century – in agriculture, technology, defense, government, communication, and trade – had led to a surge in population, and the pressure of too many mouths to feed and the factional strife that went with them was eased in the establishment of independent *poleis* elsewhere on Mediterranean coasts. The earliest Greek settlement abroad, as far as we currently know, was at Pithecusae in the Bay of Naples, from around 775, but within a century scores of new Greek towns had been planted elsewhere in southern Italy, as well as along the coasts of Sicily, Iberia, Gaul, and North Africa, and to the northeast along the Black Sea littoral, as well. Some of the colonies, such as Syracuse, Massilia, Cyrene, and Byzantium would grow to become major powers in their own right. Archeological evidence points to an intriguing amount of mixing with indigenous locals – Africans in the case of Cyrene, Sicels in the case of Syracuse, and Celts in the case of Massilia. Each *polis*'s Hellenic identity nevertheless remained strongly felt and their obligations as Greeks surfaced in times of both celebration, such as at the games, and warfare.

During the period of renaissance in Greece and Phoenicia, Egypt remained a shadow of its former self. No centralized, indigenous pharaonic authority regained control; rather, the region passed from the Nubians to a period of domination by the Assyrian Empire based in Mesopotamia and Asia Minor, beginning with the sack of Memphis in 664. When the Assyrians crumpled and failed due to civil war, their appointed representatives in Egypt became pharaohs in their own right, ruling prosperously from the city of Sais in the heart of the Delta for nearly 140 years.

1.4 Political Innovations of the Archaic Age

Over the course of the Archaic Age the vicissitudes of economy, or sometimes simply of reproductive biology, led to the diminution of old, aristocratic families and the rise of "new" ones. As a result, an entrenched stratum's monopolization of authority came to be challenged by outsiders. The evidence is particularly strong in the Greek world, where revolutions of a type were spurred by so-called *tyrannoi* (singular, *tyrannos*). It would be misleading to translate the term in English as "tyrant," since in antiquity a "tyranny" need not have connoted despotic rule, and often an individual *tyrannos* was popular with certain broad segments of the population, especially the nonelite. A *tyrannos* typically inaugurated populist reforms, such as the sponsorship of new temples, festivals, and infrastructure projects like city walls, aqueducts, and fountains. New political institutions such as councils and assemblies were often part of the scheme, put in place to enhance the voices of the previously marginalized. Examples from the mid-seventh century can be found in Corinth, Megara, and Sicyon, clustered around the Isthmus of Corinth, a crossroads for both seaborne and overland trade, where new, nonagricultural economies first took root.

Athens took its political change to the greatest extremes. It, too, experienced a tyranny, although its period of dominance came in the mid-sixth century, a couple of generations after the upheavals around Corinth. The *tyrannos* Peisistratus's two sons were challenged in 514, when the so-called Tyrannicides Harmodius and Aristogeiton managed to assassinate one of them, martyring themselves in the process and becoming symbols of a political ideology and identity in Athens that would be exploited by later leaders in Mediterranean history. The surviving brother, Hippias, was toppled completely in a civil war of 510, and he fled into exile. The ensuing melee, by turns beyond the scope of this book, resulted in the near-total empowerment of a citizen assembly over all other engines of power. A "true democracy" of adult males, Athens became an anomaly, though it was not yet in the Golden Age for which it would become famous.

The most powerful *polis* in the Greek world of the seventh and sixth centuries, by many arguments, would have been Sparta, which alone of the large city-states avoided the upheaval of a *tyrannos*. Unlike elsewhere, the nonelite citizens of Sparta enjoyed an economic status quo of relative ease, owing to an extensive, and ultimately effective, mission of enslavement against its neighbors in nearby Messene beginning in the eighth century. The helots, as the Messenians were called once subjected to Spartan overlordship, worked the land to such an extent that the typical citizen Spartiate was liberated from the anxieties of sustenance. Rather, their focus, at least according to admiring literary sources of a later age, turned chiefly to the military, and they came to perfect the phalanx form. Boys were housed in barracks and practiced drills from an early age, while girls were expected to exercise their bodies in preparation for *polis*-sustaining childbirth. A monarchy continued at Sparta as a dual institution through the end of the Archaic Age and beyond, into the period covered by this book. An assembly of citizen males was in place, but it had little control over administrative agendas, which were governed by the kings and by a council of the *gerousia*, meaning "elders" (the word has the same root as "gerontology" in English). Helotage thus made Sparta strong, but it would also prove to be a kind of Achilles's heel, as all aspects of Spartan prosperity were founded on this one institution, which was difficult to maintain.

At the time when Athens was in the throes of its tyranny and Spartan power was prominent in Greece, a new leader was rising on a much grander scale east of Mesopotamia. Cyrus, a Persian prince, had consolidated the regions of Media under his single throne by 550. Later legend ascribed near-divine significance to him, with stories of prophecies declared upon his birth that he would someday rule, prompting his jealous grandfather to order him killed, a sentence thwarted by a sympathetic lackey of the king (the tale is similar to that of Romulus and Remus in Rome, Chapter 2). From Media Cyrus went northward, bypassing the strong kingdom of Babylon to the south, and crossed Asia Minor to Lydia, which he seized in 547. This brought Cyrus up to the Aegean Sea and into regular contact with Greeks. He closed the noose around Babylon in 539, from which he returned to his Persian heartland.

The next decade was a productive one for Cyrus as he consolidated his gains and developed an imperial system that was firm in some regards, such as taxation and military recruitment, but operated with a light hand in others, such as in local administration, religious practices, and respect for indigenous languages. In something of a federal system, the realm was divided into satrapies, or administrative units whose territories were largely defined by ethnicity or by regional history. These were sometimes created with strategy in mind, such as when Cyrus liberated Judaeans from Babylon where they had been captive since 587, and transported them back to Jerusalem where they would form a bulwark against, or a steppingstone toward, Egypt on the western side of Gaza. Cyrus's son Cambyses beheld the opportunities of Egypt and conquered it in 525. Literary accounts of Cambyses's evil nature are cause for skepticism, since they level the same tropes of despotism – such as kicking his pregnant wife to death – as are deployed against other famous "villains" of antiquity (like the Roman emperor Nero). Cambyses's history was, in the end, written by his enemies: a nobleman named Darius I staged a coup in 522 and seized power, rebranding himself in the process as a true, or better, descendant of Achaemenes, the forebear of Cyrus and Cambyses (see Figure 1.3 and Primary Source 1.1). Darius's early career, from the fringe

Figure 1.3 Relief and inscription of Darius I at Mt. Behistun, 522–486 BCE.

Primary Source 1.1

The Behistun Inscription

On a rock face on Mt. Behistun in modern Iran, Darius I (ruled 522–486) recorded events related to his consolidation of power. The trilingual inscription appeared beneath a relief showing the king astride a fallen enemy.

> i.1: I am Darius, the great king, king of kings, the king of Persia, the king of countries, the son of Hytaspes, the grandson of Arsames, the Achaemenid. i.4–8: Eight of my dynasty were kings before me; I am the ninth. Nine in succession we have been kings. By the grace of Ahuramazda am I king; Ahuramazda has granted me the kingdom. These are the countries which are subject unto me, and by the grace of Ahuramazda I became king of them: Persia, Elam, Babylonia, Assyria, Arabia, Egypt, the countries by the sea, Lydia, the Greeks, Media, Armenia, Cappadocia, Parthia, Drangiana, Aria, Charasmia, Bactria, Sogdia, Gandara, Scythia, Sattagudia, Arachosia, and Maka; twenty-three lands in all. These are the countries which are subject to me; by the grace of Ahuramazda they became subject to me; they brought tribute unto me. Whatsoever commands have been laid by me, by night and by day, have been performed by them. Within these lands, whosoever was a friend, him have I surely protected; whosoever was hostile, him I have utterly destroyed."

(trans. L.W. King and R.C. Thompson, *The Sculptures and Inscription of Darius the Great on the Rock of Behistun in Persia,* London: Longmans, 1907.)

to the center of power, thus reads as a kind of Persian *tyrannos*, and when Hippias, the toppled son of Peisistratus, was staring down exile from Athens in 510, it was perhaps only natural that he hit upon Darius's court as his refuge.

The Athenian democracy; the Spartan diarchy and slave state; the participatory Persian empire – joining these oddities of politics in the sixth century was Carthage, which attained a level of stability at this time as a kind of republic, governed by elected officials. Its council of elders and assembly were not out of line with other Mediterranean city-states, but is dual executive, called the sufeture, set it apart. The two *sufetes* were elected annually, and although, according to Aristotle, all free men were eligible to vote including the very poorest, a handful of aristocratic clans dominated the office. They and other magistrates and generals were overseen by a Tribunal of 104, empowered with supervisory and judicial authority, again the bastion of elite families. The balance achieved by these various arms of government was praised later by Aristotle, who compared it with the Spartan system of dual kings (which was, dissimilarly, hereditary and lifelong) with adjutant councils and assemblies.

1.5 Greeks vs. "Barbarians"

In 499, Darius I embarked on a program of expansion into the Hellenic coast of Asia Minor, which his empire by then had abutted for nearly 50 years. After suppressing a resistance movement led by the polis of Miletus on the west coast of Asia Minor, he set his sights on the Balkans, intending to restore Hippias to power as a satrap and pawn. This marked the beginning of the so-called Persian Wars, in which luck and courage saved the Greeks on multiple occasions (see Map 1.2). A Persian fleet was shipwrecked in the current circling the Chalcidian Peninsula in 492. A second attempt in 490 traveled by way of the Cycladic Islands, ravaging *poleis* like Naxos *en route*, but the mission was stopped against all odds at the Battle of Marathon, where an outnumbered Athenian phalanx took advantage of its high ground and rushed down upon the Persians and Hippias as they were disembarking on the beach. Suddenly Athens, heretofore a middling polis with a bizarre system of government, had earned a reputation for clever courage.

A windfall in Athens's silver mines in the years after Marathon was prudently directed by the democratic citizen assembly to the construction of a new fleet, rather than to individual dispersements as some had advocated. The policy was fortuitous for in 480 the Persians returned, this time personally led by the king Xerxes, heir of Darius. The Persian army, marching overland into the heart of the Balkans through Macedonia and Thessaly, paused for a time at Thermopylae in order to dislodge a stubborn last stand by one of the kings of Sparta, but eventually descended into Attica and torched Athens, many of whose residents fled in their new ships. Xerxes's success was short-lived, for his fleet was dealt a serious defeat off Salamis, a coastal island visible from the Athenian Acropolis. In the following year, an Athenian led coalition undid the Persian generals again, at the Battle of Plataea. Allegedly on the very same day, an adventurous allied Greek fleet also defeated Persia at Mycale, on the far side of the Aegean Sea. The Persians now chose to pursue other priorities, though they would never stop meddling, at least to some extent, in Greek affairs.

Simultaneously as the Athenians, Spartans, and others were fending off Xerxes's invasion, the Greeks of the colony at Syracuse in Sicily were fighting their own version of the "Other." In 480, a Carthaginian strongman, Hamilcar, swept into northern Sicily, but was driven off by Gelon, tyrant of Syracuse, at the Battle of Himera. His victory would be embellished into epic by later writers, some of whom claimed that the battle occurred on the very same day as the Battle of Salamis. Others competed in recounting anecdotes of Hamilcar's death in battle and

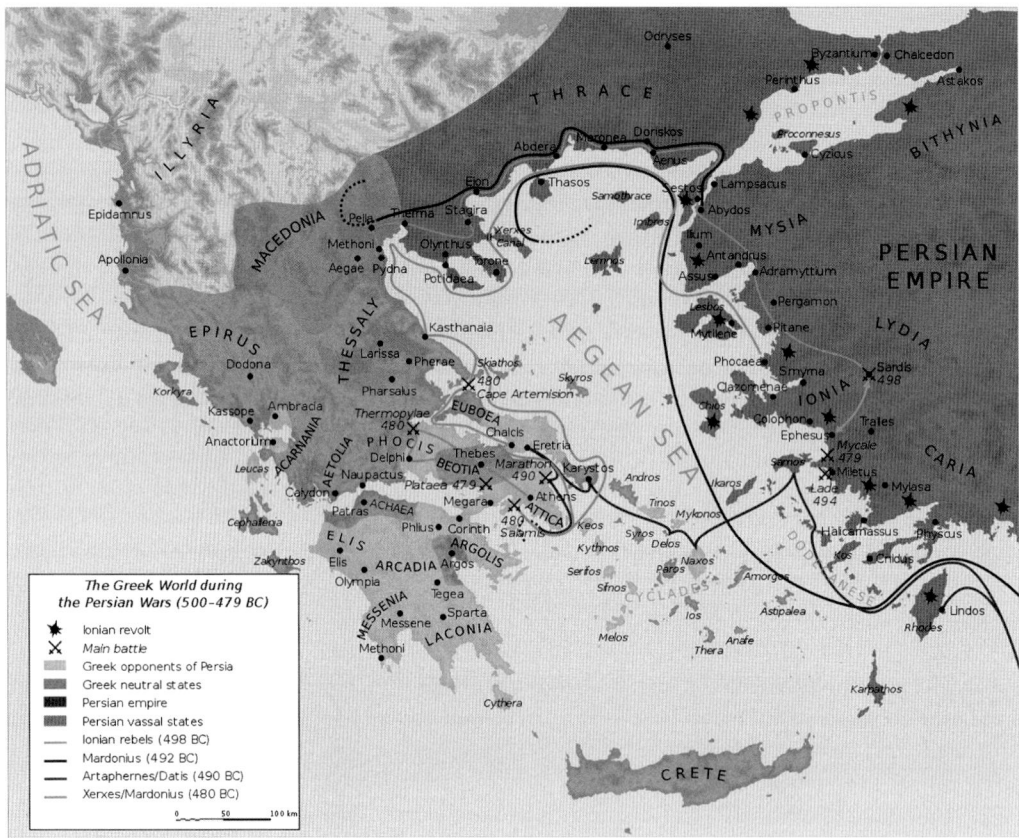

Map 1.2 The Persian campaigns against the Balkan Peninsula in 492, 490, and 480 BCE.

have in common his utter desperation in the face of superior Greek tactics. That Hamilcar had originally been invited to Himera by a Greek who had been driven off by Gelon himself is conveniently overlooked. However Hellenic the Carthaginian politics and economy may have seemed to Aristotle, and however extensive the diplomatic ties were between certain Greeks and Phoenicians, the Carthaginians came to be lumped by Greeks into the same category of existential enemies as the Persians. It was the start of a successful decade at Syracuse, which also defeated a navy of the Etruscans of northern Italy off the Bay of Naples in 474 (Chapter 2).

1.6 Athenian Prosperity and its Discontents

In the fifth century the Athenian democracy was in the hands of formidable leadership. Not satisfied with simply turning Xerxes out, they spearheaded the assemblage of a new naval confederation of Aegean *poleis* tasked with shoring up their recent gains and forming a united block. The so-called Delian League, named for Delos, a small, neutral island sacred to Apollo that became its administrative and psychological heart, was a feat of Athenian organization.

The equitable collection of tribute from member states, the fitting of fleets, the negotiation of military strategy, tactics, and logistics, and the adjudication of disputes required the immediate attention of the Athenians and they were remarkably fast learners. Money poured into Athens and it was in the course of the middle of the fifth century that the Athenians built their famous Parthenon and other buildings on the Acropolis (see Figure 1.4), as well as intensified the level of citizen participation in the democracy, which came to be funded by stipends.

Democracy is arguably at the root of new major literary activities at Athens in the fifth century, such as rise of tragedy and comedy in the theater, attended by audiences that were probably not very different in make up from a political assembly. Tragedians like Aeschylus, Sophocles, and Euripides, and comic playwrights like Aristophanes often alluded, either directly or in subtle ways, to political controversies of their day (compare Primary Source 1.2). The practice of philosophical sophistry, as perfected by Protagoras and Socrates, promoted the skills of quick thinking and penetrative interrogation, which would have taken on new value with the advent of debating among citizens. The philosophical dialogs of Plato also count among the masterworks of literature that are underpinned by a unique, democratic context.

Figure 1.4 Metope from the south side of the Parthenon, mid-fifth century, BCE. The battle between Greeks and centaurs was widely used in the Classical period as a metaphor for the struggle between "civilized" Greeks and "savage" Persians.

> **Primary Source 1.2**
>
> **Aeschylus, *The Persians***
>
> Aeschylus wrote and staged this tragedy in Athens in 472 BCE, not long after the Athenians had defeated the Persians at Salamis and Plataea and in the early years of the Delian League of Greek states, which was formed to drive the Persian presence from the Aegean Sea. In this scene, the queen of Persia, widow of Darius I (see the Behistun Inscription), not yet aware of the defeat of her son Xerxes, tells her servants of nightmares she has been having, which prompt her to inquire about the city of Athens.
>
>> Lines 159–161, 176–197, 230–245: QUEEN: "I've come from my golden palace and the bed I had in common with Darius because anxiety torments my heart. I've had many dreams every night since my son took his army to the land of the Ionians (Greece), but I will tell you about last night's – none of the earlier ones had come with such clarity. Two well-dressed women appeared to me, one wearing Persian dress and the other Doric (Greek), grand and of perfect beauty. They seemed to be sisters of the same race, but one by chance called Greece home, while the other was a barbarian. ... It appeared that they were in some kind of struggle with each other, so my son tried to restrain them and yoke them to his chariot and rein them in. One of them accepted the equipment well and held the bit in her mouth. The other convulsed and bucked and dragged (the chariot) along unrestrained and broke the yoke in two. My son fell to the ground. ... I'd like to know something, my friends: Where is the land of this "Athens," do they say?
>> CHORUS: Far off, near where the sun sinks and sets.
>> QUEEN: But my son really wanted to conquer it?
>> CHORUS: Yes, for all Greece would have then viewed him as king.
>> QUEEN: What is the manpower of their army?
>> CHORUS: It's more an army of quality (than quantity), having done some serious harm to us Medes.
>> QUEEN: Is this because they're good with the bow and arrow?
>> CHORUS: Not at all – they fight with spears and guard with shields.
>> QUEEN: What else? Are they extremely rich?
>> CHORUS: They have a strong vein of silver in their mines.
>> QUEEN: Who tends them as to a flock and leads their army?
>> CHORUS: They're not the slaving types; they're servants to no man.
>> QUEEN: How then do they resist a war of invasion?
>> CHORUS: However it is, they beat the great well-fitted force of Darius.
>> QUEEN: What you say is terrible to think about, especially for the parents (of our soldiers)."

Athenian prosperity and security depended on the Delian League, and if Athens's success called for violent suppression of the members of its league, as it did with the island of Naxos in 470 (which had been sacked by Persia just 20 years earlier) and with the island of Thasos in 465, the Athenians justified their actions by citing the need for defense against Persia, though that now was becoming a shibboleth. To many, the members of the Delian League had become no more than subjects of an Athenian Empire, and resentment grew, especially among the Spartans who were watching affairs from the outside. Allies lined up on either side of these superpowers and war broke out between them when Athens was making a bid to extend its influence west of the Balkans by forging an alliance with the island of Corcyra in the Adriatic Sea; the Aegean Sea, to their East, was already largely theirs. The so-called

Peloponnesian War was an all-encompassing, generation-defining conflict that denuded much of the Greek farmland of its productivity. Thucydides, an Athenian general in the war who was forced into exile in the midst of it, wrote a stirring analysis of the contrasts between a naval power like Athens and a phalanx such as Sparta's, between a democracy and a monarchy. For decades during the war the Athenians continued to flourish in spite of pulling back into their city walls under siege and surviving only through imports, which were untouched by the Spartans by virtue of the supplies arriving by sea into Piraeus, Athens's harbor. They managed to establish a fort at Pylos on the southwestern Peloponnese, on the verge of helot territory, from which they threatened to unshackle the providers of Sparta's livelihood.

In 415, nearly two decades into the war, Athens revived its interest in the western realm and launched a massive invasion of Sicily. In addition to increasing imperial revenue, the move stood to surround even further the enemy Spartans, rather as Cyrus had outflanked Babylon in moving first on Asia Minor. It was not to be: the Sicilian Expedition ended in colossal defeat. Still, Athens held on. The comedies of Aristophanes at the time made frequent references to prominent political leaders, the events of the war, and the hardships that the audience was enduring, but the couching of the commentary in laughter tends to create an illusion of ease. Rather, episodes like the executions of six Athenian generals in 406 for failing to retrieve the dead at Arginusae, even after they had *won* a naval contest there, bespeak the intensity of Athenian anxieties. A Spartan admiral with Persian support finally managed to wipe out the last Athenian fleet and took charge of the city in 404.

Sparta was victorious, but the parochial nature of their political, social, and economic system, dependent as it was on regional slavery, made them unsuitable for international leadership and diplomacy. In the first half of the fourth century, other *poleis* took advantage of the eclipse of Athens and made their own bids for supremacy. Thebes and Syracuse were especially successful. The Thebans reorganized their phalanx by dividing it into more flexible units and were thus able to defeat the Spartans and push them back to the Peloponnese. A Theban victory against their northern neighbors the Macedonians resulted in the taking of diplomatic hostages, which included an adolescent Philip II who would eventually go on to assume the throne of Macedonia after the end of his captivity.

As of 405, Syracuse was in the hand of a new *tyrannos*, Dionysius I, who ascended to political heights on the heels of his successful efforts against a resurgent Carthage in western Sicily. Hannibal, a grandson of Hamilcar (and not the more famous general of the same name who fought Rome), had perpetrated something of a genocide of Greek men at Himera, which he recaptured for Carthage in 409. In 397 Dionysius countered with a surprise attack on Motya, the seemingly impregnable near-island at Sicily's western tip. He also cast his eye northward, establishing colonies on the Adriatic coast and again sailing against the Etruscans (Chapter 2) and sacking one of their principal cities at Caere. Somewhat like Thebes's harboring (and mentoring) of the foreign youth Philip II, Dionysius hosted Alcetas, a fugitive prince from Epirus in the northwestern Balkan Peninsula, whom he helped retake his throne, establishing an important regional ally.

1.7 The Rise of Macedonia

After Philip II seized the throne of Macedonia, unlike previous kings of that realm he set about reforming its army and institutions to match what he experienced in the south at Thebes during his hostageship. He also made a valuable alliance with neighboring Epirus by marrying Olympias, the granddaughter of Dionysius's puppet Alcetas. The two of them turned Pella, their capital city, into a showpiece and enlisted Aristotle's services as the tutor of their son, Alexander. Philip gradually began to acquire new territory. The Greece that he encountered in the south had fragmented after the momentary interludes of Athenian, Spartan, and Theban hegemonies. Some smaller *poleis* had banded together in regional alliances, such as the Thessalian and Aetolian Leagues, but even so, resistance to Philip's creeping growth was lackluster. In 353, the Amphyctionic Council, which governed the Delphic Oracle, invited Philip's participation in repelling a move by Phocis to take over the sanctuary, and he was happy to oblige. From 349 to 348, he laid siege to Olynthus in the Chalcidice and destroyed it.

In Athens, the statesman Demosthenes tried to sound an alarm, delivering a series of speeches called the *Philippics* that denounced Philip and encouraged Athens to rethink its allocation of resources and to refit a navy equal to its glory days. Demosthenes's rival in oratory, Isocrates, argued the other side, proactively inviting Philip to do yet more to bind the Greeks under him, including by pursuing a vendetta against Persia as the Hellenes' common enemy. At the Battle of Chaeronea, Philip and his son Alexander crushed a combined force of Thebans and Athenian resistors. Macedonia was now dominant in Greece, and Philip organized a new Hellenic League, sometimes called the League of Corinth, comprised of the historically strong, but now cowed, *poleis* of the south. The League's reason for being was to seek revenge against king Artaxerxes III, a great-great-grandson of Xerxes. Philip's project must have gained traction when the Great King, or shah, died of an illness or was poisoned in 338: after an interlude of competing princes, Darius III emerged as the sole occupant of the throne, but was shaky as a newcomer Figure 1.3. Philip did not live to fight in Persia: he endeavored to set aside Olympias for another bride, but such dynastic intrigues only backfired and she, it was alleged by some, was the mastermind behind a conspiracy to assassinate Philip at the wedding of their daughter (who, to confuse matters, was set to marry Olympias's brother, also named Alexander).

Dionysius I died in 365 but Syracuse's fortunes continued to improve under the leadership of Timoleon, a general sent by Corinth to represent their interests in the region. The Carthaginians had repaired previous setbacks to some extent by the construction of a stronghold at Lilybaeum on Sicily's western coast. Punic soldiers had also populated Selinus, on the southern coast, introducing the worship of their own Phoenician gods in the process. Timoleon nevertheless obliterated a large army of Carthaginian citizens at the Crimisus River in 340. Thereafter Carthage increasingly relied on mercenaries for its Sicilian wars, and it was able to hold on by means of diplomacy with other Sicilians who shared the humbling of Syracuse as a common goal. In 338, the last in a line of several treaties between Carthage and Syracuse restored their west–east balance of power: after 150 years of on-and-off warfare, the status quo in Sicily between Carthaginian and Syracusan spheres of influence in fact had hardly budged.

1.8 Conclusions

Greek writers, whose texts have had the most influence on modern accounts of antiquity, operated largely under the ideology of Same vs. Other in their accounts of global events and trends: to their eye, the Greeks were the defenders of civilization, and everyone else, whether eastern or western, were barbarians by virtue of being foreign. And yet, a level of factional interconnectedness is unmistakable throughout the Mediterranean. The Persian Wars were fought in spite of an agreement between Hippias of Athens and Darius of Persia; Syracuse fought off the Carthaginians, but a faction of the latter was present on the scene in Syracuse to begin with, not to take over but in order to put an allied camp into power. Individual alliances tend to be subsumed or forgotten in favor of overarching narratives and imaginations of larger ethnic or nationalistic struggles. Athens liked to think that a Persian never would have heard of them (see *The Persians* of Aeschylus), but this was more to "humble-brag" about their achievement than to reflect reality. In the coming years, when Alexander finally crossed into Asia Minor (Chapter 3), many Athenians could be found fighting alongside the Persian armies against him.

Further Reading

Hall, Jonathan (2002). *Hellenicity: Between Ethnicity and Culture.* Chicago: The University of Chicago Press.

Horden, Peregrine and Purcell, Nicholas (2000). *The Corrupting Sea: A Study of Mediterranean History*. Malden, MA: Blackwell Publishing.

Llewellyn-Jones, Lloyd (2014). *King and Court in Ancient Persia, 559 to 331 B.C.* Edinburgh: Edinburgh University Press.

Miles, Richard (2010). *Carthage Must Be Destroyed: The Rise and Fall of an Ancient Civilization.* New York: Penguin.

Raaflaub, Kurt A (2009). *A Companion to Archaic Greece* (ed. Hans van Wees). Wiley Blackwell.

Roberts, Jennifer T (2017). *The Plague of War: Athens, Sparta, and the Struggle for Ancient Greece.* Oxford: Oxford University Press.

2

To 336: Roman Origins and Institutions

Timeline

753: Legendary date for the foundation of Rome
mid-seventh century: Establishment of the Roman Forum
late-seventh century: Growth of the Forum Boarium south of Tiber Island
mid-sixth century: Approximate reign of Servius Tullius
509: Foundation of the Roman Republic led by aristocratic consuls
508: Earliest known treaty between Rome and Carthage
494/3: *Foedus Cassianum*: treaty between Rome and the Latin League
494: Legendary date for the First Secession of the plebs; establishment of the tribunate of the plebs.
467: Colony founded at Antium by Rome and the Latin League
451–450: Codification of the Laws of the Twelve Tables under the Decemviri
445: Lex Canuleia establishing the military tribunate as executive offices for which plebeians were eligible
c. 396: Sack of Veii by Rome
c. 390: Sack of Rome by the Celts
348: Treaty between Rome and Carthage
343–341: First Samnite War
338: Defeat of the Latin League

Principal Themes

- The bend of the Tiber River just south of its only island was an appealing venue for settlements of various ethnicities during the Dark Ages, and the city of Rome coalesced among them in ways that preserved elements of their multiple cultures.
- Tracing the political trends evident elsewhere in the Mediterranean in the Archaic period, Rome began with an entrenched aristocracy ruled by kings, passed through a period of domination by a *tyrannos*-like figure, and ended in the sixth century with a system of elected magistrates called the Republic (*res publica* in Latin).
- Early Roman growth depended on cooperative alliances with regional powers such as the Latin League, the Etruscans, and Carthage, which enabled it to survive various incursions, including a surge of Celtic tribes from the North.

The Roman Republic and the Hellenistic Mediterranean: From Alexander to Caesar, First Edition. Joel Allen.
© 2020 John Wiley & Sons, Inc. Published 2020 by John Wiley & Sons, Inc.

- Roman society was defined by family networks that were strong yet fluid and adaptable, as marriages, adult adoptions, and patron–client relationships allowed for alliances that broadly affected politics and the economy.

2.1 Introduction

Italians participated in many of the same trends evident elsewhere in the Mediterranean from the Bronze Age through the Archaic Age, up to the mid-fourth century. The formation of new city-states took place in Italy in the eighth century, just as it had in Greece, Sicily, and North Africa (Chapter 1). Challenges to dominant aristocracies were afoot by tyrant-like figures, notably in Rome, in the mid-sixth century, at the same time that Peisistratus was doing similar things in Athens. The remnants of both Athens's and Rome's tyrannistic regimes (to coin a phrase) were overthrown and replaced by systems dependent on assemblies in nearly the same year. That Rome's new *res publica* ("Republic") of 509 was far different from Athens's absolute democracy of 508 will be explored in this chapter, but the notional similarities of their paths have still been cause for comment among scholars. Territorial expansion by the Romans also relied on shared, federal identities in its early stages in the fifth century, not unlike the leagues of *poleis* in the Greek world, such as the Thessalians and Aetolians seen in the previous chapter.

To some extent, the parallel qualities between Rome and Greece can be attributed to Rome's own historians, who worked under the influences of older Greek narratives, and who strove to imbue their Italian world with cultural legitimacy through sameness. But it is also possible that ideas traveled, in however intangible a way that may be charted against the traffic in goods and cultures that archeology has shown was increasingly the case in Italy and elsewhere in the Mediterranean in this period. Politics, society, economy, diplomacy, empire, military, religion, language, entertainment: in all respects, Italy and Rome developed their own characteristics, but never in a vacuum.

2.2 Italy in the Bronze and Dark Ages

During the prehistoric period of the Bronze and Dark Ages, Italy was a patchwork of different tribal cultures. Bronze Age settlements have been found up and down the Italian peninsula and what remains of them suggests contacts with the Balkans to the East and with Celtic Europe to the north. In the Dark Ages, the so-called Villanovan culture had a strong presence in central Italy, where Rome would eventually take shape. With cremated remains deposited in hut-shaped urns, it is possible to derive a sense of what the Villanovans expected from their typical homes – simple round structures of wattle and daub (see Figure 2.1). The first emperor of Rome, Augustus, would reconstruct one such dwelling in an outdoor diorama next to his house, which was made of marble, to assert the humble origins of prehistoric Rome and the rustic foundations of its later opulence.

In the Archaic period, just as Phoenicians and then Greeks were embarking on their colonizing activities (Chapter 1), the Etruscans and the Latins, who inhabited the region of Latium, emerged as dominant civilizations (see Map 2.1). Concentrated largely in the hills north of the Tiber River, the Etruscans would have much influence on the development of early Rome as well as make up a segment of its population. Ancient writers were divided on whether the Etruscans were indigenous to Italy or had emigrated from the eastern Mediterranean

Figure 2.1 Cinerary urn in the shape of a thatched-roof hut, Villanovan culture, eighth century BCE.

somewhere in the mists of time. Those in the latter camp were assisted in their arguments by the strong similarity between artistic styles of the Etruscans and of contemporary Greeks and inhabitants of Asia Minor to their East (compare Figure 2.2). Etruscans also sailed a fleet, which, as we have seen, engaged the Greeks of Sicily on several occasions (Chapter 1). Their language, however, was wholly distinct, even though they came to adapt the Greek alphabet for expressing themselves in written form. In any case, their urban culture was highly advanced and some of their major cities included Caere, Praeneste, Veii, and Tarquinia. The modern Italian cities of Orvieto, Perugia, and Arezzo began life as Etruscan Volsinii, Perusia, and Arretium. The people of Archaic Latium, south of the Tiber River could compete with the Etruscans in levels of sophistication, if one were to judge from their grave goods. At Castel di Decima hundreds of burials have yielded weapons, jewelry, vases, votive objects, and even chariots of impressive manufacture. Over time, regional economies grew stronger in tandem with increased opportunities in trade and exchange.

2.3 The Roman Monarchy

Trade required travel, and it was only natural, perhaps, that a central location in Italy, where prevailing north–south and east–west routes converged, would draw the attention of a variety of players on the peninsula. The city of Rome coalesced at the very spot where the Tiber River, at times an untamable gush, was most easily crossed. As its eddies swirled down from the mountains, the waters were slowed by a twofold obstacle about 16 miles from the sea: a sponge-like swamp, later called the Campus Martius by the Romans, soaked up much of the volume, and then an island, the only one in the 250-mile course of the river, halted the current further still (see Map 2.2). On either side of the river just downstream from the marsh and the island, therefore, overland herders, merchants, soldiers, and pilgrims would have paused before making

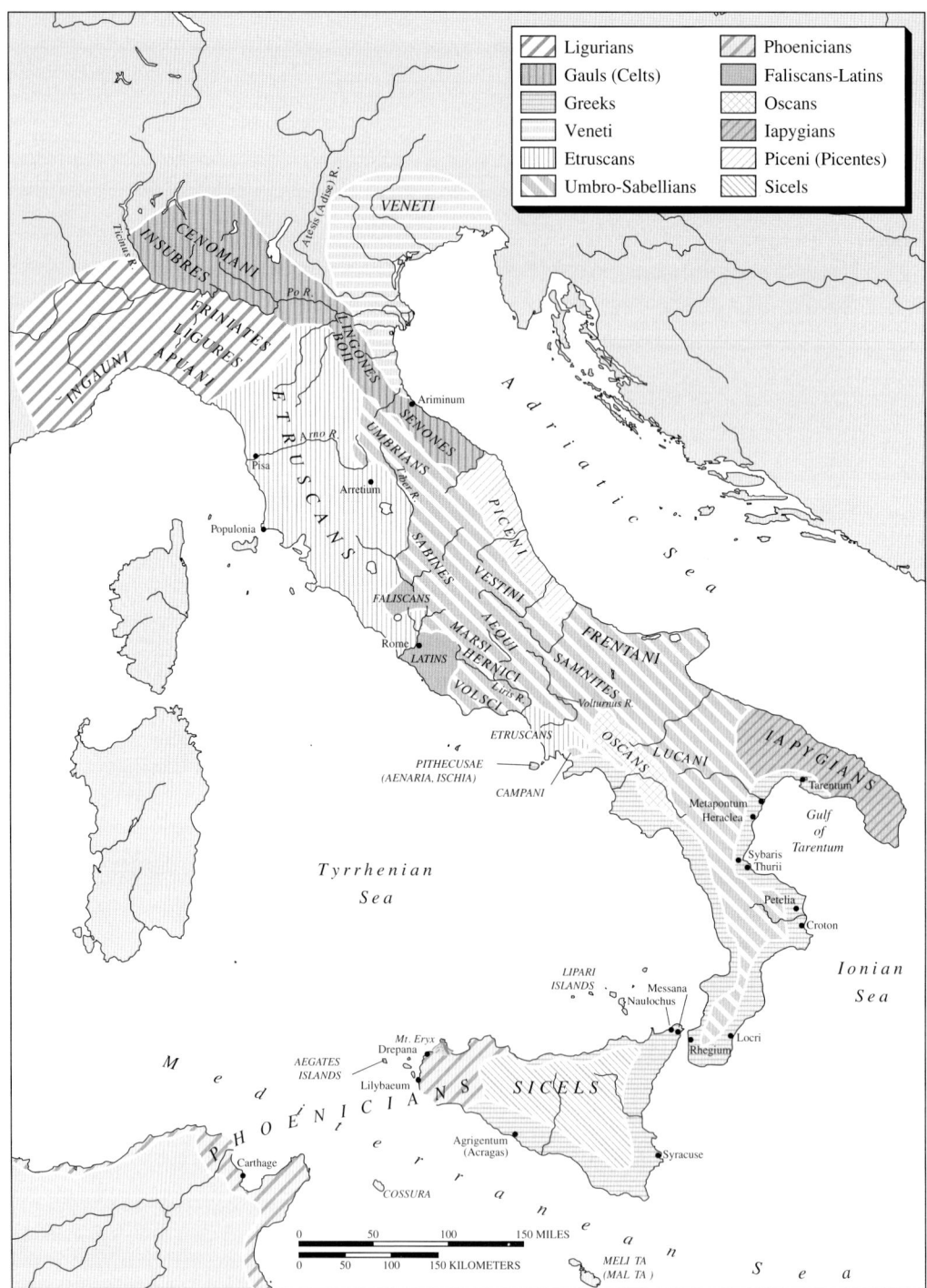

Map 2.1 The regional cultures of Italy in the sixth century BCE.

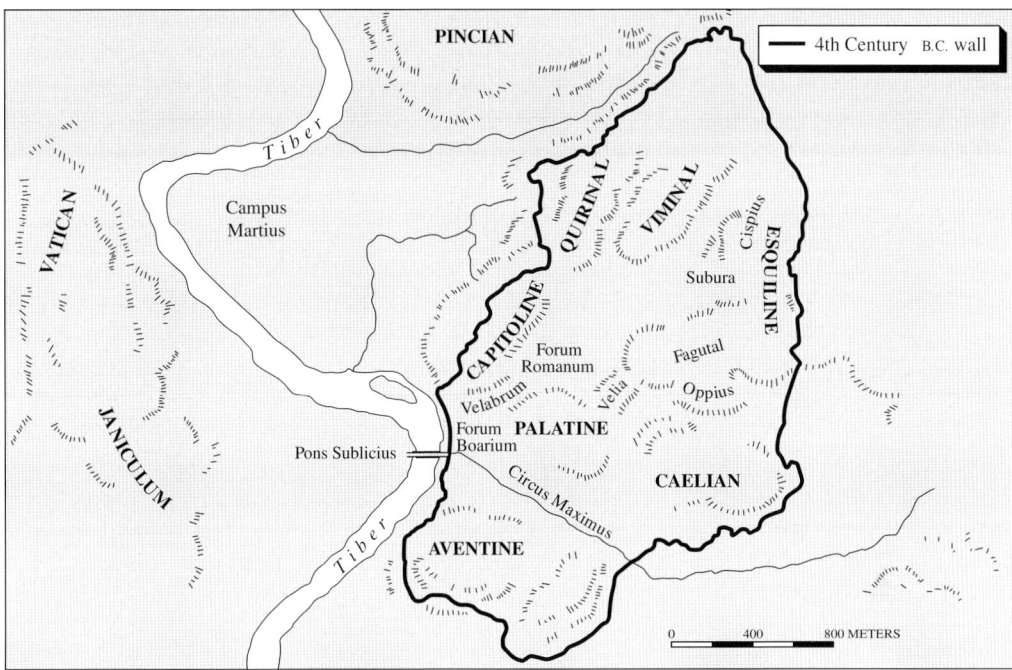

Map 2.2 Early Rome at the crossing of the Tiber.

their way across. One might imagine livestock or stores of foodstuffs or caches of tools, weapons, and other useful daily objects along the banks. From this point to the coast, the Tiber is relatively more navigable than its northern stretches, and a riparian road, later called the Via Salaria by the Romans for its role in conveying salt (*sal*) from the sea for preserving foodstuffs, came to trace its final extent. Over time, the nearby hilltops at the Tiber crossing – the Aventine, Palatine, Capitoline, Quirinal, and Janiculum Hills – were occupied by settlers; the finds from their burials, whether cremation or inhumation, suggest that representatives of several different Italian cultures were present simultaneously. The dating of the settlements to the mid-eighth century suggests that the city of Rome came about, albeit under different circumstances, at around the same time as Carthage and Syracuse elsewhere in the Mediterranean (Chapter 1).

Around the mid-seventh century, the Tiber crossing began to acquire the hallmarks of a unified state that was larger than its individual hills. The valley between the Capitoline and Palatine Hills was paved, in a sense, with beaten earth that implies regular use. For such a low-lying area to be the object of an investment of resources – difficult to defend and subject to flooding from the river – means that the surrounding communities, likely once independent, were now in cooperation with each other. What was once a cemetery became an urban core, soon to be called the Forum of Rome, a central gathering place. Soon after, the eastern bank of the crossing just south of the island was similarly organized as a public space: up and over the Capitoline Hill from the first Forum it would be called the Forum Boarium, likely reflecting its use as a staging ground and market for livestock, *bos* being the Latin word for cattle. Further archeological evidence suggests that monumental buildings soon followed in the center of the Forum, such as the Regia whose name indicates that it originally possessed some kind of royal association. It would be odd for the residential palace of a king to be down from the high ground, and so a function in religion is likely to have been the Regia's principal role, as it was the center of the chief priests of Rome, the *pontifices* (singular *pontifex*), in the historical period. Not far from the Regia and still in the Forum, archeologists uncovered the so-called *Lapis Niger* ("black stone"). Dating to the early to mid-sixth century, it preserves an elaborate inscription in Latin; its fragmentary nature and linguistic primitiveness have kept it from being completely translated, but key words, such as *sakros* and *recei* (as in *rex*) are identifiable and betray, at the very least, some kind of religion and some kind of monarchy on hand.

Kings are abundantly in evidence – indeed, central – in the Roman literary tradition for its foundation, which confirms, in part, what we find in archeology. The stories of the monarchy, as told mainly by Livy and Dionysius of Halicarnassus, both much later in the late first century BCE, are clearly fictionalized. Twins born of a "virgin" escape an evil relative by floating down a river in a basket and are rescued by a kindly mother animal, a wolf, in ways reminiscent of Jesus, Moses, King Arthur, and Tarzan (and Cyrus the Great, Chapter 1). Some amount of "cultural archeology" must be performed on the principal texts to elucidate the historical evolution of the site. Hilltops, for example, again figure prominently. When Romulus and Remus, the names of the twins, squared off against each other in a scenario akin to Cain fighting Abel, the former based his city on the Palatine Hill while the latter was on the Aventine. When Romulus prevailed, he brought the two hills under one regime. Later in his reign, when Romulus fabricated a ruse to attract women to his nascent city, he looked to the nearby Quirinal Hill, the seat of a Sabine tribe ruled by Titus Tatius. Romulus invited them to a festival and, when the Sabine men were distracted, seized their wives and daughters. As the story goes, when Tatius returned with an army, the women, now on the Roman side, rushed in between the battle lines and brokered an amalgamation, and the Quirinal, the northernmost of Rome's seven canonical hills, became part of a bifurcated regime. Roman orators for hundreds of years thereafter addressed their public speeches to "*Romani et Quirites*." It seems that these and other legends preserve the memory of a time when different communities thrived independently on the banks of the Tiber and only synoecized over time, probably in ways that were too mundane or not sufficiently episodic for storytelling. The legends came later, but still preserved the notion of distinct hilltops that archeology has theorized.

The linguistic roots of the names of the first four kings also serve to put two ethnicities at Rome's origins. Romulus and Tullus Hostilius, the first and third kings, have Latin names and toggle between Numa Pompilius and Ancus Martius, numbers two and four, which are Sabine. A literary quality also characterizes their narratives. The "Latin" kings are presented by Livy as especially martial in their outlook, leading troops and conquering new territories, while the "Sabine" kings were seen as more peaceful: Numa is credited with founding the principles of Roman religion (which he acquired from a nymph consort, Egeria) and Ancus was associated with vital infrastructure improvements, such as the first bridge over the Tiber. The fifth king, Tarquinius Priscus, has an Etruscan name and thus adds a third great regional power to the mix, at least linguistically.

Later writers understood that the Roman senate was in existence at Rome's origins. Derived from the Latin word for old (*senis*), the word suggests a board of seasoned and experienced "elders," presumably aristocratic, whose advice kings were expected to heed. The institution had analogs in the Greek world, as we have seen with the Spartan *gerousia*, also derived from a word for "elders" (Chapter 1). One of the principal tasks of the senate, at least according to Livy, was to select the new king upon the death (or in Romulus's case, deification) of the previous one: one senator was chosen by the group to serve as *interrex* for a period of five days or until the next king was elected, whichever came first. If five days were not enough for consensus, a new *interrex* was put forward, and so on until resolution of the throne. Livy also collocates the origins of the "patrician" order with the senate: the inaugural 100 members of the body constituted Rome's founding "fathers" (*patres*, and thus, *patricii*), whose descendants held on to a special status for centuries thereafter. Again, echoes from the Greek world persist: in Athens an aristocracy called the Eupatrids (*eu* with *patr-* meaning something like "well fathered") monopolized power as the *polis* emerged from the eighth century.

Greek elements continue to be found in Rome's early traditions in the nature of political conflict, especially in regard to the supposed sixth king, Servius Tullius, who bears similarities to the simultaneous *tyrannoi* of the Greek world. His name is Latin: "Servius" comes from the word for slave, which is how Tullius's mother is identified in our sources, as a prisoner of war working in the household of Tarquinius Priscus. When Tarquinius was toppled in a coup, the queen Tanaquil, whose widowhood was as yet unknown to the public since she was keeping the corpse concealed, elevated Servius Tullius as her representative until his position was secure enough to hold power. According to Livy, Servius Tullius went on to construct new temples and walls, and he has been associated with the sanctuary that housed terra-cotta sculptures of Athena and Heracles found near the Forum Boarium, which date to the mid to late sixth century.

The details are shadowy, but Livy says that Tullius also invented a new political assembly, the *comitia centuriata*, to supplement (but really, to supplant, for the most part) an older assembly, the *comitia curiata*. Whereas membership in the former "curiate" assembly was determined by a citizen's birth and could not be changed, the centuriate assembly was organized by military units, or *centuriae*, whose members were classified according to what kinds of equipment they could contribute to a shared war effort. Those who could provide horses, an expensive commodity, were at the top, and those who could fit themselves with weapons, from bronze implements on down to javelins and slings, were in descending classes from there. Movement up or down was presumably possible: a *census*, or a "counting," was to be conducted regularly to gauge wealth and thus rank. We cannot recover with certainty what the assembly's responsibilities were at this early stage (or indeed, if this reform even belongs to Servius Tullius). It seems likely that most of the details of Livy's account of the *comitia centuriata* belong to a later phase of the assembly's evolution; nevertheless, its very existence in competition with existing institutions showed that under Servius there were new ways of thinking about who could hold political power and for what reasons. This must have been seen as a challenge to the existing aristocracy, and to burnish his image and to control the damage of having been born a slave, Servius embellished his origins with a story whereby Vulcan, the god of fire, had impregnated his mother in the form of a flame that shot out from the hearth. He was thus not only the son of a god, but of a mother whose ostensibly humiliating plight – a slavewoman in the kitchen – was, in fact, integral to her destiny. Many of these attributes of Servius – an outsider who came to power in unconventional ways, who pursued populist reform, and who propagated stories of, or at least association with, divinity – are found in Peisistratus of Athens and other *tyrannoi* of Greece's peninsula, as well as among Cyrus and then Darius in Persia (Chapter 1).

2.4 The so-called Struggle of the Orders

If Servius Tullius's regime as the sixth of the alleged seven kings of Rome in fact constituted a revolution on the order of a Greek-style *tyrannos*, then what came within a generation after his death might be seen as a counter-revolution. The story of the Rape of Lucretia has been recounted for millennia for its conflation of female chastity with the ethics of the body politic. Sextus Tarquinius, in some accounts a grandson of the ex-slave Servius Tullius and son of the seventh king, Tarquinius Superbus, conceived a passion for the noblewoman Lucretia, but when she refused his advances, threatened to frame her for adultery by killing her and a slave and saying that he had found them together in bed. Cornered, she submitted to the rape, but afterwards told her patrician husband what had happened and committed suicide out of shame.

This was the spark, according to many versions of the tale, that spurred the aristocratic drive to oust the "king" (or, populist *tyrannos*?) from Rome in 509. The replacement for the monarchy, so the story goes, was a pair of so-called "consuls," elected annually from among the patricians by the *comitia centuriata* in a procedure that structurally favored the wealthiest classes. The consuls alone (at first) held *imperium*, or the right to command legions beyond Rome's borders, and also served to enforce laws enacted for domestic contexts. The first two to hold the office were Lucius Tarquinius Collatinus, the widower of Lucretia, and Lucius Junius Brutus, his cousin. The primacy of elections in this regime might seem to imply democratic underpinnings to the new Roman state, along the lines of the nearly contemporaneous democratic reform in Athens (Chapter 1), but restrictions on the consulship were, in fact, reempowering the *patricians* after a period of their eclipse by Servius Tullius. With terms of office of just one year, any ambitious demagogue would have to step down before acquiring much power. The patrician order, or factions thereof, could thus wield tremendous influence on their two peers' decisions during their brief terms in office.

The counter-revolution of Collatinus and Brutus triggered a response from the nonpatrician order, the plebeians, who, it seems, had developed a taste for power, perhaps during the interlude of populism effected under Servius Tullius. Sometime soon after the foundation of the Republic, the first of several alleged "secessions of the plebs" took place. In what was essentially a kind of labor strike, plebeians are said to have abandoned Rome to set up their own state on their own neighboring hilltop. Whether the stories of secessions are true, a degree of compromise between plebeians and patricians is clear: after 509 and perhaps as early as 494 the plebeians won the right to elect their own officials, like consuls also on an annual basis, in a kind of parallel shadow state to that of the patricians. Their leaders, the so-called tribunes of the plebs, had the right to call their own assembly, and eventually, if not right away, to interpose a veto over acts of consuls. They would also come to possess a kind of sacred inviolability, called *sacrosanctitas*, whereby it was not only illegal but also sacrilegious to harm them.

The political history of Rome in the centuries following revolution (Servius Tullius), counter-revolution (a republic governed by consuls), and counter-counter-revolution (election of plebeian tribunes) is sketchy in the extreme. What can be discerned for certain is a kind of back-and-forth between patricians and plebeians, shorthanded by modern historians with the term the Struggle of the Orders, whereby as soon as one side gained some kind of advantage or new office, the other claimed a piece for themselves. At least, that is how later Roman authors schematized the foundation of a system that, by their day centuries later, was characterized by a multiplicity of offices and assemblies, with interlocking eligibilities and confuting clusters of powers. Some signposts along the route are fuzzy, such as the creation of offices like the patrician dictator, who handled emergencies of various kinds; the plebeian aediles, who organized public works projects; and the patrician censors, who determined a citizen's social and political rank. Other episodes in the "struggle," however, acquired elements of drama and left more residual traces, such as the codification of the Laws of the Twelve Tables. According to Livy, the *comitia centuriata* agreed in 451 to suspend its powers in favor of a board of 10 men called the Decemviri for the purpose of legitimizing a formal set of laws. One tradition held that they traveled to Greece to inspect an ancient law code in Athens as a model, but in this case the parallelism with the Hellenic world is clearly a fabrication. In any case, a vast range of laws was indeed established covering topics from the mundane – whether a deceased person with gold teeth could legally be buried with the precious metal still intact (yes) – to the weighty – whether a woman could avoid becoming the absolute property of her husband (yes, if she absented herself from him for three days in a row each year). Complete texts of the laws no longer exist, but scores of them have been assembled from fragments and quotes by later authors (see Primary Source 2.1); famously, the later orator Cicero mentioned that he had had to memorize the laws as a schoolboy. The very codification of the laws, as in many societies of antiquity, may be interpreted as an advancement of nonelite interests, as the written word replaced traditions that

> **Primary Source 2.1**
>
> **The Laws of the Twelve Tables**
>
> A complete text of the Laws of the Twelve Tables, formed in 450–451, does not survive; rather, scholars have cobbled together various quotations of them from later jurists to form a skeletal sense of the code. What follows is a selection of laws relevant to an understanding of the nature of early Roman society, including the second-class status of women, freedmen, and slaves. Restrictions were also placed on political speech and on judges who accepted bribes, demonstrating that the elite were also theoretically under the laws' sway.
>
> > Table 3: (In the matter of debtors), agreements (to repay) are possible, but if there is no agreement, (the debtor) may be held in chains for sixty days. Within that time, they were brought to the Comitium (a public space in the Forum) in the presence of the praetor for three continuous market days and the judgment of the debt was made known. On the third market day they paid the penalty with their life, or they crossed the Tiber to be sold abroad (or to be hired out).
> > Table 4: If a father sells his son three times, the son shall be free from his father.…
> > (A child) born ten months after the death (of his father) will not be considered a legitimate heir.
> > Table 6: (The right of ownership) of moveable items will be established after one year; (the right of ownership) of land or a building takes two years. …If any woman does not want to fall into the possession of her husband (through right of ownership), she should absent herself for a period of three nights each year, and thus interrupt the right.
> > Table 8: If anyone has sung out or composed a song/poem which damaged a reputation or caused an insult to someone else … he should be knocked with a club.…
> > If someone has broken a limb, unless he reaches an agreement, the same damage should be done to him. If he has broken a bone of a free man with his fist or with a club, (the fine is) 300; if a slave, (the fine is) 150. …
> > If a theft should happen at night, and if (the victim) kills (the thief), the thief has been killed justly. A thief cannot be killed if it is light out, unless he defends himself with a weapon. If he does not use it and does not attack, you will not kill him. Even if he attacks, call out first. …
> > No-one shall convene a meeting in the city at night.
> > Table 9: A judge or arbiter appointed by law who is convicted of taking money in order to render a (particular) decision will be put to death.
> > Table 11: Marriage may not take place between plebeians and patricians.

were "remembered" by aristocratic officeholders in ways that were convenient to themselves when dispensing justice.

The drama in the episode of the Decemviri and the Laws of the Twelve Tables came when the board's commission was renewed for a second year, supposedly after ten of the tables had been promulgated. As Livy and others record, the Decemviri, now under the leadership of the patrician Appius Claudius, began to abuse its authority. Acting secretively, they conspired to dismantle and revoke the plebeians' right to elect their tribunes. Villainy allegedly reached a crescendo when Appius Claudius conceived a passion for a defenseless plebeian girl, Verginia. He plotted to abduct her, only to be thwarted when her father himself killed Verginia to save her from ignominy. Again, we must interpret the account for its political rhetoric rather than its melodrama: the story is clearly a politically motivated rejoinder to the Lucretia narrative, this time with a patrician devil victimizing a plebeian innocent rather than the other way around, where the low-down Sextus raped the noble Lucretia.

That the systemic political disagreements between the patrician and plebeian orders were represented by metaphors of the rape of virtuous women on the other "side" demonstrates how the issues of property and honor were twinned in the conflicts. In an ancient society, the inheritance of wealth, and also of reputation, was seen to depend on the chastity of a family's women. The establishment of legitimate birth – only achievable to ancients' eyes if women were pure and trustworthy by some fungible definition – entitled one to his ancestors' status and estate, and the desecration of a woman like Lucretia or Virginia could lead to real poverty, as well as to shame. The role of family and marriage in the patrician–plebeian conflict is further underscored by the text of Appius Claudius Decemvir's eleventh table, so far as we know it, which barred intermarriage between patricians and plebeians, thereby keeping them inextricably separate. Further demonstrating the heat of the issue of families, social order, and what defined both, the eleventh table was explicitly overturned just five years later by the *Lex Canuleia* of 445, permitting intermarriage again.

Another provision of the *Lex Canuleia* of 445 that was oriented around plebeian interests was the creation of a new executive office, the so-called consular tribunes. The magistracy is poorly understood today; what is known, as collected by Timothy Cornell, is that in the 70 years from 445 to 375, the electorate chose consular tribunes to serve in the place of the dual consulship 47 times, with the remaining 22 cases being, apparently, the consulship as designed by Brutus and Collatinus. The number of consular tribunes varied; in 444 and several other years, there were three, and in 380, there were as many as nine. Patricians still dominated the office – plebeians were elected for only eight of the years in this span – but the very eligibility of plebeians for office might have been seen as progress to some. The access of plebeians to executive roles continued as a bone of contention. New legislation of 367, proposed by tribunes Gaius Licinius Stolo and Lucius Sextius Lateranus (the Licinio-Sextian legislation), provided that one consul every year could be a plebeian. Some years later, it was stipulated further that one consul *must* be plebeian, a requirement that held nearly consistently for centuries. Plebeians eventually won access to all other major offices, too, including censor and dictator; in addition, it should be remembered, plebeians already owned the regular tribunate of the plebs exclusively.

Polybius, a Greek historian of Rome who was active in the mid-second century (Chapter 10), witnessed the end-result of these hundreds of years of political negotiations between the orders and concluded that the Romans had achieved a kind of mixed constitution, with interdependent branches. To his view, the Roman state, like those of Carthage and Sparta reviewed earlier (Chapter 1), was unusually stable because its several factions had institutional roles and were compelled to negotiate and compromise with one another, essentially per statute (though, of course, no formal document like the US Constitution existed). An equilibrium of interests, if not quite "a system of checks and balances," could thus be achieved, at least in ideal terms. As we shall see in coming chapters, at times certain social groups still tended to have an edge over others in civil disputes, and the entire system succumbed to challenges once Roman possessions included overseas territories, and political assignments became both extraordinarily lucrative and far removed from the urban center. Harriet Flower referred to this knotty period of history as one of Roman Republics, plural, in which rules changed fluidly from generation to generation in ways big and small. We should not view the Roman Republic as static politically, but we may conclude, nevertheless, that for hundreds of years it functioned more or less well, handling both grievous crises and daily concerns in satisfactory ways for, at the very least, the survival of the overall state.

2.5   Roman Diplomacy and Empire in the Early Republic

Rome was regionally strong from early in its existence, but for its first several centuries its influence was limited to the area around the Tiber crossing (see Map 2.1). This conclusion comes in spite of literary sources that describe continuous and glorious warfare between certain kings and their surrounding tribes; it will be remembered that the foundational conflict between "Rome" and "the Sabines" under Romulus and Titus Tatius was waged between two hills that are less than one mile apart. Still, the importance of Rome's river to a broader international economy gave it an outsize role relative to other Italian city-states, such as in its relationship with seafaring powers like the Carthaginians and Etruscans. Polybius reported on research that he carried out on old treaties between Rome and Carthage and cited a text of 508, just one year into the new Republic, whereby the Carthaginians were permitted to trade in the city but had to respect the integrity of Rome's allies, especially those on the coast who were otherwise susceptible to Punic incursions. The extent of Rome's negotiating power at such an early stage is difficult to confirm: Polybius struggled with the primitive quality of the Latin that he was reading, rather as modern scholars do in reference to the untranslated *Lapis Niger* above.

A more significant diplomatic milestone for Rome was the so-called *foedus Cassianum*, a treaty between the Romans and several federated cities of Latium to their south, referred to as the Latin League. The date and terms of the treaty again invite comparison with Athens: the *foedus* was struck in the early fifth century and called for Rome to be the most authoritative member in a proportional alliance, rather like Athens's role in the Delian League of 479 (Chapter 1). Allies would contribute to military efforts at a level consonant with their size, and would also reap the benefits of victories proportionately. They shared in the foundation of new colonial outposts, as well, which also had a military purpose. For example, Antium was founded on the coast in 467 under Roman leadership, with colonists not only from Rome but also from the Latin League and from the existing community; in 408, it proved its worth when the Romans defeated the Volscians nearby. Each member of the League would thus come to the defense of the other, but Rome's plurality stake meant that it typically controlled the command of forces. Rome's primacy in the *foedus Cassianum* is also indicated by its being named for a Roman consul, Spurius Cassius.

The fusion of military interests in the *foedus Cassianum* was reflected and reinforced at the level of daily society and economy: citizens in any federated city could enter into contracts with those of another, including for marriage (*ius conubii*), for residency and the purchase of property (*ius migrationis*), and for commercial agreements (*ius commercii*), and would be bound by the laws of the city of record. With each generation, such multiple bonds among the states forged a large regional power. Rome's relationships with the Latins were strong enough by the end of the fifth century for it to undertake a lengthy siege of its closest rival to the north, the Etruscan city of Veii (see Figure 2.2). Situated beyond the Tiber and fortifying a region that abutted Rome's colony at Fidenae (founded in 498), Veii posed an existential threat to Rome's economy. Later writers implicitly compared the war to Homer's Trojan saga by describing it as a 10-year affair with many tales of derring-do and divine assistance – yet again, we see the interest of later Roman authors in bringing their foundational history into line with Greek literary precedents. Upon the fall of Veii, around 396, Roman soldiers asked its goddess Juno if she would like to relocate to Rome and the statue allegedly nodded yes. The story emblematizes Rome's famous openness to foreign cultures as it grew. As for the Veians themselves, some are said to have entered into the Roman system of allies, contributing taxes and troops in the future, while, even so, other written accounts report massive bloodletting and enslavement.

The Roman success at Veii was almost immediately tempered by an invasion of Celts from north of the Apennines in the Po River Valley. Having interacted with colonial Phoenicians and Greeks for centuries (Chapter 1), these Celtic tribes were familiar with Mediterranean culture. Led by Brennus, they breached the walls and took the entire city save the Capitoline Hill. Later accounts feature patriotic anecdotes of holdouts in the citadel, including how the sacred geese of a Juno sanctuary squawked to alert the soldiers when the enemy was trying to scale the walls at night. Eventually, as the story goes, the Romans negotiated a ransom. When the time came to measure out the payment, the Romans balked at the weights the Celts were using in the

Figure 2.2 Terra-cotta statue of Apollo from Veii in Etruria, c. 500 BCE. The artistic style, distinctive of the Archaic Age, is similar to contemporaneous sculpture in Rome and on the Acropolis in Athens, among other examples.

balance, claiming they were heavier than the agreed upon standards, at which point Brennus tossed his sword onto the scale, making it heavier still; Livy says that he cried, "*Vae victis*," meaning something like, "Too bad, you've been conquered."

Following the departure of the Celts, who were apparently satisfied with loot as opposed to land, Rome's military reputation was rebuilt under the auspices of Marcus Furius Camillus, who was viewed by Roman tradition as their second founder after Romulus. Romans appear to have revered foreign conquest to a greater extent than their neighbors from early on, as conveyed by the ritual of the triumph. When a victorious general returned from battle, the senate voted on whether his accomplishments warranted an officially sanctioned celebration. The *triumphator*, as he was called, entered the city in the guise of a god, with painted face and purple cloak, shepherding prisoners of war, diplomatic hostages, and piles of treasure as he took a circuitous route to the Temple of Jupiter on the Capitoline Hill. A list of all *triumphatores*, starting as early as "752," was drafted in 12 BCE under the emperor Augustus; called the *Fasti Triumphales*, it is an occasionally useful historical tool, however late, as well as a testament to the prestige to be gained from military success overseas.

In time the voluntary nature of membership in the *foedus Cassianum* was judged to be insufficient to the Romans, and in 381, Tusculum, the federation's second city, was conquered outright and subsumed under a Roman hegemony with tax and military obligations set by Rome, rather like their settlement with the defeated Veians. Soon after, from 376 to 367, the tribunes Licinius and Sextius embarked on their proposals to reform the Roman state to do away with the consular tribunes and ensure one consul of the pair always be a plebeian (see earlier). As part of their program Licinius and Sextius also tackled issues related to territorial expansion. They required that the new parcels of land that were being acquired through the rougher treatment of Rome's Italian allies should not be concentrated in the hands of any one family or order. With limits set at 500 *iugera*, or about 320 acres, per landholder, much of the territory was divided into smaller portions and distributed to soldiers and veterans. Soon after, with Rome returned to a dual consulship as its executive, a new office of the praetorship was created. Restricted to the patrician order, the magistracy was meant to provide a governing voice in the city of Rome, given that the two consuls were at this point typically on campaign elsewhere throughout their terms. All of these measures – the reduction of powerful neighbors, the distribution of newly conquered land, the office of praetor (for which plebeians eventually were eligible, as well) – seem designed to accommodate a foreign policy geared toward general expansion and the health of Rome's soldiering class. Turning back another Celtic invasion in 349 with relative ease, the Romans seem to have hit on something.

By the mid-fourth century Rome was starting to look over the shoulder of the Latin League at the greater Mediterranean powers beyond. In 348, they renewed the treaty with Carthage that by now was over 150 years old (according to Polybius's research). The new iteration allowed for Rome to have a presence overseas, in the city of Carthage itself or in the markets it controlled in Sicily; the treaty's prohibition against a Roman presence in Sardinia, North Africa, or Spain suggests that Roman ships, likely commercial in nature, were developing a reputation. Carthage still retained the right to trade on Italian coasts near Rome. In 343, Rome entertained an embassy from Capua, a large Campanian city beyond the southern border of the Latin League's domain, and answered Capua's call to assist them against the Samnites, a collection of tribes from the mountains. The conflict, called the First Samnite War by modern historians, was short and insignificant (it was over by 341, less than two years later) except for how it revealed the irrelevance of the Latins in the enterprise: Rome was entering, waging, and resolving wars without their longtime regional friends. Cracks in Rome's relationship with the League continued to grow and finally escalated into war in 340. By 338, the Romans had reduced their erstwhile allies and curbed Latin autonomy by themselves imposing obligations. The old rights were altered so that the Latin towns could continue contracting in marriage, real estate, and commerce with Rome directly, but no longer with each other, a bold move on Rome's part toward regional supremacy. Former members of the Latin League now held the status of *civitates sine suffragio*, or "communities without the vote," which were part of the Roman dominion but not participants in its leadership or decision-making.

2.6 Early Roman Society

The reader will have noticed the use of three names, or the *tria nomina*, by Roman males – Lucius Junius Brutus, Gaius Licinius Stolo, Marcus Furius Camillus. The second name, or *nomen*, was the most significant in establishing a Roman's larger clan; by it, an individual Roman could in many cases immediately tell much about the background of the named, including whether he was plebeian or patrician. The third name, or *cognomen*, often established a branch of the clan; it could be derived from a physiognomic characteristic, such as Naso ("nose"), Caesar ("bald"), or Caecus ("blind"), or it could refer to a locality. Sometimes a *cognomen* could be awarded to a holder in recognition for a certain accomplishment, such as for Appius Claudius Decemvir, or Gaius Marcius Coriolanus, who defeated the town of Corioli. The first name, or *praenomen*, distinguished individual members within the clan and branch; about a dozen *praenomina* were in regular use. Women were generally called by the feminine form of the *nomen*, such as Tullia, the daughter of Servius Tullius, or Verginia, the daughter of Lucius Verginius. Sisters would be distinguished by their birth order, with ordinals like Prima, Secunda, Tertia, and so on.

The observation that women did not even hold their own names but were marked rather by what amounted to a filial adjective ("the first Tullian female child," for example) is just the beginning in conceptualizing their subordinate position. They could not enter into contracts without representation by some male in their family, be it a father or, if he were deceased, an uncle, cousin, brother, or even son. Voting was out of the question, and the few cases of women speaking in public were cause for much attention from historians as anomalies. The quality of *pudicitia*, or modesty, was prized, and in many female portraits, albeit later than the period of this book, heads are covered by veils and bodies, by full-length dresses and wraps. Even so, women could own property in their own right and carve out authority and prestige for themselves within hidebound conventions. For example, Vestal Virgins, priestesses who tended the sacred, eternal flame in the Temple of Vesta in the Forum, at times exercised their authority in political ways. But there were very few in number; at a more quotidian level, funerary reliefs of nonelite women demonstrate that they could be engaged in work outside the home, and some epitaphs of elite women proclaimed their role in the dedication of memorials, evidence of their manipulating their estates on their own and taking credit for it.

Family alliances were critical in early Roman society and could be achieved through women, via marriage, or through men, by means of adult adoption. The importance of the former has already been seen, both in the Struggle of the Orders between patricians and plebeians and in the formation of Rome's alliance with the Latin League, given the prominence of the *ius conubii*, or the right of intermarriage. Elaborate contracts could precede a marriage, especially among the elite. Unions where the woman fell under the absolute authority of her husband became less common in the course of Roman history, and wives came to retain a measure of independence. At elite levels, they entered the relationship with property – a dowry – that remained theirs even through divorce, which could be initiated by either partner, or widowhood. Children of the marriage, however, typically remained under the power of the father, the *paterfamilias*. In deep antiquity, a father's control over his sons and daughters was the stuff of stern legends: one general, Titus Manlius Torquatus, had his son executed for disobeying one of his military commands. In practice, however, the *paterfamilias* was mainly a position of respect, holding ceremonial status.

If a man had no heirs, or simply sought closer ties to political allies, he might arrange the adoption of a male from another family. In such cases, the adoptee took on the *nomen* of his new family while his original name transformed into an adjectival epithet as a cognomen. A prominent example, to be seen in Chapter 10, is when the adult son of Lucius Aemilius Paullus was given in adoption to Publius Cornelius Scipio: the adoptee's new name became Publius Cornelius Scipio Aemilianus, which might be phrased in English as "the Scipio with Aemilian origins." Families in Rome were fluid and adaptable and never limited by simple biology.

Beyond the level of the family, an individual Roman also likely belonged to a social network defined by patron–client relationships. Citizens of lower rank, as judged by, say, the *census* calculations, may have benefited from the support and favors of someone higher up, a *patronus*, in the form of political connections or economic opportunities. In return, the *cliens*, or client, might organize informal crowds or formal voting blocs when momentous decisions that affected the *patronus* were in the offing. Rome was a slaveholding society, especially among the elite, and if a slave were manumitted, as a freed person – called a *libertus* or *liberta* – he or she continued to function among the former owner's *clientela*. The Roman conception of mutual benefits between clients and patrons also characterized their attitudes toward the gods via sacrifice and other offering: *do ut des*, or "I give to you, [the god], so that you may give back [to me] in return" was a governing principle of Roman religion, a relationship marked by a power differential but all the while reciprocal.

Nowhere was the symbiosis of an elite Roman's family and his *clientela* more pronounced than in a funeral. As Polybius describes it, a procession of all who knew or owed some form of allegiance to the deceased accompanied the body through the city streets on the way to a tomb outside the walls. Living heirs would wear the wax masks of previous ancestors, called *imagines*, to effect a kind of cosmic reunion of the entire family, transcending time. Clients of various types would be expected to swell the procession and make a greater impression before the spectators. A new *imago* would be fashioned as a representation of the recently deceased, to be used at the next procession. All of the wax masks were housed in the entrance hall, or atrium, of a family's principal residence, to remind visitors, clients among them, of their longevity and prominence.

2.7 Conclusion

By 336, once-powerful regimes in both the Greek and Italian worlds had folded and opportunities were open for newcomers onto the scene: the dominant *poleis* of Classical Greece, be they in the Balkan Peninsula, the islands, or on the coast of Asia Minor, had succumbed to the authority of Macedonia, and in Italy, the largest towns of the Latin League and the southernmost Etruscans had been suborned under Roman hegemony. Writers in the Greek world had begun to take notice of the growing power in Italy: at some time in the fourth century the historian Alcimus of Sicily suggested Romulus was a descendant of Aeneas, a Trojan hero mentioned by Homer who escaped the fall of his city to settle in Latium. In terms of other powers, by 336 Carthage and Syracuse had agreed to a kind of draw, with wealthy Sicily still divided between them, and the Persian Empire was under the control of Darius III, who had ascended to the throne that very year (Chapter 1).

None of the above powers were static or monolithic. The internal disputes in Roman politics were far from resolved, and the ruling dynasty in Macedonia had obvious fissures undercutting it. Whatever the regime, activity overseas, whether military or commercial, could broaden a faction's prospects and shore up its position. Both Macedonia and Rome would find success in foreign wars in the next decades. While Macedonia's would be far-ranging, Rome's would be more geographically confined, directed primarily at the Samnites in central Italy. Nevertheless, both regimes, to be reviewed in the next chapter, would come to use colonization in similar ways in holding on to gains.

Further Reading

Cornell, Timothy J (1995). *The Beginnings of Rome: Italy and Rome from the Bronze Age to the Punic Wars*. New York: Routledge.

Flower, Harriet (2011). *Roman Republics*. Princeton: Princeton University Press.

Forsythe, Gary (2006). *A Critical History of Early Rome: From Prehistory to the First Punic War* (rev. ed.) Berkeley: University of California Press.

Holloway, Ross R (1996). *The Archaeology of Early Rome and Latium* (rev. ed.) New York: Routledge.

Mignone, Lisa (2016). *The Republican Aventine and Rome's Social Order*. Ann Arbor: The University of Michigan Press.

Wiseman, Timothy P (2008). *Unwritten Rome*. Liverpool: Liverpool University Press.

3

To 321: Alexanders in Asia and Italy

Timeline

336: Alexander III, son of Olympias, becomes king of Macedonia
334: Invasion of Asia Minor by Alexander III; invasion of southern Italy by Alexander of Epirus; colony founded by the Romans at Cales
333: Battle of Issus; flight of Darius III
332: Siege of Tyre
331: Death of Alexander of Epirus in Italy; visit by Alexander III ("the Great") to the Oracle of Zeus Ammon at Siwa in Egypt
330: Surrender of Persepolis to Alexander; Demosthenes, *On the Crown*
330–327: Alexander in Central Asia
328: Colony founded by the Romans at Fregellae
327–326: Quintus Publilius Philo as consul and then proconsul on mission to Neapolis; start of the Second Samnite War
326–325: Alexander in South Asia
324: Persian affectations of Alexander; mutiny at Opis; exile of Demosthenes from Athens
323: Death of Alexander the Great
321: Battle of the Caudine Forks: the Samnites defeat the Romans; loss of Fregellae

Principal Themes

- With the death of Philip II of Macedonia power was seized by his widow Olympias and her brother and her son, both named Alexander, who embarked on missions of expansion.
- Alexander the son's conquest of the Persian Empire required combat against fellow Greeks serving under Darius III to an unexpected extent, but he made headway with indigenous eastern populations by assuming preexisting vocabularies of power – satrap, pharaoh, shah – for himself and his followers.
- Alexander the brother's attempted invasion of southern Italy found some success over the course of 3 years (334–331) but dissolved with his death in battle. His campaign may have indirectly assisted in the rise of Rome to the north.
- In his later years, Alexander the Great (Olympias's son) was witness to a degree of cultural mélange between Greek and Asian populations, whose motivating factors are subject to debate, but died in Babylon in 323 just shy of age 33.
- Rome was challenged by the mountainous tribes of the Samnites, who crushed and humiliated the Roman legions at the Battle of the Caudine Forks in 321.

The Roman Republic and the Hellenistic Mediterranean: From Alexander to Caesar, First Edition. Joel Allen.
© 2020 John Wiley & Sons, Inc. Published 2020 by John Wiley & Sons, Inc.

3.1 Introduction

As of the middle of the fourth century, Macedonia and Rome were both building momentum in their respective peninsulas – the Balkans and Italy – both of which had been formerly characterized by patchworks of smaller, independent city-states, often at war with each other. What distinguished the two is that while the Romans showed little sign of looking beyond their shores at the time, the Macedonians inherited the ambitions of their Greek forebears and looked both east and west, even after the unexpected assassination of their king, Philip II. His death led to shifts in the terrain of geopolitics and court intrigue, and a successful survival strategy for Olympias, his widow, and those in her camp required both a show of strength in the present and potential for growth in the future. Military campaigns could satisfy both exigencies and to these ends, in 334 Olympias's brother Alexander went in one direction, to Italy, and her son of the same name went the other way, to Persia. That one became "Great" and the other is largely forgotten is partly a function of luck, but could also be attributed to the younger Alexander's military acumen, tactical restraint where appropriate, imperial management, and deft manipulation of public image. No one at the time was likely to have predicted that it would be the teenager, up against a huge, multinational, historically inimical empire, that would prevail, while the other would fail almost immediately against rough, upstart agriculturalists.

Historians traveling with Alexander III, remembered as "the Great," such as Callisthenes, produced elaborate tales of his accomplishments, which were embellished further by subsequent writers over the course of centuries. Accounts of him came to assume a "romantic," novelistic flair, such that interpretations of his motives and methods are difficult to establish at times and have been the subject of considerable scholarly debate.

3.2 The Ascent of Olympias and her Family

The accession of Alexander III to the throne in 336 after Philip was in no way a foregone conclusion. Olympias, his mother and champion, was both female and foreign, from Epirus; their rivals were plenty; and old allies had become untrustworthy. Alexander's cousin, Amyntas, who was also married to his sister Cynane, had blood on his side. Philip's widow, Cleopatra, who had long before supplanted Olympias (Chapter 1), had an infant son who could someday assume the throne. Philip's generals, Parmenio and Attalus, had the best of the Macedonian troops with them, and they were already in Asia preparing for the campaign. To their camps came Athenian envoys, acting under the leadership of none other than Demosthenes, who eagerly reassumed the mantle of Macedonia's most virulent opponent in the South (Chapter 1); believing that Philip's accomplishments were unraveling – as would be in keeping with the flash-in-the-pan quality of past Macedonian surges – he encouraged the generals to use their troops against Alexander. As Athens sought to capitalize on the disarray in the north, so too did Thebes, Argos, Sparta, and other *poleis* of lower Greece, which drove Philip's garrisons from their walls or otherwise protested their independence.

Using diplomacy and charm, it is said, Alexander methodically won over leagues of *poleis*, moving southward from Pella in the direction of the old bases of power. The Thessalian League responded favorably to alleged claims of shared heritage via the hero Heracles. The Amphictyonic Council also transferred its past support for Philip onto Alexander. Such pledges of support convinced Thebes to abandon its ambitions for independence, which prompted Athens to do the same. At an assembly of the Hellenic League at Corinth late in the year, Alexander sponsored a show of allegiance by representatives of the Ionian Greeks, including the great city of Ephesus, which was ever important in spite of its distance away. The audience could not have known that Ephesus was within months of shifting to the Persian column following their own civil war, but intelligence did not cross the Aegean quickly. For the time being, the Greeks came around to Alexander's side; Megara even made him an honorary citizen.

With the emergency of the southern defections in abeyance, Alexander then spent 335 largely engaged in a pincer movement against the tribes of the northern Balkans. He launched a fleet to sail through the Black Sea and up the Danube River into modern Romania to await his overland march from the south. Caught in the middle were Thracian and Illyrian tribes that had harried his and his father's forces in the past and had become even more emboldened by the transience of the Macedonian throne. The campaign was not simple, as on one occasion Alexander had to effect a bold nighttime fording of the Danube to extricate his army from a difficult position. Even after managing a victory, and thanking the god of the river for it, he confronted hostile assaults from other tribes on his return. Success here came at great cost, but the victories were decisive enough to elicit compliments from the Celtic tribes of the northern Adriatic – perhaps associated with the Celts that had sacked Rome (Chapter 2) – in the form of respectful embassies.

No sooner had Alexander turned to his northern border in 335 than Thebes and Athens again dreamed of freedom. Thebes declared its independence anew, and as Alexander was pushing through the gauntlet of Illyrian tribes on his way back home, he knew already that he would have to overshoot Pella and keep on southward before the year was out. This time he did not treat Thebes with restraint, and following a brief siege, obliterated the city. Athens escaped punishment through artful rhetoric and sycophancy and, more important, because of its large navy and its cultural prestige. Meanwhile, as Alexander was prosecuting the siege of Thebes, Olympias dealt with the distraction of Philip's surviving associates at court, contriving the deaths of both Amyntas and Cleopatra, as well as the latter's infant son.

3.3 One Alexander, in Asia

Just as Isocrates had encouraged Philip to use Persia as a common enemy to unite all Greeks (Chapter 1), Alexander sought to depict himself as a champion of Hellenic destiny against the East. At the symbolic crossing of the Hellespont in 334, he sacrificed to the hero Protesilaus who according to Homer had been the first to disembark on Trojan shores. Passing close by Troy itself he affected the pose of a second Achilles, complete with a second Patroclus, Achilles's dear friend, in the form of his boon companion Hephaestion. Later in the year Alexander would be portrayed as Zeus by the painter Apelles, wielding a thunderbolt in a stab at propaganda. Historians in his entourage were brought along to record events as they unfolded; most of their accounts are lost, but they are cited repeatedly by later writers of the Roman Empire and thus act as the filter for most of what we know about this campaign (Map 3.1).

What is striking throughout the uncertain early years of Alexander's reign is the fluidity of various political players and their associations from realm to realm, notably between the Greeks and Persians. Demosthenes had turned to Persia back when he was organizing against Philip II (Chapter 1), and the idea returned in 336: his first thought was to approach Darius III for armies against Alexander, and he only turned to Parmenio and Attalus after being rebuffed. Though Darius declined at first to become involved, later it was he who bankrolled the Hellenic resistance in 335, offering Athens 300 talents to join Thebes's rebellion. According to Diodorus, when Thebes was in the worst throes of the siege by Alexander, its heralds hinted that it was to Persia that Greeks should look for liberation. Once Alexander's position had become unassailable in late 335, his most troublesome remaining opponents, such as Amyntas of Macedonia (a nobleman different from the cousin just mentioned) and Charidemus of Athens sought refuge

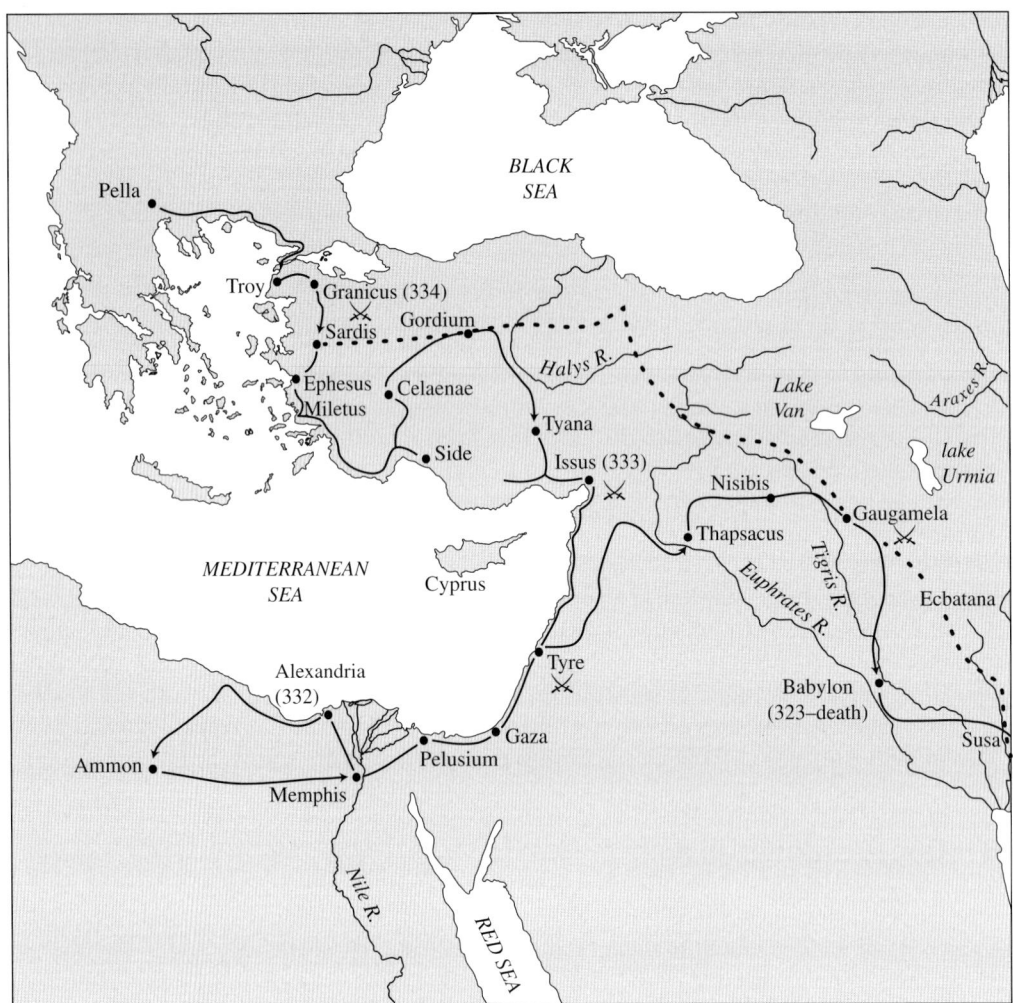

Map 3.1 Alexander's campaigns against the Persian Empire.

with Darius and were accepted gladly. At the Battle of the Granicus River in May of 334, the first major confrontation of the campaign, these two joined a coterie of the satraps of Asia Minor against Alexander and Parmenio.

As ever, the Mediterranean was a complicated arena: for all of Alexander's claims to be prosecuting a nationalistic crusade, there were, in fact, few Greeks from the centers of power in the Classical Age fighting on his behalf. The troops that marched with Alexander and his generals were largely Macedonian, and should Alexander require auxiliaries, it was to mercenaries or local forces in Asia that he looked for support. Only Alexander's naval support was largely Hellenic, but these he disbanded within months of having set out on the mission. For the first several years of the campaign, the states back West that spoke his same language and worshipped his same gods were at best unreliable, at worst antagonistic. Olympias and Antipater, an elderly general left to oversee Greek affairs while the Alexanders were away, confronted sporadic resistance movements.

Foremost among the Greeks fighting Alexander at the Granicus was Memnon of Rhodes: called a mercenary by Diodorus, he had received an army 5000 strong from Darius. Our sources

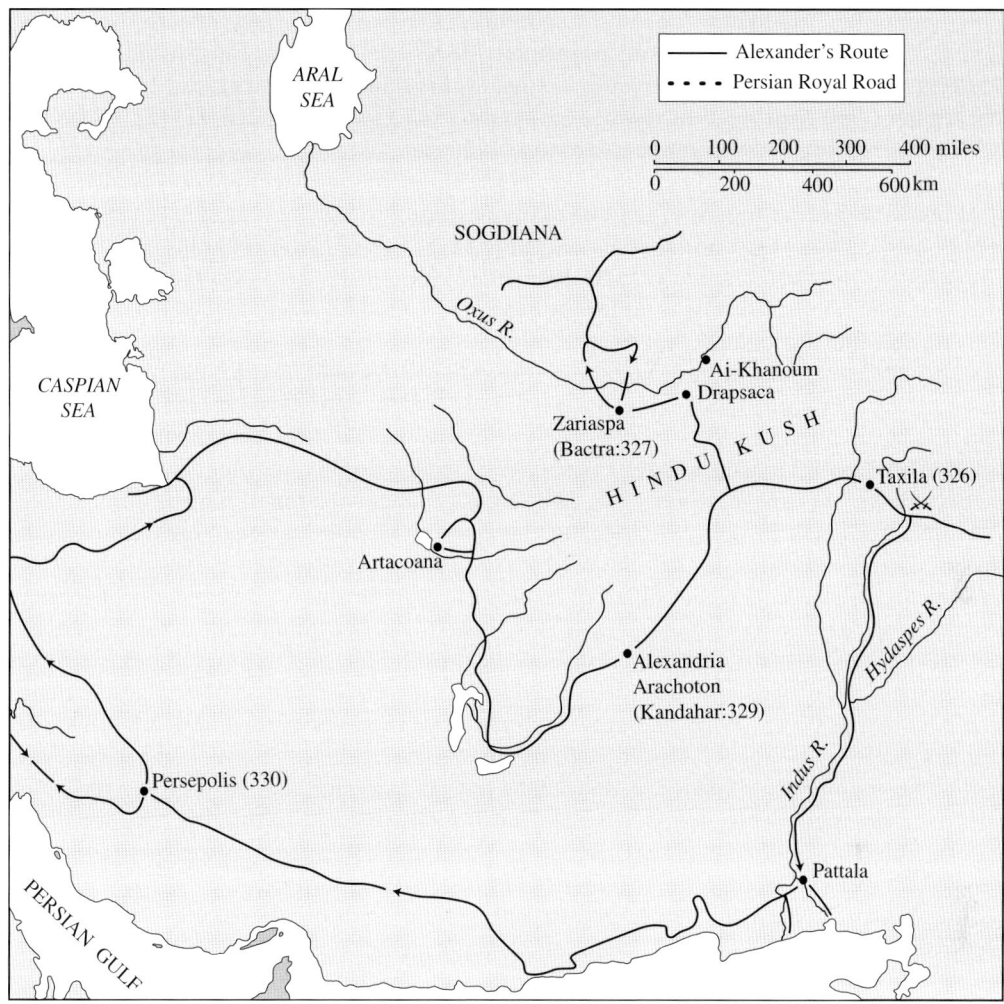

Map 3.1 (Continued)

assert that Memnon argued before the Persians for a strategy of delay, seeking to deprive Alexander of supplies as he roamed through hostile territory. It was only due to *hybris*, say these Hellenophilic sources, that the Persians disregarded his advice and engaged Alexander prematurely. The result was a victory for the Macedonians, though perhaps the hardest won of the war: Alexander himself was nearly scalped from a blow to his helmet, and Memnon managed to escape. Found among the prisoners of war were hundreds of Athenians fighting on the Persian side, which would be a sore spot between Alexander and Athens for years. In this light, Alexander's decision to *honor* Athens by sending 300 suits of armor of the defeated to the Parthenon as spoils reveals the ambiguity of any ethnic underpinnings of the conflict.

Having won at Granicus, Alexander took the unusual step of calling upon his soldiers not to pillage the defeated. He appointed one of his officers, named Calas, as a new satrap of Phrygia, but otherwise left the region with its preexisting institutions and customs. The Macedonian army then made rapid progress along the Ionian coast. Sardis and Ephesus capitulated without a fight; in the case of Ephesus, the citizens were reverting back to the Greek side after having switched to Persia just a year earlier. When Memnon of Rhodes regrouped in Miletus, the citizens petitioned Alexander that they be counted as free from *both* sides, effectively as a neutral state. Alexander balked at this and took the city (though left it intact as he had with Phrygia), and Memnon was forced to move south yet again, this time to Halicarnassus. Like Ephesus, Halicarnassus had ricocheted in recent years between Greek and Persian allegiances, and its forces were led by, in addition to Memnon, a Persian nobleman, Orontobates, and two Athenians named Ephialtes and Thrasybulus. Holed up in the city, Memnon deployed an innovative battle tower that sought to neutralize the besieging troops by raining missiles from on high, since the tight Macedonian phalanx could not be breached on the same level on land. Nevertheless, Alexander's siege was effective, and Memnon fled once again, to the island of Cos. Alexander left Halicarnassus under the control of Ada, a local noblewoman whose family had been ousted a few years before Alexander's invasion.

The promotion of Ada hints at tactics by Alexander that would characterize the rest of his war on Persia. He repeatedly relied on the collaboration of local aristocracies to hold territories as he won them, often choosing this device for imperial management over the imposition of a Macedonian overlord or garrison. For the residents, in fact, this was nothing new, given similar practices by the Persians (Chapter 1). In so doing Alexander substituted himself and his allies at the top of the Persian system while leaving the lower hierarchies in place. He exhibited a usefully fluid personal identity, for Ada adopted Alexander as her son and heir. Alexander's facility with altering his public image for different audiences as circumstances demanded – adding the Carian Ada as a second mother to the Epirot Olympias – would capitalize on an inherent weakness in Persia's management of its territories. Sharply different ethnic communities existed, at least on a day-to-day basis, much to their own taste. Local aristocracies paid homage and honoraria to a *shah*, or "Great King," and answered to satraps that represented him, but otherwise, the cities of Persian power – Babylon, Susa, Persepolis – were far off. Darius and his predecessors had been unseen and unknown, speaking a foreign language and worshipping their own gods; their aloofness, while it may have pleased the subjects and forestalled rebellions, also made the rulers susceptible to easy replacement. Alexander could gain much ground simply by presenting himself as an alternative figurehead for the existing system.

As Alexander and Parmenio converged on central Asia Minor in 333, much of the territories behind them were still unsettled. Memnon strung together a series of alliances with Cos, Samos, Chios, and Lesbos, which led to promises of support from the Cyclades and from Athens itself. If external enemies were not enough, internal espionage was an additional concern: over the previous winter one of Alexander's lieutenants, Alexander of Lyncestis, serving under Parmenio in a different theater of the campaign, was alleged to be a spy for Persia. Whether this was true or not (he was only removed from responsibility for the time being), the accusation reveals what was thought to be possible. Meanwhile in Asia Alexander's forces were spread thin: in Cappadocia, he again appointed a local as satrap and kept moving East. He had famously cut the Gordian Knot, rather than untie it, to enact the prophecy that whoever solved it would rule Asia Minor, but even so, the odds seemed to be against Alexander as he approached Issus, in the northeast "corner" of the Mediterranean Sea where Darius had himself finally taken the field.

The Battle of Issus did not begin well for the Macedonians: Alexander gambled wrong on which approach Darius would make to his position and ended up outflanked. The Persian side, some 100 000 strong as opposed to Alexander's 40 000, included a large troop of Greeks, which Darius placed in the center of his line. Still, the narrow terrain suited Alexander and defused the effectiveness of the Persian cavalry. Darius allegedly managed to wound Alexander himself when the two faced each other in the midst of battle but in the end he was forced to retreat, a scene commemorated in a famous mosaic from Pompeii crafted over 200 years after the fact. In his escape to Babylon, Darius shed his royal trappings, which would have both slowed him down and made him an easy target to spot. This royal detritus, such as treasure and harem, proved valuable to Alexander, as he pursued multiple strategies of legitimization as a substitute for, and not necessarily an avenger against, the Great King. He donned Darius's robes, occupied his tents, and took over the royal mints. He also did his best to persuade the women of Darius's family to support him, hoping that the rest of the Persian aristocracy would follow their lead. It was a prospect that Darius apparently understood well, as he offered a large ransom to retrieve his mother, wife, and others in 333, which he doubled in 332, and tripled in 331, all to no avail.

Darius had lost the battle, yet Alexander still had much to accomplish to win the war. By means of their Phoenician allies, the Persians still virtually controlled the seas, including the Aegean. Darius was fomenting a revolt among the *poleis* of southern Greece, even though Memnon of Rhodes, his best general in the region, had succumbed to an illness earlier in the year. Persian troops were also making moves on Cappadocia and Paphlagonia, whence the Macedonians had recently departed. Alexander ignored these provocations and turned south into the Levant. In Damascus, Parmenio stumbled upon ambassadors from Athens, Sparta, and Thebes who were in town to make deals with Darius's representatives. These Parmenio detained and sent ahead to Alexander, along with Barsine, the Phrygian widow of Memnon, who was also resident in Damascus as a hostage; one wonders what the conversation was like among these Macedonian soldiers, southern Greek diplomats, and a high-ranking woman of the Persian aristocracy, who reportedly had had a Greek education. Alexander would father a child by this Barsine, who would later be viewed as a potential heir to his throne. Once again, we find it a gross simplification to refer to the overall conflict as being "between Greeks and Persians."

The great Phoenician city of Sidon capitulated to Alexander readily, and Alexander hastily elevated Abdalonymus, a formerly displaced member of the local aristocracy, to the satrapy. We might count this as an otherwise unremarkable promotion, following the pattern that was repeated elsewhere by Alexander in the satrapies, were it not for the survival of an imposing artifact that has been attributed to Abdalonymus (though the association has been debated). A sarcophagus from Abdalonymus's satrapy has survived, brought out of Lebanon by imperial Ottomans in the late nineteenth century (see Figure 3.1). Now housed at the Archeological Museum in Istanbul, it depicts the deceased and his compatriots alongside Alexander and other Macedonians. Collaboration between Hellenic and non-Hellenic figures is on prominent display. Two of the panels feature hunting scenes against a lion, a deer, and a leopard (or lioness); the other two show soldiers in battle, presumably in representations of Issus. The composition is thoroughly Greek in aspect, and the material, Pentelic marble, had been imported to Phoenicia from near Athens. If the sarcophagus is indeed Abdalonymus's, its reliefs, carved in the years before his death, would serve to assert the new satrap's loyalty to Alexander and also to his way of life.

3.4   Another Alexander, in Italy

When Alexander of Epirus, Olympias's lesser-known brother, entered Italy in 334, the peninsula was experiencing a brief respite from fighting. As seen in Chapter 2, the powerful Carthaginians were satisfied with a strong sphere of influence in Sicily and with a settlement with the Romans that allowed them to trade or to wage limited war along the coast of Italy to the north. Rome had also recently vanquished the Samnites in 341 and the Latins in 338. The details of Alexander of Epirus's campaigns are not well known, but perhaps he sought to take

Figure 3.1 The so-called Alexander Sarcophagus, perhaps commissioned by Abdalonymus and depicting Alexander and an entourage of Greeks and easterners hunting a lion and a stag, late fourth century, BCE.

advantage of a perceived power vacuum following these reductions, and to capitalize on the Greek presence in southern Italy – something Athens had attempted to no avail in the midst of the Peloponnesian War (Chapter 1). The nature of his campaign as a western pendant to his nephew's was remarked upon by Justin, a late source. He pointed out that the Epirot Alexander's landing place, Brundisium, had been founded by a hero of the Trojan War, Diomedes, giving this mission as much of a Homeric flavor as the eastward one enjoyed.

The pretext for this Alexander's adventure was to assist the Greek city of Tarentum against Italian tribes that were encroaching on its territory. He had several years of success: according to Livy, he captured multiple cities, including the Lucanians' Potentia, the Apulians' Sipontum, and the Bruttians' Consentia, suggesting marches of at least 150 miles, partly over mountainous terrain (see Map 3.2). He is also said to have detained 300 hostages and shipped them back to Epirus for safe keeping, implying that he sought to build long term diplomatic relations, or even something akin to an empire. He engaged in diplomacy with the Romans, surely seeking to outflank the southern tribes by allying with their northern neighbor; in the year of Alexander's arrival, the Romans planted their southernmost colony to date at Cales just north of the Bay of Naples. Details of any Macedonian and Roman conversations would be fascinating, but our sources provide none. In 332, the Romans continued to grow, and quickly: they enrolled *en masse* tens of thousands of new citizens in Latium, creating two new electoral tribes to accommodate them and establishing a larger, more imposing domain.

Around 331, Alexander of Epirus believed he had a reliable source of intelligence in the form of Lucanian defectors and followed their advice in the field. It turned out that they were double agents of a kind, and Alexander was killed by them as he tried to flee across a river. The enemy

Map 3.2 The route of Alexander of Epirus's campaigns in southern Italy is not known, but the sites of his victories are recorded in literary sources. The pretext for his crossing to Italy was to assist Tarentum against Italian tribes.

set about mutilating his corpse, as the story goes, until a woman implored them to stop so she could use the bones to ransom her relatives held hostage overseas. It would be easy to note the contrast between the uncle and the nephew and to write off the campaigns of the former as an insignificant enterprise, but much more was in the offing: Justin says that when the Alexander that was in Asia learned of his uncle's death, he ordered three days of mourning among his troops.

3.5 In Egypt and Mesopotamia

After Sidon, Alexander, Olympias's son, faced far more difficulty against Tyre, a major city of Phoenicia, in 332, which took confidence in its position on an island redoubt surrounded by sea and guarded by a fearsome navy. In addition to their present resources, Tyre also received promises of support from their kinsmen Carthaginians. Alexander could not ignore Tyre: to move on to the friendlier cities further south would have left a refuge for Persian allies to regroup behind him. He prepared for a complicated siege that required moving mountains, literally, as he brought in wagon-loads of earth and rock to build a causeway between the mainland and the city walls. Like the battles at Granicus and Issus, the siege of Tyre implied something of a World War: Alexander recruited Jewish troops from nearby Jerusalem, while the Tyreans were assisted by Arab marauders landside, who disrupted Alexander's attempts to import timber for siege machinery. Alexander also received ships and engineering expertise from Rhodes, Lycia, Cyprus, and the Peloponnese, which proved decisive when the promised Carthaginian fleet never materialized for Tyre. Overall the victory was not elegant, engineered as it was by the blunt altering of geography itself, but it gave Alexander the cover he needed to advance into Egypt.

Alexander's entrance into the Delta in late 332 reads as child's play compared with what he endured at Tyre. He had already received the good news that Darius's efforts to ruin Macedonian diplomacy in Greece and Asia Minor had failed: Alexander's general Antigonus, who had the colorful epithet "the One-eyed" owing to a battle wound he suffered against Persia, had successfully subdued Paphlagonia and Cappadocia. The Egyptians now welcomed Alexander, who appears to have readily taken to their culture. In the course of his seven-month stay in Egypt from October to April (a wintertime retreat that would be enjoyed by Julius Caesar, too, in 47–46 when on a similarly broad campaign; Chapter 15), Alexander restored many dilapidated temples and sacrificed to Egyptian gods. In part this was his responsibility, as he received the status of pharaoh – the native godhead incarnate in the chain between Osiris and Horus (Chapter 1) – in November of 332. Greeks and Egyptians had been in contact with each other for millennia, so there was enough common ground on which Alexander could exercise his cultural habits. An oracle some 300 miles to the west at Siwa, governed by the god Ammon, had long been ranked by Greeks in the company of Delphi, and it drew Alexander's interest. In the course of a pilgrimage there he forged an alliance with Cyrene in modern Libya, which had been colonized by Greeks many centuries prior. The priests of Ammon appear to have christened Alexander as a son of their god, perhaps motivated by his near total domination of the coastline of the Eastern Mediterranean by then. Alexander seized upon the idea for its propaganda value and referred to it on coins, where his portrait included ram horns as part of the iconography of Zeus Ammon.

Once back at the Nile, Alexander set about organizing the military and civic chains of command such that Macedonians would maintain authority at the highest levels while the average Egyptian went about her affairs in much the same way as the years before. Alexander staged athletic competitions and is said to have sited out the terrain for a new, Hellenic city at the edge of the Delta. This would become Alexandria, the great city of which most readers are likely to have heard, and which will figure prominently in the chapters to come.

In 331, Alexander moved out of Egypt, back up through Tyre, and on to Mesopotamia. In the northern reaches of the Tigris River he met Darius at the Battle of Gaugemela, and again put him to flight. Again Greek mercenaries in Persian employ trailed along after their fugitive king, now to the far northeastern reaches of the swiftly crumbling empire. At Babylon, much like in Egypt, Alexander was warmly received by the ruling elite, and in exchange, he offered to rebuild fallen religious structures, in this case a ziggurat to Marduk, which had been destroyed by the Persians ages before. Forging ahead into the Iranian hinterland beyond the rivers he reached Susa and again met little resistance. Among the treasures stored there was the statue group of the so-called Tyrannicides, Harmodius and Aristogeiton, heroes who had played a role in the ousting of *tyrannoi* from Athens in 514, which paved the way for the famous democracy (Chapter 1). Xerxes had seized the sculptures in 480 during the Persian Wars, and now Alexander crated them for a return home, at once both keeping Athens happy and making a political statement that he eschewed "tyranny." These gestures, combined with Olympias's and Antipater's shrewd management of multiple fronts in quashing resistance movements in Macedonia, alleviated anxiety over the allegiance of the Greek south, which was still viewed as capable of undermining Alexander. Demosthenes, in particular, was vehement in his opposition to Alexander, and would remain so until he was exiled for allegedly taking bribes in 324 (see Primary Source 3.1).

> **Primary Source 3.1**
>
> **Demosthenes, *On the Crown***
>
> In this speech, delivered in Athens in 330, Demosthenes explained why resistance to Macedonia was justified (and thus he was deserving of a *crown* awarded by the state). Even after Alexander had scored several major victories against the Persian Empire by this point, at least one faction of Athenians preferred their own sovereignty and spoke about it openly.
>
> > 202–203, 297–300: There is no-one of the Greeks or of the barbarians who does not know that the Thebans and the Spartans who held the hegemony before them and the king of the Persians (all) would have happily and gratefully encouraged the city (of Athens) to keep what it possessed and to take what it wanted provided they did what was ordered of them and also submit to another (Macedonian) as the hegemon of the Greeks. But as far as I can tell, for our Athenian ancestors such behavior was not their patrimony, and by their nature could not be tolerated. For time eternal, it has been impossible for our city to submit to strong outsiders for the sake of safety. … I say to you, when all the leaders of the Greeks, beginning with you, were subdued, first by Phillip and now by Alexander, neither fame nor blandishments nor great promises nor wishful thinking nor fear could compel me not to think of the rights and interests of my fatherland … I did not protect the city with brick and mortar walls; that's not what occurs to me the most. Rather if you should really like to behold my defenses (for Athens), look for the weapons and cities and strongholds and the harbors and the ships and horses and the vast array of defensive troops. I set these up for Attica, such as were humanly, logistically possible, and I thus defended the entire land and not just the circuit of walls around Piraeus and our urban core."

Persepolis, eastward by another 350 miles, housed the principal throne room of the *shah*, along with the vast bulk of his riches, which were so extensive (120 000 talents, according to Diodorus) that Darius's earlier tripling of the ransom for his royal family (from 10 000 to 30 000 talents) seems less generous than on its surface. Alexander took Persepolis in 330 without a fight, and the windfall gave him yet another advantage in motivating his troops. Yet, oddly, at Persepolis Alexander departed from past practice. Rather than respecting local traditions and culture, after a four-month bivouac throughout the city he abruptly ordered his troops to torch the palace, in a way that has posed a mystery for historians from antiquity to the present. Surely Alexander had destroyed some locales throughout his campaign, such as Thebes and Tyre, but these had faced retribution for their opposition. Sleepy Persepolis did not fit that category. In obliterating the capital, was Alexander being strategic, such as by eliminating a symbol of Darius's power? Was he succumbing to his temper at some slight by the locals? Was he simply drunk? No option has been satisfactory from every angle, but the episode is important for marking a change in Alexander, as the power that he enjoyed became increasingly absolute and corruptive, at least judging by the terms of our sources.

3.6 Absolute Power

At this point, we shall abandon the year-by-year narrative of Alexander's grand campaign. For the next three years, 330–327, Alexander maneuvered around the northeastern territories of the empire in the area of modern Afghanistan and Tajikistan. Hot on the heels of Darius he eventually caught up with him, the story goes, just in time to witness his dying breath – Darius had been mortally wounded by a satrap with whom he was trying to seek refuge. Alexander announced that Darius's last wish was for him to become the next *shah*, but the convenience of this is obvious. In fact, a "true" successor emerged in Bessus, satrap of Bactria, who at least had genealogy on his side as a cousin of some kind of Darius. Renaming himself Artaxerxes, he was betrayed in turn by an underling, and soon Alexander had the title to himself. He also married a Bactrian princess at this time, Roxane, to cement his ties to the local elite.

From 327 to 325, the Macedonians came upon the verge of South Asia, campaigning across the Indus River in the Punjab. Alexander is said to have participated in some daring victories, suffering multiple wounds on the front lines, but the most powerful king that he found in the region, Porus, was still on the throne upon Alexander's departure, agreeing for the moment to the subordinate title of satrap. Alexander's troops dug in their heels at the banks of the Ganges River and would have mutinied had their general not agreed to turn back. The return home, however – part of the force crossing the desert and another part sailing in a fleet along the parched coast of the Persian Gulf – turned out to be as fatal as the previous several years of warfare. Back in the Iranian heartland by 324, Alexander spent the year shoring up the Hellenic presence in the region, partly by imbuing it with Persian characteristics, to be described shortly. Plans were under way for new campaigns in multiple directions – south to Arabia, or west to Italy and Carthage – but Alexander died of a fever at Babylon in June of 323, famously just 32 years old.

Several trends and phenomena of the second half of Alexander's expedition are worth highlighting. As he moved through Central Asia, he increasingly turned to the device of colonization for his veterans, giving his name to new or preexisting cities in the process. Herat, Khandahar, Ferah, and Ai-Khanoum, all cities of modern Afghanistan, bore the epithet Alexandria in the Hellenistic period. Ai-Khanoum, once called Alexandria Oxiana for its location on the Oxus River, is the most thoroughly excavated of these, yielding remains of houses, temples, and a large theater in the Hellenic style (Figure 3.2). Other examples of Alexandrias exist in modern Tajikistan, Turkmenistan, Pakistan, and Iran. Some, like Alexandria Margiana,

Figure 3.2 Computer rendering of a Hellenistic city in central Asia, possibly Alexandria Oxiana, whose ruins are at modern Ai Khanoum, Afghanistan.

in Turkmenistan, were so named not by Alexander himself but by a general, in this case Craterus, as an expression of loyalty and reverence.

At the same time, Alexander appears to have acted with greater paranoia concerning his underlings, in lock step with the new heights achieved by his image. In 330, Philotas, the son of Parmenio, was brought up on charges of a conspiracy and was convicted and executed. Alexander reportedly called for the death of Parmenio at the same time, to head off possible retaliation. One of Alexander's soldiers, Cleitus the Black, and his court historian, Callisthenes (see Primary Source 3.2), both identified a growing arrogance in Alexander in different ways and dared to speak out, with fatal consequences. They were objecting to a pronounced adoption of a Persian demeanor by Alexander, including his expectation of *proskynesis*, or lying prostrate before the king, something customary for a *shah* but not a Macedonian *basileus*.

Primary Source 3.2

Callisthenes, on Alexander the Great (Summary)

A continuous text by Callisthenes, Alexander's "court historian," does not survive, but what seem to be extensive quotes of his work exist in later authors. In this text, Strabo, a geographer writing at the turn of the epoch from BCE to CE, is nearly quoting Callisthenes's account of Alexander's visit to the Oracle of Zeus Ammon in Egypt, but not without some skepticism of Callisthenes's historical method and sensational claims.

> Strabo, 17.1.43: "Callisthenes says that Alexander very much wanted to journey to the oracle because he heard that Perseus and Heracles had gone there previously. He set out from Paraetonium and although the south wind was blowing against him, he powered through. When he got lost because of a dust storm, he was saved when rain fell and two crows pointed out the road to him. But this is a case of the historian's sycophancy, as is the following: The priest said that only the king could enter the temple without changing his clothes, but the others had to change. Everyone heard the oracle from the outside except Alexander who was inside. The oracles were not revealed through speech as at Delphia and at Branchidae but through nods and symbols. … The priest clearly stated that the king was the son of Zeus. To these things Callisthenes added further exaggerations: Although Apollo had abandoned the oracle of the Branchidae [near Miletus] since his temple had been pillaged by them when they joined the Persians under Xerxes, and the sacred spring had stopped flowing, now (all of a sudden) the spring was flowing again and many envoys from Miletus brought oracles to (Alexander in) Memphis about how Alexander was born of Zeus, about how he would win a victory near Arbela, about the death of Darius III, and about revolutionary movements among the Spartans."

Finally, often viewed to be of a piece with Alexander's Persian affectations are his occasional (alleged) attempts to encourage a cultural mélange of European and Asian elements that extended beyond his person. In 324, he arranged a massive wedding ceremony, where in addition to taking Persian wives himself (to add to Roxane), he paired his generals with royal women from throughout the Persian realm, aristocratic connections that were over 90 in number. He also offered financial incentives for his common soldiers to follow suit, and we are told that ultimately some 10 000 such marriages took place (though this figure is likely to be an exaggeration). Sources also make much of Alexander's recruitment of the so-called *Epigoni* (meaning something like, "those born anew"), some 30 000 Persian youths who were enlisted in the army and taught Macedonian military habits and technologies. When the Macedonian soldiers at Opis viewed these as a dilution of their own status, Alexander soon had a mutiny on his hands. The sides were reconciled, however (following some targeted executions of rabble rousers), and the new trend held. At the ensuing banquet, Alexander is said by Arrian to have proclaimed all of his men to be his "kinsmen" (*syngenes*). Further suggestions for Alexander's cultural tendencies come in a document allegedly revealed shortly after his death: he wrote that his successors should, among other things, build a Babylonian-style ziggurat to Hephaestaion, an Egyptian-style pyramid to Philip II, and transport entire populations of Greeks into the newly conquered lands in Asia. The veracity of such a testament is highly in doubt, but the very idea of it demonstrates the "multicultural" light under which Alexander was later considered.

3.7 The Second Samnite War

As Alexander prosecuted his campaign, and as Olympias maintained the home front, the Italian populations on the other side of the Adriatic acted without Macedonian interference following the demise of Alexander of Epirus. Rome continued its colonization activities: in 328 the Romans established Fregellae, at the foot of the Samnite hills and twice the size of Cales, which had been founded further south in 334. Such fortifications necessarily irked the Samnites who could see their mobility being constrained. Tensions came to a head in Naples, an old Hellenic trading post that had become something of a cosmopolitan hub over the centuries. In 327, the consul Quintus Publilius Philo was sent there to win its support against the Samnites. In 326, with the mission not yet accomplished, the Roman electorate took the unusual step of extending Philo's *imperium* for another year even as it also elected two new consuls. The process, called prorogation, demonstrates the flexibility of Rome's constitution as it dealt with emergencies; Philo's title changed from consul to "proconsul," an office that would become *de rigueur* for generals in the second and first centuries. We are told that the local Neapolitan aristocracy of Hellenic descent favored Philo while the broader segments of the population preferred the Samnites. The pro-Roman faction prevailed: it is perhaps not a coincidence that the proconsul had a Greek cognomen meaning friend (*philos*). Livy says that 3000 Roman troops thus entered Naples and a new, second war with the Samnites was on.

Livy's account is not entirely reliable, but for what it is worth, he described a bifurcated front on the part of the Romans, each led by a consul, which served to keep the Samnites from uniting into a single force. From this foundation the Romans met with success, though for the first several years their victories were mostly on the level of skirmishes. They planned a full-scale invasion in 321, but were stopped short by a tactical blunder at the Caudine Forks. Their army became attenuated as it passed through a narrow valley, and twin Samnite forces had little trouble blocking both the exit at the far end and the entrance through which they had passed. Trapped, the Romans surrendered rather than engage in a suicidal battle. The winning army extracted a promise from the Roman commanders that they would pull their colonies from the region in exchange for their lives. Even so, the prisoners would be made to depart in humiliating terms: stripped practically naked, both of tunics and more importantly of weapons, they would pass under a yoke at swordpoint, bent over in a provocative display that symbolized total submission. The army was thus disgraced, but it had at least survived. The Romans lost Cales and Fregellae, but the terms of the peace were soon dismissed by the senate as illegitimate since the proper diplomatic rituals had not been followed and the agreement had been struck under duress. The war would thus continue, but it entered a period of inactivity as the Romans recuperated from their wounds.

3.8 Imperial Styles: Persia, Rome, and Macedonia

Scholars have long attributed Rome's success in its Italian wars and beyond to the nature of its regional alliances and the methods of quasi-imperial rule that were put in place after the rebellion of Latium in 338. Like the Persians, the Romans relied heavily on the incorporation of the defeated into their systems, and on collaboration with local aristocracies. Differently from the Persians, however, as of 338 they also articulated progressive levels of citizenship for communities under their sway, paying their subjects the respect of status. Italian allies participated alongside Romans in their wars, as if part of an empire, but they were also permitted to share in like measure in the rewards. The new colonies founded throughout the south on battle-won land were populated not just by Romans but by military families of Italian allies, as well, who received their own plots. Such a reciprocity of benefits had the effect of creating a shared sense of destiny, and at all levels of society and not just the elite, which the residents of the Persian Empire lacked.

It would not be a stretch, though it is not attested directly, to consider that Alexander was aware of what the Romans were doing in Italy as he made his way through the East. There were plenty of opportunities for him to learn of Rome. We have seen how Alexander's uncle of the same name was simultaneously embarked on a campaign in Italy and was engaged in some form of diplomacy with the Romans. This Italian campaign must have required some advance planning and intelligence about Rome, of which Olympias and the younger Alexander would have been aware. Alexander was also keeping tabs on the mission's progress, if we are to trust Justin's account of the period of mourning for its failure, as well as the consensus among many sources that the Great Alexander wanted to try his own luck there in 323. Seen in the light of Roman precedent, Alexander's plotting of colonies, his plans to transfer Greek populations to the East (however vague), and even the matchmaking between his men and local wives, of a similar spirit to the *ius conubii* in Italy, seem to share aspects of what was going on in Rome. It is not possible to say that Alexander was influenced by Rome; rather, it is worth pointing out the existence of a trend in thinking about empire, which had manifestations in different areas across the Mediterranean at roughly the same time.

The comparison of Macedonia and Rome may add nuance to a scholarly debate on Alexander and his cultural policy in the East. Scholars have debated whether Alexander's attempts at acculturation were a matter of some kind of proto-liberal ideology, or rather, were the result of ad hoc arrangements to solve immediate problems of loyalty and survival. For example, was Alexander's donning of the Persian diadem and robe in 330 part of an enlightened scheme of cultural fusion (as argued by W.W. Tarn, for example), or a piece of incidental propaganda timed to compete with the claim of the Persian nobleman Bessus to the throne in that year (as according to A.B. Bosworth, among others)? And, though we know that Greek troops fought side by side with Asian soldiers under Alexander, how should we interpret scenes on the above-mentioned sarcophagus (possibly belonging to Abdalonymus), where the clothes and weaponry of the Persian figures remain distinct from those of the Greeks by their side? Evidence for ethnic hybrids may exist at the nonelite levels, as seen in the archeology of the new cities that flourished in Asia after Alexander, but we can also see clear divisions between Greek and Eastern at the level of the aristocracy: after all, in the mass marriages discussed above, it is Greek men who "took" Persian wives, and not the other way around. Moreover, of the 18 non-Hellenic satraps appointed by Alexander, Peter Green has shown that only three were still in place at the time of his death, most others having been removed for disloyalty.

The so-called "unity of mankind" thesis of Alexander's super decade of activity (as it was called by Tarn) has its limits, but so too might the opposing side of the debate. The idea that the marriages, the rituals, the recruitment, and the prayers all demonstrate an innovative and opportunistic pragmatism on the part of Alexander dissolves when we note that similar episodes of collaboration existed long before Alexander, and in the same regions. We have seen Greeks from many different *poleis* in place on either side of the conflict, just as we have seen residents of the Persian Empire alternately helping Alexander and battling him to the end. Greeks had traded with Medes, who had fought alongside Phoenicians, who had sailed with Egyptians, who had worked with Persians, who had intermarried with Bactrians, who had traded with Indians, and so on, for centuries. Seen in this light, Alexander's adaptability and willingness to dabble in all these ethnicities and to name-drop himself across a continent could be seen as a natural course.

3.9 Conclusions

While Alexander was not all that different from the world around him in his actions, what set him apart was his *story*. Tidy, complete, and comprehensible, his life followed an arc from improbable rise to rampaging success to premature, romantic demise, all while featuring colorful characters and acts of derring-do. Indeed, the mythology surrounding Alexander only increased in the subsequent centuries, finding its apogee under the Romans and carrying on into the Middle Ages, both in Europe and the Middle East, and into the Renaissance, ultimately down to Hollywood. Societies create their own Alexanders, such that he was praised by nineteenth century European scholars for his ability to bring disparate groups together, but pilloried by scholars writing in the aftermath of World War II, who saw elements of Fascism and authoritarianism in his regime. The story of Alexander should not eclipse what predicated it – a vital Mediterranean East with a multiplicity of players that had been interacting for a long time before.

In the years following Alexander's death, his empire suffered convulsions as many ambitious generals and dynasts made attempts on the throne, largely clustered around the two camps of Olympias, the dowager queen, and Antipater, the elder statesman of Macedonia. Southern Greeks had been quick to snub Alexander and never really supported him in his lifetime, but in the denouement following his death, they must have found that his victories opened new doors. Their culture, suspicious of the outside world and by turns anodyne and stagnant, would flame anew with the oxygen of cosmopolitanism. Meanwhile Rome would finally surmount the Samnite obstacle and begin to enhance its infrastructure with advanced roads, aqueducts, coinage, and a navy.

Further Reading

Brian Bosworth, A (1988). *Conquest and Empire: The Reign of Alexander the Great*. Cambridge: Cambridge University Press.

Cornell, Timothy J (1995). *The Beginnings of Rome: Italy and Rome from the Bronze Age to the Punic Wars*. New York: Routledge.

Dench, Emma (1995). *From Barbarians to New Men: Greek, Roman, and Modern Perceptions of Peoples from the Central Apennines*. Oxford: Clarendon Press.

Green, Peter (1974). *Alexander of Macedon, 356–323 BC: A Historical Biography* (rev. ed.) New York: Penguin Books.

O'Brien, John (1992). *Alexander the Great: The Invisible Enemy*. London and New York: Routledge.

Salmon, Edward T (1967). *Samnium and the Samnites*. Cambridge: Cambridge University Press.

Tarn, William W (1933). *Alexander the Great and the Unity of Mankind*. London: Humphrey Milford.

4

To 295: An Elusive Equilibrium

Timeline

323: Perdiccas as *epimeletes* (protector) of Alexander's heirs.
323–321: Marriages of Antipater's daughters Nicaea, Phila, and Eurydice to Perdiccas, Craterus, and Ptolemy, respectively.
322: Divorce of Perdiccas and Nicaea; marriage of Perdiccas to Cleopatra, daughter of Olympias and sister of Alexander the Great.
322: Suppression of revolts at Bactria and in Athens; independence of Rhodes; suicide of Demosthenes.
321: Death of Perdiccas by mutiny
326, 320, 319, 315, 313: Repeated consulships of Lucius Papirius Cursor in continuation of the Second Samnite War (326–304)
317–307: Oligarchy in Athens led by Demetrius of Phaleron
c. 310s and 300s: Comedies by Menander in Athens
316: Death of Olympias at the hands of Cassander, son of Antipater
312: Appius Claudius Caecus as censor in Rome; Aqua Appia; Via Appia
311: Siege of Carthage by Agathocles of Syracuse; Seleucus entrenched in Babylon
310: Death of Roxane and Alexander IV
306: Antigonus the One-Eyed and his son Demetrius Poliorketes proclaimed *basileus*, king
305: Ptolemy I, Lysimachus, Cassander, Seleucus, and Agathocles each proclaimed king by their respective armies
301: Battle of Ipsus: forces of Cassander, Lysimachus, and Seleucus defeat Antigonus the One-eyed and Demetrius Poliorketes; death of Antigonus
298–290: Third Samnite War
297: Death of Cassander
295: Battle of Sentinum: consuls Quintus Fabius Maximus Rullianus and Publius Decius Mus defeat the combined forces of the Samnites, Umbrians, and Celts.
c. 295: Musaion of Alexandria founded by Ptolemy I.

Principal Themes

- Following Alexander's early death, two competing family networks, led by Olympias and Antipater, contended for power in Macedonia, usually by means of allied generals.
- Ptolemy grew powerful in this era, heading up a new network of marriage alliances that spanned the eastern Mediterranean.

The Roman Republic and the Hellenistic Mediterranean: From Alexander to Caesar, First Edition. Joel Allen.
© 2020 John Wiley & Sons, Inc. Published 2020 by John Wiley & Sons, Inc.

- With gradual success against the Samnites, the Romans expanded their colonizing activities to the Adriatic coast and developed new technologies, including roads, aqueducts, coinage, and their first navy.
- Athenian culture, always influential, took on less parochial characteristics under the universalizing comedies of Menander, the philosophical allegories of Euhemerus, and the new schools of thought of Stoicism and Epicureanism.
- Carthage fell under attack by a combined force of Syracusans, Athenians, and the forces of Ptolemy, but survived, resisting an attempt to establish a monarchy in the process.
- In 306, Antigonus the One-Eyed and his son Demetrius Poliorketes were the first to claim Alexander's old title, *basileus*, followed the next year by Ptolemy, Lysimachus, Cassander, Seleucus, and Agathocles.

4.1 Introduction

The unexpected death of Alexander plunged the eastern Mediterranean into confusion as members of the nobility and military hierarchy, whether Macedonian or part of the localized communities of the recently fallen Persian Empire, wondered who would become the next *basileus*, pharaoh, or *shah*. Alexander had died young, but his accomplishments were extraordinary enough, especially his near divinization, that the aura around those in his circle – family, friends, compatriots – was slow to dissipate. After some 15 years of wrangling to be his heir, the remaining major players seem to have awoken simultaneously to the idea that they could settle with mere shares of his authority rather than the entire corpus, and could rule manageable parcels of territory in their own right rather than all of it. We use the word equilibrium in the title of this chapter with some reservation: the notion that any period of geopolitics can experience stability is unrealizable, but by 295, a certain amount of sorting-out had been achieved. The historian Hieronymus of Cardia used the term *Diadochoi*, or, Successors, as a collective term for the half-dozen or so surviving Macedonian generals who struck a balance among themselves. Another Hellenic dynast in Sicily, sandwiched between old Carthage and newly growing Rome, also made a bid to join their world of petty (as in *petit*) kings.

Compared with subsequent chapters, this one deals less with Rome and more with the rest of the Mediterranean, following the lead of our source material. This characteristic does not make the work any less relevant for students of the Republic, for many of the cultural forms that took shape in this period – philosophical schools, political theories, popular literature, artistic styles – would have a profound effect on Roman culture in later generations. It is possible also to propose that the influence of technology went in the other direction, as we shall see important advancements in Roman infrastructure that predate equivalent strides in the East. Culture aside, what we can see of Roman politics suggests a modest eclipse of the people by aristocratic interests through 295, likely owing to the state of war in Rome and the general fear and anxiety that it precipitated among the populace. It was not, some evidently believed, a time for radical elements in decision making.

4.2 The Limits of Alexander's Mystique

The anecdotes about Alexander's deathbed utterances – that he gasped out in his last breath that he was leaving his empire "to the strongest" and that he predicted a struggle for succession that would resemble funeral games on a cosmic level – have such a heroic, Homeric ring to them that scholars have suspected that they were a part of a propaganda campaign, ex post facto, perhaps pursued by the earliest contender for full power, the general Perdiccas. What is less explored is how the gendered quality of the metaphor – in antiquity, athletic events like "funeral games" by definition involved only male participants – obscures the reality of what transpired: in the decade following Alexander's death, a dozen women wielded enormous influence and were as active in the game of politics as their husbands, fathers, and brothers. The bloodline of the Argeads, which held great currency among the Macedonian infantry (a sentiment not always shared by their generals), was almost entirely manifested at this point among women – Alexander's mother, Olympias; his widow, Roxane, who was pregnant; the courtesan Barsine, who had a son by Alexander; a full sister, Cleopatra, who was the widow of Alexander of Epirus; and two half-sisters of differing rank, Cynane and Thessalonike. Cynane also had a daughter, and thus a niece of Alexander, Adea, later renamed Eurydice. With the exception of Olympias and Roxane, all of the above were part of marriage plots, whether con-summated or merely planned, that carried weight in the geopolitics of the *Diadochoi*. The males in the family, by contrast, were all problematic in some way: Arrhidaos, a half-brother of Alexander, had some kind of mental impairment; Heracles, the son of Barsine, was illegitimate; and Eumenes, Alexander's secretary, although married to Barsine's sister and therefore something of a brother-in-law, was ethnically Greek – always a cause for suspicion among the Macedonian elite – and his agnate tie was tenuous in any case.

In opposition to the women of the Argead line, three daughters of Antipater in Macedonia – Nicaea, Phila, and Eurydice (not to be confused with Alexander's niece whom we shall refer to as Adea/Eurydice) – repeatedly engaged in marriage alliances of their own. Marriages among these three at times seemed to constitute blocs of allied generals, maneuvering collectively against the interests of Olympias, her family, and the part of the Macedonian infantry that adored them. Shortly after Alexander's death, for example, Perdiccas married Nicaea, Craterus married Phila, and a bit later, yet another general Ptolemy married Eurydice. Perdiccas had fought alongside Alexander since the sack of Thebes, and it was to him that Alexander passed his signet ring. Craterus and Ptolemy both had distinguished themselves at Issus and had been with Alexander ever since. The three acted in concert for a time, and in the interests of their father-in-law Antipater, precisely up to the moment when Perdiccas put Nicaea aside for a more advantageous marriage to Alexander's sister Cleopatra, as we shall see shortly. Another general, Antigonus the One-Eyed, would arrange a marriage of his son to one of the sisters, to be discussed, to cement his place, and Lysimachus, a general in Thrace, would eventually take his turn, as a husband to Nicaea. The device of the marriage alliance was frequently a powerful reification of political allegiance.

Whether it would be the Argead remnants that seized power or Antipater's brood, something had to happen quickly, as the empire immediately began to splinter and crack. Bactria, Athens, and the important island of Rhodes all attempted to break free when they got word of the power vacuum. The situation in Babylon was tense. The soldiers favored Arrhidaos or Roxane's soon-to-be-born child, both of whom the generals rightly saw as incapable of managing great responsibilities. A compromise was brokered by Eumenes – a defender of the Argeads but also a realist – whereby Perdiccas would serve as "protector" of the boys under the new catchall title of *epimeletes* until they came of age. Once Perdiccas achieved this level of political capital, however, he used it to rid the army of the Argeads' more vocal champions. He declared a new arrangement of commands for the work of stabilization, in which his in-laws fared well: Antipater, his father-in-law, was to retain Macedonia, and Craterus, his brother-in-law, took on a new title, "guardian" (*prostates*), that was divorced from any geographical region and thus allowed for powerful flexibility. Other prominent assignments included Ptolemy to Egypt, Antigonus the One-Eyed to Pamphylia and Lycia and two more *Diadochoi*, Leonnatus and

Lysimachus, to Phrygia and Thrace, respectively. Eumenes, the Argead sympathizer, received Cappadocia and Paphlagonia, which were not top notch assignments in the sense that they were not yet fully conquered. Arrhidaos himself was largely nonfunctioning, except that he soon married Adea/Eurydice (in spite of being her uncle), and she would soon take advantage of the position to promote their family's interests. It should be noted as an aside that the pretensions to shared rule with easterners as satraps, which Alexander favored in some form, were largely abandoned for the time being, but soon to be revived in varying ways once the dust had settled among the Macedonian leadership.

With these commands in place, largely as arranged by Perdiccas, part of the army was dispatched to quell the revolt in Bactria, and a navy, led by Cleitus as commanded by Craterus, sailed to the Aegean to take on the Athenian resistance. Both of these initiatives were successful as the veterans of Bactria were silenced for the time being, and Cleitus defeated the Athenians in a battle off the coast of Amorgos. Craterus himself went on to the town of Lamia to rescue Antipater from a siege that had been undertaken by the Athenians under the leadership of Demosthenes, who had returned from exile to take these reins. Once freed, Antipater replaced the democracy in Athens with an oligarchic regime, and the leaders of the revolt were executed, a fate that Demosthenes only escaped via suicide. Now, for a citizen to participate in Athenian government he had to have a minimum estate of 2000 drachmas, which by some estimates cut the political population in half. Rhodes, which had bolted in the same year as Athens and Bactria, managed to remain independent, and as we shall see, became a major power in the eastern Mediterranean for centuries to come.

The binary quality of Macedonian politics post-Alexander, with the Argeads on one hand and Antipater's "family" on the other, was disrupted when Alexander's sister Cleopatra offered marriage to Perdiccas across the lines in late 322, and Perdiccas accepted. As the husband of Nicaea heretofore, he had been essentially, per the terms of family structures in antiquity, subordinate to Antipater the patriarch. Cleopatra, with all her symbolic power, offered him a way up; it was a route whose efficacy had been revealed the year before when Cleopatra had first tried an alliance with Leonnatus in Phrygia, which only failed because he died in battle on his way to meet her in Macedonia. By allying with Cleopatra, and presumably with Olympias, too, Perdiccas joined Eumenes, whom he then helped to take full charge of Cappadocia. He next had to figure out a way to face down all the other generals listed above, whom he himself had played a role in establishing. Antipater mounted a campaign against his betrayal, led by his son Cassander, by Craterus (Cassander's brother-in-law), and by Antigonus, who had fled Asia Minor when Perdiccas revealed his gambit. Perdiccas left Eumenes and Cleopatra in Asia Minor to face Cassander's army as it arrived from the Balkans while he made for Egypt to dislodge Ptolemy. Eumenes achieved some success, which was redoubled in the sense that Craterus died in the battle in question. Perdiccas, however, was undone by his own troops and by one of his officers, Seleucus, who mutinied on the banks of the Nile and, after assassinating their general, switched to Ptolemy.

By 320, although Olympias remained a force to be reckoned with, Antipater had fashioned a faction that held the upper hand. He himself assumed Perdiccas's old title *epimeletes*. His three daughters were at the center of a new corps of powerful generals for his cause: Eurydice was still married to Ptolemy, Nicaea now married Lysimachus in Thrace, and Phila, recently widowed by the death of Craterus, married the son of Antigonus, named Demetrius, who would soon take on a successful and colorful role in the game of geopolitics; as a result Antigonus was elevated to a kind of super command of Asia Minor. Antigonus's principal task was to hunt down Eumenes, who continued to operate in the hinterland of Asia Minor and had a knack for surviving.

The elderly Antipater died of natural causes in 319, but his network of in-laws continued to appear strong, to the extent that Adea/Eurydice abandoned the Argead side altogether and shifted her and her husband Arrhidaios's loyalties to Antipater's son Cassander. For her part, Olympias had already won over an old lieutenant of Antipater's, Polyperchon, who importantly had been the one to inherit Antipater's title of *epimeletes* upon the old man's death and thus nominal regency of Roxane's son. Affairs in the Balkan peninsula were thus in turmoil. Polyperchon brought Athens to his side by appealing to its disgruntled democratic faction, out of power since 321: with his support, the radical element seized the assembly, and the forces of the oligarchy were confined to Piraeus, Athens's harbor, as of 318. In the next year, Olympias scored a victory in Epirus when she convinced an opposing army to surrender Arrhidaos and Adea/Eurydice, who was apparently herself armed for battle, and both thus met their demise. But otherwise, Cassander's campaign was the stronger one, assisted by his Antipatrid in-laws Antigonus and Lysimachus, especially in successful engagements at the Hellespont. It was not long before the Athenians perceived Polyperchon and Olympias's shortcomings and in 317 made common cause with Cassander. This meant that once again an oligarchy would snuff out a flicker of democracy: Cassander put in charge of Athens the philosopher Demetrius of Phaleron (to be distinguished from Demetrius, son of Antigonus), a student of Theophrastus (see below) who was himself a student of Aristotle, Alexander's tutor.

To take stock, by 317, Olympias, Polyperchon, Eumenes, Cleopatra, and Roxane had held on for six full years, largely by means of the loyalty of the troops to the memory of their Alexander. On the other side were Cassander, son of Antipater, and the husbands of his three sisters, Ptolemy, Lysimachus, and Demetrius, son of Antigonus, who was also in the alliance.

By virtue of controlling more territory, the Antipatrid network, if it can be called that, had achieved a kind of primacy. Their unity would soon be riven, however, by the members' personal ambitions. Although Antigonus had worked with Cassander to secure Athens in 317, within a couple of years he was on his own in Asia Minor. Ostensibly, his mission was to destroy Eumenes, with a view toward depriving Olympias of a critical ally. As he chased Eumenes further and further East, he amalgamated smaller allies, such as Rhodes and the islands of the Ionian coast. Their allied navy not only allowed Antigonus to hunt his quarry more effectively, it also fed his desire to function for himself beyond the realm of Asia Minor. In 316, he finally managed to convince Eumenes's troops to mutiny against their commander and surrender him to execution. But Antigonus shortly followed this coup with an ironic alliance with Polyperchon and, by extension, Olympias.

Antigonus's about face stemmed not only from his ambition, but also from a sensible detection of the same quality in his supposed allies. Being geographically in the middle of things, in Asia Minor, he had many frontiers to worry about: in the west, his side of the Hellespont was coveted by Lysimachus, and in his southeast, Syria and the Levant would clearly be as useful to Ptolemy as to himself. Ptolemy had also generated suspicion recently when he seemed to set aside Eurydice in favor of a new mistress, Berenike I, who would bear Arsinoe II and Ptolemy II Philadelphus, Ptolemy's favored heirs. There was no mistaking Antigonus's total independence by 312 when he laid siege to Tyre and sent his son Demetrius to attack Ptolemy at Gaza, never mind the sisterhood of their wives.

With all this new activity, the significance of the two dynasties that once held sway in 323 reached their expiration dates. As a governing principle, one's family identity was being replaced by *sauve qui peut*, illustrated by Perdiccas's switch from the Antipatrids to the Argeads, then Adea/Eurydice's switch from the Argeads to the Antipatrids, then Antigonus's break from Cassander to join Olympias. In 316, Cassander laid siege to Olympias at Pydna; after a winter of subsisting on starvation rations, she surrendered and was swiftly done away with. But the Argead mystique still died hard: in spite of, or perhaps because of, having killed the mother of Alexander, Cassander still thought it prudent to take as his wife Alexander's last half-sister, Thessalonike, and to detain Roxane and her son in his entourage. Moreover, Antigonus gained traction by denouncing

Cassander for murdering the "queen mother," as it were, recasting the marriage of Thessalonike as a rape, for good measure. In 310 Cassander further dared to execute Roxane and Alexander IV. Antigonus and Polyperchon, still purporting to be believers in the Argead name, responded to this sacrilege by attempting to install Heracles, Alexander's son by Barsine, on the Macedonian throne, but as Polyperchon pursued this mission, he came to see Cassander's point: he decided that his prospects were better in a peace deal with Cassander than in the success of an untested teenage puppet, even if he were Alexander's son, and so he finally agreed to execute Heracles. On the other side of the Aegean, Antigonus, too, caught on: in 309 he ordered the assassination of Cleopatra in Sardis, which he controlled. For all intents and purposes Alexander's family had been snuffed out; notably it took nearly 15 years for their luster to fade. By this point, the major players were Cassander and Polyperchon in Greece, Lysimachus and Nicaea in Thrace, Ptolemy and Eurydice in Egypt, and Antigonus and his son Demetrius, now with Phila, in Asia Minor.

4.3 The Infrastructure of Conquest in Roman Italy

The post-Alexander melee in the eastern Mediterranean once again gave Italy space to develop on its own terms with relatively little eastern interference. With the *Diadochoi* and the independent cities of the Hellenic world trying to figure out their places in relation to one another, they largely eschewed the investments in Italian adventures that characterized previous generations. An exception can be found in squabbles for Sicily between Syracuse and Carthage, which drew some glancing attention from easterners, such as Ptolemy and the cities of Sparta and Athens.

Following their abject humiliation at the hands of the Samnites at the Caudine Forks, the Romans were quiet for a time. For two years in a row, 320–319, the electorate returned the same man to the consulship, Lucius Papirius Cursor, a sign of dealing with an emergency (and he would again be consul in 315 and 313). There is some evidence that the Romans took advantage of the lull to explore options in diplomacy, establishing ties with tribes along the Adriatic coast, such as the Frentani, as a means of opening up a second approach to the inland Samnites from an eastern flank. The Samnites accordingly made a move on Rome itself but were stopped at Ardea, one of the original colonial enterprises that was by then 125 years strong. In 314, the Romans had sufficient confidence to plant a colony at Luceria in Apulia on the far side of the Samnites, another attempt at encirclement. They also rebuilt Fregellae in 313, which had been a catalyst to the Second Samnite War back when it was founded in 328, and which had been lost to them since the Caudine Forks.

In 312, a remarkable senator was elected censor: Appius Claudius Caecus used his office to launch initiatives that capitalized on the momentary advantage held by the Romans in their sphere. To improve the quality of life in the growing urban core, he sponsored the Aqua Appia, an aqueduct that brought fresh water from springs over 10 miles east of Rome. What is more, likely mindful of the logistical failures that contributed to the defeat at the Caudine Forks, he invested in a new, highly engineered road from Rome to Capua called the Via Appia. Like the system of interstate highways in the United States, the project was borne of strategies for defense: soldiers and supplies could be taken straight to the front along its paved surface with greater efficiency and protection. Around the same time the Romans fitted out their first fleet, albeit a miniscule one: with just 20 triremes, the plan was likely meant to provide a coastline escort for troops along the new road. Finally, Rome minted its first silver coin in 310, the didrachm, produced outside the city in Campania and based on a Neapolitan weight standard; a one-time issue, it likely served to facilitate the new public expenditures on the aqueduct and the road.

The Aqua Appia and the Via Appia set precedents that spurred new infrastructure improvements that continued in the Roman world for centuries: the Via Valeria soon followed in 307, connecting Rome to the Adriatic Sea, and in 272, the Aqua Anio Vetus carried water to Rome from the Anio River, a large tributary of the Tiber north of the city. All of these projects demonstrate a burgeoning interest in science in Rome as a means of facilitating the state's survival and future prosperity. In essence, the city of Rome was being recognized as a physical space; as we shall see, these advancements were nearly exactly contemporaneous with the construction of dozens of new cities in the East by the *Diadochoi*, including the great Alexandria in Egypt.

Perhaps it was the very plotting of the Via Valeria in the years before its completion that prompted an uprising of Etruscan towns, which were located on the northern shoulder of its route. In 311, the Romans fought the highlander Etruscans that lined the Tiber – the cities of Perusia, Cortona, and Arretium – and in 308 the consul Quintus Fabius Maximus Rullianus subdued Volsinii (modern Orvieto), closer to home. An anecdote in Livy demonstrates the extent to which acculturation could contribute to an ancient state's success: in 308, the consul's brother allegedly was able to traverse enemy Etruscan territory to a northern ally because he was fluent in their language as a result of having received his education at Caere. In the following year, to see the crisis through, the Roman electorate extended Rullianus's *imperium* to another year, as it had done for Philo in 326 (Chapter 3), and as a proconsul he scored new victories. By 306, the Samnites and the Etruscans remained intact, but Rome had used ingenuity in building its influence anew after the disaster of the Caudine Forks.

In the course of clawing its way back, Rome experienced a rightward tilt in its domestic politics. According to some scholarly interpretations the Lex Ovinia of the 330s (its date is uncertain) provided that the senate become a lifetime position except in cases of moral turpitude of some unspecified kind. By the decade of the 310s, the significance of this reform would begin to take root, as aristocratic voices in Rome achieved a level of constancy and independence from popular vagaries. At the same time the practice of repeated consulships, or iteration, began to wane. A law of 342, the Lex Genucia, had compelled consuls to wait 10 years before running for a second term; the law was suspended from time to time as emergencies warranted (as with Papirius Cursor), but when crises subsided, the prohibition appears to have been back in effect. With the consulship no longer easily repeatable, the lifetime nature of the senate's membership increased its authority a step further. Senators may have argued that as Rome's territory grew, the extent of responsibilities outpaced what a popular assembly of amateurs could address.

4.4 Athens under Demetrius of Phaleron

If Rome indeed underwent a conservative tilt in its politics in the late fourth century (and the interpretation of the evidence is contested), it would be contemporaneous with similar trends in Athens. Demetrius of Phaleron, who had been appointed to govern Athens by Cassander, initiated reforms that can be called conservative both in the sense that they resisted change and that they favored the elite. Around the start of his tenure, a board of "guardians of the laws" (*nomophylakes*) was created with the task of ensuring that new legislative proposals did not contradict past practices or laws that were already in force. He also seems to have favored the authority of the Areopagus, an old council of aristocratic Athenians holding lifetime tenure, which had dominated the *polis* in the Archaic period. Some of the financial burdens on the elite were also curtailed, and simultaneously Demetrius cut back on state programs that allocated resources to the poor. To wit, he ended the practice of funding Athenian public works, such as

Figure 4.1 (a) The Lysicrates Monument, commemorating an award of first place in a theatrical competition in Athens in 335/4 BCE. (b) Engraving of a detail of the frieze depicting a memorable special effect in the production, of a man transforming into a dolphin. The performance was likely funded through a liturgy assigned to Lysicrates.

the fitting of triremes and the staging of festivals, through so-called liturgies, or, compulsory donations by the wealthy to the public good (see Figure 4.1). The drop in revenues from the cancelation of liturgies was offset by discontinuing the practice of paying poorer Athenian citizens to attend the assembly or to serve on juries. Participation in the organs of government was in turn restricted by property qualifications once again: only citizens with a net worth of 1000 drachmas could vote. Notably, this was not as extreme as the 2000 drachma requirement of the oligarchic regime of 321–318; the Athens of Demetrius of Phaleron charted something of a middle course.

Another feature of this unique decade in Athenian history is its universalist tendencies. That is, the right to citizenship, which was so hotly prized in the Classical period, was relaxed, such that it could be shared with worthy immigrants. The trend is as evident in the culture of the period as it is in its politics. The decade of Demetrius of Phaleron saw the rise of his good friend Menander as a premier comic playwright. Menander was noteworthy for abandoning plotlines about Athenian political life. Rather than disguise his characters as thinly veiled references to contemporary public figures, as Aristophanes had often done during the Peloponnesian War (Chapter 1), Menander's hero was the everyman or everywoman, from slave to soldier to strumpet, and audiences would find much that was familiar to their day-to-day lives (see Primary Source 4.1). Because of the de-emphasis in the plays on place and context, they were performed successfully throughout the Greek-speaking world, including Egypt where long fragments of his plays have been found on papyrus scraps. Menander thus represents an important change that was occurring in his generation – the increased fluidity of national or cultural identity. His plays would eventually have a profound influence on early Roman literature, as we shall see.

> **Primary Source 4.1**
>
> **Menander, *Perikeiromene* (or, "She Who Was Shorn")**
>
> This comedy of Menander, performed in Athens around 310–300, tells the story of a soldier in Corinth named Polemon ("War," in Greek) who shaved the head of his beloved, Glykera, in a jealous rage over her (alleged) attraction to their neighbor, Moschion. The play was popular in antiquity, but today it exists only in fragments, many, such as the one translated below, recovered from chance finds of papyri scraps in Egypt. In this scene, Moschion's slave, Daos, is leading his master to their house to reveal that Glykera has sought refuge with them. Overjoyed, Moschion asks Daos what reward he would like. Note the pessimism of Daos's response, a contrast to the virtues of courage and patriotism espoused by Demosthenes (Chapter 3).
>
> MOSCHION: Daos, you god forsaken con man, you've often made declarations to me that weren't true. If you're leading me astray now…
> DAOS: If that's the case, go ahead and string me up.
> MOSCHION: Now you're talking.
> DAOS: Wage war on me, so be it. But if it's true, and you see her (Glykera) inside, well, MOSCHION, I made it happen, everything – convincing her to come here; deploying thousands of arguments; making your mother take her in – everything you wanted. So, now what will I become?
> MOSCHION: What kind of life would you prefer, Daos, of all the options? Think about it.
> DAOS: Ok, wouldn't it be grand to be a miller?
> MOSCHION: You would go to a mill (?)
> DAOS: Don't assign me to any other craft.
> MOSCHION: I would like to see you as an overseer (*prostates*, see above in reference to Craterus) of Greek affairs, and in charge of an army!
> DAOS: It does not interest me to have my throat cut at any opportunity.
> MOSCHION: But think of the tax contracts! You'll be able to skim seven talents out of every eight (you collect).
> DAOS: I just want a bodega, Moschion, or a cheese stand in the marketplace. I swear I'm not interested in being rich. That's who I am; that's what I prefer."

Another innovative writer in Athens at this time, Theophrastus, like Menander also took steps to view the human experience as divorced from ethnic identity. He had inherited the leadership of the Lyceum, Aristotle's school, upon Aristotle's death in 326 and led it until 290. His work, *Characters*, composed in the decade of the 310s, is a compendium of personality categories, all of them flawed or annoying in some way – the reckless man, the gossip, the braggart, the coward, the idiot, among others. In Theophrastus's telling, ethnicity was not a cause of natural traits, but rather circumstance and context determined how one behaved. He still held an affection for Athens, but his "characters" had little interest in the Athenian *esprit de corps*, instead hiring foreign servants, obsessing over luxurious foreign imports, and looking down on the native Athenian assembly.

4.5 Other Western Powers: Syracuse and Carthage

Sicily in this period became more of interest to the great Greek powers, including Sparta, Athens, and eventually Ptolemy, and it experienced some tumultuous civil wars. At the center of the storm was Agathocles, the son of a potter who had taken power in Syracuse as an informal *tyrannos* in 317. His reign brought to an end some 20 years of oligarchic competition, and his rise, of course, was not uncontested. In 314, the Spartan king Acrotatus, backed by Tarentum, attempted to launch a campaign against him from nearby Agrigentum, which failed. Part of Agathocles's success on this score, we are told, came from his negotiations with the Carthaginian general Hamilcar, who promised at least not to abet Sicilian missions against Syracuse. In this sense Agathocles benefitted from Carthage's loose management of its generals in the field, who tended to act autonomously. It is a testament to how important this détente was to his survival that as soon as Hamilcar died, in 311, and was replaced by a less friendly, more assertive Punic general, Agathocles promptly fell under siege, a low point in his career. Trapped in this corner, he effected a remarkable escape and relieved the siege by a bold maneuver: he planned to attack Carthage itself, the first Hellenic general to do so. Carthage had to scramble to defend itself.

The unprecedented nature of Agathocles's expedition created a stir among the eastern powers who were just emerging from the Argead mystique. Ophellas, a governor of Cyrene further down the African coast from Carthage and an ally of Ptolemy, sent help to Agathocles. Athens, too, sent ships, partly because Ophellas was married to Euthydice, an Athenian woman descended from Miltiades, the victorious general at the Battle of Marathon (Chapter 1). There is evidence that a Punic delegation was on the scene in Athens around the same time, most likely to rebut the friends of Ophellas and to plead that the Athenians stay out: while Euthydice may have inspired Athens's patriotic dreams, the Carthaginians could have pointed to productive trading relationships with them, if the extensive archeological evidence of Attic artifacts in Carthage is any judge. The Carthaginians were also surely aware of the praise heaped upon their political system by Aristotle, Alexander's tutor, it should be remembered, whose analysis of their constitution concluded that it was strong. Nevertheless, Athenians flocked to Ophellas's campaign, and perhaps to Euthydice's side.

Carthage was lucky to survive Agathocles's game-changing assault. In the midst of the siege, an opportunistic nobleman Bomilcar tried to overthrow the government and establish something approximating a monarchy, but he was somehow put down. A windfall for Carthage came in the form of unrest among Agathocles's soldiers. He was having difficulty feeding them in this foreign land, plus some of the Cyrenaean reinforcements were displeased to say the least when their commander Ophellas was murdered, we are told, by Agathocles himself. The end of the expedition came when Agathocles had to return to Syracuse to shore up his "throne": he left his son in charge in Africa, who spread their forces too thin and ended up defeated and having to negotiate. Notably the Carthaginians were not as vituperative as would have been their right: some of the surrendering Greek soldiers were said to have been allowed to join the Punic army, and still more accepted land in western Sicily as part of a Punic settlement. Sicily, Carthage, Sparta, Cyrene, Athens, Egypt (the Ptolemies) – the rise of Agathocles yet further demonstrates the interconnectedness of the Mediterranean, and the multiplicity of players trying to make sense of the vacuum after Alexander's eclipse.

4.6 Political Epiphanies

As Demetrius of Phaleron held steady in Athens, his important allies – Cassander, Lysimachus, and Ptolemy, all siblings-in-law – contended with Antigonus with varying degrees of success. Antigonus, for the most part in possession of Asia Minor and Mesopotamia, had the advantage of the residual wealth still present in the old Persian metropolises even after Alexander's predations. With such vast treasure, he was able to maintain his vital relationships with Rhodes and other naval powers. Still, he needed to remove at least one of his many rivals if he were to step into Alexander's role as sole king. As mentioned earlier, he sent his son Demetrius to do just that at Gaza, the entrance passage to Egypt and the Nile Delta. Ptolemy, with critical assistance from the superior generalship of Seleucus, managed to turn back Demetrius. Meanwhile,

Seleucus saw an opportunity in the momentary disarray of Demetrius's failure to make a run for Babylon, which he took for himself relatively unchallenged. A delicate *status quo* obtained in the eastern Mediterranean from 311 to 308 with Ptolemy in Egypt, Lysimachus in Thrace, Cassander in Macedonia, Antigonus in Asia Minor, and now Seleucus in Mesopotamia.

Much of this changed when Demetrius, son of Antigonus, came into his own in 307 with an aggressive and creative agenda. First Demetrius's naval allies helped him encircle Athens by taking Andros, Corinth, Sicyon, and Megara. Then he sealed the deal by placing Munychia, the fortress protecting Athens, under siege. Athens soon capitulated and Demetrius of Phaleron retreated from his homonymous attacker, Demetrius Poliorketes, to the protection of Cassander. The new Demetrius in Athens promptly reinstalled the full democracy, wiping away many of the reforms from the previous decade. He also set the city on a path to unprecedented prosperity, with timber at subsidized prices for shipbuilding, contracts to rebuild the Long Walls connecting Athens to Piraeus, control over some strategic islands, and the removal of all garrisons. The Athenians responded with gratitude that was unprecedented in its level of sycophancy: the assembly decreed games in honor of Poliorketes; established two new voting tribes in his name and that of his father Antigonus; set up statues of them adjacent to the Tyrannicides (recovered from Susa by Alexander; Chapter 3); and even assigned priests to devise a scheme for worshipping them as gods.

One of Demetrius Poliorketes's few failures was an attempt to control Athens's philosophical schools, which he rightly viewed as supplying intellectual fodder for oligarchies in the recent past. A law forcing all such schools to register with the state was passed at first, but was soon repealed, which gave rise to the foundation of two new philosophical schools, Epicureanism in 306 and Stoicism in 301, to be discussed shortly. Nevertheless, in spite of Demetrius's inability to quash Aristotle's old Peripatetics and the others, the mutual admiration between Athens and the Antigonid generals, at least on the surface, was unmistakable: in addition to all of the above, Demetrius Poliorketes took as a second wife Euthydice, the walking symbol of past Athenian glory who was newly widowed after the death of Ophellas. The irony is that even as Euthydice's marriage elevated Athenian fortunes, the values that her forefather Miltiades had championed – a democratic ethos; equitable political participation – were eclipsed by the city's strange new adoration of a near-monarch.

Demetrius Poliorketes's remarkable year was not yet finished: after settling affairs in Athens, he sailed for Cyprus where he defeated a navy led by Ptolemy's brother. His and his father's successes were undeniable, and now they both felt comfortable enough to forego the euphemisms of power, such as *epimeletes*, *prostates*, or some other moniker, and had themselves proclaimed kings, *basileis* (singular, *basileus*) in their own right. With Alexander's family largely dead and buried (disregarding for the moment Cassander's two sons by Thessalonike, who were still children), there was, practically speaking, little reason not to. The royal proclamation in 306 tipped a line of dominoes in the following year. Ptolemy, Lysimachus, Cassander, Seleucus, and even Agathocles in Syracuse all took on the title of *basileus* in 305.

What did it mean to be "king," especially when many others shared the title? For one, it may have helpfully clarified the nature of a ruler's status when dealing with the outside world. For example, in 303 Seleucus embarked on an important diplomatic deal with king Chandragupta, the founder of the Mauryan Dynasty in India. By its terms, Seleucus would rescind all claims to the land so tenuously held by Alexander some 20 years prior, and in exchange, receive herds upon herds of battle elephants; we are told that there were 500 in number, the scale of which takes some effort to imagine. Seleucus must have been satisfied to sign the relevant missives with the title of "king"; the evidence does not survive, but one wonders what he called himself in 308, when he is known to have first entered into negotiations with Chandragupta.

The political epiphany of kingship appears to have played a role in a florid phase of city-building around this time, akin to Alexander's many Alexandrias some 20 years prior. Antigonus, in need of a showpiece capital, founded Antigoneia on the Orontes River, strategically policing the northeast Mediterranean in the corner where Asia Minor met the Levant. Ambitions for the city's future were profound: it is said to have been plotted within a perimeter of over 7 miles, and the first wave of settlers came from Athens, still in the throes of Antigonomania. Other new cities from the period similarly bespeak his self-aggrandizement: the name Antigoneia was given to a small town in Bithynia on Lake Ascanius near the Sea of Marmora, and it was enlarged to suit the honor; another was founded near the site of Troy, known as Antigoneia Troas, effecting a synoecism of smaller villages around a new urban core. Cassander simultaneously embellished the Macedonian capital at Pella, commissioning a new grid of streets that expanded its size and gave it the ordered regularity that was prized in this period. The famous mosaics of Pella, featuring Alexander the Great on a hunt, date to around 300 (see Figure 4.2). He also founded Cassandreia, in Chalcidike, not far from Olynthus, the town that had been destroyed by Philip II in 348 (Chapter 1). For Seleucus's part, he established Seleuceia in 305 on the Tigris River at its closest remove from the Euphrates, where Babylon still stood, as well as another Seleuceia in the northern Levant, called Seleuceia Pieria.

Ptolemy I also marked the trend: though the great Alexandria is said to have been founded by Alexander the Great, it was the Successor who made it a city worth visiting, laying out its grid and the Heptastadion, an artificial land bridge connecting the mainland with an offshore island called Pharos. Easily discerned zones of the city defined certain purposes, such as a palace quarter and military barracks occupying one quadrant. The palace also included the famous Museum. Demetrius of Phaleron, who had fled to Ptolemy's guardianship in 297 when Cassander died, is said to have been an initial advisor to the formation of this institution, a library and research institute that was opened in 295. Funding came from Ptolemy's

Figure 4.2 Mosaic from Pella depicting a stag hunt, c. 300 BCE, perhaps featuring Alexander the Great. A similar scene appears on the so-called Alexander Sarcophagus, Figure 3.1.

largesse, and as the collection of scrolls and other resources grew, scholars, writers, and artists soon followed, and Alexandria quickly became a rival to Athens as the cultural hub of the Greek-speaking world.

4.7 New Philosophies of Politics and Participation

Another sea change that was related to the expansion of the title *basileus* was a change to broad conceptions of politics and power in general. This manifested itself in changes to both religious practices and intellectual pursuits. As if Athens had not heaped enough praise on Demetrius Poliorketes already in 307, the sycophancy reached new heights when he returned in 304 following an ingenious though ultimately unsuccessful siege of Ptolemy's allies at Rhodes. The siege of Rhodes had taken a year and involved an elaborate blockade of the harbor and a huge camp of infantry outside the gates (the epithet Poliorketes means "Besieger"). All of it failed, and the materials of Demetrius's abandoned siegeworks were eventually used by Rhodes to build their "Colossal" statue of Helios, one of the seven wonders of the ancient world; nevertheless, Demetrius presented the siege as a victory in the sense that he had compelled Rhodes to remain neutral. As *basileus* he was nearly elevated to godhead by the Athenians. Though he was now married to both Phila and Euthydice, he also married Deidameia, an Epirot princess related to Olympias; Deidameia's younger brother Pyrrhus was on the verge of coming into his own in the region (Chapter 5).

The monopolization of politics by multiple *basileis* led to existential dilemmas, for lack of a better term, among the Athenians, a populace that was accustomed to participatory self-government. New philosophers were inspired to rethink the role and nature of the individual in the cosmos. In 306 Epicurus gave radical lectures on the apathy of the gods toward the human experience, stating that divine beings existed but cared not about the turmoil and vicissitudes of human life. For that reason, he argued, one should strive to absent himself from situations that caused stress or tension, and seek to achieve a state of *ataraxia*, or "freedom from anxiety." Often his movement was associated with a life lived free of politics, a significant departure from the culture of Athens to this point.

Coming shortly after the advent of Epicureanism, the philosophy of Stoicism was borne in the teachings of Zeno, an immigrant to Athens from Cyprus who lectured in the Stoa Poikile, or "Painted Stoa," a monumental porch overlooking the Athenian agora from its northern boundary. Similar to the Epicureans, he believed that much of what transpired in the world was beyond one's control, but rather than advocating a departure from anxiety, he and his followers taught that fear and desire were impulses that distracted men from virtue, and one must find ways to control these passions and accept one's fate.

Contemporaneous in Athens with Epicurus and Zeno was Euhemerus, who joined them in their rejection of the notion that gods might respond to human prayers. In his conception, as recounted in his story, *The Sacred History*, the gods were once earthly, mortal kings (*basileis*) who achieved divinity through fantastic deeds. They now lived on a distant island beyond Arabia, not coincidentally in the direction of the world in which Alexander himself had perished. The island now housed a universalizing Utopia, where language, dress, cuisine, and other facets of life bore features found throughout the known world, from Crete, Egypt, and Persia, for example. The resonances with the recent elevation of the *Diadochoi* to kingship across many terrains are clear.

At the root of all these trends in philosophical thinking was the new veneration in the Hellenistic period of the goddess/personification Tyche, the Greek conception of Fortune or Chance (see Figure 4.3). As Greeks reached far beyond both the physical and intellectual confines

Figure 4.3 (a) Roman copy in miniature of the Tyche of Antioch, originally sculpted in the late fourth century BCE. The original featured the figure of the personified Orontes River at the goddess's feet and a crown fashioned as Antioch's walls – a metaphor for the city's reliance on Tyche/Fortune. (b) Plaster cast of a metal emblem from Ptolemaic Egypt featuring Isis with aspects of the pose and iconography of the Tyche of Antioch. The popularity of the goddess was widespread and was adapted for different contexts.

of their recent ancestors, they saw that the universe was governed – or not governed at all – by principles that were unruly or unknowable, and not in keeping with old Hellenic expectations.

4.8 The Battle of Ipsus and its Aftermath

Being called a *basileus* at this time no longer implied absolute power, as was evident to all. Antigonus now faced a united front of fellow "kings," Lysimachus, Seleucus, and Ptolemy, as organized by Cassander. In 301 a battle was joined at Ipsus, near the geographic center of Asia Minor, with only Ptolemy absent owing to a miscommunication. Antigonus was killed and his army was routed; Seleucus's elephants were said to have been decisive. Demetrius Poliorketes escaped thanks to his command of the seas, probably taking his teenaged brother-in-law Pyrrhus with him, but his departure meant surrendering his massive holdings in Asia Minor to be divvied up among the victors. Lysimachus absorbed most of Asia Minor, which brought him closer to the border with his old brother-in-law Ptolemy, who held a rich part of the Levant called Coele-Syria uncontested (apart from a few coastal strongholds still loyal to Demetrius Poliorketes). Two of the cities named Antigoneia mentioned above – in the Troad and Bithynia – accordingly fell to Lysimachus's control, and he renamed them Alexandria Troas and Nicaea, respectively, the latter memorializing his wife, the daughter of Antipater, who died around this time. With Nicaea's death, and since Ptolemy had demoted, in a sense, his first wife

Eurydice in favor of his mistress Berenike I, the two kings reinforced their old marriage tie with a wedding between Lysimachus and Arsinoe II, Ptolemy's daughter by Berenike. Cassander, still holding Macedonia, agreed for his son also to marry a daughter of Ptolemy, articulating another tripartite union. Agathocles of Syracuse, now self-proclaimed to be a "king," married into Ptolemy's family, too, via Theoxena, who was either Ptolemy's daughter or stepdaughter. Around this time Agathocles had managed to seize Corcyra along Greece's northwest coast, a vital bridge between western and eastern spheres that betrayed his ambitions beyond Sicily. Seleucus received the region of northern Syria around Antigoneia, finally in possession of a land bridge between his Mesopotamia and the sea. He had no use for a city so named, however, and so in 300 he founded a new settlement nearby, called Antioch after his son Antiochus, and simply transferred much of Antigoneia's population to it, the original Athenian settlers included. Antioch would grow quickly and become one of the great cities of antiquity, with its representation of Tyche becoming widely revered (above).

After 301, Demetrius Poliorketes was thus poised to lose everything. He took flight; though he lacked land he still had treasure, which was sufficient enough to hire mercenaries and navies to carry him west. His former abode, Athens, which had feted him with zeal a few years earlier, now rebuffed him. Cassander had wasted no time in capitalizing on the reversal of fortune to back a new regime in the city supported by mercenaries of his own, and Demetrius ricocheted a few miles down the coast to Corinth. From his perch on the Acrocorinth, Demetrius could have seen Athens on the horizon on any clear day, and he plotted his return. He set about arranging various rapprochements with the powers that could help him: to Seleucus he sent in marriage his and Phila's daughter, named Stratonike, and to Ptolemy he sent Pyrrhus, the talented brother of his wife, Deidameia, as a diplomatic hostage. Diplomacy was thus afoot for Demetrius Poliorketes, but it would turn out that his next step forward would be facilitated by chance: the hated Cassander died of natural causes in 297. Cassander's two surviving sons, nephews of Alexander, were divided against themselves, and Demetrius was able to retake Athens, although not at all easily, by siege in 295.

4.9 Rome vs. Italy at the Battle of Sentinum

An illustrative piece of evidence for the growing importance of Italy at this time is the attention it was beginning to receive among historians in the East. Timaeus, born in Sicily but writing as an immigrant in Athens, took up Rome as his subject, and by now he had much to report. Following the reduction of Etruscan power in 306, the Romans pivoted south where they confronted the Hernici and Aequi who still clung to their mountaintop fortresses in the spine of Italy. Many of their communities were incorporated into the system of allies as states without the vote, *civitates sine suffragio*. In 304, the Samnites formally sued for peace, ending the so-called Second Samnite War but in reality only taking a hiatus from fighting. New Roman colonies were planted at Sora and Alba Fucens in 303, and in 299, a colony at Narnia occupied a commanding hilltop near the center of the Italian peninsula, thus useful for supporting campaigns on both sides of the mountains. Tarentum, situated in the instep of Italy's boot and the largest of the old Greek colonies, thought it prudent to enter diplomatic negotiations with Rome, whereby if the Romans respected Tarentum's primacy in its gulf, Tarentum would not interfere with Rome's presence inland.

With the Etruscans subdued and following the Samnite peace, Roman activity further south along their coast increased. Another Spartan king was active in support of Tarentum: just as Acrotatus had tried to help the Greeks in Sicily against Agathocles in 314, in 303, Cleonymus took to the field against the Lucanians, in the toe of Italy's boot, so to speak. Romans participated in the defense of Lucania, and Cleonymus was forced to quit Italy entirely. The Lucanians turned to Rome again in 298 when Samnite raids in their territory threatened their sovereignty. It is likely that around this time the number of legions in the Roman army expanded from two to four. The leadership of the Lucanian campaign is in dispute among historians owing to contradictory strands of evidence, but it is worth drawing attention to the role played by the forefather of a famous clan of Roman generals: Lucius Cornelius Scipio Barbatus, consul of 298, is said by an inscription to have captured key cities and to have extracted hostages (see Primary Source 4.2 and Figure 4.4). In this, the so-called Third Samnite War, the Romans pressed every advantage. The capable and clever Rullianus was returned to the consulship for 297, with Publius Decius Mus as his colleague. They held their *imperium* as proconsuls in the following year (just as Rullianus's command had been extended from 308 to 307, above), and the venerable Appius Claudius Caecus was elected consul. In 296 Appius demonstrated as keen an awareness of the inspirational power of religious architecture as he had realized the value of infrastructure investments in 312: he promised a new temple to Bellona, a war goddess, between Tiber Island and the Capitoline Hill.

Primary Source 4.2

Epitaph of Scipio Barbatus

The inscription on this sarcophagus (Figure 4.4) honors Scipio Barbatus, consul of 298. Though the events it describes are from the Third Samnite War, it is likely that it was carved by Barbatus's descendants a couple of generations later, perhaps during the Second Punic War when the Scipiones were distinguishing themselves in Spain and in Africa (Chapter 7). Still, it is one of the earliest Latin inscriptions recording an historical event. The Latin text is in verse and would have been sung, a quality that is not preserved in the English translation.

> "Lucius Cornelius Scipio Barbatus, born to Gnaeus his father, was a brave and wise man whose appearance was equal to his courage. A consul, censor, and aedile among you, he seized Taurasia Cisauna from Samnium, conquered all Lucania, and detained hostages."

By the start of the Third Samnite War, through a combination of alliance and colonization, in a process that had been as piecemeal as it was deliberate, the Romans had assembled a protected zone over the mountains that connected the Tyrrhenian and Adriatic Seas, and the only hope for the Samnites lay in forming a coalition of their own. Under the leadership of Gellius Egnatius, they tried to organize a pan-Italian resistance that would unite the Etruscans and Celts of the north with the Oscans and themselves in the south. A Samnite army managed to negotiate passage north of the Via Valeria to join the Celts at Sentinum, where both awaited reinforcements from the Etruscans. Rullianus and Decius Mus, now reelected to the consulship of 295 (having thus held *imperium* continuously as consuls, then proconsuls, then consuls again, all on an annual basis) hastened to join the battle before the Etruscans arrived. Decius Mus's side suffered some initial losses that seemed liable to demoralize his troops, and so he sacrificed himself to the gods in the name of victory by charging into Celtic lines in spite of impossible odds against survival – an act of self-immolation called *devotio*. Rullianus was thus the only consul to return to Rome, where he celebrated a massive triumph and promised to build a temple to Jupiter in his role as bringer of victory. The war was not yet over, but the Samnites were all but lost.

Figure 4.4 Sarcophagus of Scipio Barbatus, with inscription.

4.10 Conclusions

Rome became the focus of Greek attention. The Battle of Sentinum was described not only by Timaeus but by his contemporaries as well, including Duris of Samos and Philinus. Rome was an oddity – it brushed up against multiple Greek-speaking powers, and existed in Greek mythology, including the Trojan War saga, as a weigh station for wandering heroes on their way home. Yet, it had its own language, its own way of fighting (without a navy, for the most part), and its own gods and traditions. Most notably, it eschewed the tendency toward *basileus*, which was continuing along a trickle-down from the major *Diadochoi*: Zipoites, a local landowner in Bithynia, proclaimed himself *basileus* in 297. An equilibrium of sorts had been achieved by 295 among Ptolemy in Egypt, Seleucus in Mesopotamia, Lysimachus in Thrace, and Agathocles in Sicily, yet even so, the growth of Rome portended that new ways were opening up for the balance to come under pressure. Pyrrhus in the next generation would tread a path that included both east and west, proving that a pan-Mediterranean realm, while not achieved by him, could be a legitimate aspiration.

Further Reading

Anson, Edward (2014). *Alexander's Heirs: The Age of the Successors*. West Sussex: Wiley-Blackwell.
Billows, Richard (1990). *Antigonus the One-Eyed and the Creation of the Hellenistic State*. Berkeley: University of California Press.

Carney, Elizabeth (2006). *Olympias: Mother of Alexander the Great*. New York: Routledge.

Cornell, Timothy (1995). *The Beginnings of Rome: Italy and Rome from the Bronze Age to the Punic Wars, c. 1000–264 BC*. London: Routledge.

Grainger, John (1990). *Seleucus Nikator: Constructing a Hellenistic Kingdom*. New York: Routledge.

Habicht, Christian (1997). *Athens from Alexander to Antony*. Cambridge, MA: Harvard University Press.

Hölbl, Günther (2000). *A History of the Ptolemaic Empire*. New York: Routledge.

Lape, Susan (2004). *Reproducing Athens: Menander's Comedy, Democratic Culture, and the Hellenistic City*. Princeton: Princeton University Press.

Lund, Helen S (1992). *Lysimachus: A Study in Early Hellenistic Kingship*. New York: Routledge.

5

To 264: The Path of Pyrrhus

Timeline

295: Marriage of Pyrrhus to Lanassa, daughter of Agathocles of Syracuse
293: Colony founded by Rome at Venusia
291: Marriage of Lanassa to Demetrius Poliorketes; Temple of Aesculapius in Rome
289–287: Failed attempt by Demetrius Poliorketes to expand into Asia Minor, defeated by combined pressure of Lysimachus, Ptolemy I, and Pyrrhus
287: Lex Hortensia in Rome gives resolutions of the plebeian assembly the force of law
283: Deaths of Ptolemy I and Demetrius Poliorketes; Romans support garrison at Thurii close to Tarentum
281: Battle of Corupedium: combined force of Seleucus I, Antigonus Gonatas, and Ptolemy Ceraunus defeats Lysimachus; death of Lysimachus, assassination of Seleucus I
280–275: Pyrrhus's wars in Italy against Rome and in Sicily against Carthage
279: Celtic invasion of the Balkans; death of Ptolemy Ceraunus
274–271: First Syrian War: Ptolemy II against Antiochus I, heir of Seleucus I
273: Roman colonies at Cosa and Paestum; fall of Tarentum; embassy of Ptolemy II to Rome
272: Death of Pyrrhus at Argos
270: Campanian mercenaries seize Rhegium

Principal Themes

- Individual *Diadochoi* still dreamt of total domination and made bids for Alexander's old realm – Demetrius Poliorketes in 289, Lysimachus in 281, and Seleucus I also in 281 – but each time, the other *basileis* rallied against the striver and restored the multipolar quality of the East.
- Pressure from Rome led states in southern Italy to invite Pyrrhus of Epirus to fight on their behalf.
- Pyrrhus won a reputation for military excellence, but the allied forces of Rome and Carthage stopped his progress and he returned to the Greek world much reduced.
- A brief war between the Ptolemies and the Seleucids for control of Coele-Syria went in favor of the former. Called the First Syrian War by modern historians, it marked a conflict that would reignite from time to time for generations to come.
- The Library at Alexandria found its footing under Ptolemy II's sponsorship of innovative intellectual projects in medicine, engineering, and literature.
- Celtic tribes took advantage of the disarray in Thrace and Macedonia to invade the Balkans and Asia Minor, in the second case settling into the long-lasting kingdom of Galatia.

The Roman Republic and the Hellenistic Mediterranean: From Alexander to Caesar, First Edition. Joel Allen.
© 2020 John Wiley & Sons, Inc. Published 2020 by John Wiley & Sons, Inc.

5.1 Introduction

For many reasons it might seem misleading to list Pyrrhus among the *Diadochoi*. Born in 319, he obviously never knew Alexander and was at least one generation younger than the major players with whom he dealt for most of his career. Hailing from Epirus, sparse and mountainous, and often barely holding on to that, he did not have strong territorial foundations for his exploits. Whatever boost he had in early life came from his blood relationship with Olympias, though the feuding between the respective branches of their clan meant that their alliances were never simple. And yet, Pyrrhus was highly revered in antiquity for his generalship, commonly ranked as second only to Alexander in his grasp of tactics and strategy. And it was with *his* death – not Ptolemy's, or Lysimachus's, or Seleucus's – that Hieronymus of Caria chose to end his influential history of the *Diadochoi* (Chapter 4). In many ways, as we shall see, his career marked a turning point in Mediterranean geopolitics. As Pyrrhus criss-crossed the sea without a secure base from very nearly his birth, he was open to whatever opportunities afforded him a chance for advancement. The flexibility of his worldview is emblematic of new possibilities for the exercise of power in the mid-third century.

Pyrrhus became famous for his tussles with Rome, but in fact these came late in his life and lasted for only a few years. It was Pyrrhus who elevated Rome's profile and not the other way around, as their handful of battles prompted the Romans to deepen ties with Carthage, then its ally, and resulted in new diplomatic contact with the Ptolemies. The Roman experience of Hellenic culture continued to broaden as war booty was imported into the city at this time, including the poet Livius Andronicus who would go on to translate Homeric epics into Latin. For their part, the Ptolemies came under the leadership of Ptolemy II Philadelphus, the heir by Berenike I, rather than Ptolemy Ceraunus, the son of old Antipater's daughter Eurydice; effectively ousted, Eurydice and Ceraunus fled Alexandria. Egypt flourished under its creative and forceful new monarch, achieving some of Alexandria's most famous glories at this time. Seleucus I also managed to pass power smoothly to his son, Antiochus I, in Syria and Mesopotamia, even as he was killed, ironically, by his ally the renegade Ceraunus, right after a military victory. With Antigonus Gonatas, the son of Demetrius Poliorketes, governing Macedonia following the death of his father, the eastern Mediterranean was dominated by these three major canonical dynasties.

5.2 The Education of Pyrrhus

Glimpses of Pyrrhus's early career came in the previous chapter. To back up to the beginning: he was born to an aristocratic family in Epirus related to Olympias. When Olympias was besieged by Cassander at Pydna in 316 Pyrrhus's father had to flee, taking his toddler son with him. They found refuge with Glaucias, the king of Illyria and a constant rival of Cassander. Years later, in 307, Glaucias attempted to make use of Pyrrhus, whose father had died, by planting him on the Epirot throne as an 11-year old puppet. The same year saw another newcomer to Greece, it will be remembered, when Demetrius Poliorketes took Athens from Demetrius of Phaleron. Now a boy-king, Pyrrhus would have watched as generals proclaimed their royalty, first Antigonus in 306, and then the others in 305 (Chapter 4). In 303, Demetrius Poliorketes married Pyrrhus's sister, Deidameia, presumably also backed by Glaucias, creating a useful alliance for Pyrrhus, now aged 16. The next year, as Pyrrhus was attending a wedding in Illyria (which he perhaps viewed as a comfortable second homeland given his youth spent there), he was knocked from power by a relative in Epirus, forcing him to seek refuge with his sister and powerful brother-in-law in Athens. As we have seen, Pyrrhus was present with Demetrius on the Antigonid side of the Battle of Ipsus in 301, and following that loss, was deployed as a diplomatic hostage to Ptolemy I. Thus, before the age of 20, Pyrrhus had been all over the Balkan peninsula; had fought a massive and bloody engagement in the heart of Asia Minor; and ultimately found himself on the edge of the Nile Delta. Both at Ipsus and in Ptolemy's court, Pyrrhus would have developed a familiarity with elephants – the start of a long and productive relationship.

The two or so years of Pyrrhus's hostageship in Egypt saw a shift in his loyalties and associations. During this time his sister Deidameia died, thus removing the filial link to Demetrius Poliorketes. At the same time, he received as wife Antigone, a daughter of Berenike I, Ptolemy's powerful consort. Thus, when Cassander died in Macedonia in 297 leaving a divided dynasty in Greece, it was to Ptolemy I, not Demetrius Poliorketes, that Pyrrhus turned for help in retaking his throne. Shortly after Pyrrhus's reinstallment with the help of Ptolemy's navy, Antigone died, and by 295, the end of the previous chapter, he had taken on another strategic marriage, to Lanassa, the daughter of Agathocles of Syracuse, by whom he gained access to the island of Corcyra as a kind of dowry (Chapter 4). Demetrius Poliorketes soon retook Athens, and the two former allies and in-laws would now have seen each other over their horizons as, at best, rivals, but more likely as enemies.

When Cassander died Pyrrhus backed one of his sons, named Alexander, who took the throne with his help. He did not hold it for long: Demetrius Poliorketes was able to murder the youth at a banquet, and, still married to Phila, the sister of Cassander and aunt of this Alexander, he was able to convince the soldiers to proclaim him king. Thus began a successful period of several years for Demetrius Poliorketes: he managed to subdue rebellions by Thebes and Thessaly and sought expansion into Thrace after its king Lysimachus was momentarily held prisoner by the Celts in 292. Demetrius's appointed representative and quasi-governor in Thebes was Hieronymus of Cardia, the influential historian of the *Diadochoi*. Demetrius's and Phila's daughter, Stratonike, who had been married to Seleucus I, divorced the old man to marry his son, Antiochus I, who was elevated to joint king. It was a strange but peaceful hand-off of power, father to son via a shared wife; the constancy and centrality of Stratonike as queen suggest the powerful role that she played in the regime. As her father, Demetrius Poliorketes must have experienced enhanced prestige in the process. One of the high-level players to recognize that the winds were in Demetrius's sails was Pyrrhus's wife, Lanassa: in 291 she offered herself in marriage to Poliorketes, taking the island of Corcyra and her status as heir of Agathocles with her. With this loss Pyrrhus had the same enemy both west and east of him.

5.3 The Collapse of Demetrius Poliorketes

With a break for the moment in his battles with Pyrrhus and others in the Balkans, Demetrius Poliorketes believed in 289 that he, like the Great Alexander in 334, occupied a suitably pacified foundation from which to launch an invasion of Asia. He began constructing a massive new fleet for which he founded a new harbor city, of course calling it Demetrias (modern Volos). For Athens, he performed an about-face in his preference for its political regime: once the restorer of democracy (Chapter 4), he now supported an oligarchy in the interest of keeping the assembly under control. If the reform was unpopular in Athens, we have to guess at it from their later actions, for a principal literary source for the moment of Demetrius's return – a hymn revering him as a god – implies abject obeisance (see Primary Source 5.1). Preserved by Duris of Samos, the hymn was composed on the occasion of the Eleusinian Mysteries, which honored Demeter

> **Primary Source 5.1**
>
> **Hymn in Praise of Demetrius Poliorketes**
>
> This text was quoted by the historian Duris of Samos as the hymn that was composed in Athens in honor of Demetrius Poliorketes when he held the city in 291. It would seem that the determination to resist outsiders in Athens, as once extolled by Demosthenes (Chapter 3), was not universally held, or could at least be concealed in the name of expediency.
>
> "The greatest of the gods and the most beloved in the city are here. The season (of the Eleusinian Mysteries) has brought together Demeter and Demetrius. She has come to complete the sacred rites of her daughter, and he is present in benign countenance, fair and cheerful as a god should be. A sacred thing it is to behold, all his friends in a ring about him, who occupies the center as if they were the stars and he were the sun. Be well, o son of most powerful Poseidon and Aphrodite! The other gods are far removed, or have no ears, or don't even exist, or aren't paying attention, but you, we see, are here, not made of wood or stone, but genuine. So we pray to you: first bring about peace, dearest one; that's within your power. That Sphinx that's lording it over us (and not just [a Sphinx] over Thebes but over all of Greece) – the Aetolians, perched on their cliff like the old legend, grab all our bodies and carry them off… Would that you would punish them."

from whom the king's own name was derived. Demetrius was likened to Poseidon for his victories at sea, and Phila, still his primary wife, as Aphrodite. Most important, it obliquely called on him to defend Athens against the predations of the Aetolian League. Demetrius took up the challenge by founding new athletic competitions in Athens, which were fashioned as the new Pythian Games, supplanting the ones that had been held at Aetolian-controlled Delphi for almost 500 years. Ever the opportunists, the Athenians yet further intensified their reverence for the person strongest enough to defend them: a late source claims that Demetrius took up residence in the Parthenon at this time, and that the Athenians turned a blind eye to sexual escapades on their holiest site (though one would be wise to discount such a scurrilous account).

The tables turned quickly. Since Demetrius's designs on Asia were obvious, the other *Diadochoi* maneuvered against him in staggered unison. In 288, three fronts gradually opened on Demetrius's domains. First, Ptolemy I sent ships into the Aegean, having already won Tyre, Sidon, and Cyprus. It is possible that among his goals in the region was pursuit of his former first wife, Eurydice, the sister of Phila, who had abandoned Egypt when it became apparent that Berenike I was favored; Eurydice had settled near Miletus with her son Ptolemy Ceraunus and her daughter Ptolemais. While Demetrius Poliorketes was losing influence in the islands and coastal cities in the face of attacks by Ptolemy, he was attacked by land from the east by Lysimachus. What must have surprised Demetrius the most, and what led to his undoing, was a third front, opened on his west by Pyrrhus in clear violation of a pact of 289. We are told that the Macedonian army then effected the gentlest of mutinies: they pointed out to Demetrius that his situation was untenable, that they were unwilling to follow him, and that he should make his escape while he could. Demetrius agreed: he ordered his son Antigonus Gonatas (meaning, "Knock-kneed," another memorable epithet) to hold on to their remaining fortresses in Greece, such as Demetrias, Piraeus, and Corinth, among others, while he worked on plans to go east in search of conquest and aid. Along the way, in Cassandreia, Phila ended her role in their shared flight by suicide. In 287, the Athenians overthrew Demetrius's oligarchs and reestablished their democracy, even though Antigonus Gonatas still held Piraeus: a latent insincerity was thus revealed behind the hymn to Demetrius, which had been sung in Athens just three years prior

Figure 5.1 Roman copy of a portrait of Demosthenes. The orator, a staunch defender of democracy in Athens, died in 322 (see Chapters 1 and 4), but this image was not created until the early third century BCE, as a rebuke against the Macedonian monarchy in Athens.

(for another rebuke of the Antigonids at this time, see Figure 5.1). Pyrrhus was proclaimed king of Macedonia in Demetrius's absence and received the western division of territories while Lysimachus got the eastern reaches. Pyrrhus arrived in Athens soon after its independence to make a showy sacrifice to Athena.

Demetrius landed in Asia in 287 and bounced around various territories, largely unable to convince any of the loosely confederated strongmen to switch to his side. Under Lysimachus, the regional powers of Asia Minor had operated with relative independence and saw no reason to change trajectories, and Sardis was the only city of note that crossed to Demetrius's side. Near Miletus, he found his once sister-in-law Eurydice, and accepted her daughter Ptolemais in marriage – his fifth in this narrative after Phila, Euthydice, Deidameia, and Lanassa – but with few material prospects and with Lysimachus's army trailing behind, he turned to head deeper into the hinterland of Anatolia. Eventually he was captured by Seleucus and detained, although "detention" may not be the right word, given that his and Phila's daughter Stratonike was still queen. Demetrius was said to have been maintained in style until his death in 283, allegedly from alcohol poisoning.

After the swift collapse of Demetrius Poliorketes, Lysimachus held many powerful cards, not least of which was his experience as a soldier and a king, honed for over 40 years of not just survival but of prosperity, too, in his corner of the Mediterranean (see Primary Source 5.2). As widower of Nicaea, he had long ties to the Macedonian throne, and now married to Arsinoe II (Chapter 4), he had a strong alliance with Ptolemy I. What is more, any potential rivalry with the Ptolemies was neutralized when old Ptolemy I died, in 283. Though the accession of Ptolemy II Philadelphus, the son of Berenike I, was smooth in Egypt (Ptolemy II had held the title of co-king since 285), the dynasty still had to contend with the fugitive Eurydice and her legitimate children in Asia Minor. Unopposed in the main, Lysimachus quickly usurped Pyrrhus's half of Macedonia and held the kingdom for himself. As if to pattern, the remaining *Diadochoi* combined against him, this time led by Seleucus, who assembled a new network of alliances – with Antigonus

> **Primary Source 5.2**
>
> **Letter of Lysimachus to the Island of Samos**
>
> This decree reports the preamble of a decision by the *basileus* Lysimachus in 283/2 concerning a land dispute between the mainland town of Priene and the coastal island of Samos. The text breaks off before the verdict is reached, but its existence demonstrates the role a regional *basileus* played as an arbiter of international disputes, as well as the role of historical texts as evidence and exhibits in court cases.
>
> "Lysimachus, *basileus*, to the Samian council and people, greetings. Ambassadors from you and from Priene appeared before us (to make petitions) about the land that they happened to have disputed previously before us. If we had known that you had held and worked this land since many years ago, we would not have taken up the case. We considered you to have been in possession (of the land) for a short time, since the delegation from Priene had previously made statements to that effect. (In any case,) when envoys from you and from Priene were both present, it made a critical difference to hear presentations from each (at the same time). The Prieneans endeavored to show by means of histories and other witnesses and documents, including the Six Years' Truce, that the Batinetis (parcel of land) from the start had been theirs…"

Gonatas, who was still clinging to a few but powerful fortresses in Greece; with Philetairus, one of the regional strongmen of Asia Minor, based at Pergamon, who had previously been loyal to Lysimachus; and with Ptolemy Ceraunus. Seleucus's troops defeated Lysimachus at the Battle of Corupedion in 281; the latter was 80 years old and is said to have died of a javelin wound in the field. Seleucus, age 77, was thus on the verge of winning Macedonia when, plot-twist, he was murdered by the treacherous Ceraunus, supposedly at the very moment when they were disembarking to Europe. Demetrius Poliorketes, Ptolemy I, Lysimachus, and Seleucus I thus all died within a couple of years of each other, having navigated tricky geopolitical shoals for equally long periods against equally difficult odds. A new world was going to confront the next generation.

5.4 Pyrrhus and Rome

In 280, Pyrrhus decided to try his luck in Italy. There was, after all, little reason to stay in Greece: Ptolemy Ceraunus's murder of Seleucus had yielded him a huge army that had momentum behind it. This Ceraunus also lent Pyrrhus troops, demonstrating his own interest in the West, even if, as some have suggested, Ceraunus only helped out so that he could be rid of a rival in the region. The pretext for Pyrrhus's move was once again an invitation by Tarentum to help them ward off Roman encroachment onto their sphere of influence (similar invitations had been extended by Tarentum to Acrotatus in 314 and to Cleonymus in 303; Chapter 4).

In the years following the Battle of Sentinum of 295, Rome had enjoyed growing security and prosperity; skirmishes with the remnants of the Samnites had continued until 290 when the last of the tribes was conquered. The Romans consolidated their supremacy by means of colonial bookends – Venusia south of the Samnites in 293 and Hadria north of them in 290. The material benefits of the peace for Rome are indicated by occasional references in literary sources to economic improvements and scientific discoveries: Livy tells us that a terra-cotta representation of Jupiter in a four-horse chariot which stood atop the Temple of Jupiter Capitolinus was replaced with a bronze version; this is also the period to which art historians ascribe the iconic bronze sculpture of the Roman she-wolf (see Figure 5.2c). In 293, a temple to Quirinus, the name that Romulus assumed upon deification, was supplemented with a *horologium*,

Figure 5.2 A selection of coins from the third century BCE. (a) Silver tetradrachm of the Seleucids depicting Zeus (obv.) and Athena driving a chariot drawn by elephants (rev.), early third century BCE. (b) Gold decadrachm of Syracuse depicting Persephone (obv.) and a chariot (rev.), 288–279 BCE. (c) Silver didrachm from southern Italy depicting Hercules (obv.) and the Roman she-wolf with Romulus and Remus (rev.), 269–266 BCE.

or monumental sundial, which had been brought as war booty from the Samnites by Lucius Papirius Cursor, son of the consul of the same name (Chapter 4). In 291, the first Temple of Aesculapius (Roman Asclepius), the Greek god of healing, was erected in Rome on Tiber Island and functioned as a kind of sanctuary-cum-hospital. If Pyrrhus and the Tarentines wanted to check Roman progress, they were going to have to do it soon.

The balance of political power in Rome also saw changes in the years after Sentinum, although the interpretation of the ancient evidence is controversial. On the one hand, it would seem that the gradual empowerment of the senate with its lifetime tenure (Chapter 4) was checked in 287 with the passage of the Lex Hortensia. This law established that resolutions of the popular assembly were to be binding on the entire state. The reform seems democratic enough on its surface, but some scholars have pointed out that in the generations following its enactment, the oligarchic senate only came to assert itself more. Perhaps this was the result of structure: the plebeian assembly did not meet regularly but had to be called to order by a magistrate, and it could not amend legislation but rather voted yes or no to proposals that were put to it. Moreover, voting in the assembly was conducted by tribes, which were 33 in number as of 299. Only four of them existed in the city with the others representing agricultural lands at an inconvenient remove in the periphery. The citizens who voted in the so-called rustic tribes tended to be among the wealthy, since only they had the leisure to travel to Rome on short notice for legislative purposes. The continued rise of the senate might partly be seen in the extensive power sharing evident in the highest executive office: as Timothy Cornell has shown, in a 35 year period from 289 to 255, the 70 available consulships were held by 65 different people (p. 372). In such a context, a constant body like the senate would have a more consistent voice.

The Romans were mainly concerned with the Etruscans and Celts along their northern borders in the years around 285, but these were pacified to their satisfaction, at least for the moment, with victories at Lake Vadimon and Populonia. This freed the Romans to respond to requests for help from small Greek cities in their south. Rome's status in the region had most likely increased in any case when Agathocles of Syracuse died in 289 and left Sicily without a strong leader. First Thurii in 283, and soon after, Locri, Croton, and Rhegium, sought Roman alliances of protection. The powerhouse in the region, Tarentum, resented the competition, which they saw as a violation of an agreement by which Rome would avoid "their" gulf (Chapter 4). The Tarentines successfully dislodged the Roman garrison from Thurii and destroyed a small fleet in its harbor. The Romans sent an embassy demanding restitution, but the Tarentine democracy was allegedly not above slinging feces at them. The Romans should not be seen as blameless, given that the terms they were proposing amounted to a near total loss of Tarentine sovereignty in Rome's favor. In 281, the Romans still held a strong position – their garrison in Rhegium, for example, was still in place, populated mainly by Campanian allies – and so they invaded Tarentine territory, which was the immediate cause for Tarentum's appeal to Pyrrhus. A strong argument in Tarentum *against* war was that Pyrrhus had demanded both manpower and money to prosecute his mission and had extracted a promise that he could invest Tarentum with a garrison after the campaign's completion, implying that he had long range territorial goals, perhaps smacking of empire. The population was divided, but the war faction won the day, prompting a number of elite Tarentines, we are told, to defect to Rome.

In 280, one of the new consuls, Publius Valerius Laevinus, marched south to join the recent ex-consul Lucius Aemilius. The latter contended with Italian tribes to prevent them from joining Pyrrhus's forces. It appears that the allied Campanian garrison in Rhegium perpetrated a bloody putsch of a faction of locals who were suspected of plotting to betray them to Pyrrhus. The mass execution was remembered as especially brutal and would weigh on the Roman conscience in the future, as we shall see in Chapter 6. Meanwhile, Laevinus marched straight for Tarentum; Pyrrhus intercepted him at Heraclea. The Romans had succeeded in depriving

Pyrrhus of his Italian allies, but were inexperienced at handling crucial features of Pyrrhus's panoply, such as arrays of battle-elephants and soldiers armed with long Macedonian thrusting pikes. Once the battle was engaged Pyrrhus unleashed his 20 elephants, and the horses of the Romans scattered in disarray. One concession for the retreat was that on the way out a Roman soldier managed to wound an elephant and noticed that its cries had a profound effect on the morale of the rest – intelligence that would come in handy before long. What remained of the Roman force gained refuge at Venusia, justifying its usefulness as a colony, while Pyrrhus seized their camp in the field.

Eager to reach a settlement Pyrrhus sent his leading negotiator, Cineas, to Rome to offer peace. We are told that he approached the city with money to bribe the senators and fine garments to win over their wives, but the anecdote (in Plutarch) appears to be designed mainly to set up an antidote: the Romans displayed rustic simplicity by rejecting such luxury, in keeping with a superior sense of honor, at least in the story. Cineas proclaimed that Pyrrhus would rather have Rome as an ally than an enemy, but the question that was left unanswered by the sources is at what cost. According to one source, all Pyrrhus asked for was Tarentine independence, but according to another, he demanded, too, that the Romans evacuate Lucanian and Samnite lands, which would have been repugnant following the over 60 years of warfare in southern Italy up to that point. Old Appius Claudius Caecus (Chapter 4), now around 70 years of age, argued against peace: in one source, he is said to have based his argument on the observation that although Pyrrhus had won one engagement, he had many troubles back home against his neighbors, Ptolemy Ceraunus, Antigonus Gonatas, and others. If the story is true, it is interesting to see the Romans taking stock of the larger Mediterranean in devising their approach to an enemy at home.

Also relevant in regard to Rome's growing international profile is a reference in our literary sources to the arrival of a Carthaginian contingent to Rome as the case was being debated, offering the assistance of 120 ships. The Romans declined, we are told, so that they would not fall under any obligation to Carthage, but perhaps such sourness reflects a later source's bias against what would become Rome's defining enemy (Chapters 6 and 7). One might just as well suggest that the Romans declined because this was largely a land war and that they, if anything, took heart that a naval ally was available to them should they need it: as we shall see, Rome would seize the opportunity to ally with Carthage in only the next year.

In 279, Pyrrhus changed tack, electing to pursue a campaign along the Adriatic coast, directly across the sea from his native Epirus, rather than head to Rome directly. The Romans were desperate to protect their valuable colony of Venusia and so marched to intercept Pyrrhus; they met at the town of Asculum. By all accounts, the Battle of Asculum was much larger than Heraclea the year before, and literary sources go into greater detail about how troops were arranged and conducted themselves, especially in their quest to occupy terrain suitable for their own technologies. Pyrrhus sought open ground for his elephants, while the Romans sought the opposite of that, preferring wooded conditions or hills. At a decisive moment, Pyrrhus again sent in the pachyderms, but this time the Romans were prepared: they countered with armored wagons drawn by oxen that carried artillery towers, swinging spears, cranes, and long, burning torches, by which they hoped either to wound or to frighten the animals. The Roman innovations would have been fearsome, had it not been so easy for Pyrrhus's army simply to kill the poor oxen. Still, Pyrrhus suffered grievous losses, being wounded himself in the arm and losing his own camp, which was torched by an Apulian ally of Rome in a surprise attack. Opinion in antiquity was divided about the outcome and who ultimately was the victor. The *Fasti Triumphales* excludes mention of Asculum, so it would seem that Pyrrhus got the "honor". Nevertheless, the costs of the victory for Pyrrhus were legendarily severe, such that it was practically tantamount to failure – the meaning of our term, Pyrrhic victory.

In thinking about his next move, Pyrrhus had reason to look elsewhere than to return home. In early 279, before the Battle of Asculum, tribes of Celts, which we have already seen as a significant force in northern Italy, descended into the Balkans. Ptolemy Ceraunus was the king who stood in their way. Newly in control of Macedonia, he had recently made a useful marriage alliance by essentially compelling his half-sister, Arsinoe II (they shared Ptolemy I as their father), now the widow of Lysimachus, to marry him. Hardly a romantic proposal, Ceraunus made the offer while Arsinoe was under siege by his own troops, and she only agreed if she could be attended by guards and conduct the ceremony outside her own fortress. She was not a fool: indeed, Ceraunus killed two of her children soon after the wedding, and Arsinoe II had to run for her life to her full brother Ptolemy II Philadelphus in Egypt (see Figure 5.3).

Ptolemy Ceraunus was not prepared for the onslaught of multiple Celtic tribes at once, and what is more, our sources ascribe overwhelming *hybris* to his disdain for them as barbarians: he was killed in one of the first engagements. With Lysimachus gone, as well, and with the Macedonian throne unoccupied, no strong king remained in Thrace to keep the Celts in check, and they swiftly made it as far as Thermopylae. Leagues of cities held the narrow pass – the Boeotians, the Aetolians, and the Phocians. Even the Athenians and Antigonus Gonatas cooperated in sending contingents, though the democracy in charge of the city remained staunchly opposed to Antigonus's garrison in Piraeus. Bottled up at the narrow pass, the Celts tried alternate paths to the rich cities of the south, going over mountainous terrain in the direction of Aetolia and Delphi, but they were blocked by unseasonable snowfall. The Celtic leader fell, either by a mortal wound or by his own hand, and without him the movement shriveled. As we shall see, a different Celtic tribe had better luck in the following year en route to Asia Minor.

Figure 5.3 Limestone portrait attributed to Arsinoe II, c. 278–270 BCE.

5.5 Pyrrhus and Sicily

With Epirus an unappealing location due to the Celtic nuisance, Pyrrhus had incentive to take advantage of a different opportunity outside Italy. At the end of 279, ambassadors from Syracuse, Agrigentum, and others in Sicily asked for his help in driving the Carthaginians from their island. Pyrrhus perhaps listened to the Syracusans most keenly: not only was it the storied metropolis of the island, but he also had legitimate claims to leading it across many generations of ties, since his grandfather had once retired to Syracuse when forced out of Epirus by Olympias, and since he himself had fathered a son by Lanassa, who was thus a grandson of the great Agathocles. Pyrrhus's mission – an assault on the Carthaginian presence in Sicily – could be seen as an outgrowth of his antipathy toward Rome, for the two cities had expanded their old alliance shortly after Asculum. By the new terms, the Romans and Carthaginians agreed to help each other against Pyrrhus and would not enter into treaties with him without the other as part of the same negotiations. In late 279, they already began to act in concert as a combined Romano-Punic force took Messina in Sicily. It was a strong start, but Carthaginian successes stop here. The sources are not thorough for these years in Sicily, but we are told that in one city after another, Pyrrhus faced little difficulty in brushing away the Carthaginian army – Syracuse, Leontini, Agrigentum, Selinus. Scholars have suggested that with the majority of urban populations in Sicily being Greek, Pyrrhus's arrival may have been viewed as a liberation. In addition, Carthaginian armies, when overseas from North Africa, relied heavily on mercenaries rather than citizen-soldiers, which may also have hurt them. Even Mt. Eryx, which stood a greater chance of holding out owing to its high acropolis, capitulated when Pyrrhus used siege machines to clear the walls. The mountain was sacred to the Phoenician god Melqart, as was Tyre, which Alexander the Great took in 332, also by a famously innovative siege: it is one of several echoes between Pyrrhus's Sicilian campaign and Alexander's larger successes in a previous generation.

The last Punic holdout in Sicily was the fortress at Lilybaeum. On the westernmost coast, it was washed on two sides by the sea, which Carthage controlled. Along the landward walls, a ditch was dug to provide an obstacle to Pyrrhus's now-famous siegeworks. Reinforcements were brought in from a number of Punic allies, including Italians. Here Pyrrhus finally met his match: he was forced to abandon the siege in late 277 after two months. Plutarch says that at this point, Pyrrhus began to treat his Sicilian allies with increasing harshness and impatience; at the same time, he grew paranoid of the loyalty of his lieutenants, and since he had demanded much from the locals by way of supplies for his campaign, he may have been right to worry. But the stories of Pyrrhus's late-in-life anxieties again strike of Alexander writ small and may be suspicious. In any case, when Tarentum summoned him back to Italy in the face of mounting pressure from a resurgent Rome, Pyrrhus readily obliged.

5.6 Celtic Migrations to Asia Minor

During Pyrrhus's years in Sicily, Antigonus Gonatas catapulted from an untenable position among a few Hellenic outposts to the heights of the Macedonian throne. In the main, he was capitalizing on the chaos wrought by the Celtic invasion. He led a troop of mercenaries (for he had no state from which to recruit) and met the Celts at the eastern mouth of the Hellespont. Allegedly he made the Celtic greed for plunder work against them by dangling an abandoned camp before them like bait. When they loaded up on loot, it was easier for him to trap them against the coastline (they had no navy) and cut them down. But this story is told by Justin, a much later source who may have had the primary goal of casting unfavorable characteristics upon the Celtic Other. In any case, the result was a decisive victory for Antigonus, and the

Macedonian armies rewarded him with the royal title; he could now command a native army in addition to his mercenaries. His new status made him eligible for one of the high-level marriage alliances to which we have become accustomed: in 276, he married Phila, the daughter of Seleucus I and Stratonike, who was now both stepdaughter and half-sister of the sitting king Antiochus I (since he had married his father's wife); Antigonus thus acquired his own niece as a wife (Stratonike was his sister), who had the same name as his mother: readers would be forgiven for being confused. Antigonus Gonatas and Antiochus I accordingly struck a grand bargain that defined their two realms geographically with Europe for the former and Asia for the latter. Pyrrhus would have to contend with an immensely more powerful and stable king if he ever returned to Epirus.

Antiochus I's large realm consisted of three regional capitals by the 270s – Sardis, overseeing western Asia Minor; Antioch, where Asia Minor met the Levant; and the region of Mesopotamia around Seleuceia-on-Tigris near Babylon. The first of these was soon jeopardized by yet more detachments of migrating Celtic tribes. A large contingent was finally helped across the Hellespont by Nicomedes I of Bithynia, who sought their aid in contending with a brother for the throne following the death of their father Zipoites, a minor *basileus* (Chapter 4). The tribe is known today by their Greek name, the Galatians, derived from the same root as "Gaul." Propaganda states that they functioned as vicious, cheap mercenaries with little by way of a moral compass, but in reality they remained settled in the region for centuries and mixed into the local populations; one could argue that they held their position for the rest of antiquity. Antiochus I thus lost ground as they advanced; he simultaneously felt pressure from Ptolemy II, who managed to win Samos and Miletus, and continued pressure on Cyprus, coastal Asia Minor, and Phoenicia. Ironically, Antiochus seemed to have the least trouble with the satrapies that were farthest away, such as Bactria, which appears to have sent money and manpower as needed, but it should also be pointed out that we know less about these regions in any case.

5.7 Alexandrian Erudition

For his part, Ptolemy II, by 274, had taken as wife his full sister Arsinoe II, that intrepid dynast who had managed to survive her first husband Lysimachus and to elude her murderous second, Ptolemy Ceraunus. The sibling marriage suited the Egyptian population, who were familiar with pharaohs marrying within their families. In terms of their own dynastic concerns, the bond closed off routes to power by rivals, allowing for a period of prosperity and stability, which in turn fostered an explosion of scientific and artistic creativity in the next generation. Among the thinkers whose research was sponsored by the royal court at this time was Euclid, whose work on geometry is well known and whose main contribution to mathematics may be the methodology of the "proof." His work may have been of immediate use to Sostratus, a contemporary engineer who designed the famous lighthouse of Alexandria, completed under Ptolemy II and later counted as one of the so-called seven wonders of the ancient world.

Great strides in medicine were being made simultaneously by Erasistratus and Herophilus, whose studies of anatomy clarified the functions of arteries and veins and the different roles of the heart and the brain. A maxim attributed to Herophilus observed that art and wisdom were impossible without physical health first. Herophilus would have had reason to know what he was talking about: in addition to doctors, engineers, and scientists, the Library had by now attracted many poets. Lycophron is credited with dozens of tragedies from this period, and Theocritus wrote lyric poetry on themes of love, including a celebration of the marriage of Ptolemy II and Arsinoe II. Ptolemy II was also praised by Callimachus, a Young Turk of a poet who disdained classical forms and called for experimentation in form and content. "A big book

Figure 5.4 Limestone relief from Cyprus depicting Zeus, Apollo, and perhaps Hermes above a philosophical text inscribed in Cypriot script. Multiple writing systems coexisted in the eastern Mediterranean at the time of the foundation of the Library at Alexandria.

is a bunch of crap" is the literal translation of a famous Callimachan quip – *mega biblion, mega kakon* – in reference to ponderous epic poetry. His witty epigrams would get a second life later in the Roman Republic as a new generation of Latin poets mimicked his style and admired his ethos (Chapter 14). Experiments in language thrived in the cosmopolitan Ptolemaic realm (see Figure 5.4).

5.8 The Mediterranean Without Pyrrhus

While Pyrrhus was in Sicily, the Romans kept up pressure on the Tarentines and the indigenous south Italian tribes, apparently focusing their efforts on towns not garrisoned by Epirots. Pyrrhus struggled even to set foot back in Italy: Carthaginians attacked his transports near the Straits of Messina and sank over half of his already depleted fleet. Within a year, Carthage had reacquired Agrigentum and Panormus. Pyrrhus also had to contend with a band of rogue mercenaries called the Mamertines, who adventured in and around Rhegium on the mainland. It is possible that the Mamertines, who were based in Messina, had crossed to Rhegium to help the allied garrison that had so brutally terrorized the local aristocracy (see earlier): both groups were originally of Campanian extraction. Pyrrhus appealed to Antigonus Gonatas for help, but he did not participate. Short of money, Pyrrhus resorted to the desperate act of robbing a temple treasury at Locris, for which, we are told, he faced divine retribution in the form of unfavorable winds and ultimately defeat at the hands of Rome. The latter happened at the Samnite town of Maleventum. The consul Manius Curius Dentatus, with two legions plus auxiliaries, was outnumbered by Pyrrhus, but in the ensuing battle, a wounded elephant led a reverse stampede against its overseers. It was an obvious victory for Rome, in honor of which they changed the name of the town to Beneventum.

Pyrrhus was forced to return to Epirus, defeated. He lost no time in going on the offensive against Antigonus Gonatas in Macedonia. He probably did not have a choice given his sagging reputation, his lack of funds, and the relative newness of Antigonus on the throne: all of these made swift action important. Pyrrhus did well at first, which convinced many Macedonian soldiers to defect to his side (or, as is likely, revert back to his side); he also artfully trapped some of Antigonus's elephants and thus rebuilt that part of his old force. Both sides had Celtic mercenaries in their employ; what distinguished Antigonus was his possession of a navy. As successful as Pyrrhus was inland, he never could budge Antigonus from the coastal cities, which afforded the latter the benefits of trade, communication, fast transportation, and diplomacy. Pyrrhus next turned south, responding to the invitation of Cleonymus, the Spartan who had invaded Italy on Tarentum's behalf (Chapter 4) and who now sought help in taking back the throne from which he had been recently expelled. What ruined Pyrrhus in the end were both the arrival of a relieving force from Antigonus Gonatas and the return of one of the Spartan kings from campaigning abroad.

Pyrrhus next went to Argos, but a similar sequence of events as at Sparta occurred, to his misfortune. His goal, once again, was to help a statesman on the outs seize power against the ruling faction. But, again, a relieving force dispatched by Antigonus slowed his progress. He managed to infiltrate the city, but the narrowness of the streets worked against his elephants, one of which blocked a passageway and thus prevented infantry from offering assistance. An Argive soldier wounded Pyrrhus slightly, and when the king turned to counter-attack, the Argive's mother, watching from above, pelted Pyrrhus with a roof tile in order to rescue her son. The end was violent: while Pyrrhus was incapacitated, one of Antigonus's men decapitated him. We are told that Antigonus rebuked the men who brought him Pyrrhus's head as being disrespectful to their fellow Greek: this is surely a trope of historiography, similar to Alexander's last respects for Darius (Chapter 3) and repeated, as we shall see, with Pompey and Caesar (Chapter 15). The main purpose of such an anecdote is to reify the chivalry of men-in-charge: such sentiments may have had everything to do with winning over the supporters of the defeated.

In the same year as Pyrrhus's death at Argos, in 272, according to a late source Rome and Carthage laid siege to Tarentum, the former by land and the latter by sea; Pyrrhus's garrison had no choice but to surrender. In the few years since Pyrrhus's departure, the Romans had lost no time in securing their south, now that its vulnerability to armies from overseas had been cast in sharp relief. The device of colony foundation again played a role: in the Etruscan north the Romans founded Cosa and in the Lucanian south, Paestum. Both came in 273, 16 years after the most recent colony, at Hadria, had followed the victory over Samnium. Paestum today is a particularly picturesque site for its well-preserved Greek temples from the Classical era, when it was called Poseidonia; in its Roman period, it was especially loyal to Rome, even as it enjoyed a degree of autonomy. Rome's interest in Greek culture, always evident, was expanding: it is possible that Livius Andronicus, the first Latin author whose work survives was enslaved at the fall of Tarentum. A new temple to the agricultural god/personification Consus was built on the Aventine Hill in 273 with spoils from an unknown victory.

Rome's growth now drew the attention of Ptolemy II Philadelphus, perhaps largely because it had come at the expense of Pyrrhus, who was well known in Egypt. He dispatched an embassy to Rome in 273; we know nothing of what transpired beyond establishing diplomatic relations. Around this time the Ptolemies and Seleucids became embroiled in what modern historians call the First Syrian War, which ranged over much of their naval strongholds throughout the East. The king in Cyrene, Ptolemy II's former officer Magas, had declared his independence, and what is more, had received aid from Antiochus I, whose daughter, Apama II, he married. Ptolemy II naturally resented Antiochus's interference and himself went on the march, to Coele-Syria and other rich Seleucid territories. The war ended by 271, with Ptolemy having the upper hand: Theocritus, his court flatterer, sang that year of new acquisitions in Syria, Phoenicia, Cilicia, Lycia, and Caria, all of which had previously spent time under Seleucid control (see Primary Source 5.3).

> **Primary Source 5.3**
>
> **Theocritus, *Idyll* 17**
>
> This poem was likely composed in 271 in celebration of Ptolemy II's victories over the Seleucids in the First Syrian War. Theocritus, a scholar in the Library at Alexandria who was supported by the king's largesse, goes to great lengths to equate Ptolemy with Zeus, worthy to be worshipped as a god (see Figure 5.4). Notably, the women of the dynasty, including Ptolemy II's mother, Berenike I, and sister-wife, Arsinoe II, receive similar attention.
>
>> Lines 1–8, 18–21, 74–92, 121–128: "From Zeus let us begin, and with Zeus let us draw to a close, Muses, whenever we remember to sing of the greatest of the gods. As for men, let Ptolemy be mentioned first, last, and in the middle, for he surpasses all. Heroes born of demigods in the past had wise poets singing of their great deeds, but it will be I who writes a hymn for Ptolemy, and hymns are the prizes of gods. ... Next to him (Ptolemy II) sits Alexander with an approving gaze, the god with his glittering diadem, scourge of the Persians. And opposite them, the throne of Heracles the centaur-killer, made of impenetrable adamant. ... (Ptolemy II) stands out, whom (Zeus) has loved since his first birth, and much success attends him; he rules over many lands and many seas. Countless, boundless people grow and flourish from the rain of Zeus, but nothing like the marshes of Egypt when the Nile overflows and saturates the soil, and none has as many cities with men skilled at crafts. Three hundred cities are built there, and three thousand more, on top of three times ten-thousand, and thrice three with nine times three on that – over all of these valiant Ptolemy II is king. And now he has cut off a chunk of Phoenicia, of Arabia, of Syria and Libya, and the swarthy Ethiopians. He holds forth over all Pamphylia and the Cilician spearmen, and the Lycians and Carians and Cycladic islanders, since the greatest ships that plow the sea are his; all the seas and rushing rivers are ruled by Ptolemy. ... He alone of those past and those whose imprinted footsteps are still warm on the earth has set up shrines to his beloved mother (Berenike I) and father (Ptolemy I). In beautiful gold and ivory are they positioned there to aid mankind. On many red altars he sacrifices juicy cuts of meat, both he and his strong consort (Arsinoe II). No better woman throws her arms around a groom, she who loves her brother, her husband with all her heart."

5.9 Conclusions

By the year 270 Antigonus Gonatas and Antiochus I were firmly in control of Macedonia and Syria, respectively, and to some extent had squared off against Ptolemy II through a marriage alliance. Ptolemy II endeavored to bring Rome to his side through which means he may have hoped also to win over their allies, the Carthaginians, and thus even out the Mediterranean balance. Ptolemy II could not have known that the alliance between the two western powers would spectacularly explode in the coming years. Rome's position in Italy had grown increasingly secure, not only by military victories but by shrewd colonizing activities that followed these. The city was growing, but it was still land based; that would change as the Romans took to the sea in the subsequent generation, opening up new frontiers but, of course, not without opposition.

Further Reading

Anson, Edward (2014). *Alexander's Heirs: The Age of the Successors*. West Sussex: Wiley-Blackwell.
Carney, Elizabeth (2013). *Arsinoë of Egypt and Macedon*. Oxford: Oxford University Press.
Cornell, Timothy (1995). *The Beginnings of Rome: Italy and Rome from the Bronze Age to the Punic Wars, c. 1000–264 BC*. London: Routledge.
Habicht, Christian (1997). *Athens from Alexander to Antony*. Cambridge, MA: Harvard University Press.
Hölbl, Günther (2000). *A History of the Ptolemaic Empire*. New York: Routledge.
Miles, Richard (2010). *Carthage Must Be Destroyed: The Rise and Fall of an Ancient Civilization*. New York: Penguin Books.
Rosenstein, Nathan (2012). *Rome and the Mediterranean, 290 to 146 BC: The Imperial Republic*. Edinburgh: University of Edinburgh Press.
von Staden, Heinrich (1989). *Herophilus: The Art of Medicine in Early Alexandria*. Cambridge: Cambridge University Press.

6

To 238: The Three Corners of Sicily

Timeline

265: Hiero II of Syracuse lays siege to the Mamertines, a group of Campanian mercenaries holding Messina in Sicily
264: The consul Appius Claudius Caudex invests Messina in support of the Mamertines
264–241: First Punic War
260s: Under Nicomedes I Bithynia achieves independence from the Seleucids
263: Under Eumenes I Pergamum achieves independence from the Seleucids
262: Roman siege of Agrigentum
261: Battle of Mylae: Rome defeats Carthage for its first naval victory
259–253: Second Syrian War between Ptolemy II and Antiochus II
255, 253, 249: Major shipwrecks of the Roman fleet around Sicily
250s: Under Ariarathes III Cappadocia achieves independence from the Seleucids
246: Deaths of Ptolemy II and Antiochus II
246–241: Third Syrian War between Ptolemy III and Laodike, widow of Antiochus II and mother of Seleucus II and Antiochus Hierax
241: Battle of the Aegates Islands: Rome defeats Carthage, which sues for peace; Roman annexation of Sicily
240–238: War between Carthage and its mercenaries
240s: Latin renderings of Greek drama and epic poetry in Rome by Livius Andronicus
238: Roman annexation of Sardinia

Principal Themes

- The Romans developed an interest in lands overseas in spite of the new investment in naval technology that it required – whether for the purpose of empire or other opportunities is debatable – and went to war with Carthage for greater influence in Sicily in the so-called First Punic War.
- Seleucid control of Asia Minor evaporated with the rise of smaller, independent kingdoms, including Galatia, Bithynia, Pontus, Pergamon, and Cappadocia, while Parthia and Bactria also won a greater degree of autonomy from Hellenistic power in the East.
- Antigonid forces of Macedonia declined in the face of assertive leagues of *poleis* in southern Greece, especially the Achaean League as led by Aratus.

- Ptolemy II Philadelphus, and then his son Ptolemy III Euergetes who ascended the throne in 246, held their own against Seleucid and Antigonid rivals through proxy wars and in the Second and Third Syrian Wars.
- By the late phases of the First Punic War, Carthage was worn down by the disgruntlement of its mercenaries and allies, and by the resilience of the Romans in recovering from naval defeats and shipwrecks; the contrasts between the two city-state's systems of diplomacy and empire were thus cast in stark relief.

6.1 Introduction

Sitting like a bull's eye in the middle of the Mediterranean (see Map 1.1 and Map 6.1), Sicily as of 265, was something like a land-mass manifestation of the arrangement and distribution of major powers in the larger sea around it. In the southwest, the Carthaginians held sway once again, easily taking back what had been lost to Pyrrhus ten years before. In the southeast, as we know, was Syracuse, a Hellenic jewel that had housed its own *basileis* in the Hellenistic stripe, like Agathocles and Pyrrhus, both of whom had extensive ties to the Ptolemies, Seleucids, and Antigonids; it was now held by Hiero II, who had risen through the ranks during the wars with Pyrrhus. To the north of both of these was Messina, which was at the time in the hands of the Mamertines, already encountered in the previous chapter when they menaced Pyrrhus's forces as they attempted to return to Italy in 276. As Italian Campanians, they had roots in a region that had long been in Rome's sphere of influence and part of its vital network of allies.

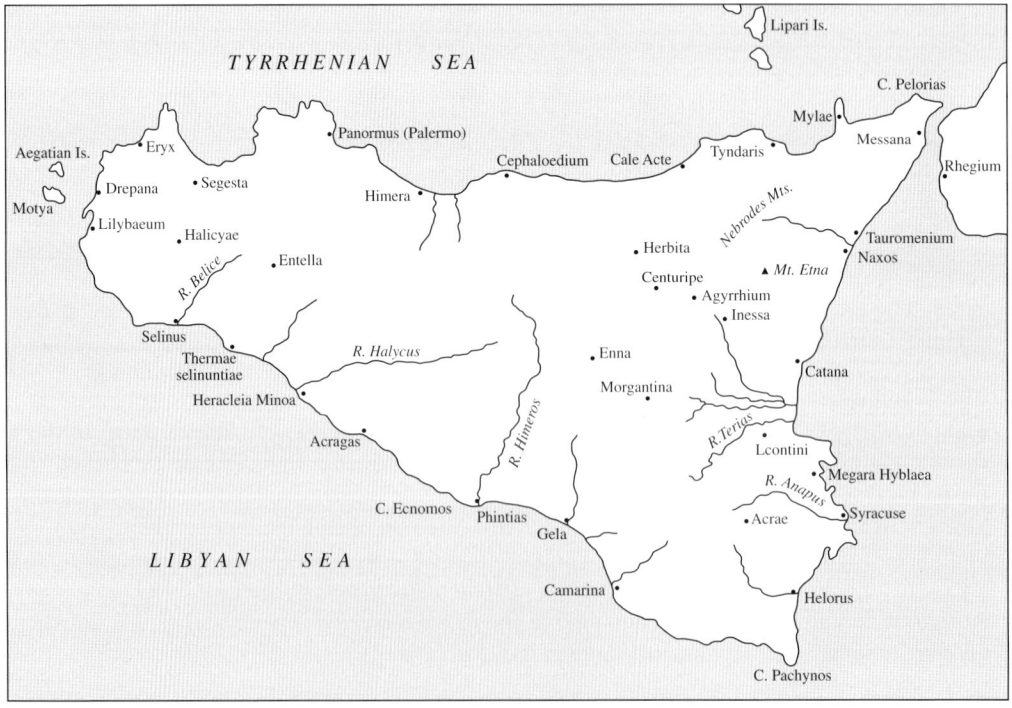

Map 6.1 Sicily during the First Punic War.

From 264 to 241 the island became a battleground between Rome and Carthage, formerly allies. Both sides absorbed enormous losses, but Rome proved more adept at fielding new armies, stocked and funded by its Italian allies. In taking to the sea for the first time in a serious way, Rome entered a new era. The Hellenistic world experienced internecine warfare that would be familiar, except that the Seleucids were particularly constrained by the end of the period. Asia Minor would essentially be lost to them after no fewer than five new kingdoms – in Galatia, Bithynia, Pontus, Pergamon, and Cappadocia – asserted themselves (see Map 6.2). These kingdoms, especially Pergamon, would grow to make major contributions to Hellenistic culture and, ultimately, to Roman identity, as well. Some years later, the Seleucids would suffer the loss of their Far East, as Parthia and Bactria also peeled off under their own *basileis*.

6.2 The Origins of the First Punic War

A number of historical uncertainties bedevil our understanding of the origins of the first war between Rome and Carthage. As so often happens, it arose out of a smaller conflict between allied states. In 265, Hiero II, the strongman of Syracuse (it is debated whether he had assumed the title of *basileus* yet), defeated the Mamertines (Chapter 5) at the Battle of the Longanus River, and laid siege to them at Messina, just across from the Italian mainland. Trapped behind their walls, the Mamertines appealed to Rome and Carthage for help. Our sources have difficulty in fathoming a circumstance where a city would enlist aid from both of these powers simultaneously: writing after not only the First Punic War but the Second, as well, by which

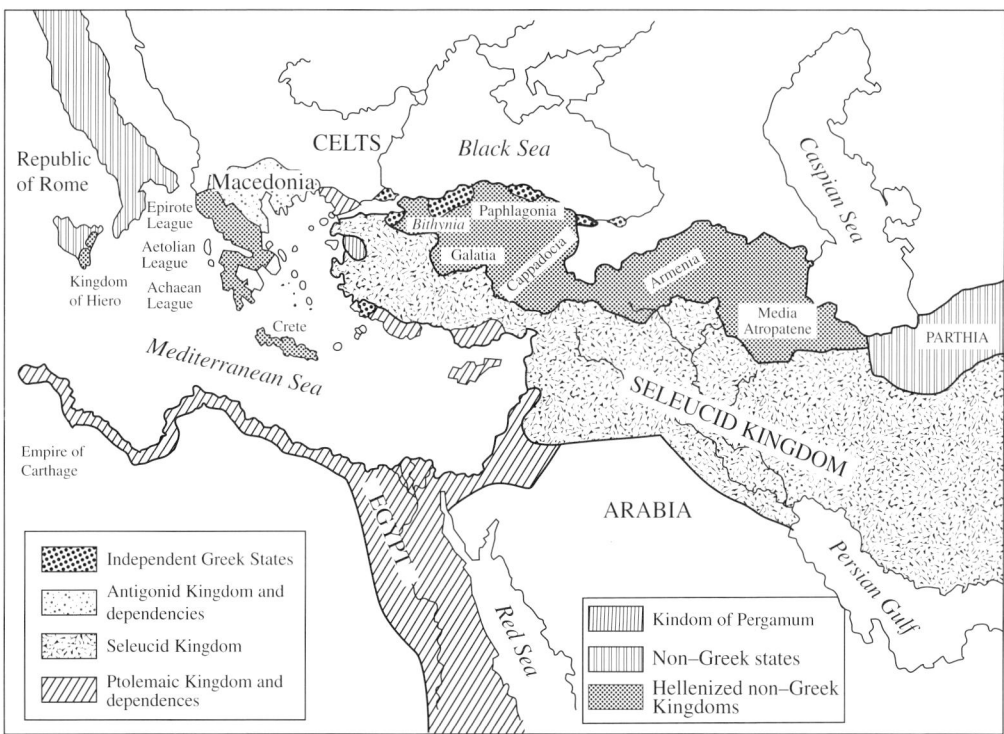

Map 6.2 Local powers in Asia Minor, c. 240 BCE.

point Rome and Carthage were famous foes, the historian Polybius, for example, presupposes hostility between them. The result is that we are told of some confusing scenarios and odd chronologies, such as the notion that the Mamertines first applied to Carthage and then applied to Rome, later and separately. Rather, given the many treaties between Rome and Carthage and their recent cooperation in dispelling Pyrrhus, it is likely that the Mamertines thought the two would act in concert. Carthage arrived first and established a garrison, and Hiero accordingly abandoned his siege. The Romans also sent aid, led by the consul of 264, Appius Claudius Caudex (of uncertain relationship to Appius Claudius Caecus; possibly none at all). Polybius says that the people of Rome were divided on the question of the morality of helping people who were as low-down and dirty, evidently, as the Mamertines. In 270, the Romans had had to punish the Campanian mercenaries at Rhegium for executing its leading citizens (Chapter 5); nearby and of similar ethnicity, the Mamertines might have been lumped in the same category. We are told that it was the urban masses, and not the senate, who were eventually convinced to help them but out of greed for easy plunder with no sense of moral compunction. But the accounts of populist appetites being diametrically opposed to aristocratic restraint are often the result of social bias in our sources and should be taken with a grain of salt.

Key elements are missing in our accounts of what happened when Caudex arrived in the region. On the one hand, the Carthaginians withdrew their garrison in deference to Rome; perhaps this makes sense if one remembers that both powers were allies to that point. But on the other hand, Diodorus says the Punics then pitched camp outside the walls and tried to bar the Romans from entering, implying that they viewed Rome as their enemy. But if that were the case, why had they withdrawn in the first place? Indeed, a skirmish between Roman and Punic forces brought tensions to a head, but then Hanno, the Carthaginian general, returned the Roman prisoners of war and captured ships to Caudex, as might be expected if diplomatic relations were current. When Caudex managed to enter the city anyway by means either of a ruse or of cover of darkness, Rome and Carthage still turned first to negotiations to figure out the situation, not to siege warfare. Polybius, Diodorus, and others are not in agreement as to precisely when, but at some point around this time the Carthaginians decided to work in the open with Syracuse against Rome. In the battle that ensued Caudex managed to drive off both armies and then moved south to lay a temporary siege to Syracuse itself. At what point did Rome and Carthage become enemies? When did Carthage and Syracuse become allies, and why, and to what extent? Answers to these questions are not forthcoming and remain the subject of debate. One thing that is certain from the *Fasti Triumphales* is that Caudex did not receive a triumph for this year. In spite of some florid literary accounts, we might conclude that Caudex did not achieve much beyond an investment of Messina, and this was likely not worthy of note.

In the following year, 263, the new consul Valerius Maximus focused his efforts on Syracuse. He conquered, or received the peaceful surrender of, many of the towns along the coast or slightly inland between Messina and his objective. So fast came his success that Hiero offered him terms beneficial to Rome: he would pay out 100 talents and return all the prisoners that he held to date. This time we know that a triumph was awarded to Valerius Maximus, now called Messala in recognition of his accomplishment. In 262, the Romans initially ordered only one consul to Sicily. We are told that they changed their minds and sent the second, as well, when word arrived that the Carthaginians were increasing the forces in "their" third of the triangle. Up until this point, there had been little armed conflict between Rome and Carthage, apart from the possible dust-up surrounding Rome's initial arrival at Messina (which, we have seen, is imperfectly known in any case). But in the face of a looming threat, both consuls marched to Carthaginian-controlled Agrigentum and pitched camp. The Romans held the siege for much of the summer, and as the city was in increasing danger of starvation, reinforcements arrived by sea from Africa. The Romans won the ensuing battle and enjoyed a massive windfall from the sale of the population of Agrigentum into slavery. Polybius records that it was this battle (and not the defense of the Mamertines) that inspired the Romans to try for the whole island.

6.3 The New Roman Navy

An irony of the years following the siege of Agrigentum is that although the Romans had scored a major victory on land, their subsequent achievements came at sea. In some sense, the Carthaginians brought this on themselves: desperate to do damage to Rome in some way after their major loss, under the new general Hamilcar they attacked the coastline in Italy. It became apparent that Rome needed a larger navy than the 20 or so ships that Livy ascribed to 311 (Chapter 4). Polybius relates the famous tale of how the enterprising Romans copied a Carthaginian warship plank for plank, which had run aground as they were crossing to Messina in 264, and churned out a sizeable fleet over the winter from 262 to 261. Polybius adds that for the crews, the Romans enlisted sailors and marines from the *proletarii* of Rome. Aristotle argued in his *Politics* that such populations were ideally suited for naval service because expensive bronze armor and weaponry were not needed: these men were "armed" simply with oars. It is perhaps not a coincidence then that one of the consuls elected for 261, Gaius Duilius, was a *novus homo*, or "new man," who had no aristocratic pedigree. Landlubbers to the core, the Romans tried via benches on dry land to practice what it meant to row in synchronized fashion. The goal was to learn how to maneuver a ship so that, when timed right, it could sail at an angle into the broad side of an opposing vessel: battering rams affixed to the bow would tear a hole in the side and sink it, or at least shave off the other's oars. Anyone who has rowed in a crew knows both how difficult such synchronicity can be, and how vital it is: if rowers do not keep time, their oars may bang into one another and get tangled or stuck. If an oar, out of sync, is pushed into the water against the momentum of the ship, the countering force can thrust the dry end against the rower's chest: the phenomenon, called "catching a crab," can crack ribs or worse. Add to this hazard high winds or undersea currents and one realizes the full nature of the difficulties for Rome, and also the shortcomings of practicing on land.

The first consul to take a fleet on a mission, Gnaeus Cornelius Scipio, demonstrated just how dangerous a lack of experience could be. While sailing to Sicily with a small advance guard, he thought it would be a small matter to seize the main harbor of the Lipari Islands along the way. The Carthaginians, under the command of Hannibal (different from the famous general to be discussed in Chapter 7), had no trouble in trapping his ships and taking him prisoner. The other consul, Gaius Duilius, already in command of land forces, had to take charge of the rest of the fleet. Now fully acknowledging that they could not match wits in traditional naval warfare with Carthage, who had been at it for centuries, or for millennia if one considers their Phoenician roots, Roman engineers created elaborate machinery for boarding enemy ships, regardless of their nimbleness of seafaring. The device consisted of a plank with a large spike on one end, which was raised by a rope against a pole standing perpendicular on deck. This could be swiveled to point in any desired direction, and when dropped, would pierce the deck of the targeted ship and provide a bridge for soldiers to cross. Since the spike on the raised plank resembled a beak, the device was called a "crow" in Greek.

The Carthaginians perhaps viewed the Roman vessels with more amusement than concern when Hannibal's fleet sailed against Duilius's off the coast of Mylae. The contrast between them could not have been more pronounced: not only did the Romans possess what looked like crude, top-heavy floaters – bobbing in resting position more like vicious ducks than crows – but also the Carthaginians, for their part, led with the grand flagship of Pyrrhus, which they had captured around 276. Nevertheless, the Roman innovation won the day: the grappling spikes did their job, and the Carthaginians were forced to retreat, losing some 50 ships including Pyrrhus's. The Battle of Mylae thus went down in history as Rome's first naval victory, and a column was erected in the Forum honoring Duilius. According to the *Fasti Triumphales*, Duilius also won against Punic armies on land in Sicily, though it is uncertain whether this campaign came before or after Mylae.

In the following year, Rome's successes at sea continued, this time in the waters off Corsica and Sardinia, led by the brother of the Scipio who lost at the Lipari harbor and was most likely still a prisoner of war. This Scipio was awarded a triumph; in gratitude to the gods he dedicated a temple to the weather, which is not surprising given that his effort entailed crossing the open sea and not just hugging the shoreline as Rome had done the previous year. The other consul, Gaius Aquilius Florus, had less luck on land in Sicily as Hamilcar advanced east and seized towns within a few days' striking distance of Syracuse. Florus was forced to stay in the field through the winter; when joined in 258 by the new consul, the two were able to take back much of what they had lost. At sea, the action remained in Sardinia: from among our scant sources we learn that Hannibal, the admiral, was defeated, put to flight, and subsequently killed by his mutinying men. There appears to have been a slight lull in the fighting in 257, but it is worth noting that one of the consuls for that year, Gaius Atilius Regulus, took advantage of the lack of action to try sailing to Malta, the furthest a Roman navy had yet ventured.

6.4 The Emergence of Minor Kingdoms in the Hellenistic East

As Rome, Carthage, and Syracuse stumbled haltingly and then moved full throttle into war, the eastern Mediterranean maintained a tentative status quo. An outlier was the so-called Chremonidean War. Late in 268, the Athenians voted to declare war on Antigonus Gonatas to challenge his control of Piraeus and the Acrocorinth. Led by the arguments of Chremonides, whose decree has survived, the effort became a full-blown collaboration among Sparta, Athens, and the Achaean League, with assistance from Ptolemy II, who had just emerged from the First Syrian War with Antiochus I (Chapter 5). The decree highlighted Ptolemy II's sister-wife, Arsinoe II, recently deceased, and her role in fighting for Macedonia when she was the wife of Lysimachus. The decree also alluded to historic efforts against Persia on behalf of the "freedom of the Greeks," lending the conflict an epic quality, but as the war was prosecuted Antigonus Gonatas was never seriously at risk. He never lost control of Corinth, which enabled him to keep Sparta bottled up and Athens under siege. Antigonus went on to add the large island of Euboea to his territory and led a direct assault on Rhamnous, just a score of miles north of Athens. Evidence of hard fighting by Athens exists: an inscription reveals that a metic (a type of resident alien) received citizenship for his service, and coins found in Attica suggest that a Ptolemaic force attempted to help in its defense but did not last long. Due to Antigonus's blockade, Athens was forced to surrender, and Chremonides fled to Alexandria. The only serious threat to Antigonus on the Greek mainland was from the Aetolian League, which was capitalizing on its control of Delphi and its success against the Celts to maintain a kind of diplomatic authority.

The Ptolemies and Seleucids experienced different fortunes in the aftermath of the First Syrian War. For his part, Ptolemy II held tight to his Nile basin and buffered it with strong activity in Athens, as we have seen, and Cyprus, Syria, southern Asia Minor, and the islands. In Cyrene, Magas now wielded a royal title and remained married to a daughter of Ptolemy's rival Antiochus I (Chapter 5), but the regime had been chastened in the First Syrian War. By contrast, the Seleucids faced serious challenges in the decade from 265 to 255. The Galatians who successfully migrated to northeast Asia Minor at the invitation of Bithynia were becoming fully entrenched. The current king of that state, Nicomedes I, was nominally an ally of the Seleucids, but at the same time used the title *basileus*, implying independence; his relationship with Antiochus II, the heir who would soon rise to the throne in 261, would not be genial. Earlier, in 280, a *basileus* named Mithridates I had also identified himself in Pontus, east of Bithynia on the southern shore of the Black Sea. And in 263 the city-state of Pergamon, to Bithynia's south, wrested itself from the Seleucids' direct control: Philetairus, the guardian of Lysimachus's old royal treasure, died and was succeeded by his more assertive nephew Eumenes I. Eumenes (not to be confused with the *Diadochos* of the same name in Chapter 3; no relation) stopped short of taking the title *basileus* for the time being, but he did begin minting coins depicting Philetairus and not the Seleucids, and he was able to defend this autonomy against Antiochus I in a battle near Sardis. Under Eumenes I and the dynasty that he inaugurated – called the Attalids after his grandfather Attalus – Pergamon would grow to become a major power, as we shall see. Thus, at the time of Antiochus I's death in 261, northern and western Asia Minor were slipping from Seleucid control.

With Antiochus II being a new and untested king, and one in the midst of a crisis to boot, Ptolemy II saw an opportunity to gain yet more of an edge in the contest for Syria and the Levant and sent troops into the region in 259, inaugurating the so-called Second Syrian War. In order to deal with this new problem, Antiochus II had to marry off one of his daughters to the son of a local nobleman in Cappadocia to keep that region loyal. This entailed sharing royal status even further, and yet another region in Asia Minor thus had its own local *basileus*, Ariarathes III, in addition to the Seleucid one.

Meanwhile, around this time, Ashoka, the grandson of Chandragupta (Chapter 4) and now king of the Mauryans on the far eastern border of the Seleucids, declared in an inscription that he had sent Buddhist missions, of a kind, into the Greek world (see Primary Source 6.1 and

---

Primary Source 6.1

Decree of Ashoka about Buddhist Missions in the Mediterranean

This decree was an inscription in Magadhi Prakrit, a language of eastern South Asia, and was set up by the Mauryan king Ashoka. It refers to Buddhist proselytizing efforts, as sponsored by the king, which were undertaken in the Hellenistic kingdoms in the mid-third century BCE. Though the text proclaims the success of the Dhamma (or, "law" of Buddhism) overseas, no texts from the Mediterranean world offer confirmation.

> Major Rock Edict 13 (see Figure 6.1): "Now it is conquest by Dhamma that the Beloved-Servant-of-the-Gods (Ashoka) considers to be the best conquest. And it has been won here, on the borders, even six hundred yojanas away (= approximately 4000 miles; at is happens, the distance from Pakistan to Greece) where the Greek king by the name of Amtiyoko (Antiochus II) rules, beyond whom are the four kings, Turamaye (Ptolemy II), Amtikini (Antigonus Gonatas), Maka (Magas of Cyrene), and Alikasudaro (Alexander, son of Pyrrhus) rule, likewise in the south among the Cholas, the Pandyas, and as far as Tamraparni. Here in the king's domain, among the Yonas (the Greeks), the Kamboyas, the Nabhakas, [and five more tribes are named] everywhere people are following Beloved-of-God's instructions in the Dhamma. Even where Beloved-of-God's envoys have not been, those people too, having heard of the practice of Dhamma and the ordinances and instructions of Dhamma given by Beloved-of-God are following it and will continue to do so.
>
> (trans. S. Dhammika, "The Edicts of King Ashoka: An English Rendering," *The Wheel Publication*, no. 386/387, Kandy, Sri Lanka: the Buddhist Publication Society, 1993)

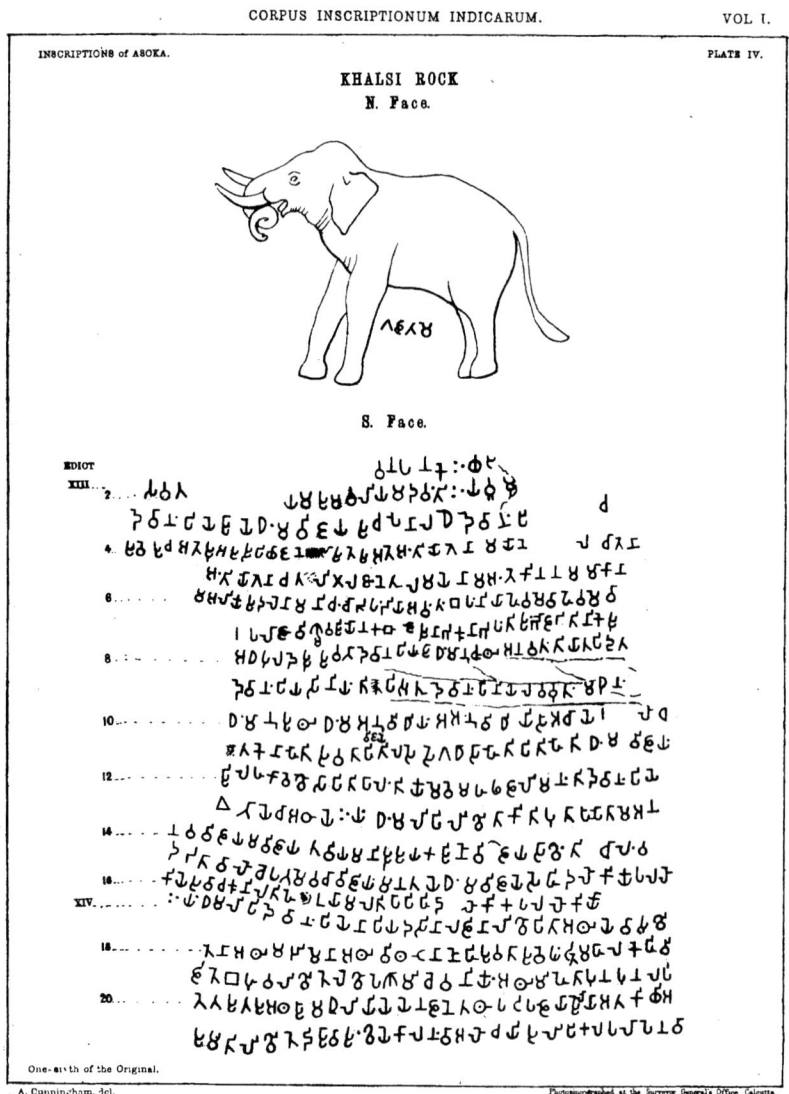

Figure 6.1 Line rendering of Major Rock Edict 13 of Ashoka, emperor of the Mauryans in South Asia.

Figure 6.1). The decree mentioned by name Antiochus, Ptolemy, Antigonus, Magas, and even Alexander, the otherwise unremarkable son of Pyrrhus ensconced in a much diminished Epirus. Another edict of Ashoka, found in Kandahar, Afghanistan (called Alexandria at this time), is a bilingual text in Greek and Aramaic; it records Ashoka's efforts to proselytize Buddhist beliefs of nonviolence toward both man and animal. No evidence survives in a Mediterranean context for such embassies and missions, but there is no reason to doubt that envoys from South Asia were able to move through the Greek-speaking world, in spite of the several wars upon which the preceding pages have concentrated. In addition to much else, the Ashoka Edicts provide proof enough, if it is needed, that cultural exchange continued apace, and that "life went on" in quotidian ways for the nonelite, even as agents in the upper echelons of power contended with each other.

6.5 Romans in North Africa

If Ashoka's Buddhist missions indeed visited Magas in Cyrene, then they would not have been far removed from an odd flotilla of Romans and Italians as they made a bold move on Carthage itself in 256. After inconclusive warfare for years in Sicily, and following closely on the heels of an experimental voyage to Malta, the Romans took a page from Agathocles's playbook (Chapter 4) and assembled a massive fleet at Messina for a mission to Africa. It was led by the consuls Manlius Vulso and Marcus Atilius Regulus, who was the older brother of the admiral to Malta. Simultaneously, the Carthaginians fitted out, we are told, some 350 ships to transport their own major force to Italy. The two navies met in the waters off Ecnomus, a hilltop village on the southern coast of Sicily. Since the Romans were towing horse transports at the time, it appears that they were taken by surprise, and perhaps the Carthaginians were, as well, given the slow pace of intelligence gathering. The "crows" continued to be effective. Polybius reports that nearly 100 Punic ships were lost to inundation or capture, compared with 24 on the Roman side. Overall, it was a net gain of around 40 ships for Rome; now unopposed, they set off for Africa.

Vulso and Regulus landed at the town of Aspis on the east coast of Cap Bon. With the summer dwindling, they could not do much more than establish a garrison and prepare stores for the winter, mainly by ravaging the surrounding Carthaginian estates. Regulus stayed behind and Vulso returned to Rome where he celebrated a triumph. Over the winter, the Carthaginians hatched plans to dislodge Regulus, planning to attack as soon as possible and avoid a repeat of Agathocles's campaign on their turf, which had dragged on for four years. Foremost, they secured the leadership of Xanthippus, yet another adventurer from Sparta. We are told that it was Xanthippus's gambit to fight the Romans on flat terrain, and to eschew the usual instinct of operating from high, hilly ground. In this way, the Carthaginians maximized the impact of their elephant corps; scholars have suggested that Xanthippus would likely have witnessed elephant warfare in 273, when Pyrrhus had laid siege to Sparta. The result was a total rout of the Romans; Regulus was captured alive. All of this transpired before the Roman fleet could reach Africa in early 255. With the garrison in Aspis barely holding on, the 364 ships could only rescue the few thousand survivors and sail back. To make matters worse for Rome, all but 80 of their ships were subsequently wrecked by a storm in the return trip; some 100 000 Romans were said to have perished.

Again, we hear of the rapid constitution of a new fleet over the winter, and in early 254, the Romans put another 300 ships to sea. It is a testament of the scale and reliability of their resources in Italy that they recovered this quickly. The Romans attacked Panormus on the northern coast of Sicily (modern Palermo), and the Carthaginians attacked Agrigentum in the south. In 253, the Romans again sailed for Africa, but this time restricted their activities to raids along the eastern coast down from Cap Bon, as far as the coastal island of Djerba. But on their return to Italy, another storm devastated the fleet, sinking some 150 ships. With this second catastrophe, the Romans appear to have grazed the bottom of their deep well of reserves: for the next several years, campaigns on both sides were desultory.

The Carthaginians had their own problems in dealing with unrest among their African neighbors, the Numidians. In 250, Carthage reinvigorated its army and tried to take Panormus back from the Romans with a direct assault, but it was a failure. The usual tropes of ancient warfare appear in our sources: the Punic elephants were terrorized into trampling their own, and their Celtic mercenaries were plied with wine and were ineffective when drunk. Both of these phenomena reflect well on the Romans in suspicious ways. Additional patriotic Roman anecdotes, of equally dubious veracity, say that the Carthaginians allowed Regulus to lead a peace embassy to Rome, though he was a prisoner, so long as he swore an oath to come back if the treaty were rejected. In the story, not only did Regulus, once in Rome, argue *against* the peace contrary to his "orders," he also stayed true to his word and returned to Carthage though he faced certain execution. Again, this smacks of later Roman propaganda.

6.6 Boxing Matches, Part 1: The Ptolemies and the Antigonids

During the half-decade lull in the war for Sicily, Antigonus Gonatas faced direct pressure from southern Greece and indirect pressure from the Ptolemies, who supported the Greek initiatives. Perhaps Ptolemy II's antipathy stemmed from a major defeat that he suffered at the hands of Antigonus's navy off the island of Cos, but the date for the battle is uncertain. Or, perhaps it was because Ptolemy II and Antiochus II had resolved their differences in the Second Syrian War, which had ended in Antiochus's favor; he married Ptolemy II's daughter Berenike Syra in 253 to seal the deal. (For the marriage to proceed, Antiochus II had had to divorce Laodike, a granddaughter of Seleucus I and thus a powerful cousin; we shall hear more from Laodike shortly.) In 253 (though again, the date is imperfect), a nephew of Antigonus Gonatas who was managing his garrisons at Corinth and on Euboea had himself proclaimed *basileus*, and Ptolemy II recognized his legitimacy to do so. Soon after, in 251, Ptolemy again backed a regional challenger: the nearby city of Sicyon expelled its tyrant and was now led by the remarkable, 20-year old Aratus, a member of the nobility who had been raised in exile in Argos. He traveled to Egypt to receive the assistance from Ptolemy II in person. Here we see Ptolemy yet again exploring war by proxy – low-cost initiatives that had the potential to yield massive dividends.

Antigonus Gonatas was not without his own means of waging proxy wars. In 250, he sent a half-brother to Cyrene to seize both the throne and Berenike II, the daughter of Magas, who had died. Antigonid control of Cyrene posed a threat to Ptolemy II for a number of reasons: it was obviously on his doorstep and it had been in rebellion before, but moreover, this half-brother was the son of Demetrius Poliorketes and Ptolemais, and thus through his mother's side could legitimately claim the Egyptian throne as a grandson of Ptolemy I (and a nephew of Ptolemy II). Berenike II was the granddaughter of Antiochus I, and so it would seem that Ptolemy II was being boxed out in a second way, through a form of alliance between the Antigonids and Seleucids. It is probably not a coincidence that shortly thereafter, Antiochus II set aside Berenike Syra, whom he had only just married in 252, and returned to his Seleucid ex-wife Laodike.

Around this time Berenike II demonstrated a boldness that would make her a celebrated figure among Alexandrian poets: by many accounts she orchestrated the murder of Antigonus's half-brother, which she followed by seeking the hand of Ptolemy III, the crown prince, of a sort, in Egypt who ascended to the throne in 246 when Ptolemy II died. At her own initiative she had thus thwarted both the Antigonid and Seleucid encroachments in Cyrene and rendered all of northeastern Africa Ptolemaic once again. Recent scholarship has seen allusions to her actions in masterworks of Hellenistic literature at the time, such as the poetry of Callimachus (see Primary Source 6.2) and the *Argonautika* by Apollonius of Rhodes (Chapter 7).

6.7 Boxing Matches, Part 2: Rome and Carthage

The year 249 saw renewed activity in Sicily, as the Romans made a concerted effort to take Lilybaeum once and for all. The fortress was the key to Carthaginian success, as we have seen in the campaign of Pyrrhus (Chapter 5): it had superb defenses both manmade and topographical. Against this tough foe, the Roman electorate turned out experienced seamen as consuls – Gaius

> **Primary Source 6.2**
>
> **Callimachus, *The Lock of Berenike***
>
> Callimachus wrote this poem toward the end of his long career at the Library of Alexandria, around the 240s shortly after Ptolemy III's campaign against the Seleucids in the Third Syrian War. Scholars have argued that the patron for the work was Berenike II herself, the wife of Ptolemy III and daughter of Magas, king of Cyrene. For centuries the poem was known only by a Latin translation of it by the Roman poet Catullus (Chapter 14), but substantial papyrus fragments were found and published in the early-twentieth century. It recounts how Berenike II dedicated a lock of her hair to the gods in gratitude for her husband's safe return from war, and that the lock, which here speaks for itself in first person, was miraculously taken up to heaven and now appears as a constellation. The poem has been seen by scholars as a form of propaganda (not unlike Theocritus, *Idyll* 17, Chapter 5) by the queen, to shore up support from the newly combined realm of Egypt and Cyrene.
>
> > Lines 7, 51–56, 75–78: "Conon (the court astronomer at Alexandria) beheld me in the heavens, the lock of hair of Berenike which she dedicated to all the gods. … My sisters (other locks of hair) missed me, newest of them, when quickly (Zephyr, the west wind), … Locrian steed of purple girded Arsinoe II, nurturing breeze waving his swift wings, placed me with his breath through the damp air on the lap of Cypris (Aphrodite). Such things do not bring me joy so much as I fear that I'll no longer touch her head, whose many unscented oils I partook when she was still a maiden, from which I am now cast off, missing the perfumes of womanhood."

Atilius Regulus, of Malta fame, and Manlius Vulso, who had won at Ecnomus. They pitched two camps on either side of Lilybaeum and encircled its landward side with siegeworks, all the while shielding their labor from Carthaginian missiles with portable shelters. They also tried to block the harbor by submerging obstacles beneath the surface of the water. We are told that the bulk of the Carthaginian forces behind the walls were Greek and Celtic mercenaries, and with these ethnicities come the usual stereotypes in the literary evidence: Polybius says that the Celts, typically treacherous, were about to betray the city to the Romans until a Greek soldier who hailed from the Achaean League (Polybius's own state) informed on them; the Carthaginian general accordingly raised the Celts' salary so that they would stay "loyal."

Those Carthaginians not trapped at Lilybaeum, as led by Adherbal, proceeded to provide the Romans with a master class in how control of the sea could make one practically invincible. Numerous relieving fleets from Africa eased the conditions inside Lilybaeum (evidently avoiding the underwater obstacles without difficulty), and allowed for raiding parties against Roman assets along the coast. Time was thus on the Carthaginians' side: after months, the wooden siegeworks of the Romans had become dry and brittle and when the winds were favorable, the soldiers inside Lilybaeum were able to set them aflame from afar.

The new consul of 249, Publius Claudius Pulcher, discerned the nature of the problem and endeavored to attack the Carthaginian fleet at its base at Drepana further north. He launched a secret attack at midnight so that by morning they could take the enemy unaware. A famous anecdote for this campaign is likely apocryphal, but worth recounting for its color: a priest aboard the fleet allegedly informed Pulcher that the gods were against him on the basis that the sacred chickens would not peck at the food put in front of them. Pulcher replied that if they would not eat, then let them drink, and tossed them overboard. Readers can probably guess what happened next: Adherbal was indeed surprised, but he was fast, too, and he escaped the harbor before Pulcher was within reach. For some reason, perhaps because of their experience of storms, the new Roman fleet had abandoned the "crow" technology. This returned the advantage to the Punic side, as Adherbal maneuvered his ships so as to have plenty of room in which to ram the Roman flanks. It was a huge victory for Carthage. To make matters worse, the second consul, Lucius Junius Pullus, wandered into the rough seas of the southern coast. We are told that a nearby Carthaginian fleet could see that the weather was changing and dashed behind a protective cape just in time to avoid a massive storm. Pullus was not so fortunate and the devastation of 249 is said to have far outpaced the shipwrecks of 255 and 253.

Perhaps himself bored with his own narrative, Polybius cuts short the rest of his account of the First Punic War with a memorable metaphor: like two boxers, the Romans and Carthaginians exchanged punch and counter-punch for the next several years, but neither could deliver a death blow. After all, the Romans had suffered staggering losses at sea and decided to stick with what they knew best, a land war, for the time being. For the Carthaginians' part, they appear to have redirected their attentions to the African hinterland, which was still rebellious, perhaps more so following the revelation of Carthage's vulnerability at the hands of the Romans. The new commander in Sicily, Hamilcar Barca, restricted himself to harrying the Italian coast and maintaining their forces at Lilybaeum and Drepana.

6.8   Boxing Matches, Part 3: The Ptolemies and the Seleucids

Boxing is as also an apt a metaphor for competitions elsewhere in the Mediterranean. The years 246–241 comprise both the Third Syrian War between the Ptolemy III and the Seleucids and, roughly, a war between Antigonus Gonatas and the Achaean League, as led now by Aratus. The Third Syrian War erupted shortly after the deaths in 246 of both Ptolemy II Philadelphus and Antiochus II. The two kings had brokered an uneasy truce in 253, but this had weakened, it will be remembered, when Antiochus II left Berenike Syra, Ptolemy II's daughter, to return to his powerful cousin Laodike. Both women had sons who could make a bona fide bid for the Seleucid throne, but Berenike Syra's was still a child, and Laodike had more than one: neither situation was stable or compelling. Ptolemy III, the new king in Egypt with the epithet Euergetes, backed Berenike Syra, his sister; however, he was not fast enough to rescue her, and she and her son were assassinated in Antioch in 245. Ptolemy III still ultimately won the city – a major prize – and then pressed into Anatolia in the west and Mesopotamia in the east, perhaps raiding as far as Bactria. The eastern regions went into upheaval, as the Parthians, led by Arsaces, declared independence. Bactria followed suit, if we accept the presence of its own *basileus* around this time as a reflection of autonomy. But Ptolemy was never comfortable beyond the safety of Egypt, and he returned home quickly; although he did not hold onto any Mesopotamian territory, he did retain Seleucia-Pieria, the port of Antioch. Ptolemy III also secured the loyalty of several powers further west, including Ephesus and the Achaean League. The widowed queen Laodike's strengths lay in Asia Minor: not only were her two sons, Seleucus II and Antiochus Hierax, sharing power over Seleucid dominions there, she was also mother-in-law to kings in both Cappadocia and Pontus. She needed to persuade this generation to cooperate, for after the peace with Ptolemy III in 241, which ended the Third Syrian War, Seleucus II and Hierax became bitter rivals.

In forming alliances with Ephesus and with Aratus of the Achaean League, Ptolemy III was making inroads against Antigonus Gonatas just as much as against Laodike and her brood of Seleucids. Aratus had dealt Antigonus a serious blow in 243 when he freed the Acrocorinth. Achaean possession of this stronghold convinced other local powers, such as Megara and even

Sparta, to ally themselves with Aratus in various ways. Sparta had changed considerably from its Classical past. A wealth gap had opened up between a small population of elite Spartans and the remaining majority, many of whom apparently faced destitution. Such a dynamic stood to devastate the uniquely Spartan sense of shared military responsibility. One king, Agis IV, had tried to correct the imbalance by redistributing landholdings, but he was assassinated by his fellow king in 241. The Sparta that joined Aratus was thus riven by faction. Aratus's troops attempted to take Piraeus from Antigonus; his campaign failed, but the expansionist policies that it betrayed led Antigonus to make an alliance with the rival Aetolian League.

6.9 No Peace

To alter the balance struck between Carthage and Rome in Sicily in the 240s, either Carthage had to increase its land forces or Rome would have to try its luck at sea again. The latter is what happened: we are told that the Roman aristocracy solved the problem of funding a new fleet by sponsoring ships individually, with the understanding that they would recoup their investments should Carthage fall. It is possible that such contributions were mandated by the state, rather like the practice of naval liturgies in Athens described above (Chapter 4). The fleet took to the sea in 241, led by the new consul Gaius Lutatius Catulus. The Romans also elected, perhaps for the first time, a *praetor peregrinus*, who, imbued with *imperium* of his own, sailed with Lutatius as a kind of second in command: the new office again demonstrates the flexibility of the Roman constitution in times of war. The Roman and Punic navies met at the Aegates Islands off the coast of Lilybaeum. The Carthaginians had the wind on their backs, but were also hindered by a number of lumbering transport ships in their train, since they were apparently ferrying supplies to their garrisons. Lutatius Catulus won the battle, with the Carthaginians losing some 120 ships, three-fourths of which were captured by the Romans.

Carthage finally sued for peace. The war had gone on for too long and without clear command of the sea Carthage could not sustain a Sicilian force. They agreed to pull their entire army from Sicily, precious Lilybaeum included, and not to challenge Syracuse on their turf again. Moreover, they were to pay Rome an indemnity of 3200 talents over 10 years. Further clauses in the treaty are disputed by modern historians, but relevant for events that will be reviewed in the next chapter. Polybius later states that both sides agreed to honor each other's existing holdings and diplomatic arrangements; that is, neither side would send war ships to the other's territory, and would not try to recruit troops or establish settlements or back rebels in the other's sphere. How those spheres were defined, specifically, is obviously important, but we have no details.

In all, the year 241 saw three major peace negotiations: between Rome and Carthage from the First Punic War; between the Ptolemies and the Seleucids from the Third Syrian War; and between Antigonus and Aratus of the Achaean League.

After 241 Carthage struggled with massive debt burdens, not only to Rome as part of the treaty but also to its own mercenaries: their plan to pay them off with booty from Sicily was a failed gamble. Two leaders of differing ethnicities – Spendius of Campania and Mathus of Libya (as ever, we notice the ease of movement around the Mediterranean) – roused disgruntled Punic soldiers into an assault on their own capital in 240 and won support from non-Punic neighbors along the way. Polybius refers to the rebel group as "mixhellenes" (1.67.7), which to his mind was an appropriate label for a single category that included soldiers from Spain, Gaul, Libya, Sicily, Italy, and Thrace. Literary sources such as Polybius who write off the motley crew as drunkards and rapists again discredit the organization necessary to manage a population characterized by multiple languages and to muster them for battle. The mercenaries fought

Hamilcar Barca using a combination of concentrated sieges, such as at Utica and Carthage itself, and guerilla tactics worked by small fighting groups. Hamilcar Barca eventually managed to trap a large number of his enemy in a narrow pass and butchered them. Spendius was crucified, to which Mathus responded by torturing *his* prisoner of war, a Carthaginian general. Hamilcar rallied and suppressed the uprising once and for all in 238. But, mercenaries in Sardinia had also by now rebelled against Carthage. Part of their strategy was to invite *Rome* to take possession of the island, and thus join it with Sicily as their prize from the preceding war. The Romans declined for a time, and their merchants profited from selling supplies to both sides. With all that was going on, the Carthaginians could mount no sort of resistance against the Romans beside moral condemnation for their clear violation of the treaty of noninterference in each other's realm. At the end of the so-called "Mercenary War" Sardinia was annexed to Roman control.

In the Greek world, the treaty binding Aratus and Antigonus appears to have been a dead letter from the start. Aratus attacked Athens in the very next year, and when Antigonus Gonatas died in 239, he convinced the Aetolian League to leave the Macedonian side and join him in driving Antigonus's heir from their southern end of the Balkans.

6.10 Rome's Cultural Mélange

In terms of its culture, Rome continued to absorb what its neighbors and allies had to offer. The staging of combats between gladiators, for which the later empire would become notorious, began in the mid-third century. Subsequent writers attributed the custom to the Etruscans, but tomb paintings from further south in Paestum, which Rome had recently colonized in 273 (Chapter 5), suggest that the ritual was more pronounced in Campania (see Figure 6.2). Initially gladiatorial combatants appear to have been prisoners of war, and their fight to the death was viewed as both a form of penalty for the enemy and a means of avenging the Roman war-dead. The displays grew as a form of popular entertainment and came to shed any religious or even

Figure 6.2 Fresco from a tomb near Paestum in southern Italy depicting a boxing match and gladiatorial combat, third century BCE.

nationalistic significance. Fighters would specialize in certain weaponry and techniques of fighting, and a few achieved celebrity status, purchased their freedom, and retired with their aches and pains.

A new literary form of entertainment of the period constitutes a sharp contrast from the physical grit of gladiators. A Greek poet, Livius Andronicus, who seems to have been taken prisoner from southern Italy, perhaps from Tarentum in 272 (Chapter 5), began to publish Latin verse translations of Greek classics. His versions of Greek tragedies and comedies, such as popularized by Menander (Chapter 4), were said by Cicero to have been first staged in 240 shortly after the conclusion of the First Punic War. Very few fragments of these plays survive; the known titles of some of his tragedies demonstrate that the saga of the Trojan War was a source of inspiration – *Achilles*, *The Trojan Horse*, and *Aegisthus*, to name a few. Livius Andronicus's interest in Troy is also confirmed by the work of his that is most extant – a translation of Homer's *Odyssey* into Latin. In this case the surviving fragments show an artistic approach to the project, switching the meter from the Hellenic dactylic hexameter to Saturnian verse, apparently to accommodate the Latin language, and using periphrasis to convey some aspects of Homer's composition (see Primary Source 6.3). That Andronicus was also said to have been a teacher of Roman children suggests that Rome at the time aspired to a broader knowledge of the world around them, worth an investment in new kinds of training for their next generation.

Primary Source 6.3

Livius Andronicus, *Odyssia*

Livius Andronicus's Latin translation of Homer's Odyssey, like so much of early literature both Greek and Latin, is frustratingly fragmentary today. The following are a selection of some of the lines that survive as quoted by later authors, along with the book and verse of Homer that the lines are believed by scholars to translate.

> Line 1.1:
>   Virum mi, Camena, insece versutum…
>   Proceed for me, Goddess of Song, (in the story of) the shrewd man…
> Line 1.65:
>   Neque enim te oblitus sum, Laertie noster…
>   For I have not forgotten you, our son of Laertes (Odysseus)…
> Line 3.110:
>   Ibidemque vir summus adprimus Patroclus…
>   There is the man, great and prime Patroclus…
> Line 4.495:
>   Partim errant, nequinent Graeciam redire…
>   Some wander (the earth); they cannot return to Greece…
> Line 19.225:
>   Vestis pulla porpurea ampla…
>   A garment dusky, purple, wide…
> Line 20.19:
>   Cum socios nostros Ciclops impius mandisset…
>   When the cruel Cyclops chewed up my friends…
> Line 22.91:
>   At celer hasta volans perrumpit pectora ferro…
>   But the swiftly flying spear broke into his chest with its iron tip…

6.11 Conclusions

Carthage was cowed in the course of the First Punic War, making plain the shortcomings of their reliance on mercenaries for foreign warfare and of their style of management of imperial territories. Rome, by contrast, was saved by its Italian allies, and systems were now in place to explore more opportunities overseas. As with the systems of roads in previous generations, the new Roman navy allowed faster movement, broader horizons, and a new frontier. Easier travel along the coasts of the western Mediterranean led to contacts in Spain, a traditional Carthaginian sphere, which would go on to trigger another war.

Of the major eastern dynasties, the Ptolemies were in good hands under Ptolemy II and Ptolemy III, who both marched deep into Seleucid territory. The Seleucids had experienced major setbacks in the course of a generation, and this chapter ends with Laodike's two sons uneasily sharing a dual throne over territory that was much reduced. Antigonus Gonatas died in 239 and power passed to his lesser son, Demetrius II. Just as Asia Minor broke up into smaller kingdoms, the southern Greek mainland also fragmented with the eclipse of the Macedonians, with the various *poleis* experimenting with the limits of their autonomy under the growing power of the Achaean League.

Further Reading

Acosta-Hughes, Benjamin and Stephens, Susan A (2014). *Callimachus in Context: From Plato to the Augustan Poets.* Cambridge: Cambridge University Press.

Clayman, Dee (2014). *Berenice II and the Golden Age of Ptolemaic Egypt.* Oxford: Oxford University Press.

Eckstein, Arthur M (2008). *Rome Enters the Greek East: From Anarchy to Hierarchy in the Hellenistic Mediterranean, 230–170 BC.* Oxford: Blackwell Publishing.

Feeney, Dennis (2016). *Beyond Greek: The Beginnings of Latin Literature.* Cambridge, MA: Harvard University Press.

Green, Peter (1990). *Alexander to Actium: The Historical Evolution of the Hellenistic Age.* Berkeley: University of California Press.

Hoyos, Dexter (ed.) (2015). *A Companion to the Punic Wars.* Oxford: Wiley-Blackwell.

Lazenby, John F (1996). *The First Punic War.* New York: Routledge.

Sherwin-White, Susan and Kuhrt, Amelie (1993). *From Sardis to Samarkhand: A New Approach to the Seleucid Empire.* Berkeley: University of California Press.

7

To 201: The Expanding Roman Horizon

Timeline

230s: Naevius writes the *Bellum Poenicum* in Rome, and Apollonius of Rhodes writes the *Argonautica* in Alexandria
230–228: War between Rome and Illyria
227: Praetors in Rome increased from two to four
225: Battle of Telamon: the Romans defeat a Celtic incursion
220s: Attalus I of Pergamon commissions the Greater Attalid Monument celebrating victories over the Celts
219–217: Fourth Syrian War and the Battle of Raphia (217): Ptolemy IV blocks Antiochus III from entering Egypt
219: Sack of Saguntum by Hannibal
218–202: Second Punic War
216: Battle of Cannae: Hannibal obliterates a large Roman army
215–205: First Macedonian War and the Peace of Phoinike (205)
212: Sack of Syracuse by Marcellus
205: Rome's importation of the cult of Magna Mater from Asia Minor
202: Battle of Zama: Scipio Africanus defeats Hannibal in North Africa
202–195: Fifth Syrian War: Antiochus III against the child-king Ptolemy V

Principal Themes

- Rome's expansion into the rest of the Italian peninsula, including the Celtic north, became more systematic following the First Punic War, and new contacts in Greece and Spain betrayed even farther-flown interests.
- Weaknesses among the Antigonids, Seleucids, and Ptolemies enabled both the rise of Pergamon and a momentary restoration of prestige to Athens and Sparta.
- Hannibal of Carthage surprised Rome with a direct assault on Italy (the Second Punic War), with the goal of turning the Romans' Italian allies against them, but enough remained loyal for Rome to survive despite devastating losses.
- Nearly every Hellenistic power was involved in the Second Punic War, with Philip V of Macedonia, the Achaean League, and Bithynia in support of Hannibal, and the Aetolian League, the Ptolemies, and Pergamon on Rome's side, to an extent. The so-called First Macedonian War was entirely contained within the Second Punic War and essentially marks a concomitant theater in the larger conflict.

The Roman Republic and the Hellenistic Mediterranean: From Alexander to Caesar, First Edition. Joel Allen.
© 2020 John Wiley & Sons, Inc. Published 2020 by John Wiley & Sons, Inc.

- Rome's alliance with Pergamon led to new cultural forms, as did Rome's victories over large Greek cities, even as the importation of the new and the "exotic" prompted social conflicts within the city.

7.1 Introduction

In the last quarter of the third century Rome was at war with Carthage again, but the experience was a thoroughly different species from the First Punic War. Neither side could enjoy the security of a far off front like Sicily but instead confronted the enemy, at times, right outside their gates. Multiple foreign theaters compounded problems for both sides. Spain saw hard fighting, and Roman legions cruised to Greece for the first time, at least to monitor the new Macedonian king who allied with Carthage against them.

All three of the major Hellenistic dynasties – Ptolemies, Seleucids, and Antigonids – enjoyed relatively long-lived monarchies through their first three generations; all three would see an end to this trend around the same time in the mid-third century. By contrast, the newcomer Attalids in Pergamon started their own stable, "first three" kings – Attalus I (r. 241–197), Eumenes II (r. 197–159), and Attalus II (r. 160–138); in many ways, the mid-third to the mid-second century was Pergamon's Golden Age.

In the city of Rome the pace of Hellenization picked up dramatically. Evident already in earlier temple construction and in the translations of Livius Andronicus, Greek culture became more visible following conquests of high profile cities like Syracuse, Tarentum, and Ambracia. No one in the city or the senate could have considered the Italian shoreline as the limit of their horizon by the end of the Second Punic War.

7.2 Historicism in Literature: Naevius and Apollonius of Rhodes

One of the Roman soldiers who fought in the First Punic War went on to become a prolific writer. Gnaeus Naevius, like Livius Andronicus (Chapter 6), dabbled in many genres from drama to epic, but unlike his predecessor, he was a native Roman citizen who wrote original verse about Roman themes, as opposed to translations or transpositions of Greek literature. His *Bellum Poenicum* glorified Rome's very recent victory over Carthage in epic terms (see Primary Source 7.1). Several of its fragments deal with the arrival of the Trojan Aeneas to Italy and his ancestry of the Roman people. Naevius thus inserted his historical work into a frame of myth and imbued it with Homeric status, perhaps taking a lead from experimental poets in Alexandria who were tying Ptolemaic monarchs to the world of the gods (note Theocritus in Chapter 5 and Callimachus in Chapter 6). He also uniquely put versions of "current events" on the stage – a genre of Latin Literature called the *fabula praetexta*. A prominent example is his tragedy, *Clastidium*, which was about a Roman general, Marcus Claudius Marcellus, who killed an enemy chieftain of the Celts in hand-to-hand combat. The battle in question occurred in 222 (see below), and it seems that the performance took place not long after. The political value of the play to the real-life heroes it depicted, likely still living and even in the audience, is obvious, and it is interesting to see this poet of the plebeian order engaging the leading statesmen of his day. Naevius also wrote comedies, some of which skewered Roman leaders in the way Aristophanes had done in the Classical period (Chapter 1), and it is possible that later references to an unnamed poet of this period who was detained for libel allude to him, although that is not certain. Latin Literature thus had strong political dimensions from its very inception.

> **Primary Source 7.1**
>
> **Naevius, *Bellum Poenicum***
>
> Naevius's poem about the First Punic War was apparently composed in the lead-up to the Second Punic War. It is fragmentary, but enough survives to demonstrate that references to known historical figures and the offices they held in the Republic were presented alongside tales of gods. The reverence of Neptune might be compared with the association of Demetrius Poliorketes with Poseidon in Athens's hymn to him from 291 (Chapter 5).
>
> Book 1, fragment: "Nine concordant daughters of Jupiter, sisters…" (This is apparently the poem's opening line, typical of epic, calling upon the Muses for inspiration.)
> Book 1, fragment: "The old man, forthright in his piety, then addressed Neptune, brother of the king of the gods and ruler of the seas." (Context uncertain.)
> Book 3, fragment: "Marcus Valerius, consul, leads part of his army out on an expedition." (A reference to Valerius's campaign in Sicily? Chapter 6)
> Book 4, fragment: "The Roman crossed to the fulsome island of Malta. He burns, he razes, he devastates it; in such a way did he render the affairs of the enemy." (A reference to Regulus's campaign in Malta? Chapter 6)
> Book 7, fragment: "This also they agreed to, that their walls should be in a way that satisfies Lutatius. He agreed that the Sicilians would give back the many prisoners they held as hostages." (A reference to Lutatius's preparations for the Battle of the Aegates Islands? Chapter 6.)

Writing around the same time as Naevius (though the dates are not certain in either case) was Apollonius of Rhodes, based in Alexandria. His masterwork, the *Argonautica*, tells of the wanderings of the magnificent Argo, loaded with heroes in support of Jason and his quest for the Golden Fleece. Unlike the *Bellum Poenicum* the *Argonautica* exists in its entirety, and readers are treated to tales of gods and monsters and miraculous escapes and deeds. References to historical figures are not explicit as in Naevius's work, but scholars have seen in the work references to Apollonius's context. The cosmopolitanism of the Argo's crew has been cause for comment, as the collection of heroes in one place from many scattered *poleis* – from Argos, Miletus, Sparta, Samos, Thrace, Thessaly, Aetolia, and others – brings to mind the Library itself, or Alexandria's ruling aristocracy, which were also made up of Greeks who traveled to a locus of new opportunities. Many of the landing places of the Argo on its adventures include hotspots of Hellenistic history, including sojourns in the lands of the Adriatic coast and northern Italy, whence came the bogeymen Celts that figured as the opposite of Hellenic civilization in the new propaganda of Attalid Pergamon (see below). Scenes in Book 4 on Mt. Eryx and at Lilybaeum in Sicily seem to demonstrate an awareness of major battles of the First Punic War. Dee Clayman has argued that Apollonius's accounts of Medea and Jason were influenced by the careers of Berenike II and Ptolemy III: the former had killed her Macedonian husband en route to marrying the Ptolemaic heir in Egypt (Chapter 6) in ways that are reminiscent of Medea's acquiescence to the murder of her brother in order to join Jason. If Apollonius were indeed making references to the politics of his own world within the fantasy of the epic (and the interpretations presented above are subject to debate), nevertheless, the contrast with Naevius's explicitness of allusion, where living Romans were named directly, is telling. In Rome, artists viewed the military stories of their contemporaries in the same way that Alexandrian poets considered the feats of gods and heroes.

7.3 Rome's New Neighbors

After the First Punic War and the annexation of Sardinia (Chapter 6), the Romans faced the same crucial task that nearly destroyed Carthage – how to pay, or at least to reward, their returning soldiers. That the Roman solution was to dole out parcels of land, and not simply coin like the Carthaginians with their mercenaries, reveals intrinsic differences between their empires: just as with their network of Latin allies, as seen in the joint colonial projects throughout Italy in Chapters 2–4, with their returning soldiers Rome realized that loyalty could be forged by generosity in land allotments. According to Polybius, the Romans looked further out in Italy to territories recently won from the Celts, Samnites, Etruscans, and Tarentines. The colonies at Ariminum on the northern Adriatic coast, at Brundisium on the southern, and at Spoletium in the mountains on the way to both were no more than a generation old by 238, and they bespeak Roman intentions for the length of the Italian coast between them. In 232, a tribune of the plebs, Gaius Flaminius, officially earmarked the land of Cisalpine Gaul – northern Italy up to the Alps – for distribution among Roman veterans. Such advancements of their borders gave the Romans yet newer neighbors – additional Celtic tribes to their north and the Illyrians and Epirots on the other side of the Adriatic.

A competition for resources soon escalated into warfare between Rome and the Illyrians. Some sources have viewed the Illyrians as little more than "pirates," but one reader's bandits and pirates are another reader's heroes and patriots, and there is little reason to differentiate the Illyrian navy's quest for prominence from contemporary or near-contemporary invasions by Ptolemy III, Antigonus Gonatas, or Antiochus I into lands not their own, or from Rome's seizure of Sardinia. The Illyrians' reputation was equally compromised in the eyes of ancient authors because their ruler was a woman, Teuta, acting as widow regent of the child-heir following the recent death of the king. She pursued a campaign of expansion, taking her most significant prize, the island of Corcyra, around 230. The threat was severe enough that the Achaean and Aetolian Leagues, which had been frequent adversaries (Chapter 6), formed an alliance of convenience against her, but with equivocal success. When a Roman embassy to Teuta was rebuffed the senate ordered a large fleet to her waters, which was surely based out of Rome's new Adriatic strongholds. The mission comprised nearly 200 ships, which was around the same size as the invasions of Africa in recent memory (Chapter 6). The Roman victory was decisive, though hardly dramatic: the Illyrian governor at Corcyra turned it over without a fight. A treaty was agreed to in 228 by which Illyria's activities were curtailed. Roman envoys then traveled throughout the major powers of southern Greece to share with them the terms of the peace and to join in victory celebrations. Polybius makes much of these contacts, including an episode where the Romans were admitted to the Isthmian Games, which had been nominally limited to Greeks (2.12.8).

The horseshoe of land around the northern Adriatic was also in competition with the new Romans in the region. Migrations of Celtic tribes were particularly horrifying to Rome owing to the sack of 390 (Chapter 2), and when word arrived that more were on the move, anxiety prompted a ritual human sacrifice in 228 of a Greek and a Celtic couple. The invasion came nonetheless: after building a coalition of smaller tribes on both sides of the Alps, in 225 the Boii and Insubres, led by Aneroestes and Concolitanus, marched south toward Rome. One of the consuls, Lucius Aemilius Papus, followed them from Ariminum; the other, a son of Regulus, the hero of the First Punic War, had been stationed in Sardinia but set sail to return to face the Celts. The Romans also empowered a praetor with *imperium* to raise fresh recruits among noncitizen communities. The corps of praetors had only recently been expanded in 227, from two to four, another adaptation of the constitution to military exigencies. Listed among the new praetors' troops were Etruscans, Samnites, Umbrians, and even other Celts that were opposed to the tribes marching from the

North. The sense of solidarity among Italians, forged in the fourth century and put to the test by Pyrrhus 60 years earlier and again by Carthage 30 years before, continued to strengthen. Aneroestes and Concolitanus reportedly thwarted the praetors army, but they began to withdraw upon the approach of Papus, only to run into Regulus as he was disembarking from Sardinia in front of them. Caught between two consuls at the town of Telamon, the Celts were soundly defeated. Each side lost a general – Regulus and Aneroestes – and Papus took Concolitanus prisoner.

For the next three years, both of the annual consuls were assigned to northern Italy with a brief to eliminate any Celts who would not cooperate. In 223, one of the consuls was Gaius Flaminius, the once-tribune who had set his sights on this territory for its settlement potential. In 222, the historical episode that inspired Naevius's *Clastidium* took place, as one of the consuls, Marcus Claudius Marcellus, killed the enemy commander himself and was accordingly awarded the *spolia opima*, a special designation of personal bravery. In 220, Flaminius was elected censor, and he used the office in ways similar to Appius Claudius Caecus in 312, commissioning a new road, the Via Flaminia, to reach Ariminum, and founding new colonies at Placentia and Cremona, on the far side of the Po Valley, effectively encircling this rich agricultural treasure. In Rome, Flaminius's ideas for infrastructure included the first architectural racing track, or *circus*, in Rome, which was built in the Campus Martius.

7.4 Successors to the Successors

Pergamon started to come into its own just as the Romans were shoring up their eastern coast. Eumenes I had died in 241 and power passed to his cousin, Attalus I. Attalus defeated the Galatians around 238, upon which victory he finally assumed the title *basileus* for his regime, giving form to what was becoming obvious since Eumenes I. Later he would memorialize the victory with a series of sculptures that spoke of his ambition: in the 220s he commissioned a sculpture group depicting dead and dying Galatians, which was located in a sanctuary to Athena on his acropolis (see Figure 7.1). The so-called Greater Attalid Monument (to distinguish it

Figure 7.1 Later Roman marble copy of an original bronze sculpture (c. 220s BCE) of a dying Celt from the Greater Attalid Monument in the sanctuary of Athena on the acropolis of Pergamon.

from the Lesser Attalid Monument in Athens, Chapter 8) intentionally cited the Parthenon and its depictions of dead and dying Persians, centaurs, and Amazons, which commemorated the victories over Xerxes in the Classical era and which cast that city as the very guardian of civilization itself (Chapter 1). Attalus self-consciously claimed the same status for himself in this new, Hellenistic context – another sanctuary to Athena atop another acropolis with images of yet more defeated "exotics."

Shortly after dealing with the Galatians, Attalus turned to Antiochus Hierax, the one of the two Seleucid heirs (Chapter 6) that was local to him in Asia Minor. The brothers Hierax and Seleucus II had made peace between themselves in 236 by agreeing that the Taurus mountain range would divide their spheres of influence, but in coming to this arrangement Hierax had discounted the capabilities and drive of Pergamon. Put to flight, he sought grounding in his brother's Babylon since Seleucus II was on campaign in the far eastern reaches of his kingdom at the time, trying to keep Parthia and Bactria in the empire. But Babylon had been Seleucus's home base for too long and Hierax got nowhere: he was killed in Thrace in 227. Like his grandfather, Seleucus I, Seleucus II was now alone atop the powerful throne, but also like his grandfather he lost it almost immediately to a freak occurrence, falling from his horse in 226 and dying from the wounds. His son, Seleucus III, had a short reign, from 226 to 223, as he was assassinated by his own soldiers while fighting Attalus I, and power passed to his brother, Antiochus III. Based in Babylon far from the trouble spots in the West, Antiochus III had the time and space he needed to rebuild Seleucid forces.

Meanwhile, the Antigonids also muddled through a period of fleeting leadership from 239 to around 220. Demetrius II who took over from his father Antigonus Gonatas after his death in 239 alienated the Aetolian League with a marriage alliance with Epirus. In 229, he appears to have been a victim of the same northern Celtic movements as bedeviled Rome at Telamon: he died on the battlefield while trying to hold them at bay. His son, Philip V, was still a child so Antigonus III Doson, an older cousin, took over as regent. He laid a strong foundation for Philip V during his time on the throne, taking the Acrocorinth, but he too died fighting the Celts, in 221. Philip V then became king in his own right in his late teens.

In the late 230s, Cleomenes III of Sparta embarked on a total reorganization of his state and society, purportedly to restore Spartan idealism and self-sacrifice and, concomitantly, their aura of invincibility. Picking up where Agis IV left off (Chapter 6), he broke up the largest estates and redistributed the land so that more families would be secure enough to put their sons through the highly regimented military training called the *agoge* that made Sparta famous to generals and philosophers. Cleomenes's reforms were more radical than Agis's in that they included political institutions as well as the economy, in ways that brought Sparta more into line with Hellenistic monarchies. In his regime there would be no ephors, the officials who had the power of veto over the kings in some situations. He also declared that the second throne of the dual kingship could be held by someone from his own family, which was previously forbidden; Cleomenes appointed his brother. The *agoge* was to be administered not by an elder Spartan veteran but by an outsider, and a philosopher at that – Sphaerus, a student of Zeno's Stoicism (Chapter 4). Cleomenes III's mother, unlike the strong and patriotic Spartan matriarchs of old, moved to Alexandria, ostensibly as a hostage, but as we have seen, in antiquity such a status had more to do with high-level diplomacy and relationship forming than coercion or blackmail. Cleomenes also plotted northern movements for his army, departing from the southern Peloponnese in a way uncharacteristic of Sparta. This concentration of power in Cleomenes's own person has led scholars to see in him a nascent *basileus* in the broader sense of the Hellenistic world of the past century. In 222, he lost a pitched battle just north of Sparta at Sellasia and fled to join his mother at the court of Ptolemy III.

In 227, the island of Rhodes was leveled by a devastating earthquake, toppling the Colossus that had stood since the departure of Demetrius Poliorketes in 304 (Chapter 4). The famous Hellenistic dynasties had been bickering for generations, to say the least, but they seemed to agree that this vital node of trade and naval power should be rebuilt: the Ptolemies, Antigonids, and Seleucids all sent food and supplies to Rhodes in relief. Mithridates II, *basileus* in Pontus and an in-law of the Seleucids, also sent aid, as did Hiero II of Syracuse, demonstrating at least some level of cooperative affinity among the competitors for power.

7.5 The Origins of the Second Punic War

Blocked from Sicily and essentially defrauded of Sardinia (Chapter 6), a faction in Carthage led by Hamilcar Barca and his son-in-law Hasdrubal looked to Spain to recover their lost glory, not to mention their empire's lost revenues. They eventually founded the city of New Carthage (modern Cartagena) in 228 and led their armies almost as a splinter state, divorced from the Carthaginian elite back in the capital.

Spain should have been far west enough not to have concerned the powers further east, except that Rome had established an alliance with Massilia (modern Marseilles), a Hellenic city on the southern coast of Gaul; both powers were likely cooperating against the Celtic tribes further north. Now in Spain's orbit, the Romans, likely working with the Massilians and in their interests, grew concerned with the successes of Hasdrubal such that they negotiated an agreement whereby he would not campaign north of the Ebro River, beyond which would be the Massilian – and lightly, by extension, the Roman – sphere of influence (see Map 7.1). Somewhere in time – the date is highly in question, as is even the veracity of the episode – the Romans also made an alliance with the coastal Spanish town of Saguntum, even though it was to the Ebro's *south*. Our sources for this alliance are weak: Polybius does not mention its details, and yet it is crucial for understanding the start of a major war.

The sequence of events is relatively straightforward. In 220, the Saguntines reportedly attacked some tribes near them, which were under Carthaginian protection, now led by Hannibal, son of Hamilcar Barca. Hannibal accordingly laid siege to Saguntum the next year. The Saguntines applied to Rome for assistance, but in that year both of the consuls were stationed in Illyria, restoring conditions that had deteriorated when their appointee to Corcyra, who once betrayed Teuta to Rome, now began to imitate her policies and was attacking ships in his waters. After a prolonged siege, Saguntum fell to Hannibal who, it is alleged by unfriendly sources, completely massacred the population. In early 218, the senate awoke to its Saguntine diplomatic obligations and sent envoys to Carthage to protest. Perhaps aware of the factional nature of Punic politics at the time, they demanded that Hannibal be turned over to them. As our sources say, the anti-Hannibal faction was either unwilling to deliver, or, equally likely, *unable* to deliver: with a bitter war against their mercenaries in recent memory, there may not have been the stomach in Carthage to provoke civil strife. Faced with this recalcitrance, the Romans declared war.

It is not entirely clear why Rome cared so much about Saguntum as to allow the conflict to escalate into a major war. They had little reason to be in Spain, and it is hard to see what they had to fear from chaotic Carthage; they had instead been devoting their recent attention to Celtic activity. One solution by scholars has been to suggest that it was Massilia that was really the driving force, and their role was obscured in accounts written after the war. Another solution has been to suggest that the Romans did not think the war would amount to much. With their bases in Sicily and Sardinia, and with their alliance with Massilia, they had the seas under good control, and how else could Hannibal become a threat from Spain? They likely believed that the war would be fought

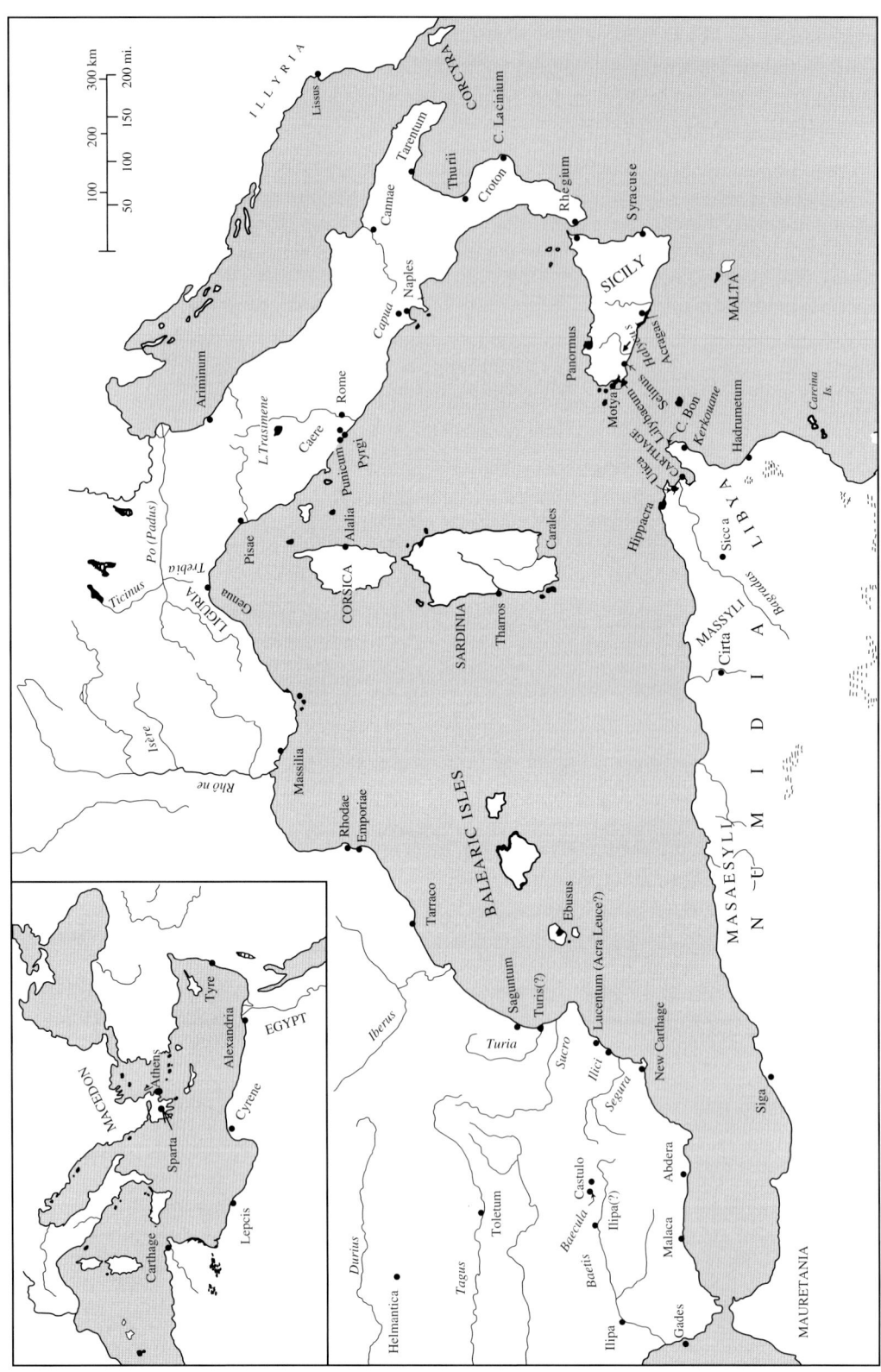

Map 7.1 The Roman and Carthaginian spheres of influence at the start of the Second Punic War.

in a zone around the Ebro; after all, the consuls for 218 were assigned to Spain and to Africa. Win or lose, neither Italy nor Rome would suffer much, or so they (may have) thought.

7.6 Rome's Initial Failures

Famously, Hannibal dared the unpredictable and attacked Italy over land, effecting a dangerous off-season crossing of the mountains. However treacherous the Alpine terrain was, the choice of route made sense for a number of reasons. First, the sea was not an option, given Rome's strategic bases. Second, Hannibal, who had had success in diplomacy with the Celtic populations of Iberia, may have expected to pick up support among Celts on the other side of the Alps, as well, to smooth his path. Third, once Hannibal's African, Spanish, and (with any luck) Celtic troops arrived in Italy, their numbers alone could generate snowballing defections among Rome's allies, which Hannibal must have understood were the source of the Roman victory in the First Punic War after one catastrophic shipwreck after another had been remediated through manpower.

Perhaps the only surprising dimension of Hannibal's transalpine march was its timing: he set out near the start of winter. Snow and ice made his task Sisyphean both figuratively and literally as elephants were marched up steep slopes only to tumble back down. Furthermore, in spite of Hannibal's efforts at diplomacy, some tribes remained hostile. When Hannibal finally descended from the mountains, it was with a much reduced force. Still, his feint had the effect of pulling the consuls from their original assignments in Spain and Africa to face him in northern Italy. We are told that both consuls were driven by a desire for glory, which led to rash actions. The first of many examples may be the Battle of the Trebia River in 218, where one of the consuls, Tiberius Sempronius Longus, was eager for a pitched battle before Hannibal could recover from the stress of the crossing. He drove his soldiers to wade across the river to engage Hannibal's troops, who, dry and not at all tired, put him to flight. In the following year, 217, the Romans turned to a hero of the era, Gaius Flaminius, whose tribunate, consulship, and censorship had been enormously productive (see above). Flaminius led his army to the shores of Lake Trasimene, but the Carthaginians had made it there first and had hidden themselves from view. Thick fog helped even more in giving them the element of surprise, and once again, the Romans were crushed. Flaminius himself died in the battle.

With these defeats, the Romans appointed a dictator to handle the growing emergency. Quintus Fabius Maximus (consul in 233 and 228; censor in 230) sought to avoid the mistakes of his predecessors and spent his term following Hannibal, but not engaging him. This strategy of delay forced Hannibal to stay on the move for supplies and to remain constantly vigilant against guerilla tactics. The senate was impatient, however, as the downside of allowing Hannibal to ruin the Italian countryside were obvious. The new consuls for 216 included Lucius Aemilius Paullus, who had triumphed in 219 for the Illyrian victories that had kept Rome from helping Saguntum, and Marcus Terentius Varro. Our sources make Varro out to be a villain in a story of Roman disorder, though his lower social status relative to his colleagues may be the true impetus for his negative reputation. As the story goes, he badgered the more cautious Paullus into joining battle with Hannibal before they had ideal terrain. The two held the overall command on alternating days, and Varro, the more aggressive of the pair, used "his" command days to advance further toward Hannibal, building a momentum that Paullus could not fruitfully reverse when it was "his" turn. Thus, the Romans marched to a flat expanse near the town of Cannae that favored Hannibal's cavalry. Hannibal drew the Roman line forward in such a way that the legions became knotted in a concentrated area and not arrayed in a long line, which made it easier for Hannibal to surround them. The result was even higher casualties than at Trebia and Trasimene, including Aemilius Paullus himself. What is more, a few months after Cannae, a praetor L. Postumius Albinus was defeated and killed in Celtic Italy. The Italian allies had seen enough: numerous cities of the Samnites, Lucanians, and Greeks joined the Carthaginian cause. A notable loss for the Romans was the large city of Capua, which not only went over to Hannibal but confined a large crowd of resident Romans to a bathhouse where they were suffocated.

Hannibal could have marched on Rome, perhaps even bringing the war to an end, but he did not press his advantage. His decision need not be seen as foolish: Rome still had allies, as well as excellent walls, and sieges were not as straightforward for an army ranging around enemy territory as outright battles were. Indeed, a new dictator, Marcus Junius Pera, adeptly cobbled together two legions from slaves and those imprisoned for excessive debt and thus put up a credible defense. Livy tells the story of one Decius Magius, apparently a Roman leader of some kind in Capua, who was singled out for special imprisonment at Carthage. En route to Africa, his ship was blown off course to Cyrene and he thus ended up in the hands of Ptolemy IV (who had ascended the throne in 221; below), who protected him – a sign of the growing sense of alliance between Egypt and Rome.

7.7 Adolescent Kings in Syria and Egypt

While Rome's involvement in Illyria and Spain was adding a new dimension to Hellenistic history, the Seleucid and Ptolemaic regimes were locked in a struggle that was congruent with trends to that point – that is, they were fighting for control of Syria. As of 221, both the Seleucids and the Ptolemies had new teenaged kings in Antiochus III and Ptolemy IV, and both were dominated at the start by influential administrators, rather like their contemporary Philip V of the Antigonids, also just 17 at this time. In the case of Ptolemy IV, given both his adolescence and, apparently, his interests in hedonistic pursuits (though such accusations in our sources should always be taken with a grain of salt), the multiple ethnicities of the advisors are notable: they included Sosibius, an Alexandrian; Agathocles, from a line with origins in Samos; and Theodotus, an Aetolian who commanded Ptolemaic forces in the Levant. Cleomenes III of Sparta was also now resident in the capital (above), and was sufficiently involved in politics that he could at least harbor an ambition to govern: he was killed in 219 while attempting a coup in Alexandria.

Sosibius was the most powerful of the Alexandrian advisors; fragments of poems by Callimachus survive in which he was celebrated for his victories, probably in horse-racing, at a number of prestigious Panhellenic athletic games. Since these associates were ruthless in their style of management (they eliminated Ptolemy IV's family members to forestall competition, including his mother Berenike II), they had to look elsewhere to survive the simplest of disagreements: this is what Theodotus did when, in flight from Sosibius, he offered his armies to Antiochus III in 219, the start of the short-lived Fourth Syrian War. The Seleucid army marched toward the Delta, against which Sosibius mounted an effective resistance at Raphia south of the Gaza Strip in 217, an impressive feat since it entailed the recruitment of native Egyptians to the largely Macedonian army. Present at the battle, though probably not contributing much, were Ptolemy IV and his sister-wife, Arsinoe III. Though the Battle of Raphia went their way, the Ptolemies lost Seleucia-Pieria, the harbor of Antioch. Apart from some high level diplomacy with Rome and a network of unlikely allies (to be discussed), Ptolemy IV was for a time largely occupied with native insurrections and breakaway kingdoms, especially in the highlands south of the Nile Delta, rather like the Seleucids in the Far East.

7.8 The Five Fronts of the Second Punic War

As bad as 216 was for Rome with its defeat at Cannae – thereafter commemorated as a *dies ater*, or "black day" in the Roman calendar, to be mourned rather like September 11 in the United States – the following year, 215, might have seemed even worse. In the spring of that year word came that Hiero II of Syracuse had died and that his successor, a teenaged grandson Hieronymus, was in the hands of administrators, not unlike the recent history of the Antigonids, Ptolemies, and Seleucids. Hiero, the father, had been a Roman ally for nearly 50 years, but the new powers-behind-the-throne, a pair of brothers who were half-Punic owing to a Carthaginian mother, took Syracuse in a profoundly different direction and offered an alliance to Hannibal. Hieronymus went along but was assassinated early the next year. The loss of Syracuse robbed the Romans of a great advantage that they had possessed over Hannibal – his isolation without a decent port. To make matters worse, Roman soldiers happened to apprehend an embassy between Philip V of Macedonia, now aged 23 and ambitious in his own right, and Hannibal that implied diplomacy was at work between them (compare Primary Source 7.2). The Illyrian Wars had already revealed how dangerous a cross-Adriatic belligerent could be for Rome.

Primary Source 7.2

Letter from Philip V to the Town of Larisa

In this decree from Philip V, set up in the city of Larisa, the king extols the benefits of being liberal with grants of citizenship, citing the Romans as his model.

> Lines 26–29, 31–34: "Philip, *basileus*, to the *tagoi* (magistrates) and the city of Larisa, greetings. I learn that those enrolled as citizens in keeping with my letter and with our decree, whose names were inscribed on the stelae, have been stricken (from the citizen rolls). If this indeed transpired, those who advised you have failed to understand the benefits that my decision (in this regard) would have brought to your country. … It is possible to observe others who enroll citizens in similar ways, whose number includes the Romans. [They] bestow political rights and a share in the office even to slaves whom they free. In such a way they have not only enhanced their own country, but they have also sent out colonies to almost seventy sites…"

With all this misfortune coming at once, bad omens seemed to confirm the displeasure of the gods. It was discovered that some of the Vestal Virgins had not upheld their vow of chastity, and the election for one of the consulships was disrupted by an inauspicious thunderclap. The offending Vestals were buried alive, as was dictated by tradition for such slips, and a Greek couple and a Celtic couple were sacrificed to curry favor, as had been done in 228. For further clarification of the will of the gods, the logical place to seek answers was at the Oracle at Delphi, which the Roman embassies following the Illyrian War had surely encountered in the 220s. Quintus Fabius Pictor, a senator and son of a consul, led the mission. We do not know how his questions were answered, but we might suppose that he sharpened his language skills in the process: he would soon undertake the first prose history of Rome, which he composed in Greek (Chapter 8).

The human sacrifices and other religious rites, however macabre, may have been a comfort to the distressed Romans, but reforms in the temporal realms of fiscal policy, military science, and leadership brought more thoroughgoing solutions to their emergencies. Incredibly, there were now five fronts to handle: the Romans had to stem tides in Sicily, Greece, Spain, and Italy, both in the south against Hannibal, and in the north against the Celts. The complexities of logistics must have presented a fatal puzzle: legions upon legions were needed quickly, and they had to cross seas, don armor, be fed, and be led. To deal with expenses the Romans passed the Lex Oppia in 215, which set limits on expenditures for luxury items like fine clothing, jewelry, and conveyances. To address the leadership vacuum – having just two consuls and four praetors no longer sufficed – the Romans perfected their deployment of promagistrates, or, past praetors and past consuls who could be imbued with *imperium* upon appointment by the senate as propraetors and proconsuls, charged with handling a particular task, or a *provincia*. The device had first been used in the Samnite Wars as we have seen with Quintus Publilius Philo in 326 (Chapter 3) and had been repeated sporadically when the need arose. Now the practice became more systematic. Varro's consulship was accordingly extended; Pomponius Matho's praetorship was extended; and Marcus Claudius Marcellus, the hero of Clastidium, was given a special proconsulship, not an extension of a previous year's office but a new appointment.

The front in southern Italy took priority for the Romans by a long way. Hannibal had established a base of operations near Capua. He was likely seeking another engagement with a full force of Roman legions, but the generals had learned their lesson and simply watched and waited through 214 and 213. In 212, Hannibal made a move on Tarentum: with its Greek population, position on the coast, and history of bad blood with Rome, he hoped to exploit an advantage. As Hannibal departed, the Carthaginian forces around Capua fell into apparently lesser hands. The Romans completed a circumvallation of Capua's walls and devastated its farmland in order to induce famine. Starved into submission in 211, the leading senators of Capua paid for their defection with their lives. The lower orders were allowed to live and the physical city, to stand, only now without any of the autonomy Capua had enjoyed in the past. At Tarentum, Hannibal used an array of disguises, feints, and conspiracies, worked out amid a force of Africans, Celts, and Greeks, to take the city under cover of darkness. The citadel held out, but other major towns, like Thurii and Metapontum, went over to Hannibal's side and nearly the entire Bay of Tarentum was his.

In 213 Roman forces were dispatched to Sicily. Marcus Claudius Marcellus, now proconsul, led an initial invasion with speed and ingenuity, creating floating siege towers to broach the walls from the water. His gimmicks were thwarted, however, by equally clever devices on the Syracusan side, as designed by the mathematician and engineer Archimedes. These included both the elegant – iron cranes that lifted enemy ships out of the water and dropped them back until they broke apart – and the crude – mechanical arms that simply dropped heavy lumps on ships from directly above, obviating the guesswork of parabolic catapult shots. Later claims that Archimedes fashioned huge concave mirrors to concentrate the sun's rays into laser beams have been discredited: this detail is not in Polybius, and modern attempts to replicate the technology have failed. The Romans were forced to settle into a long siege. Carthage sent reinforcements from the south via Agrigentum, and the Romans answered with supplies from the north via Panormus.

The fall of Syracuse was the result of a series of small steps. A Spartan serving among the Syracusans (part of a trend of Spartans overseas, if one thinks of Acrotatus, Cleonymus, and Xanthippus, Chapters 4 and 6) was captured while trying to sneak out from the city. He was important enough to generate ransom negotiations, and as the Romans drew close to the city for the discussions, they scrutinized the walls and figured out a way of scaling them. Soon after, when the Syracusan guards were celebrating a festival, Marcellus's soldiers made their way up and over to open the gates. Another source describes a kind of diplomacy of ethnicity in Marcellus's campaign: a Spaniard fighting on the Roman side was sent to persuade a Spaniard in Hannibal's army to open the gates. Whichever story be true, perhaps neither, the Romans took the city and transported many treasures of Greek art back to their parochial capital; Archimedes died in the melee.

A Roman army had been in Spain since 218, when Gnaeus Cornelius Scipio supported Massilia in landing at its sister-colony at Empuriae (modern Empuries; both cities had been founded by Greeks from Phocaea in Asia Minor). In 217, he was joined by his brother Publius, an ex-consul, and the two advanced relatively easily across the Ebro and down to Saguntum. The Scipios freed the hostages that had been detained by Carthage to ensure the loyalty of the local tribes – a kindness that was evidently more effective in winning their support than detaining them in the first place, according to Polybius (who himself wrote as a hostage in Rome some 50 years later; Chapter 10). The Carthaginian forces were pushed further and further west in Iberia, such that the Scipios felt comfortable enough to pursue an opportunity in Africa itself, by negotiating with the Numidian Syphax to attack Carthage at its doorstep. The two Spanish legions plus auxiliaries experienced much success for some seven years, surely contributing to Roman momentum in Italy in the sense that they deprived Hannibal of a source of supplies. But in 211, the Scipios in an overabundance of confidence ventured further south than they had to date and were both killed in their first serious defeat.

As for Greece, a fourth front, the Romans may have been intimidated at first by the news of an alliance between Hannibal and the storied Macedonians, but it would turn out not to be a troublesome theater of operations. The only proactive movement we know of in 215 and 214 was the anchoring of a navy in Brundisium to protect against an invasion, if it should come. It did not: rather, Philip V sailed along the Illyrian coast, eventually seizing Oricus, the port town of a greater inland prize, Apollonia. But even this was half-hearted: the Roman fleet easily freed Oricus in late 214, broke up the siege of the larger city, and planted its own garrison, which sat quietly there for a couple of more years without action. Only in 211, which, as we have seen, was the year that affairs at home were going Rome's way, did the Romans enter into a formal alliance that demanded more responsibility from local powers in the area. They contracted with the Aetolian League to drive Philip from central Greece, with any moveable booty going to Rome and any land (which was more valuable) to the Aetolians. Other regional powers were listed as likely collaborators should circumstances require, including Sparta, the Illyrians, and the Attalids of Pergamon. The alliance bore fruit: with Rome and Aetolia stepping up their pressure and with Celtic aggression in their north, Macedonia was quiet for a time. Modern historians refer to these operations as the First Macedonian War, starting in 215, but its early years were not tumultuous.

> The front in northern Italy – a fifth theater of the war – would also prove not to be a problem, though Italians on Rome's side, of course, would not have known that in 215. An army was permanently stationed at Ariminium to keep watch, but the Celts remained quiet until 207 when they were spurred to action again by the Carthaginians.

7.9 Rome, Triumphant and Transformed

With the loss of Capua and Syracuse, Hannibal's position in southern Italy was deteriorating as of 210, but the Romans still largely left him alone so they could act in the other theaters. No evidence for Rome's growing sense of security in Italy is more illustrative than records of the disbanding of multiple legions for that year: they evidently were not felt to be necessary, and keeping them in the field could damage the allies' morale. More action was to be found in the

Greek world. The Roman-Aetolian-Attalid alliance was able to take the island of Aegina, which in turn triggered the defections of the large cities of Elis and Messene to their cause. Later that year they also received pledges and troops from Sparta. Livy mentions in passing that this year also saw a new embassy from Rome to the Ptolemies, which would be natural given Egypt's historic ties with Rome's new Greek friends.

The problems in Sicily lingered and the Hellenic nature of the island perhaps contributed to the Roman decision to shift Marcus Valerius Laevinus, the commander of the fleet in Greece for the past several years, to a mission against Agrigentum, which still held out for Carthage. Laevinus must have been especially desired for this purpose because the Romans broke with precedence in electing him to the consulship in absentia. Laevinus got word to Mottones, a Carthaginian officer, that, should he betray Agrigentum he would be rewarded with full citizenship rights in Rome. He did so, and Livy says that he accordingly took the name of his patron; an inscription from Delphi confirms his new identity in the spelling of Hellenic epigraphy, Maarkos Oalerios Mottones. He will appear in the next chapter fighting on Rome's behalf in Greece. We thus see another innovation of the Second Punic War – the offer of citizenship to individual, non-Italian leaders for the purpose of building an international coalition. From Agrigentum, Laevinus continued his aggressive press by sending raids to the African coast.

In Spain, the year 210 was one of rebuilding following the shock of the demise of the Scipio brothers. Sent to replace them was Publius Cornelius Scipio, son to one and nephew to the other. Our sources, which tend to remember Scipio fondly owing to what he was to accomplish at the end of the war, describe his arrival in the region as something of a charm offensive, winning over both the Roman soldiers who had been demoralized the year before as well as the local Iberian tribes. His command, like Laevinus's election to the consulship, was awarded in absentia; it was further innovative in that he was only 26 years old and had yet served neither as praetor nor as consul. The senate's granting of *imperium* to someone untested and in command of legions hundreds of miles away at a time of war attests either to Scipio's military reputation or to the role of sentimentality in allowing him the chance to rebuild not only Rome's reputation but also that of his family.

The following year, 209, witnessed new boldness and vigor on the part of the Romans in Italy, in Greece, and in Spain. Quintus Fabius Maximus was returned to the consulship for a fifth time. Part of the skill of his famous strategy of delay was to know when the circumstances were right to shift back to offense, and Fabius judged now to be the time: three armies made a coordinated assault on Hannibal's forces in southern Italy. Marcellus kept Hannibal occupied in Bruttium; the second consul, Fulvius Flaccus, campaigned in Samnium; and Fabius himself led an assault on Tarentum. He managed to sack the city, and once again Rome would get a taste of Greek art and culture when a trove of treasures was sent back as trophies, just three years after the fall of Syracuse.

It is possible that one reason for Fabius's success was that Hannibal had finally honored his pledge to help Philip and sent part of his Tarentine navy to the Macedonian army in Greece. Philip was desperate as his principal ally in the region, the Achaean League, was now being attacked from the north by the Aetolians and from the south by Sparta. In addition to the Punic ships, he was also expecting a fleet from Bithynia, whose king Prusias I had joined him probably in an effort to stifle the Attalids of Pergamon. The Ptolemies, Rhodes, and Athens were also involved tangentially in the conflict, offering their services as neutral arbiters. The so-called First Macedonian War was finally building, and the Gulf of Corinth became the locus of a true world war, as far as the Greek-speaking powers were concerned. Negotiations went nowhere, dismissed, we are told, by Aetolian optimism in their position. Philip tried to attack Elis, but Rome came to its rescue, and Philip ended the year decamping for his home turf because, to make matters worse, the Celts had invaded once again.

Even with the renewal of Roman potency in Italy and Greece, it was the feats in Spain that were perhaps the most surprising for 209. Young Scipio surveyed his options for action south of the Ebro and became aware that the three Carthaginian armies were dispersed to such an extent that Carthago Nova itself was unguarded. With the element of surprise, Scipio marched deep into Punic Spain and laid siege before any armies could block him. He took the city in a two-pronged assault: in the morning he sent a conventional force to storm the landward walls, which drew the Carthaginians away from the sections that fronted a lagoon; in the afternoon, aware through intelligence that the waters receded for some reason (it could not be the tides; perhaps it was strong winds), he sent a second force to wade through the shallows and scale the walls. So quick was his victory and so benevolent was his handling of the Iberian hostages that he found on the premises (once again), local tribes switched to his side in droves. Polybius recounts that there was a movement to bestow upon Scipio the title of *basileus* in keeping with Hellenistic political norms (10.40). Declining that, he favored purely military accolades. In many ways Scipio's 209 was much like Hannibal's 218, with its surprising march through enemy territory and its plot to turn alliances through persuasion.

In 208, the pendulum started to swing back to Carthage, but was stopped dead. The two consuls, our famous Marcellus who was joined for the year by Titus Quinctius Crispinus, were both arrayed against Hannibal in Italy, but they wandered into an ambush and were killed, Marcellus immediately and Crispinus after suffering from his wounds. Meanwhile Carthaginian reinforcements were sent from Spain, led by Hannibal's brother Hasdrubal (who had the same name as Hannibal's brother-in-law, above). The new consuls for 207 thus had as their chief goal the prevention of a reunion between the two Punic armies. One consul, Gaius Claudius Nero, headed south to contend with Hannibal, and the other, Livius Salinator, went north to face Hasdrubal. But, Claudius Nero divided his army, as secretively as he could, and himself led a contingent on a rapid march to join Salinator. As he neared his colleague's camp, he awaited the cover of darkness before effecting the final amalgam, so that Hasdrubal would not know how large the opposing Roman army was. In the ensuing battle at the Metaurus River, the Romans routed Hasdrubal's force of Africans, Spaniards, Celts, and elephants, which went berserk on their own armies, as so often happened. Nero (not the emperor, obviously) then dashed back south to face Hannibal and to deliver to him his brother's decapitated head.

In 206, Hannibal was stranded. He had no hope of help from Africa, where the Roman fleet had begun conducting periodic coastal raids. The news from Spain was even worse: Scipio had won a pitiless victory at the Battle of Ilipa against the remaining Carthaginian armies. In so doing, Scipio managed to muster a Numidian cavalry force led by Masinissa from the Punic side to join the broader Numidian rebellion in Africa itself, first undertaken by Syphax. Carthage would never again have a presence in Iberia: Scipio also founded colonies for veterans – Italica, near Seville, is a particularly well-preserved example today – and Hannibal's other prominent brother, Mago, was lucky to escape with his life from Cadiz to the island of Minorca. In Greece, Hannibal's ally Philip V had finally achieved something useful and forced the Aetolians to the table after a successful invasion, but his sense of obligation to Carthage had long since evaporated. All of the Hellenic parties agreed to a treaty at Phoinike in 205, which thus brought an end to the so-called First Macedonian War.

Scipio returned from Spain a hero and was elected consul for 205. He applied the same energy and wit that he displayed in Spain to planning a new campaign against Carthage on its African turf. According to Livy, Fabius Maximus, now elderly, expressed skepticism and doubted whether Scipio understood the challenges of an overseas campaign. Nevertheless, Scipio gathered a massive force in Sicily in preparation for a crossing to Africa.

7.10 An Imperial Culture

Rome underwent cultural change in organic ways in the course of the First Punic War, where slaves (Livius Andronicus) or soldiers (Naevius) made names for themselves with innovative literary works. In the Second Punic War, more examples of Hellenism appeared in the city, but in the more nationalistic context of the military and empire. Triumphal festivals celebrating victories over Syracuse and Tarentum were elaborate affairs: Romans had surely seen Greek works of art previously, but in these contexts they doubled as trophies. The new works drove change; some scholars have seen a nascent generation gap between old-timers who would have demurred at the Hellenic nudity of the statuary, and the youth who found it to be cutting edge.

In 205, the Romans looked even further East and deeper into Asia Minor for a cultural touchstone. Their Sibylline Books, sacred and prophetic, predicted that an enemy on Italian soil (in this case, Hannibal, of course) could be dispelled if Rome imported the cult of Cybele, who would receive the Latin name Magna Mater, or Great Mother (see Figure 7.2). Her sanctuary was at Pessinus, east of Pergamon, not coincidentally under the sway of Rome's most powerful and likeminded ally Attalus I. Publius Cornelius Scipio Nasica led the mission, having received the blessing to do so from the Oracle at Delphi, and as he was returning with the black stone, the abstract manifestation of the divinity, his vessel ran aground where the Tiber met the sea. A Roman matron suspected of loose morals – in some sources, she is a Vestal Virgin and thus potentially on the verge of horrific execution – proved her honesty by miraculously pulling the ship free on her own. The cult was strange for a Roman context: with eunuch priests celebrating the principle of fertility among women, it was both distinctively gendered and foreign. Its primary attraction may have been its origin in the vicinity of Troy, home of Rome's forefather Aeneas, and its association with Pergamon, for which the Romans had great affinity. Notably, when the stone finally reached Rome it was housed in the Temple of Victory until its own dwelling could be completed.

Figure 7.2 Plate from Ai Khanoum (see Figure 3.2) depicting Cybele drawn in a chariot drawn by lions beneath a sun god, third century BCE.

7.11 The End of the Second Punic War

In 204, Scipio finally made the crossing to Africa, and having organized Masinissa as his chief Numidian ally since Syphax had returned to the Carthaginian fold, began the campaign in earnest in 203. His original consulship, for 205, had expired; in 204, he had been prorogued for a year; in 203, a divided senate took the unusual step of proroguing the office for an indeterminate period of time – however long it took to defeat Carthage. Scipio's main base of operations was near Utica, which remained walled up for Carthage. He scored some impressive victories regardless, and Masinissa eventually captured Syphax alive. Meanwhile, in northern Italy, one of the sitting consuls, Marcus Cornelius Cethegus, defeated Mago's army, which had sailed there from Minorca, and Mago died of his wounds on board a ship back to Africa.

Desperate, Carthage now agreed to the principles of a new peace proposal, part of which required the recall of Hannibal from Italy. Hannibal thus embarked in the late fall, ending 15 years in Italy, which itself followed over 20 years in Spain. For some reason – the sources assign treachery to either Rome or Carthage based their own series of events – the peace was scrapped and a state of war was returned. Hannibal risked all in a pitched battle, located by a later source at Zama though better authorities place it in other locales. Among the ethnicities present on Hannibal's side, according to various accounts, were Africans, Numidians, Spaniards, Ligurians, Celts, Balearics, Moors, and even Bruttians, who presumably left Italy with Hannibal rather than face reprisals from Rome. Scipio won the battle; different sources have different details, but in every case the Carthaginians are said to have lost some 20 times more soldiers than the Romans.

Scipio quickly moved his land army to the very gates of Carthage, and his fleet to the harbor, and set about negotiating a peace. Factions of Carthaginians were received at the Temple of Bellona in Rome where they blamed Hannibal for the war, but their arguments were rejected: the Romans were not looking for a deal. It took a year, until 201, for the treaty to be ratified, but Carthage was ultimately to be limited to a swath of Africa alone, and a smaller one than it had possessed before, as Masinissa was rewarded with territories for his Numidians. The state was rendered inert: with the burning of almost all of its ships, the surrender of all of its elephants, and the dismissal of all of its mercenaries, Carthage would not be able to expand. Moreover, Carthage would owe 10 000 talents to be paid over 50 years, and would submit for Roman supervision a population of 100 hostage youths between the ages of 14 and 30, regularly refreshed as they died or aged in residence in Italy. Scipio took on the name Africanus for his victory and celebrated a triumph.

7.12 Antiochus III Becomes "Great"

We have seen above references to almost all of the major Hellenistic powers through the course of the Second Punic War, to the extent that they were sucked into, or chose to join, the conflict between Rome and Carthage. Philip V entered into an outright alliance with Hannibal but did not do much about it. Attalus I allied with Rome against him. Ptolemy IV seemed to be sympathetic with Rome but was largely limited to facilitating diplomacy. The major absence here is the Seleucid dynasty: for the bulk of the war years in the West, Antiochus III was on the opposite side of the *oikoumene*, campaigning in Parthia, Bactria, and even India. If success can be defined by marching a large army through distant terrains, supplying them all the while and maintaining morale, then Antiochus earned his new epithet *Megas*, "the Great," obviously mimicking Alexander. He may not have won any epochal battles, as the previous Great One had done, but he was able to send back much treasure that had been paid as tribute by various eastern kings. In 205, he turned his attention to the old bone of contention with the Ptolemies,

Syria. As mentioned above, the Ptolemies had been weakened by a series of breakaway regions in their south, doubly so in the sense that they lost taxation revenues and yet had to fund campaigns to keep the rebellion from spreading. In 204, Ptolemy IV died; the throne went to the infant Ptolemy V but power as usual fell to an internecine council of regents and advisors. Antiochus III entered into an alliance with Philip V for the purpose of ousting the Ptolemaic regime from Egypt, but the treaty was mainly useful simply for keeping Philip from opening a second front against the Seleucids as Antiochus III marched south in 202. He thus embarked on the so-called Fifth Syrian War, and in its state of weakness, Egypt lost much territory. But the most significant result of the war was the spirit of cooperation between Philip V and Antiochus III, who would soon house the fugitive Hannibal.

7.13 Conclusions

The Second Punic War, more so than the First, became a defining moment in Roman identity for centuries, perhaps for the entire life of the culture. A signpost on a continuum, it looked backward to Rome's rise in the West, finally eclipsing its most organized rival in that sphere, but also to the future as Rome held its own in conflicts with Macedonians and in negotiations with Aetolia, Pergamon, and the Ptolemies. The Hellenistic East took time to realize Rome's growing importance and would function for another decade or two before an epiphany of the new significance of the Italian power would occur to them. With new Hellenic cultural forms – literature, sculpture, architecture – whetting their appetite, the Romans could dare to partake in the patrimony of Alexander the Great, but they did so on their own terms, pointedly eschewing the leadership of a *basileus*.

Further Reading

Fronda, Michael (2010). *Between Carthage and Rome: Southern Italy during the Second Punic War.* Cambridge: Cambridge University Press.
Green, Peter (1990). *Alexander to Actium: The Historical Evolution of the Hellenistic Age.* Berkeley: University of California Press.
Gruen, Erich (1984). *The Hellenistic World and the Coming of Rome* (2 vols.) Berkeley: University of California Press.
Harris, William (1985). *War and Imperialism in Republican Rome.* Oxford: Oxford University Press.
Hoyos, Dexter (ed.) (2015). *A Companion to the Punic Wars.* Oxford: Wiley-Blackwell.
Lazenby, John F (1998). *Hannibal's War: A Military History of the Second Punic War.* Norman, OK: University of Oklahoma Press.
Levene, David S (2010). *Livy on the Hannibalic War.* Oxford: Oxford University Press.
Miles, Richard (2010). *Carthage Must Be Destroyed: The Rise and Fall of an Ancient Civilization.* New York: Penguin Books.
Thalmann, William G (2011). *Apollonius of Rhodes and the Spaces of Hellenism.* Oxford: Oxford University Press.
Walbank, Frank W (1940). *Philip V of Macedon.* Oxford: Oxford University Press.

8

To 186: Hercules and the Muses

Timeline

202–195: The Fifth Syrian War
200–197: Second Macedonian War; Battle of Cynoscephalae (197): Flamininus defeats Philip V of Macedonia.
196–189: Hostageship in Rome of Demetrius of Macedonia, son of Philip V
196: Flamininus's declaration of the "Freedom of the Greeks"
196: The Rosetta Stone marking attempts to shore up the reign of Ptolemy V
190: Battle of Magnesia: the brothers Scipio defeat Antiochus III
190–180s: Comedies of Plautus in Rome
189: Roman siege and sack of Ambracia; Ennius's poem in praise of Marcus Fulvius Nobilior
188: Peace of Apamea
188–178: Hostageship in Rome of Antiochus IV, son of Antiochus III
c. 187: The Temple of Hercules and the Muses commissioned by Fulvius Nobilior
186: The Bacchanalian controversy

Principal Themes

- In the short Second Macedonian War, Rome joined with Athens, Aetolia, and Pergamon in permanently subduing Philip V, who retained his throne but in a much reduced capacity.
- Antiochus III of the Seleucids mistook for disinterest Rome's evacuation of Greece behind a mantra of "Freedom for the Greeks" and sought to fill the vacuum left by the defeat of Macedonia. The Romans and their allies drove him from the region and then pursued him beyond Asia Minor, reaching a settlement for war indemnities that dwarfed even those from the Second Punic War.
- Cato the Elder rose to prominence in Roman politics as consul serving in Spain; his brand of conservatism sought a greater role for Italian characteristics in the emergent cosmopolitanism in Rome.
- New art forms flourished in Rome, in step with greater levels of imperial revenue. The popularity of non-Roman forms of entertainment, such as were found at Fulvius Nobilior's Temple of Hercules and the Muses, at Plautus's comedies, and in the worship of Bacchus, rankled Romans of Cato's stripe.

The Roman Republic and the Hellenistic Mediterranean: From Alexander to Caesar, First Edition. Joel Allen.
© 2020 John Wiley & Sons, Inc. Published 2020 by John Wiley & Sons, Inc.

8.1 Introduction

The wealth that Rome won from its victory over Carthage would soon pale in comparison with the revenues achieved from its rapid defeat of the Antigonids, the Seleucids, and other Hellenistic powers. Rome's simultaneous campaigns in Spain are less understood today, but they too were successful in the main and yielded treasure and diplomatic hostages just as the wars in the East. With wealth and new ideas, Roman culture became more cosmopolitan, with an abruptness that would make the experiences of a younger generation dramatically and unsettlingly different from their forebears'. New works of literature and new public buildings, all of which engaged with Hellenic prototypes, attempted to accommodate Hellenic innovation with the Roman embrace of rusticity and strength. But a hybrid of Same-with-Other could be as revolutionary as the Other alone, and in at least one episode – panic concerning the popularity of the cult of Bacchus – violence ensued and reportedly engulfed the entire Italian peninsula and was based solely on cultural anxieties.

8.2 Philip V Faces East, Then West

In the five or so years following the Peace of Phoinike in 205, Philip V appears to have made some fatal assumptions about Rome. As Scipio was fighting a make-or-break engagement in Africa from 203 to 201, Philip figured either that the Romans would lose and thus no longer be a threat, or if they won, they would be war weary and not seek campaigns across the Adriatic. In either scenario, he would be left alone in an eastward expansion to the lands around the Aegean – Thrace, Asia Minor, and the many islands. We have seen already that he effectively neutralized the traditional superpower in the region, the Seleucids, by combining with them against Egypt (Chapter 7). Add to these calculations the fact that the arrangement at Phoinike dealt exclusively with the Balkan Peninsula, and Philip would be forgiven for concluding that activity in the East should not upset the Roman cosignatories with regard to the peace.

However sensible Philip's justifications for eastward expansion, his execution of it was rough and ill-advised. He achieved a microburst of activity from 205 to 201 by means of a technology not heretofore known as a Macedonian strong suit – a navy. A capable new admiral in Philip's employ, Heracleides, a Tarentine who had been exiled from Italy following the Second Punic War, quickly numbered successes, darting around victories at the Chersonese, Thasos, and the Hellespont, plus Samos, where he captured a Ptolemaic armada, and at Lade, near Miletus, where he defeated the famous navy of the Rhodians. On the mainland Philip benefited from the support of the king of Bithynia who continued to despise the principal regional power, Pergamon; a city in Bithynia was renamed Apamea for Philip's sister who had become the wife of Prusias I. The Macedonians marched right up to the gates of Pergamon and even cut down trees sacred to Athena. As primarily a land-based soldier-general to that point, Philip may have reveled in the unfamiliar swiftness and flexibility of military seafaring. What Philip understood less was that retaliation could also be swift by sea: Rhodes, Pergamon, Byzantium, and Chios – all prominent sea powers – banded together and crushed him at a naval battle in 201, and blockaded his remnants at Bargylia.

Philip also underestimated Roman resilience, but only just. He was correct that the Romans were not eager for a new overseas campaign. When they were asked for help against Macedonia in the early second century by Aetolia, Rhodes, Pergamon, and Athens, Rome at first only sent warnings. In the course of 200, Athens in particular was suffering at the hands of Philip, who had eluded the Bargylia blockade early in the year and returned to his raiding ways. Still in possession of Corinth, Chalcis, and Demetrias, the so-called "Fetters of Greece," Philip ravaged

Attica. Rhodes and Pergamon came to Athens's defense; Attalus I was especially interested in the region given his control of Aegina, the large island in the Saronic Gulf. In Rome, when the question of war in Macedonia was put to a vote in the *comitia centuriata*, the electorate decided on peace; Zama and all the trials of the Second Punic War were fresh in people's minds. It was only on a second vote that the *comitia* approved action, and only with the proviso that veterans of Africa could opt out if they so wished. A Roman army was accordingly in place in Epirus before the end of 200, led by Publius Sulpicius Galba, who had commanded the legions in Greece from 210 to 205 in the First Macedonian War after the departure of Marcus Valerius Laevinus for Agrigentum (Chapter 7). Galba soon sent ships to guard Piraeus, and with powerful allies now on their side, the Athenians watched as their precious Attica was liberated. For the rest of the so-called Second Macedonian War, the Athenians exercised their skills as diplomats: they were instrumental in winning Aetolian support in 199 and, in 198, they persuaded the Achaean League to forsake their current alliance with Macedonia. Present at the conference was a Roman envoy, Lucius Quinctius Flamininus, the brother of the new consul for that year, Titus.

Athens also effected symbolic gestures, such as a total assault on the very idea of Macedonia: public portraits of past Antigonid kings were destroyed; the two tribes called Antigonis and Demetrias, formed in honor of the One-Eyed and the Besieger (Chapter 4) were disbanded; and even references to Macedonians in public inscriptions were chiseled out, leaving glaring blank spaces amid otherwise intact sentences. To compensate for the loss of tribes, Athens cast their lot with the Attalids: a new tribe was called Attalis, which welcomed Attalus I and eventually all four of his remarkable sons as citizens. A deme – a hinterland village that was part of the democracy – was also renamed Apollonis after Attalus's wife. A decree of the Athenian assembly survives from this period honoring Hicesius, an Ephesian who was governing Aegina on Attalus's behalf.

Attalus returned the compliments by commissioning a new monument on the south side of the Acropolis, the so-called Lesser Attalid Monument (see Figure 8.1; for the Greater Attalid Monument, see Chapter 7). It featured dozens of sculpted depictions of dead or dying enemies of Hellenism, mythic and historic: included in the composition were Amazons, Giants, Persians, and, new to the catalog on the Acropolis, Celts. How the sculptures were grouped and presented is debated among scholars. Some have suggested that the arrangement evoked a battlefield, such that the memorial became a kind of diorama where the visitor could personally witness the barbarian casualties in a cosmic, superhuman war for culture, right at the foot of the Parthenon. The presence of the Celts was particularly relevant to Attalus I given his projects against the Galatians in Asia Minor. The overall message of the piece was to align Pergamon even more with the defining spirit of Athens in the Classical Age.

By 197, Philip was without serious allies, and diplomatic momentum was favoring Rome. At Cynoscephalae, Titus Quinctius Flamininus, now as proconsul, was joined by an Aetolian force against Philip's phalanx for a pitched battle. At the start, one half of Flamininus's line fell back while the other half advanced. The soldiers who had advanced soon found themselves on the far side of the Macedonians who had pressed the retreating half of the line; thus a large part of the Macedonian army was surrounded and cut down. Flamininus's victory was decisive and he dictated terms similar to those presented by Scipio to Carthage just five years before: Macedonia could go on existing, but as an inert entity with only a small swath of territory in its traditional homeland. This meant that the Macedonians would finally be forced to evacuate the "Fetters of Greece," forsaking all opportunities to grow again and torching their fleet for good measure. Philip was to pay 1000 talents over six years and submit hostages, including a son, another of the many Hellenistic princes named Demetrius.

(a)

(b)

Figure 8.1 Roman marble copies of original bronze sculptures (a and b) (c. 200 BCE) depicting dead and dying enemies, both legendary and historical, of Hellenistic culture, including Amazons, Giants, Persians, and Celts. Originally displayed south of the Parthenon in Athens as part of the Lesser Attalid Monument (compare Figure 1.4).

8.3 "Freedom of the Greeks"

Philip had been defeated, but the Romans did not intend to linger in Greece: in 196 Flamininus famously declared the Greeks to be free and autonomous, in keeping with the glorious past now newly reified in the contemporaneous Lesser Attalid Monument. The announcement was made at a prime Hellenic venue, the Isthmian Games near Corinth, which would have been attended not only by the southern and central Greeks in question, but by all others, including representatives of the Seleucids, Ptolemies, and Attalids. A committee of ten Roman senators, bearing commissions as *legati*, was tasked with implementing the policy of emancipation. Surviving inscriptions provide a glimpse of some of the tricky legal disputes that they faced as adjudicators. Given the long tenure of Macedonian rule, claims to ownership of property were beyond human memory and had to be investigated from many angles. We know that some Greeks freed Roman slaves who had been purchased as prisoners-of-war, probably from Hannibal's various successes; the fact that they were praised for doing so voluntarily implies that there were other cases of enslavement in which the "owners" were not so forthcoming, thus requiring Roman involvement. It would take two years, but the Romans in Greece were largely demobilized and extracted by 194, which is the year Flamininus finally celebrated his triumph.

Scholars have long proposed that the exit from Greece was a case of opportunistic generosity whereby the Romans still expected allegiance, or a kind of clientage, from the various *poleis* and leagues in future conflicts. Some cities simply traded masters: Eretria, in Euboea, was placed under the control of Eumenes II, the new king of Pergamon who had ascended the throne when his father Attalus I died in late 197. Meanwhile, the remaining Roman soldiers that were necessary, if only as guards for the committee of ten, took on the task of freeing Argos from the control of Sparta. Philip V himself, now an ally, contributed troops to the effort, which was ironic given that he was the one who turned Argos over to Sparta in the first place. Sparta was ruled by a tyrant-like figure, Nabis, who had violently supplanted the dual kingship in the course of the Second Punic and First Macedonian Wars. He had taken up the populist reforms first attempted by Agis IV (Chapter 6) and Cleomenes III (Chapter 7) and endeavored to restore vigor to the Spartan phalanx. He resisted Rome but was defeated in 195; like Philip, he had to give up his navy in the form of ceding Sparta's only harbor to the Achaean League, and had to tokenize the deal by giving his son and other aristocratic youths to Rome as diplomatic hostages. In spite of their claims to have left Greece, the Romans could have faced justifiable suspicions from certain parties: whereas Athens reportedly defended the Roman settlement, the Aetolians accused them of a kind of crypto-tyranny.

With their activity in the Greek world stepped up in these decades, the Romans were on the receiving end of a species of honors in the Hellenistic vein that was new to them – religious veneration. Flamininus was treated to some of the same quasi-divine honors that had been bestowed on *basileis* (compare Demetrius Poliorketes, Chapter 5). His own portrait appeared on gold coins in Greece – a phenomenon that Rome would not permit for a living person until Julius Caesar, and even then to much grumbling (Chapter 15). The city of Argos created a new religious festival in his honor, the Titeia: while not a case of outright worship, it came close. The city of Chalcis did take the ultimate step, creating a priesthood for the worship of Flamininus and joining his name with that of Heracles in the dedication of a gymnasium. On the other side of the Aegean, in 195 the mixture of religion and politics became more disembodied at Smyrna: rather than worshipping Flamininus specifically, that city inaugurated a new cult to the goddess Roma complete with a temple. It is unlikely that the Romans expected such honors, but it is also unlikely, at least in terms of their eastern geopolitics (if not necessarily in their domestic policy), that they objected strenuously.

Even if the evacuation had an opportunistic dimension, it may still have been motivated by wholly different exigencies on Rome's own turf in Italy. The Celtic tribes of the Boii and Insubres, whose ancestors had long beleaguered both Macedonians and Romans, were on the move once again and required military attention. As Flamininus had been prorogued for Greece in 197, both of the new consuls for that year were assigned to the north. A renegade Carthaginian, yet another Hasdrubal, no relation to Hannibal, had roused the local tribes to a sack of Placentia and an assault on Cremona, both Roman colonies from 220 (Chapter 7). The two consuls divided their quarry and fought the tribes separately. One even managed to capture Hasdrubal, but even so, the tribes did not surrender, and consuls continued to be sent to the region through 191.

8.4   Romans in Spain

It should be remembered that at the start of the Second Punic War, before Hannibal's surprise, the Romans fully expected that they were entering a contest for Spain: that is where their first corps of troops had been assigned in 218. Now that Carthage was out of Iberia, the Romans took full measure of their task. In 197, they decided that the effort had to become systematized, and the *comitia centuriata* elected two new praetorships with the pacification of Spain as their brief. The duality of the task has a consular ring to it. Their mission was soon divided geographically with one praetor assigned to Spain's east coast as Hispania Citerior ("Nearer" Spain) and one to the south coast around Gibraltar, Hispania Ulterior ("Further" Spain). The fighting turned out to be difficult, perhaps more so than expected, as one of the praetors succumbed to battle wounds in the next year.

In 195, one of the consuls Marcus Porcius Cato was assigned to the region. He would eventually be remembered as Cato the Elder, to distinguish him from an active descendant over a century later and to acknowledge his long career, past even the Third Punic War (Chapters 9 and 10). By then Cato had developed a reputation as a fearless soldier and a tough senator. He was present at the battle against Hannibal for possession of Capua and had served under Scipio, not yet Africanus, in Sicily before the launch of the invasion of North Africa at the end of the Second Punic War. As praetor governing Sardinia, he won a reputation for stern and economical administration. Luxury seemed to him not only frivolous but also dangerous, as it drew resources from military defense: one of his first acts as consul, before setting out for Spain, was to try to retain the Lex Oppia that limited women's jewelry and cosmetics purchases (Chapter 7) when others sought to repeal it (he lost). In Spain, he prosecuted a campaign that was as brutal as Scipio's in the Second Punic War was diplomatic. He is also credited with developing new mining operations, which enabled him to display an unusual quantity of precious metals at his triumph in 194, the same year that Flaminius celebrated his victory at Cynoscephalae after a three-year delay.

8.5   The Roman Wars with Antiochus III and Aetolia

As mentioned before, Philip V at first must have been glad when his ally, Antiochus III, went off to fight the Ptolemies in pursuit of their pact to share Egypt. But then Rome surprised everyone in ways fatal to Macedonia, and it was Antiochus III who thrived in the late 190s. Egypt was still in disarray following the rise of the toddler king, Ptolemy V. The revolving door of advisors continued to spin, with contenders from powerful aristocratic clans that hailed from all over the Mediterranean. First were Sosibius of Alexandria and Agathocles of Samos (Chapter 7); after they died in episodes of political violence, Tlepolemus of Lycia replaced them only to be toppled by Aristomenes of Acarnania and Polycrates of Argos, a past governor of Cyprus. It was in this context of pandemonium that the decree of the famous Rosetta Stone was promulgated (see Primary Source 8.1 and Figure 8.2). It venerated Ptolemy V, who was still an

> **Primary Source 8.1**
>
> **The Rosetta Stone**
>
> The so-called Rosetta Stone is famous for its simultaneous rendering of the same decree in three languages – Greek, hieroglyphics, and Demotic – which made it possible to decipher hieroglyphics elsewhere. In terms of its historical context, the decree came at a time, 196, when Ptolemy V's court was riven by internecine conflict. In spite of this, or more likely because of it, the decree takes steps to legitimize the king's status, citing his benefactions to the people, campaigns against the enemy, and suppression of a rebellion. Instructions for new ways of worshipping the king are also decreed. The parallelism of the three texts is itself historically relevant, demonstrating the means of communication to a population of multiple native languages. The following is a translation of parts of the Greek version of the decree.
>
>> "In the reign of the young one, who received the throne from his father, lord of crowns, glorious, the one who established Egypt, and pious toward the gods, superior to his opponents, the one who restored the life of men, lord of the thirty-years' feasts just as Hephaestus the great, king just as Helios the great…
>>
>> Decree: Whereas king Ptolemy … being beneficially disposed toward the gods, has dedicated to the temples revenues in both silver and grain, and has undertaken many expenses for the sake of bringing Egypt into a state of prosperity and establishing the temples, and has been generous with all his own means, and of the revenues and tax collections existing in Egypt he entirely remitted some and others he has lightened, in order that the native people and all the others might be in a state of security during his reign, and the royal debts, which both those in Egypt and those in the rest of his kingdom owed, and which were many in number, he remitted, and those who had been led off to prisons and those who were since long ago under accusation he freed from their charges…
>>
>> …And he provided that cavalry and infantry forces and ships should be sent out against those who attacked Egypt by sea and land (The Fifth Syrian War), submitting great expenses in silver and grain in order that the temples and all those in them might be in safety; and going to Lykonpolis in the Busirite (nome), which had been occupied and fortified against a siege with an abundant collection of arms and with all other provisions – for long standing was the disloyalty of the impious men gathered there, who had wrought much evil against temples and those dwelling in Egypt – and encamping over against it, he surrounded it with mounds and trenches and remarkable fortifications…
>>
>> …With good fortune, resolved by the priests of all the temples in the country … to set up in each temple in the most conspicuous [place] an image of the Ever-Living king Ptolemy, god manifest (and) gracious, which shall be called (that) of "Ptolemy the Avenger of Egypt," beside which shall stand the principal god of the temple…"
>
> (trans. Roger S. Bagnall and P. Derow, *The Hellenistic Period: Historical Sources in Translation*, Blackwell, 2004, no. 137.)

adolescent at the time, for his benefactions to the people, attributing to him military actions that could not have been possible for someone his age. The inscription is important in Egyptology and to the history of epigraphy for providing parallel texts in multiple languages, which assisted in translating hieroglyphics. In terms of politics, it bespeaks of a weakness on the part of Ptolemaic authorities, which were trying to reestablish a measure of respect.

Figure 8.2 The Rosetta Stone, 196 BCE.

Flamininus dispatched a warning to Antiochus III to change course. With attractive targets tracing the corner of the Mediterranean from the Levant to southern Asia Minor in Cilicia, Lycia, and Caria, Antiochus was reasonably willing to leave Egypt behind. The so-called Fifth Syrian War, which had begun in 202 (Chapter 7), drew to a close with Antiochus III in a strong position, in possession of Coele-Syria and key coastal cities like Sidon (although the decree of the Rosetta Stone implies, propagandistically, that young Ptolemy V had performed well against them). Josephus reports that Antiochus III forged a cordial relationship with the Jews of Jerusalem at this time. His permissive outlook on their customs reads as a case of catching flies with honey (compare Primary Source 8.2).

In 196, with Philip V reduced and no longer an equal partner, Antiochus III sent troops into Macedonia, endeavoring to reestablish Lysimacheia as a Seleucid base of operations. The Romans, under their slogan of "Freedom of the Greeks," again tried to move him around like a chess piece, back across the Hellespont and out of the Greek cities of Asia, which the Romans meant to be as free as the Balkan cities. Antiochus is said by a later source to have been defiant, delivering to Roman ambassadors a lesson in Hellenistic history and dynastic management with three principal arguments: his ancestor, Seleucus I, had conquered this region in 281, and

> **Primary Source 8.2**
>
> **Letter of Laodike III to the City of Iasos**
>
> This decree, dated to 197, the year before the Rosetta Stone, demonstrates the kind of benefactions that the Seleucids could bestow upon a local community. Laodike III and her husband, Antiochus III, were not siblings; scholars have suggested that the reference to Antiochus as a "brother" in the text either reflects metaphorical closeness and equality, or deploys the vocabulary of power current among the Ptolemies in Egypt. The prominence of the queen also resembles the nature of the Ptolemaic dynasty.
>
> > "The queen Laodike sends greetings to the council and the people of Iasus. I have often heard from my brother about the support that he gives to his friends and allies and that he has restored your city that was damaged by unforeseen calamities. He has given liberty to you, and has established laws and taken other measures to enlarge the commonwealth and bring it into a better condition. I have also made it a priority, following his example, to act with his zeal and earnestness, and therefore to establish something to benefit both the poor citizens and to be advantageous to the entire population. I have written to Strouthion, the director of finances, that for ten years annually he should convey to the city 1,000 Attic *medimnoi* of wheat and turn it over to men chosen by the city … [T]he profits (should) be used to constitute dowries for the daughters of needy citizens. They are to give not more than 300 drachmas of Antiochus to each of those who are married. If the Iasians continue to be well disposed toward my brother and our entire household and are mindful of our benefactions, I will try to accomplish other benefactions which I devise, proceeding in every way in harmony with the will of my brother, for I understand that he is very eager for the restoration of the city. Farewell."
>
> (trans. Sarah Pomeroy, "Charities for Greek Women," *Mnemosyne* 35 (1982), 121–122).

so Antiochus had a legitimate claim; his daughter, Cleopatra (aged 10), was about to marry Ptolemy V, and that is how the kings shared territory in this part of the world; and the Romans should observe that there were Greek cities in their own realm, in Italy, and Antiochus would agree not to bother them (suggesting that Rome, lest it appear hypocritical, should leave Asia to him). History, unity, ubiquity: Antiochus III was contrasting the characteristics of the Seleucids from those of Romans – young, parochial, and outside Hellenism.

And then Hannibal arrived. Ever since the defeat at Zama and subsequent treaty Hannibal had endeavored to rebuild Carthage from within. Nervous about his fate as Rome's grip remained tight, he fled for Antiochus III. Much of Antiochus's aggression toward Rome in the years 194–193 was attributed by historians in antiquity to Hannibal, but they wrote from hindsight and savored the romance of Hannibal as Rome's white whale. In truth, Antiochus had already demonstrated an independent and ambitious spirit, as we have seen. It was, rather, the Aetolians in 193 who triggered a chain reaction that culminated in war between Rome and Antiochus. The Aetolians felt that they had not been adequately compensated for their contributions at Cynoscephalae, and so they invited Antiochus to help them reassert themselves in the region. In 192, in a burst of success the Aetolians took both Demetrias, one of the "Fetters" whose possession would allow Antiochus to land unchallenged, and fabled Sparta, killing Nabis in the process. But the success ended there: the Spartan army rebelled against the Aetolian usurpers and drove them out. Moreover, the Aetolian abnegation of the Roman grant of freedom alienated those who were benefitting from it, such as the Achaean League, the large independent cities, and Philip himself.

Antiochus, in spite of travelling many miles through the eastern reaches of his empire and two wars with the weakened Ptolemies, had seen no serious military threat since the Battle of Raphia in 217 (which he lost; Chapter 7). He was defeated at Thermopylae by the Romans and Philip in 191, for which Philip was rewarded with lands in Thessaly – yet more cities that slipped quietly from the "freedom" Rome purported to enforce. Antiochus retreated to Asia Minor, and the Romans followed, now led by a pair of brothers, Lucius Cornelius Scipio and the more famous Scipio Africanus. Joining Rome were what was becoming a productive pair of partners, Rhodes and Pergamon. Rhodes provided valuable naval leadership and expertise, while Eumenes II was proving to be an effective general. Pergamon itself fell under siege for a time by Seleucus IV, the son of Antiochus III, but with a small detachment of fresh soldiers from the Achaean League, Eumenes II was able to relieve his city. A major naval battle was fought off Myonnesus. Rhodian and Roman navies, commanded by Eudamus and Lucius Aemilius Regillus, respectively, defeated Antiochus the Great's largest fleet, ironically commanded by another Rhodian, Polyxenidas, sailing for wages as a mercenary. Once Antiochus's remnants were trapped at Ephesus, he felt it necessary to withdraw from lands accessible by sea, such as Thrace and the Hellespont, and to focus his strength elsewhere, such as on north-western Asia Minor.

Even with winter approaching, the Scipios preferred a pitched battle to resting on their laurels, and the armies met at Magnesia in Asia Minor in 190. Appian presents many details of the Seleucid menagerie of elephants carrying towers, camels bearing Arabian archers, and the usual horses of any cavalry, a testament in zoology of Antiochus's lifetime journey through the world and his "global" support. In spite of superior numbers, Antiochus was put to flight, first to Sardis, then to Apamea, and then over the Taurus Mountains to the safety of Antioch. Lucius Scipio took on the epithet Asiaticus, a nice pendant to his brother Publius Africanus.

In 189, both consuls, Gnaeus Manlius Vulso and Marcus Fulvius Nobilior, were stationed in the East. Vulso took over for Scipio in Asia Minor and followed Eumenes II on a campaign against Celtic tribes, which the Pergamenes liked to project as their own special adversary. Along the way, Vulso fined Ariarathes IV of Cappadocia 600 talents for lending help to Antiochus. The sum was ultimately reduced by half when Eumenes II married Ariarathes's daughter, Stratonike, to build up his friendships in the Asian sphere. The other consul, Fulvius Nobilior, policed the Peloponnese, watching as the Achaean League destroyed Sparta, a wild card in the region as far as Rome was concerned. Nobilior's main focus was on the Aetolian League. He laid siege to their showpiece city, Ambracia. Athens sought to avoid more bloodshed in its proximity and joined Rhodes in negotiating a peace between the two. Leon of Athens sailed for Rome to present Nobilior's proposed terms to the Roman Senate, which voted in his favor. The Aetolians thus surrendered and were punished with a disadvantageous treaty whereby they would pay a total of 500 talents over six years. They also submitted a crowd of 40 hostages between the ages of 12 and 40 from among their aristocracies, to be housed in Rome for six years. The siege of Ambracia accordingly became the subject of an epic poem by Quintus Ennius (see below).

In 188, Antiochus III was forced into a treaty with the Romans that formalized his expulsion from Asia Minor: in a stark reversal of fortune given his ease of passage just a few years earlier, under the so-called Peace of Apamea Antiochus would lose all of Asia Minor, which was divided by Pergamon and Rhodes roughly in respect to their sides of the Maeander River. Per the terms of the treaty, Antiochus would also have to pay 15 000 talents, a staggering sum that was 50% more than mighty Carthage (and 25 times the Aetolian penalty), a prize that would make Rome rich beyond belief. He would also have to surrender 20 hostages to be held for 20 years, with the population rotated every three years, except for Antiochus's own son, Antiochus IV, who would have to stay for the duration. All Seleucid ships were to be burned, and Antiochus would be made to retreat, essentially, to Mesopotamia, the Levant, and Cilicia. Hannibal escaped to Bithynia and the court of king Prusias I. To compensate for the loss of wealthy Ionia, Antiochus had to find more revenues in his Mesopotamian heartland: it was on a campaign to Susa in 187 that he was killed by resistors.

8.6 Rome and the Other: Embrace and Rejection

The Aetolian and Seleucid hostages that were sent to Rome joined a growing crowd of similar diplomatic tokens in the city. We have seen similar hostage stipulations for Carthage and Sparta. To these one could add simultaneous groups attested in the literary sources from Spain and the Celts. Within the next decade, 188–178, more hostages would be added from Corsica, Sardinia, and Ligurian tribes. The evidence for hostages' experiences in Rome is limited, but what glimpses exist imply a comfortable, even dignified existence. Antiochus IV, the son of Antiochus III, was provided with his own house on the Palatine Hill, the most expensive district in the city. As we shall see in the next chapter, Demetrius of Macedonia, the son of Philip V, made many friends among the senatorial elite, which would become both a blessing and a curse in his later life after returning home. Many sources speak of the acculturation of the detained to Rome's way of life – language, religion, even diet – although the nationalistic qualities of such accounts should inspire caution.

While the hostages and other international travelers likely contributed to the cosmopolitan evolution of Rome, a backlash to the Other flared up from time to time. Within a decade of the detention of the hundreds of Punic hostages following Zama, the comic playwright Titus Maccius Plautus staged "The Little Carthaginian" (*Poenulus*), about a Punic boy who had been kidnapped from his home and raised in Greece (see Primary Source 8.3). When his uncle coincidentally passed through town on business, the youth was unable to understand his Punic speech, so complete had been his transformation. The humor must have been predicated on Romans' own experiences of the Punic boys in their presence, whose ethnicity may have been seen as problematic and worthy of alteration. Twenty other plays by Plautus survive and attest to the growing popularity of Greek New Comedy, already in evidence with Livius Andronicus. Haunted houses, twins separated at birth, braggadocio soldiers – Plautus's settings, plotlines, and characters are familiar from Greek predecessors, most notably Menander (Chapter 4), but his plays also feature innovative metrical interludes amidst the dialog, suggesting spectacular musical effects.

Primary Source 8.3

Plautus, *Poenulus* (or, "the Little Carthaginian")

This comedy by Plautus tells the story of Carthaginian youths kidnapped from their homes as children and raised in "Aetolia" (though the script is in Latin, not Greek) in a new culture. In this scene, an old man, Hanno, the uncle of one of the youths, named Agorastocles, has arrived to find and retrieve him. They do not recognize each other. Agorastocles and his slave Milphio discuss how to approach the elderly Punic. Readers should note the ethnic humor of the play, based on the appearance and language of the Carthaginian man; the play was performed around 188, in the aftermath of the Second Punic War when over 100 youths aged 14–30 were serving as hostages from the Zama treaty, presumably themselves forgetting the Punic language.

Lines 975–988: MILPHIO:	What is that bird, the one coming here in nothing but a tunic? Did they con him out of his cloak at the baths?
AGORASTOCLES:	By his face he certainly looks Punic. Some kind of scavenger.
MILPHIO:	He's got some pretty old and broken-down slaves, by god.
AGORASTOCLES:	How so?
MILPHIO:	See those men following on, burdened down by their packs? And I don't think they have any fingers on their hands.
AGORASTOCLES:	How so?
MILPHIO:	Because their rings are in their ears, as they trundle along.
HANNO (aside to audience):	I'll go up and talk to them in Punic. If they reply, I'll keep talking Punic. If not, then I'll change my tongue to fit theirs.
MILPHIO (to Agorastocles):	What do you say, do you remember any Punic?
AGORASTOCLES:	None, by god. Tell me, how could I, I who was snatched from Carthage as a six year old.
HANNO (aside to audience):	Oh god, a good many free born lads have been snatched from Carthage like that recently."

Some of Plautus's contemporaries dwelt on more patriotic themes, largely in service to the Roman aristocracy. Quintus Fabius Pictor, who led an embassy to Delphi after the disaster at Cannae (Chapter 7), wrote a history of Rome, which was in prose and in Greek. He gravitated toward the accomplishments of members of leading families, a category to which he himself belonged. Quintus Ennius also praised contemporary Romans, but in meter and in Latin. A poem of 200, called the *Scipio*, likely celebrated the hero of the Punic War, and another, the *Ambracia*, recounted the feats of Fulvius Nobilior's siege (see above). Ennius and Fulvius Nobilior reportedly took heat from Cato the Elder, who objected to the use of literature for purposes, as he saw it, of political propaganda. There may have been more than a tinge of hypocrisy to Cato's remark, if true, given that it was he who singled Ennius out when Ennius was serving under him in Sardinia in 204, during the Second Punic War.

The rivalry between Cato and Fulvius Nobilior spilled over into the urban fabric of the city as each sponsored large, beautiful buildings in competition with one another. Cato, in spite of his occasional bromides against fancy Greek culture, built the Basilica Porcia in 184 at the northwestern corner of the Forum. The name itself – *basilica*, derived from *basileus* and meaning something like, "a king's hall" – implied an affinity for styles from the Hellenistic East. Airy and light, the large interior space was ideally suited for public business or court proceedings of different kinds and became the architectural form of choice for major buildings around the Forum for centuries. Within a decade, two other, more elaborate *basilicae* went up on the north and south edges of the Forum. One was commissioned by Fulvius Nobilior when he was censor in 179; originally the Basilica Fulvia, it would be renamed the Basilica Aemilia by the senator who completed the construction. Across the square, Tiberius Sempronius Gracchus, who like Cato would earn his name from military service in Spain (Chapter 9), built the Basilica Sempronia, also in the 170s.

Fulvius Nobilior's greatest donation to the city was the Temple of Hercules Musarum, or, Hercules in his role as the leader of the Muses. Again, we see the mixture of a Greek idea with Roman self-regard: works within the complex included a statue group of the nine muses retrieved from Ambracia, wealthy and Hellenic, alongside a small, rough shrine to Numa Pompilius, the second king of Rome. The temple also somehow displayed an annotated list of Roman leaders and their accomplishments called the *Fasti*. By cataloging episodes from deep in Rome's past, the *Fasti* would have catered to antiquarian tastes. Hercules brought two strands of culture together, as the pan-Mediterranean hero was thought to have spent time at the Tiber crossing during one of his many journeys and thus had a Roman affiliation. His leadership of the quintessential women of the arts suggested the proper way for Greek culture to be deployed – in service to Roman muscle. The orator Cicero (Chapter 13) would later cite the temple as the culmination of Roman and Greek identities when he was defending a Greek poet accused of faking Roman citizenship.

An *improper* way to engage in Greek culture was identified in Italy around the same time and was violently suppressed. In 186, Rome and Italy became gripped with panic over rumors that occultists were performing heinous acts in their worship of Bacchus. Two strands of evidence survive for the so-called Bacchanalian Affair. An inscription purports to be the transcript of a senatorial decree against the religion, and Livy records a version of the decree in his histories, with slight but interesting variations (Plautus also refers to the controversy in his play, *Casina*). Bacchus himself was a welcome part of the Roman pantheon, but a few extremists, reportedly, had been holding their rituals at night, rather than the day, and had introduced sexual elements and violence. Livy identified the nonelite – slaves, women, simpletons, the poor – as the most egregious offenders, suggesting further that interest in Greek culture could only be acceptable along lines established by the powerful. The senate clamped down on the practices and rounded up perpetrators; some 7000 were said to have been executed. Hellenism had thus become a characteristic that could be praised or vilified depending on the context.

8.7 Conclusions

While the Punic Wars had been a terrible slog lasting multiple generations, in just a decade-and-a-half from 200 to 185, the Romans brought down the dynasties of two of the most famous Diadochoi, the Antigonids of Macedonia and the Seleucids of the East. Kings from those realms still occupied their thrones but at the cost of literally tons and tons of treasure, which shifted to Italy. The Aetolians and the Spartans were also done for, in spite of Rome's earlier declaration of their freedom.

It is difficult to grasp the propulsive power of such immediate and massive wealth in Rome. New buildings were everywhere, as well as new cultural forms. For some, the change threatened to be fatally destabilizing, while others only drew inspiration for yet more experiments in overseas interference. In the next generations, Romans began to take their role in the East seriously, flexing their muscles at times but also adopting responsibilities in geopolitical diplomacy.

Further Reading

Allen, Joel (2006). *Hostages and Hostage-Taking in the Roman Empire*. Cambridge: Cambridge University Press.
Grainger, John D (2002). *The Roman War of Antiochus the Great*. Leiden: Brill.
Gruen, Erich (1990). *Studies in Greek Culture and Roman Policy*. Berkeley: University of California Press.
Gruen, Erich (1992). *Culture and National Identity in Republican Rome*. Ithaca: Cornell University Press.
Kay, Philip (2016). *Rome's Economic Revolution*. Oxford: Oxford University Press.
Richlin, Amy (2005). *Rome and the Mysterious Orient: Three Plays by Plautus*. Berkeley: University of California Press.
Stewart, Andrew (2004). *Attalos, Athens, and the Akropolis: The Pergamene "Little Barbarians" and their Roman and Renaissance Legacy*. Cambridge: Cambridge University Press.

9

To 164: Hostages of Diplomacy

Timeline

180: Death of Ptolemy V and regency of Cleopatra I over Ptolemy VI
180s: Altar of Zeus in Pergamon
179: Death of Philip V, accession of Perseus
179–177: Tiberius Sempronius Gracchus governor in Spain
178: Exchange of Antiochus IV for Demetrius Soter, son of Seleucus IV, as hostage in Rome for the Seleucids
176: Death of Cleopatra I; shared rule in Egypt of the sibling children Ptolemy VI, Cleopatra II, and Ptolemy VIII
172: Accession of Jason as High Priest in Jerusalem
171–168: Third Macedonian War; Battle of Pydna (168): Aemilius Paullus defeats Perseus
170–168: Sixth Syrian War: Antiochus IV invades Egypt
167: The "Day of Eleusis": Rome orders Antiochus IV out of Egypt
167: The four republics of Macedonia established under Roman authority
166: Triumph of Paullus in Rome; Procession of Antiochus IV outside Antioch; Romaia festival on Delos
165: Maccabaean Revolt in Judaea

Principal Themes

- Having "freed the Greeks," Rome maintained a largely supervisory role in the East through the mid-170s, keeping especially close tabs on the competition for power in Asia Minor.
- The Seleucid kingdom, having suffered for generations under assaults by the Ptolemies, Attalids, and Rome, was reinvigorated for a time under Antiochus IV, a former hostage in Rome who moved against Egypt and Jerusalem in the Sixth (and final) Syrian War.
- Another former hostage, Demetrius of Macedonia, nearly became *basileus* among the Antigonids, but was removed in a conspiracy led by his brother Perseus, against whom the Roman prosecuted the Third Macedonian War.
- Conflicts between Judaism and Hellenism bedeviled Jerusalem as the Maccabaean revolution sought to undo reforms wrought by neighboring Hellenic dynasts.
- In Rome, foreign poets such as Caecilius, Terence, and Pacuvius joined Ennius (continued from Chapter 8) in exploring Roman identity through their adaptations of Greek genres and works.

The Roman Republic and the Hellenistic Mediterranean: From Alexander to Caesar, First Edition. Joel Allen.
© 2020 John Wiley & Sons, Inc. Published 2020 by John Wiley & Sons, Inc.

9.1 Introduction

The community of powerful non-Roman leaders, or rather sons of leaders, who had been assembled in Italy by Roman policy in the course of the previous chapter – Demetrius of Macedonia, Antiochus IV Epiphanes, Armenes of Sparta, and others – began to repay investment. Former hostages brought their intimate knowledge of Rome to their home dynasties and steered affairs in ways that, while not always successful for themselves, gave Rome more latitude for movement. At least that is what is alleged in later sources that glorified Roman achievements in its empire in this period. After a short war with Rome, Macedonia ceased to be a kingdom at all and instead was organized into four administrative zones that were self-governing but essentially manipulated from Italy. The squabbling between the Seleucids and the Ptolemies over their borderlands would come to an end: this chapter sees the sixth and final of the "Syrian Wars" for control of the fertile Levant. The Romans were now firmly a part of Mediterranean politics, best and most famously emblematized by the episode of the "Day of Eleusis," when a Roman legate threw off any pretense of sidelined objectivity to compel Antiochus IV to abandon an attempted conquest of Egypt, which he was on the verge of completing. Questions of whether the Romans should follow the prevailing eastern model of monarchies that were nearly divine – Prusias II of Bithynia is said to have hailed the senate with deific epithets heretofore reserved for *basileis* – were nipped in the bud by conservative figures like Cato the Elder, who hewed to a sense of Roman exceptionalism.

9.2 Rome as Referee

With Philip V cowed, Antiochus III gone, and Eumenes II of Pergamon reliably allied (Chapter 8), Rome settled into the role of referee for various geopolitical contests in the remainder of the 180s. Ambassadors from much of the Greek-speaking world descended upon the upstart city in Italy and its senate to sing their congratulations and, soon, to voice their grievances. The most thoroughgoing example of Rome's status as an arbiter of borders came with the Peace of Apamea, which bestowed at a single stroke vast swathes of territory to Pergamon and Rhodes (Chapter 8). The logistical details, however, by which those states would gain access to, and derive benefit from, their new possessions is another story. What Rome offered when it assigned the territories to those states was not guaranteed land but free rein for them to make an attempt for it, followed by a geojudicial role for Rome in any secondary phases of conflict. Eumenes II for example had to fight a war with both Bithynia and Galatia as early as 187, largely under his own steam, in order to close in on the parts of Phrygia that Rome had "awarded" him. He did not achieve his objective until 179, and it is interesting to find that Rome sent a representative only at the settlement phase, when the fighting had been concluded. Flamininus himself was in attendance, perhaps not to favor his ally from the Aetolian War and the war with Antiochus III so much as to demand the extradition of Hannibal who was being sheltered by Prusias I of Bithynia. With nowhere to run for a change, Hannibal committed suicide rather than face detention, which would have been followed most likely by torture, humiliation, and execution in public.

Rhodes, too, found that the Peace of Apamea was a less dramatic document in practice than in theory. The regions of Caria and Lycia were its twin prizes, but both were stubbornly independent. Documents from Lycia show towns, at best, acting of their own accord or, at worst, openly taunting Rhodes with *their* favorable treatment by Rome. The town of Xanthus, for example, bristled so much at Rhodian oversight that it appealed to Rome as a higher power to get their way, and indeed Rome preferred their arguments. Another Lycian inscription reveals a town making its own foreign policy decisions, this time a treaty with the Ptolemies, with evidently no input from Rhodes. Moreover, a dispute between Miletus and Magnesia-on-Maeander was settled not by Rhodes alone, but also by delegates from Athens and the Achaean League.

The Achaean League also struggled to capitalize on its victory, or at least its presence on the victorious side, following the war with Aetolia (Chapter 8). Its pride in its independence in the region was made apparent when it refused a gift of philanthropy from Eumenes II in 185, lest it would become beholden to the state that still needled them with its retention of the island of Aegina in the Saronic Gulf. Nominally, the League had almost complete control of the Peloponnese, but in 183, the rich polis of Messene sought to secede. The Romans offered to arbitrate, but the League's general, Philopoemen, refused their participation, doubtlessly keeping an eye on Rome's self-serving decisions elsewhere in the East with regard to Pergamon and Rhodes. He marched on Messene but fell into enemy hands where he soon died. His political colleague, Lycortas, sought revenge by attacking Messene, capturing its leadership, and forcing them to suicide, again contrary to Rome's wishes. None of these flashes of defiance prevented Rome from muscling into mediating roles: in 180, Rome heard arguments from both Sparta and the Achaean League when the former was pushing for greater freedom. Rome's compromise was that Sparta had to remain in the League, but that it could rebuild its walls. There could be no doubt as to who held power, and Callicrates, an Achaean statesman, rose to prominence by sponsoring Rome-friendly policies. At times, it seemed that Fortune was against the independence-minded Achaeans: in 180, when Lycortas's son, Polybius, not yet a historian of Rome, was to set sail to Alexandria to receive 10 teams of rowers for their navy – important not just for manpower but as a token of diplomatic support – his trip was canceled due to the untimely death of Ptolemy V.

Rome also involved itself in eastern affairs when in 183, an allied son-in-law of Antiochus III, king Pharnaces I of Pontus, seized Sinope, the dominant city on the Black Sea coast of northern Asia Minor. Pergamon, Cappadocia, and Rhodes all joined forces to free it. Envoys from all sides, including Pharnaces, appeared in Rome to state their case. We do not know specifically how the senate ruled, but later events show that Sinope itself remained with Pharnaces, but he was not active against the coalition in any other way for the rest of his reign.

Philip V, too, was subject to close Roman oversight. In 186, when Pergamon protested the Macedonian occupation of two Thracian towns that had been "given" to Eumenes II, Rome heard embassies from both sides. Philip V sent his son Demetrius, a former hostage who had been either in Rome or with the Romans from 196 to 189 (Chapter 8), to represent him, thinking rightly that Demetrius had made fruitful contacts among key senators in his youth. Demetrius's deputation eventually lost, but so, too, in a way did Pergamon: the towns were declared free and independent, under neither side's sovereignty. What is more, regardless of the decree, Philip continued to enjoy de facto possession for an additional three years, until 183, before he was finally forced to leave. The towns were evidently too valuable as bulwarks against northern migrants for Philip to cede them in any blithe way. Having to think without soldiers, Philip tried a couple of other time-honored Macedonian devices – the marriage alliance and city foundation. In the late 180s, one of his daughters married a Thracian prince, and his son Perseus married a Bastarnian princess from the Danubian region. Philip also founded the city of Perseis along the route to his son's bride's tribe. In these ways, he sought to preserve his kingdom's integrity, but he never pressed the limits of Rome's patience.

9.3 The Power of Pergamon

It is likely that Rome's stinginess with its aid to these Hellenic allies was motivated by an interest in seeing the region divided into smaller pieces. The Peace of Apamea had replaced a sole superpower, the Seleucids, with a binary pair – Pergamon and Rhodes – and the senators preferred that neither rise beyond a half-station. If this were indeed a concern, Pergamon gave ample reason to test Rome's resolve: their city was booming in a number of realms, from infantry to navy, from science and medicine to art and architecture. We have already seen the stakes to Hellenic prestige that the Attalids claimed via the Greater and Lesser Attalid Monuments (Chapters 7 and 8). During this period, Eumenes II also set up endowments in a number of towns to support gymnasia as educational institutions for citizen youth. Just like the libraries in the United States sponsored by Andrew Carnegie, the funds had as much to do with the donor's glory as with achieving a social mission. He and his three brothers represented the new Pergamon by participating in major Philhellenic games: all four took prizes at the Panathenaea of 178.

Just as he took Pergamon out into the world, Eumenes II also set the stage for the world to come to Pergamon. A fine new circuit of walls, built in the 180s, encompassed a larger urban space. A major new festival, the Nikephoria, drew athletes, artists, and spectators from all over the Mediterranean. The locus of the festival was a massive new Altar to Zeus, completed in the 170s but likely planned and undertaken in the heady decade of the 180s. Perched on a terrace below the Temple of Athena, jutting out from the steep conical hill of the acropolis, the altar's sides were carved with a fantastic frieze, sculpted in deep relief with figures larger than life size and painted in bright colors. Visible today at the Pergamon Museum in Berlin, snakes and monsters writhed through the composition amid beautiful gods doing battle against earthy Giants. A variety of creative ways of killing monsters is presented in the over 100 m of scene: Nyx, the goddess of night (or, she may be one of the Furies), crushes a pot full of poisonous snakes on the head of one giant (see Figure 9.1); Artemis sets her hunting dog on the neck of another; and still another succumbs to a torch thrust perpendicularly into his face by Hecate. Cybele rides in astride a lion, pulling an arrow from her quiver and getting ready to shoot. The

Figure 9.1 Scene from the Altar of Zeus at Pergamon, c. 180 BCE, depicting the goddess Nyx confronting a Giant in battle.

sculptures spilled onto the wide staircase itself, up which pilgrims would have ascended, themselves now "part of the action" in a way similar to how visitors to the Lesser Attalid Monument in Athens may have experienced a cosmic battlefield firsthand (Chapter 8). There was nothing to rival it in Athens or in Alexandria, and certainly not in Rome.

9.4   A New Balance of Power in the East

At the start of the 170s, Rome had to adapt to momentous changes in geopolitics. In Egypt, Ptolemy V died in 180 at a surprisingly young age; his throne passed to another infant son, Ptolemy VI, overseen by the widow, Cleopatra I, as regent; she was a daughter of Antiochus III and thus sister to the sitting king of the Seleucids, Seleucus IV. In the previous chapter we saw Ptolemy V as weak and indecisive in his youth, but he was just coming into his own upon his death, having finally regained Upper Egypt and defeated the insurrection there in 184. In the previous year he had augmented his forces by dispatching a eunuch, Aristonicus, to Greece to recruit fresh troops.

Around the same time Macedonia also experienced a regime-change: in 179 the now-docile Philip V died and was replaced by his son Perseus. Perseus had reportedly risen to power by exploiting anti-Roman sentiment in Macedonia, whipping up suspicion surrounding his brother Demetrius, whose hostageship in Rome had marked him as a potential sympathizer with the enemy (see above). Demetrius had indeed collaborated closely with Roman senators in 184 to gain an edge for Macedonia's territorial objectives, but this had been with Philip's blessing. Perseus nevertheless spun Demetrius's mission as an act of treason, forging incriminating documents of secret deals with Rome, with the result that Demetrius was brought up on charges and executed shortly before Philip's own death. Now Rome could not be certain of Antigonid loyalty, just as it also had questions about the "new" Ptolemy.

Meanwhile, the Seleucids were adjusting to a new straitened reality. Seleucus IV could not do much with his reign beyond lying low and working out a way to pay the war reparation obliged by the Peace of Apamea. At some point, he was compelled to send his son to Rome as a hostage, another Demetrius, often called Demetrius Soter by modern historians to distinguish him from other Demetriuses, using an epithet bestowed on him later in life. It will be remembered that in the treaty at Apamea, it had been Antiochus IV who was detained as a royal hostage for his father (Chapter 8), but since Antiochus III was now dead, the arrangement had to be brought up to date: a son of Seleucus IV would better tokenize loyalty than his brother. The date for the switch of hostages is not certain, but a decree from Athens puts Antiochus IV in that city by 178, likely en route back to Syria.

By contrast with much of the region, Athens was doing well and enjoyed Roman protection. It had not been seriously damaged in any of the recent wars, apart from Philip's invasion of 200 (Chapter 8), and it made much of its prestige to lead processes of diplomatic arbitration across the Greek-speaking East. The city was also assuming an ever more prominent role in the management of the Delphic Oracle now that the Aetolians had been reduced. Inscriptions reveal that the great Panathenaea had a more enhanced profile globally, as the lists of champions in this period include participants from far flung places like Numidia in North Africa, Liguria in northern Italy, Mesopotamia, Egypt, Cyrene, and the Levant, in addition to the usual Ionians and islanders. Antiochus IV, coming from the cosmopolitan community of high-level hostages in Rome, where he had grown to maturity since the age of 16, must have felt somewhat at home there in 178. His sojourn in Athens had a profound effect on him: later, after he assumed the throne at home, he sent gifts back to Athens, most notably underwriting renewed construction of the massive, unfinished Temple of Zeus Olympius, which had been begun by the tyrant Peisistratus nearly

400 years earlier (Chapter 1). The architect that he employed was reportedly an Italian named Cossutius (although the evidence is not conclusive), whom surely he had met as a hostage.

In 175, Antiochus IV would get his chance to return to Antioch. In that year, Seleucus IV sought to make up for overdue tribute payments by sending a minister, Heliodorus, to Jerusalem to see about raising funds from its wealthy Temple. In much the same way as Antiochus III met his demise trying to extract special treasure from Susa to pay Rome (Chapter 8), Seleucus IV's bid to exploit the Jews backfired fatally: Heliodorus's mission failed, but he used his momentary command of troops to organize the assassination of Seleucus IV upon his return. Antiochus IV thus hastened to Antioch to assume a regency of Seleucus's preadolescent son, whom he did away with relatively quickly in order to take power for himself. We are told that he was assisted in the move by Eumenes II, who was surely happy to see a friendly leader of the kingdom that had bedeviled him and his ancestors for generations, either directly or through proxy wars with smaller neighbors like Bithynia and Pontus.

One of Antiochus IV's first acts as king was to send his reliable lieutenant Apollonius, who hailed from Miletus, to Egypt to investigate the state of affairs in the Ptolemaic court. Cleopatra I had died in 176, the year before Antiochus's own accession. She had, by then, been regent over her son Ptolemy VI for four years; it should also be remembered that she was Antiochus IV's sister, and therefore the child-king on the throne was his nephew. Apollonius found the royal siblings – not just Ptolemy VI but also his younger sister Cleopatra II and younger brother Ptolemy VIII – being deftly manipulated by a pair of advisors, Lenaeus and Eulaeus. They were identified in our sources as a freedman and a eunuch, respectively, which social statuses carried pejorative connotations in elite-authored histories; our record is generally hostile to their regime, though in truth all the players, royals included, had similar objectives. Lenaeus and Eulaeus were certainly ambitious to restore Egypt's fortunes and reputation, beginning with, as always, Coele-Syria, and both sides began to prepare for war.

9.5 Spain as the Laboratory of Empire

Even after Cato's successes in Spain (Chapter 8), the region continued to offer sporadic resistance to the Roman presence. Acknowledging that Rome's efforts there required greater systemization, a tribune proposed the Lex Baebia in 181, which would have extended the terms of the two governing praetors there from one year to two. Tiberius Sempronius Gracchus held the command of Nearer Spain in 179 and set about pacifying rebellious tribes; as the son-in-law of Scipio Africanus, who had cut his teeth in Spain in the course of the Second Punic War (Chapter 7), this Gracchus may have received advice at family gatherings. He is said to have been more magnanimous with the defeated than his predecessors, especially in the awarding of land grants. Again, the influence of Scipio is discernible, since Africanus was said to have won over the locals through his generous policies toward hostages there. The plan worked, and Spain became less difficult for Rome in the coming decades, not interrupted by uprisings until the late 150s. In the meantime, the fertile farmland became a reliable source of revenue for Rome.

9.6 The Plight of Perseus

As the new king of Macedonia in 179, Perseus largely followed his father's policy of shoring up their circumscribed kingdom through a variety of means. After Cynoscephalae, Philip's military options had been limited, and he pursued diplomacy in his realm's interests, as we have seen.

With Thrace relatively secure by the time of his rise, Perseus looked to his other neighbors. To his east, he forged a couple of additional marriage alliances, as his sister Apama wed Prusias II of Bithynia and Perseus himself married Laodike, a daughter of Seleucus IV. To his south, he sent two representatives to occupy seats on the Amphictyonic Council, and himself visited Delphi with an impressive entourage. Internally, he stabilized social unrest by granting parcels of land to, or forgiving the financial obligations of, those who had been dispossessed by either exile or debt.

To Eumenes II and to certain senators in Rome, it appeared as if Perseus was inching back toward the glories of his Macedonian forebears. Eumenes personally visited Rome in 172 to ask the senate for a declaration of war, which indeed came the following year. Whether the hawks in the debate had just cause to fear Perseus or were opportunistically seeking an easy victory against a hobbled innocent is an open question. Evidence for the former might be found in a remarkable inscription from Delphi in which the reasons for war, called the Third Macedonian War by modern scholars, are outlined (see Primary Source 9.1). In this letter to the Amphictyonic Council from the Roman senate, many of Perseus's governing principles are interpreted as hostile: treaties with his northern neighbors become devices by which to facilitate an invasion of Italy; attendance with a troop at Delphi is imagined as a bullying show of force; and Perseus's populist forgiveness of debts to ordinary Macedonians is construed as a blow to the landowning elite, who generally supported Rome. Eumenes II even claimed that assassins hired by

---

Primary Source 9.1

Letter from the Roman Senate at Delphi against Perseus

Inscribed and set up at Delphi in 171, this letter from the Roman senate enumerates the crimes Perseus is alleged to have committed. It served to justify, to a Panhellenic audience at their holiest shrine, Rome's declaration of war that year. The decree plays upon well-known anxieties of the Greeks, including fear of invasion by Celts, political assassinations, financial upheaval, and violence against envoys. Livy provides the extra detail that the attempt on the life of Eumenes II was carried out by the assassin rolling a boulder down a cliff as he passed by.

"Contrary to what is proper, Perseus came to Delphi with his army during the Pythian truce (when military activity is suspended for the sake of athletics); and it was altogether wrong to permit him to enter or to participate in the oracular rituals, the sacrifices, the games, and the Amphictyonic Council of the League of the Hellenes. He called in the barbarians (the Celts) who dwell across the Danube – those who also on an earlier occasion, massing for no good purpose but in order to enslave all the Greeks, invaded Greece and marched against the shrine of the Pythian Apollo at Delphi, intending to plunder and destroy it. … Of the ambassadors sent to Rome by the Greeks and the kings concerning an alliance, he drowned the Thebans and attempted to put others out of the way by other means. Indeed he came to such a point of madness that he planned to get rid of our senate by poison. … He undermined the leading men and cultivated the masses, promising cancellation of debts and launching revolutions, thus making perfectly plain his policy toward the Greeks and the Romans. … Being long since desirous of a war against us, so that while we were thus rendered helpless, he might enslave all the Greek cities with no one to oppose him, he bribed Genthius, king of the Illyrians, to rise against us. King Eumenes (of Pergamon), our friend and ally, when he visited Delphi to fulfill a vow, (Perseus) plotted to kill through the agency of Evander …" (trans. Naphtali Lewis and Meyer Reinhold (eds.), *Roman Civilization, Selected Readings, Volume 1*, third edition, New York: Columbia University Press, 1990.)

Perseus had, somewhat cartoonishly to our modern eyes, rigged a landslide to crush him in 172 near Delphi as he passed through on his way home from Italy. The inscription also alleges an attempt by Perseus to poison the Roman senate en masse, the logistics of which would be baffling and are conveniently left out.

Given the fantastic complaints and conspiracy theories of the charges against Perseus, it might be preferable to follow the second strand of evidence for the origins of the Third Macedonian War, which is that Rome was seeking an easy target. By 172 the difficult campaigns in Spain were in abeyance and Rome had liberty to turn its attention elsewhere. The wars had yielded tremendous booty, for which the Romans, having also drawn fortunes from Syracuse, Tarentum, Carthage, Ambracia, the Seleucids, and the Aetolians, were developing a taste. Nothing but justice was stopping Rome from a unilateral assault on a weakened neighbor, and that could be had through creative spin. The balance of the evidence implies that the Roman view of the East, or even of the entire Mediterranean, had turned a corner around the mid-170s, into a proactive, preemptive policy of war making – perhaps not in every case, but in some very prominent ones. Given that by 173, the Romans had received all the tribute payments from Antiochus IV that had been deferred for a time, and the treaty of Apamea was coming to an end with the Seleucids occupying a strong position, it may be that the Romans saw new reasons to act at this moment.

For each of the first three years of the Third Macedonian War, one of the two consuls was assigned to the Macedonian theater and engaged in skirmishes. Perseus repeatedly pleaded for diplomatic talks but was rebuffed. Eumenes II and even Masinissa of Numidia (who had risen to prominence with Rome's favor during the Second Punic War, Chapter 7) contributed cavalry to help the Romans, and Athens played an active role in procuring and delivering provisions. Ambracia, which Fulvius Nobilior had won in 189 (Chapter 8), was a critical depot for operations, demonstrating how the Romans could make more of their conquests as long-term investments than just as short-term plunder. The final battle came in 168, when Lucius Aemilius Paullus led his troops into southern Macedonia. He met Perseus's phalanx, already compromised by the terms of the settlement after Cynoscephalae, near the town of Pydna, where Olympias had died nearly 150 years earlier (Chapter 3). Defeated and apprehended one year later, Perseus was brought back to Rome for a triumph in the capacity of a prisoner of war, a far more degraded status than that of his younger brother who had been a diplomatic hostage. A second triumph was awarded to Lucius Anicius Gallus, whose navy had defeated Perseus's ally Genthius of Illyria, who joined Perseus as a prisoner of war.

9.7 The Sixth Syrian War and the "Day of Eleusis"

In the late 170s, both the Seleucids and the Ptolemies (or at least the advisors to the child-monarchs) had reason to be optimistic at the prospects of war with each other. Lenaeus and Eulaeus had the dynasty firmly to hand: they elevated not just Ptolemy VI but also his sister Cleopatra II, now his wife, and their younger brother Ptolemy VIII, approximately 12, 10, and 8 years of age, respectively, to a kind of tripartite throne. On the part of the Seleucids, Antiochus IV had rebuilt his empire's finances and had begun stockpiling military necessities. Part of his confidence stemmed from the accession of a new and reliable ally in Jerusalem. In 172, a nobleman, Jason, asked Antiochus IV to help him seize power as High Priest. In exchange Jason offered almost 600 talents in all, plus a promise to encourage the Hellenization of Jews through new educational institutions such as gymnasia and an *ephebeia*, a Hellenic-style curriculum of education for adolescents. Money and loyalty were things that the Seleucids had not had much of from Judaea since Antiochus III had won it in 200 and had granted it de facto autonomy (Chapter 8). Add to this the incentive that Antiochus IV was the uncle of the sibling-monarchs in Egypt and a path for expansion of Seleucid influence became obvious. Both sides notified Rome of grievances toward the other and both took notice that Rome's involvement with Perseus kept its senate from interfering.

Antiochus IV began in 170 by moving on Pelusion, a fortress that guarded access to the Delta, and defeated Lenaeus and Eulaeus there. He had elephants at his disposal, which had been forbidden by the now expired Peace of Apamea. Moving swiftly, he was welcomed in Memphis, where he met with the now rudderless young Ptolemy VI. The new royal advisors were open to negotiations, and they declared Antiochus IV to be the king's official regent. The city of Alexandria, however, remained closed and defiant: in possession of Ptolemy VIII, they set him up as a rival king, prompting Antiochus to lay siege. Antiochus's position was strong, but word came from Jerusalem that a political rift there could jeopardize his exit strategy for return to the Levant. A rival to Jason for the High Priesthood, with the equally Hellenic name of Menelaus, offered Antiochus even more money than had Jason, and Antiochus gave him his blessing, but when Menelaus's promise was not met, Antiochus abandoned Alexandria to return to Syria at the end of 169. With Antiochus IV out of sight and out of mind, it did not take long for the malleable Ptolemy VI to be reconciled to his younger siblings and to rejoin them as an independent council of monarchs.

At the start of 168, Antiochus IV seized Cyprus: rather like the illegal elephants of Pelusion, this campaign required a fleet of ships, which the Peace of Apamea had prohibited of the Seleucids. He again breezed into the Delta and planted siegeworks at Alexandria. But timing is everything: in July of that year, a Roman envoy named Gaius Papilius Laenas arrived on the scene. June had been the month of Perseus's defeat at Pydna, and Rome was no longer preoccupied. Antiochus, doubtlessly proficient to a degree in Latin from his hostageship, went to welcome the Roman whom, again, he probably knew firsthand. Many authors savor the irony of the scene: Laenas is said to have rebuffed the greeting, and rather demanded that Antiochus go home to Syria at once and leave the Ptolemies to their own devices. Antiochus asked for time to think about it, upon which Laenas scratched a circle in the ground at Antiochus's feet and threatened that he could not leave that spot until he gave an answer. Antiochus had no choice: he called off the entire, expensive campaign, we are told, just like that. The episode has come to be called "The Day of Eleusis," after the suburb of Alexandria where the exchange took place. It is cited as a symbolic turning point in Mediterranean history: Rome had just cheated many Spanish tribes of tons of treasure; had just won a war, unprovoked, against Perseus; and now threw down the gauntlet for two storied kingdoms in the East, the Seleucids and the Ptolemies, essentially depriving them of independent action.

9.8 The Year 167

It would be too much to say that as of the Day of Eleusis, a new world order had been established in Rome's favor. Rather, one had been *proposed*, in effect, by the Romans, and the task remained for it to be accomplished. A new trend of the tightening of control by Rome is unmistakable, and the victims of their policies included their erstwhile friends as well as their stated enemies. The defeated Macedonians and their allies faced revolutionary conditions: the Antigonid monarchy in Pella was abolished completely, ending a run of 140 years if one counts from Antigonus the One-Eyed (Chapter 3). In its place, the Romans organized four distinct republics that were institutionally separated: residents of each region could not move to another one; could not marry into another one; and could not do business with another one. One might compare the new settlement in Macedonia with the Roman division of Asia Minor in 188 among Pergamon, Rhodes, and the independent cities (Chapter 8): where once there was a single power, now there were separate, weaker states, which were inherently designed for competition and a lack of unity. Both arrangements may themselves be productively compared with the much earlier situation in Italy where the Latins possessed the rights of marriage, movement, and markets with Rome but not with each other (*iures migrationis*, *coniubii*, and *commercii*, Chapter 3).

Meanwhile, allies of Perseus faced extreme brutality. The Molossians of Epirus, age old foes from the days of Pyrrhus, ceased to exist as a people. Their property was seized by the Romans; their villages torched; and all survivors, some 150 000, we are told, were sold into slavery. Prusias II, Perseus's brother-in-law, was allowed to live, but only after displaying what Polybius (admittedly his enemy) described as a humiliating display of groveling. In Polybius's account, Prusias addressed the senators as *theoi soteres* ("savior gods"), which had been an official epithet for the Ptolemaic monarchs. As Polybius was construing it, Prusias was pointedly defining Rome as a Hellenistic power.

Perhaps one reason why Prusias II was allowed to remain was that Rome wanted to punish Pergamon. Rumors had circulated that Eumenes II had been in secret talks with Perseus – at once hard to imagine given Eumenes's role in bringing about the war against him in the first place, but perhaps less so if one considers Hellenistic opportunism. Eumenes had tried to appear in Rome in person in 167 to burnish his image, but was turned back at Brundisium. The senate declared Galatia – not only a regional rival of Pergamon's, but the very source of its Hellenic credentials in the sense that it was promoted a barbaric foil to Pergamene culture – to be free. Rhodes was also punished, this time for trying more than once to negotiate a path for Perseus to stay in power: Caria and Lycia on the Asian mainland were both declared free. A faction in the Achaean League was also brought to an end. Callicrates, the general who had always argued strenuously for allegiance to Rome (Chapter 8), named names of those who disagreed with him, and some 1000 statesmen were arrested and sent to Italy as veritable hostages. The dragnet ensnared Polybius, who would stay under Roman control for 17 years, where he would be inspired to write most of what survives today of his histories. Lucius Aemilius Paullus appears to have recognized Polybius's talent as a writer, borrowing some of his library and arranging for him to tutor his sons in spite of their having been on opposite sides at Pydna. Finally, the Ptolemies, or at least the Alexandrians that controlled them, sent an embassy to Rome to express gratitude for their rescue.

All the while, Paullus, the champion of Pydna, enjoyed a victory lap of sorts through the major sites of the Classical Greek world. Starting in the north, he toured Aulis, whence the mythic thousand ships were launched for Troy in the Homeric epics, and Chalcis, one of the famous "Fetters." He also visited Delphi where an equestrian likeness of him was set atop a platform that previously supported a portrait of Perseus. A relief at the base of the tower, now displayed in the Delphi Museum, depicts scenes from the Battle of Pydna (see Figure 9.2). A circuit of the Peloponnese rounded out his travels – Olympia, Sicyon, Corinth, Argos. Paullus also visited Athens, which was rewarded heartily for its service against Perseus: Athens received control of the islands Delos and Lemnos, and most likely Imbros and Scyros, as well, thus reviving its fortunes as a major commercial power in the Aegean. Around this time, our evidence picks up for the festival of the Theseia in Athens, a kind of second Panathenaea that revered the city's mythological hero Theseus. With its newfound glory and with an absence of serious rivals in the region following Rome's reordering, Athens more and more took on an arbitrating role in disputes. In 167 it settled a case between Ambracia and Acarnania over how each should offset the losses of the other when Roman soldiers had bivouacked in their homes during the war with Perseus.

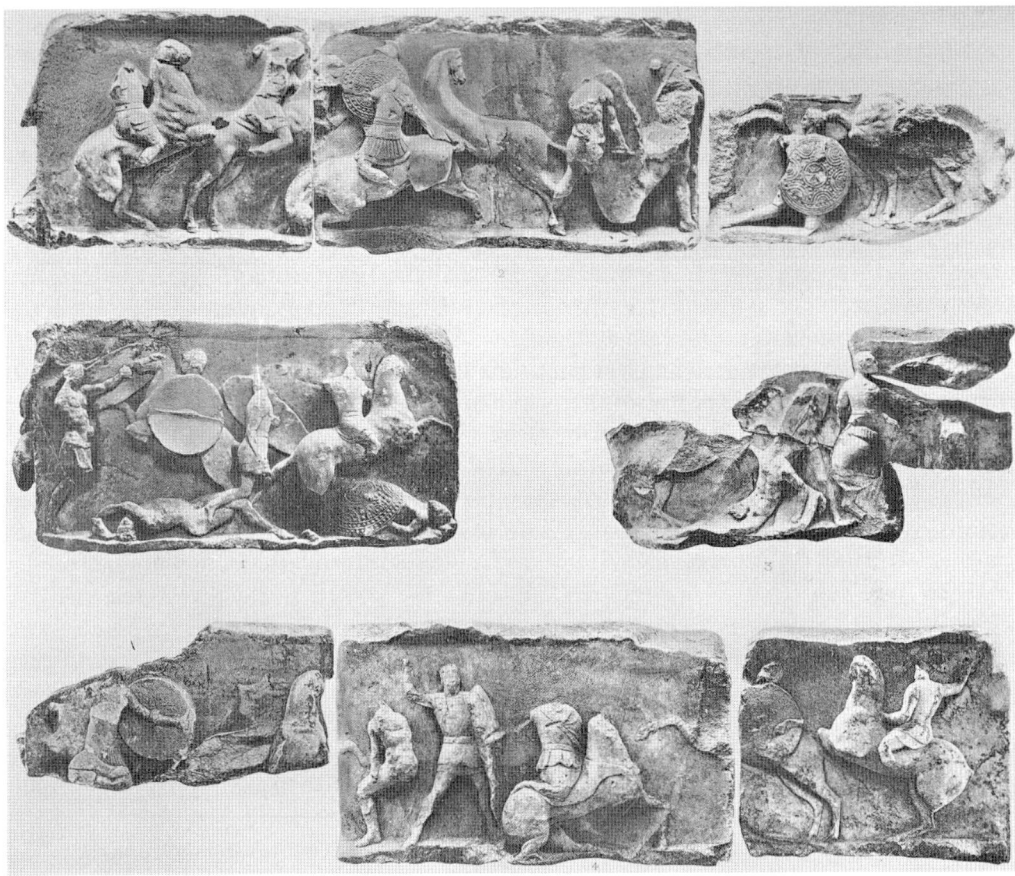

Figure 9.2 Relief from the victory monument of Lucius Aemilius Paullus at Delphi, 160s BCE, depicting scenes from the Battle of Pydna in 167.

9.9 Three Celebrations

Records of three major celebrations held at sites across the Mediterranean in 166 demonstrate a new balance of authority and prestige among the traditional Hellenistic powers. Virtually simultaneously, Antiochus IV staged a pageant at Daphne, a suburb of Antioch, to advertise his feats in Egypt, however illusory; a new governing order on Delos created a new festival called the Romaia to pay homage to the champion of the island's newly enhanced status; and Rome itself was witness to a *ne plus ultra* of triumphal processions, as Lucius Aemilius Paullus took stock of his conquest over Alexander's homeland of Macedonia. All three are emblematic of a kind of national momentum that was to carry their states forward, some longer than others.

In the remaining years of his reign, Antiochus IV walked a line between vassalage to Rome and his own independent ambitions. On his way back to Syria he exacted terrible vengeance on Jerusalem for deposing his representatives, outlawing Jewish practices in the process. In terms of his attitudes toward Rome, later sources remember him as a devoted acolyte. He is said to have worn a toga and to have moved throughout the crowd of his subjects as would an elected official of the Roman Republic – an activity that was viewed as completely insane by a population used to hereditary rule: Antiochus's epithet, Epiphanes, was playfully tweaked as Epimanes, or "out of one's mind." Livy attributes to him the sponsorship of gladiatorial style combats at

Antioch and claims that he built a Temple to Jupiter Capitolinus. But given that these images are conjured by Livy alone, who wrote at a time of Roman nationalistic fervor some 150 years later, and not by Polybius who was a contemporary, modern readers should temper their understanding of Antiochus's Roman-ness. Indeed, no temple to Jupiter has been found; perhaps later sources were conflating Antiochus's known support for the new Temple of Zeus in Athens (see above) with reverence for Jupiter in Antioch. If anything, Antiochus's procession in Daphne implies independence of ambition. In his "victory" parade tens of thousands of infantrymen and cavalry marched amid treasures of all kinds – gold, silver, fine fabrics and perfumes, exotic slaves, living elephants, and raw ivory tusks from dead ones. The parade, even if smacking of a Roman practice, spoke of his own greatness, to the exclusion of other influences. If word of the humiliating Day of Eleusis was present, it could only have been a rumor.

In the following year, Antiochus was back on a war path, but now prudently in directions opposite from Rome and the rest of the geopolitically saturated Mediterranean. In 165 he moved on Armenia to his north and from there turned east toward Mesopotamia. He gave harbor to Menelaus, his man in Jerusalem who had been toppled and driven out by a set of brothers of the Maccabaeus clan. Judaism, at least as the Maccabaei conceived it, had thus been restored. Many scholars date the *Book of Daniel* to this early Maccabean period and associate the book's "prediction" of wars between the kings of the north and the south with the conflict that had just ended between Antiochus IV and Ptolemy VI, respectively (see Primary Source 9.2). The text goes on to predict a spectacular fall for the "king of the north," and in true form, Antiochus succumbed to an illness while on campaign in 164; the coincidence implies that the text was written shortly thereafter. Antiochus IV had done much to revive the flagging vigor of the Seleucid realm, even within the new confines of the Roman presence. The throne passed for a time to his son, Antiochus V, and more significantly, to the boy-king's regent, a general named Lysias. Their regime did not last long, as we shall see, but one of their policies – a slackening of Seleucid interference in Judaea – provided an even stronger foundation to the rebel leader Judas Maccabaeus's hold on the territory. He lost no time in rebuilding the Temple and reestablishing kosher practices, at times experiencing miracles such as the endurance of a single day's worth of lamp oil over an entire week, which gave rise to the light festival of Hanukkah.

> **Primary Source 9.2**
>
> *The Book of Daniel*
>
> *The Book of Daniel* in the Hebrew Testament was written in the late 160s, but purports to be a much older text in which "future" calamities, which were current events in the 160s, were predicted to come about (compare the *Oracle of the Potter*, Chapter 11). This excerpt likely refers to the rise of Antiochus IV (a "king of the north," relative to Jerusalem) among the Seleucids. The text mentions his war against a "king of the south," apparently referring to the Sixth Syrian War against Ptolemy VI, followed by withdrawal due to the arrival of the "ships of Kittim," which may refer to Rome and the Day of Eleusis. The king of the north goes on to exploit factions in Jerusalem and to desecrate the Temple, as Antiochus IV did, and the text "predicts" that he will die fighting in his north and east, again, features of Antiochus IV's biography. The sacred quality of the text serves to render the king's downfall as divinely sanctioned before a Hebrew audience.
>
> 11.21–33, 44–45: "A contemptible person shall arise on whom royal majesty had not been conferred; he shall come in without warning and obtain the kingdom through intrigue. Armies

> shall be utterly swept away and broken before him, and the prince of the covenant as well. And after an alliance is made with him, he shall act deceitfully and become strong with a small party. Without warning he shall come into the richest parts of the province and do what none of his predecessors had ever done, lavishing plunder, spoil, and wealth on them. He shall devise plans against strongholds, but only for a time. He shall stir up his power and determination against the king of the south with a great army, and the king of the south shall wage war with a much greater and stronger army. But he shall not succeed, for plots shall be devised against him by those who eat of the royal rations. They shall break him (the king of the south), his army shall be swept away, and many shall fall slain. The two kings, their minds bent on evil, shall sit at one table and exchange lies. But it shall not succeed, for there remains an end at the time appointed. (The king of the north) shall return to his land with great wealth, but his heart shall be set against the holy covenant. He shall work his will, and return to his own land. At the time appointed he shall return and come into the south, but this time it shall not be as it was before. For ships of Kittim shall come against him, and he shall lose heart and withdraw. He shall be enraged and take action against the holy covenant. He shall turn back and pay heed to those who forsake the holy covenant. Forces sent by him shall occupy and profane the Temple and fortress. They shall abolish the regular burnt offering and set up the abomination that makes desolate. He shall seduce with intrigue those who violate the covenant; but the people who are loyal to their God shall stand firm and take action. The wise among the people shall give understanding to many; for some days, however, they shall fall by sword and flame, and suffer captivity and plunder. ... But reports from the east and the north shall alarm him, and he shall go out with great fury to bring ruin and complete destruction to many. He shall pitch his palatial tents between the sea and the beautiful holy mountain. Yet he shall come to his end, with no one to help him." (New Revised Standard Version.)

In Delos the Romaia festival of 166 was one part of a raft of sudden changes that made the small island the figurative center of the Hellenic economy. We know little of what transpired at the festival – it likely included ritual banquets and athletic and artistic competitions – but its articulation of Rome's centrality is unmistakable, even as the site fell under the formal jurisdiction of Athens. Many native Delians were forced out as Athenian *cleruchs* – colonial outsiders who governed while still holding citizenship in Athens – took over real estate both public and private. The well-excavated site has yielded inscriptions attesting to newly founded cults, new power structures, new landowners, new ethnicities, and new political institutions. The office of *epimeletes* (or, guardian, the same term passed around among the *Diadochoi* in charge of Alexander's heirs; Chapter 3) was voted on by the cleruchs. Rome's authority, however, was never in doubt, as an anecdote reveals: a certain Demetrius (nonroyal and of no relation to the Hellenistic monarchs) set up inscriptions explaining how the Romans granted him, a priest of Serapis who was likely descended from many generations of similar priests, the right to oversee his cult, and that in so doing they were overruling an Athenian decree that had initially supplanted him. Rome was also behind the declaration of Delos as a tax-free harbor, which led to an explosion in mercantile activity and which dealt another blow to Rhodes nearby. Merchants from all over the Mediterranean, from Italy to Phoenicia, settled on Delos and formed guilds to promote and protect their several interests. Slave trading is particularly well attested in surviving texts, in part a result of warmongering and piracy of various types in the era. Delos's central location made it a convenient place to liquidate large crowds of prisoners.

In Rome in 166 Lucius Aemilius Paullus's triumph gave that city its own opportunities in slave trading, and on a hyperbolic scale. We have already seen how Paullus was said to have detained 150 000 prisoners of war from the Molossians of Epirus on his way home, a staggering number even if exaggerated, and even as it sets aside Macedonia itself. We do not know whether the procession included the thousand Achaean statesmen, including Polybius, who were detained after Pydna. Our sources do say that Perseus's wife and children played prominent roles, with the children now receiving instructions on how to beg, which reportedly elicited sympathy from the crowd. One son willingly shed his royal identity and became a staff record-keeper for the Republic. His father Perseus, however, starting from too great a height, could never have that option: he was packed off to a dungeon in the snowy Apennine fortress of Alba Fucens, not far from the dungeon that housed his ally Genthius of Illyria. The triumph served to advance the already gathering notion that Rome's role overseas was expanding.

9.10 Outsiders Regarding Rome

Roman literature in this period continued to be dominated by outsider voices that had likely come to the city as a function of warfare. Caecilius Statius, like Livius Andronicus, catered to Rome's interest in Greek New Comedy; only titles of his works and a few fragments survive, but they imply the influence of Menander (Chapter 4). Whereas Livius Andronicus came from Italy's Hellenic South, Caecilius originally came from the Celtic North.

Far more is known about Caecilius's near contemporary, Quintus Ennius, about whose earlier career we have already heard. In the period of the Third Macedonian War, Ennius moved beyond the ad hominem poetry that characterized his initial work (such as the celebration of the sack of Ambracia by Fulvius Nobilior, Chapter 8) and began to focus on an all-encompassing Roman epic poem. Titled the *Annales*, it tracked the rise of Rome on an annual timeline. He began with Aeneas but moved quickly to the wars of living memory with the majority of his books dealing with conflicts that had occurred since Pyrrhus, some 80 years before Ennius's *floruit*. He used the Homeric meter of dactylic hexameter, the first to put Latin into that Hellenic form. An irony thus emerges: Ennius's Rome may have dominated the Greek world physically, but its quarry constituted the operative influence on Roman intellectual pursuits. Ennius's nephew Pacuvius was also a writer. His *fabula praetexta*, the *Paullus*, praised the general who won at Pydna, following in the footsteps of his uncle; Pacuvius was otherwise known for his tragedies.

Shortly after Paullus's triumph and the extirpation and imprisonment of Perseus, another writer, this time apparently from Africa, traded in plots about the displacement of populations through warfare, piracy, and enslavement. The playwright Terence wrote many comedies, six of which are extant, mainly dating to the 160s. The hint of his African roots comes from his full Roman name, Publius Terentius Afer, the cognomen of which could refer to any region along the southern Mediterranean coast – Cyrene, Numidia, or even Carthage. He is said to have learned Latin as a second language and to have earned his freedom through his writing. A generation younger than Plautus, he produced plays that, while building on Greek prototypes of Menander and New Comedy, nevertheless reflected realities of his Roman world. One of his plays, the *Self-Tormenter*, is about a father who is remorseful for having forced his son to enlist in an army headed for Asia Minor (see Primary Source 9.3). As a result, the father is left behind to work the land, even in his old age. Terence's theme was prescient: the phenomenon of the farm that fails because a son is displaced by military obligations in the prime of life will be at the root of economic difficulties in Italy within a generation of the play's production (Chapter 10).

Primary Source 9.3

Terence, *Heauton Timoroumeos* (or, "The Self-Tormentor")

Like Plautus, the comic playwright Terence worked under the influence of Menander but created his own unique compositions. The title of this play is shared with a Menander original, but some of the themes relate directly to what we know of social and economic problems in Rome. Namely, in this excerpt an elderly character complains about what will become of his family farm with his son off fighting in wars in Asia Minor. The pain is especially acute because it is the father, Menedemos ("The unbending people," in Greek), who drove his son to leave, thus "tormenting himself." In this scene, Menedemos's neighbor, Chremes ("Wealth"), asks him to explain why he is working as hard as he is, at his age.

> Lines 53–71: CHREMES: "Although our acquaintance with each other is recent (from the time when you bought the field nearby), and although hardly any serious matter has come up, nevertheless, your worthiness and your proximity to me, which I think is nearly the same as friendship, steels me to warn you that you are working beyond your age, and beyond what your circumstances dictate. For, by all things holy and just, what do you want, and what are you trying to achieve? You were born sixty years ago or more, I conjecture. No-one has a better farm in these parts, nor of more value. (I see) lots of slaves here, but still as if none are around, you attentively perform all their tasks. Never do I set out in the morning or return at dusk when I don't see you on your plot digging or plowing or lugging something around. Finally, you take no breaks and you're not caring for yourself. I know this cannot be pleasant for you …
> MENEDEMUS: You want to know (why I work like this)?
> CHREMES: That's why I said what I did.
> MENEDEMUS: There's an impoverished old immigrant woman here from Corinth. My son came to love her daughter with abandon. He considered her almost as one would a wife. All of this was kept secret from me. When I discovered the affair, I started to berate him inhumanly, not as was appropriate for the love-sick soul of a teenager, but with force, along the lines of all fathers … "When I was your age," I told him, "I didn't pay attention to love, but I went to Asia Minor on account of my poverty and there I found both wealth and glory at the same time, with weapons of war." Afterwards it all came back (to bite me), for he was just a teenager and he was convinced after hearing the same weighty speech (from me) so often, that I, on account of my age and my care for him, understood more than he did. Chremes, he ran off to fight some king in Asia."

Polybius, the one-time adversary of Rome who became the tutor of Paullus's son, apparently took notes during his hostageship and embarked on a history of Rome. Unlike the Latin authors described above, he wrote in Greek, likely for a Greek audience. He endeavored to explain the nature of Rome's success, citing the nature of its political system with a mixture of a populist tribunate, an aristocratic senate, and a monarchical consulship. He also drew attention to Rome's proclivity for processions, whether in triumphs or for funerals, and how competition for glory in both contexts spurred activity overseas. Whereas Terence's *Self-Tormentor* pointed out the sorrows for a family that was riven by a youth's military service, both emotional and economic, Polybius saw the intertwining of family honor with overseas victory as a key to Roman prosperity. In many ways, to be explored in the next chapter, they were both right.

9.11 Conclusions

The Ptolemies, Seleucids, and Attalids remained nominally independent by 164, but the Antigonid dynasty was now a thing of the past. Rome replaced that monarchy with a new system of government in Macedonia, but still did not claim it as theirs: all of Rome's formal provinces at this time were in the West – Sicily, Sardinia, and the two Spains. What distinguished the period, however, was the increasingly personal relationships and familiarity that Romans were developing with individual agents in the East. To see easterners, as well as westerners for that matter, walking through the streets of Rome, speaking at the senate house, performing on the stage, dining in banquets, or trading in the market was becoming commonplace. Not all Romans embraced the change, and conflicts continued in this period between old and young, rich and poor, and to some extent, between the military way of life and the civilian.

Ambition begat ambition among the Roman senatorial elite and their success mushroomed in the subsequent period. Soon, the restriction of gross prosperity to a select few led to discontent and dangerous impoverishment among the many. Political change became necessary, as well shall see, in redressing their grievances, and not at all peacefully.

Further Reading

Astin, Alan (1978). *Cato the Censor.* Oxford: Oxford University Press.
Eckstein, Arthur (2006). *Mediterranean Anarchy, Interstate War, and the Rise of Rome.* Berkeley: University of California Press.
Evans, Richard (2012). *A History of Pergamum: Beyond Hellenistic Kingship.* New York: Continuum.
Marshal, CW (2006). *The Stagecraft and Performance of Roman Comedy.* Cambridge: Cambridge University Press.
Reiter, William (1988). *Aemilius Paullus: Conqueror of Greece.* London: Croon Helm.
Rosenstein, Nathan (2004). *Rome at War: Farms, Families, and Death in the Middle Republic.* Chapel Hill: University of North Carolina Press.

10

To 133: The Price of Empire

Timeline

163: Rome supports Ptolemy VI on the throne in Egypt and Ariarathes V on the throne of Cappadocia
162: Murder of Gnaeus Octavius in Antioch; escape of Demetrius Soter from hostageship in Rome
161: Rome recognizes the Maccabbean regime in Jerusalem
155: Delegation of Athenian philosophers to Rome to argue against claims of the Achaean League
150: Death of Demetrius Soter; accession of Alexander Balas, alleged son of Antiochus IV
150–148: Fourth Macedonian War: Rome defeats Andriscus, alleged son of Perseus
149: *Lex Cornelia de repetundis* in Rome, against corruption in the provinces
149–146: Third Punic War
146: Destruction of both Carthage and Corinth
135–132: Slave rebellion in Sicily led by Eunus (also called Antiochus)
133: Tribunate of Tiberius Sempronius Gracchus; death of Attalus III and bequest of Pergamon to Rome

Principal Themes

- In an irony of geopolitics, Rome took strides to enforce the just management of its growing overseas territories, including the creation of a new court of law tasked with handling provincial corruption, and yet new Roman aggression led to the destruction of Carthage and Corinth with little provocation.
- Rapid imperial growth disrupted the economies of Italy as agricultural production shifted from soldier-farmers to vast landowners who benefitted from the exploitation of provinces.
- Leaders in Rome began to redefine the sources of legitimacy in politics: existing magistracies, such as the tribune of the plebs, were held by men who claimed to have greater rights and privileges in the office than previously exercised.
- Leaders in the Hellenistic East began to redefine the sources of legitimacy in politics: existing dynasties, such as the Antigonids, Seleucids, and Attalids, were infiltrated by men who claimed to be blood-relatives of past monarchs and thus members of dynastic networks – so-called "pretenders" to the thrones.

The Roman Republic and the Hellenistic Mediterranean: From Alexander to Caesar, First Edition. Joel Allen.
© 2020 John Wiley & Sons, Inc. Published 2020 by John Wiley & Sons, Inc.

10.1 Introduction

The previous chapter saw the eclipse of large, storied Hellenistic dynasties by Rome. In this chapter Rome's victories come at the expense of the smaller satellites, such as independent city-states, federated leagues, and the already much reduced Carthage. The concomitant, ongoing surge in wealth in Rome led to political controversies and, ironically, economic crises, which combined to destabilize the state. The soldier class grew to resent the massive enrichment of their generals and senatorial governors who controlled the resources of the new provinces. "Income inequality" (for lack of a better term and at the risk of being anachronistic) spurred activism and a search for new ways of exerting power within Rome's oligarchic institutions. The unrest gives the lie to Polybius's analysis of an ironclad stability in Rome's "mixed" constitution, which he wrote about just a decade before the splinters began to fly. Rather than the constitution being balanced by monarchical, aristocratic, and populist elements, it was undermined by vigorous competition among them. The office of tribune of the plebs was redefined as the disgruntled and dispossessed sought to manipulate its veto power in new ways.

Likewise, the entrenched dynasties of the Hellenistic East confronted challenges from competitors who, too, used their own legitimizing institutions against them – the hereditary right to rule. That is, so-called "pretenders" recognized the power to be had in blood relations with old, dead monarchs, and so, they simply claimed to be the long, lost heirs of any king or other, and thus won legitimacy in the eyes of large crowds. Five such pretenders appear in this chapter, and more will surface beyond that. Thus in both Rome and the East, ambitious outsiders were seizing power, though not quite in revolutionary ways since they kept within existing political vocabularies – in Rome, a new conception of the tribunate, and in the dynasties, the fabrication of family ties.

10.2 Internationalized Family Networks in Rome

Aristocratic clans in Rome were becoming as byzantine in their interlocking ties as the dynasties of the East. For example, the sons of Aemilius Paullus, the victor at Pydna, were adopted out to other prominent clans, both to reduce Paullus's number of heirs, thus preserving his estate, and to establish political ties (see Figure 10.1b). Quintus Fabius Maximus and the son of Scipio Africanus, both carrying names famous from the Second Punic War, became the new "fathers" of two of Aemilius's adult children, who were accordingly renamed Fabius Maximus Aemilianus and Scipio Aemilianus. Scipio Aemilianus's new father had no children of his own, and so the adoption allowed Africanus's line to continue, in a way, to a third generation. Yet, Scipio Aemilianus also kept ties to his biological father; from him he inherited, in effect, the patronage of the historian Polybius, whom Paullus had brought from Greece along with his library (Chapter 9). Scipio Africanus also had a daughter, Cornelia, whose fecundity set her apart from her brother – two of her sons, Tiberius and Gaius Gracchus, would go on to famous careers, as we shall see, and her daughter, Sempronia, would marry Scipio Aemilianus, even though, through adoption at least, they were now also cousins. The Hellenistic royals themselves, with centuries of experience in dynastic management, felt affinity for the new Roman phenomenon: Ptolemy VIII, while on an embassy to Rome in 155, is said to have proposed marriage to the widowed Cornelia, which would have added an interesting dimension to Roman domestic political intrigues, but he was rebuffed.

These Romans were also increasingly becoming patrons to Hellenistic heirs, who after initially arriving as hostages were now coming of their own volition, as students or quasi-ambassadors

(a)

Hellenistic dynasts in Rome

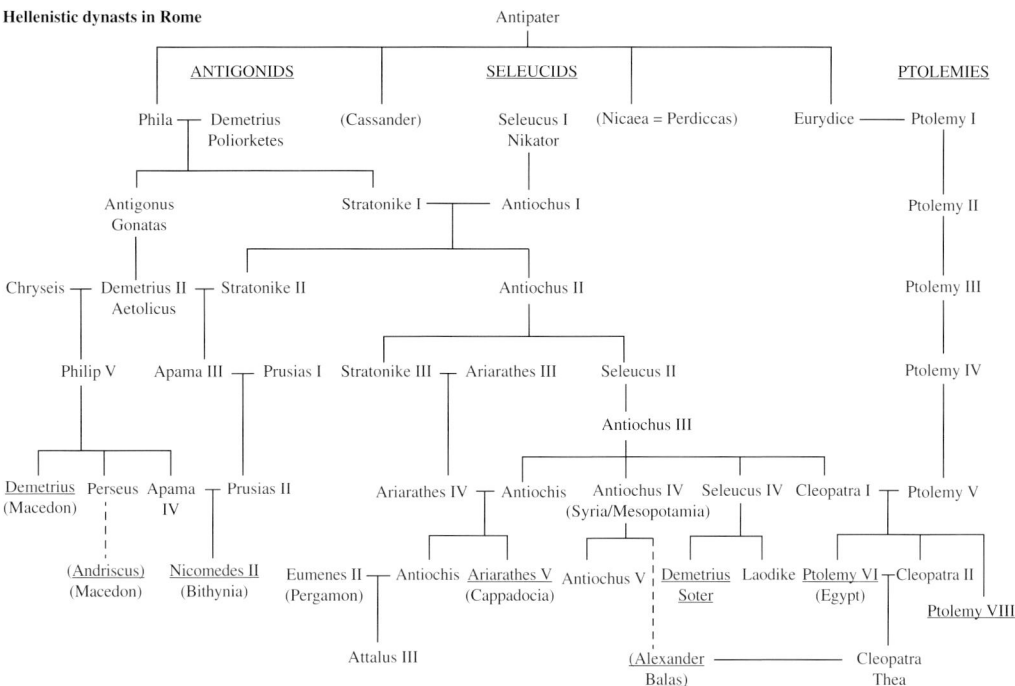

Note: The underscored spent time in Rome in the 170s to 150s BCE (except Demetrius of Macedon, who was there in the 190s). Parenthesis and dotted lines indicate so-called pretenders.

(b)

The Scipionic-Aemilio-Fabian network

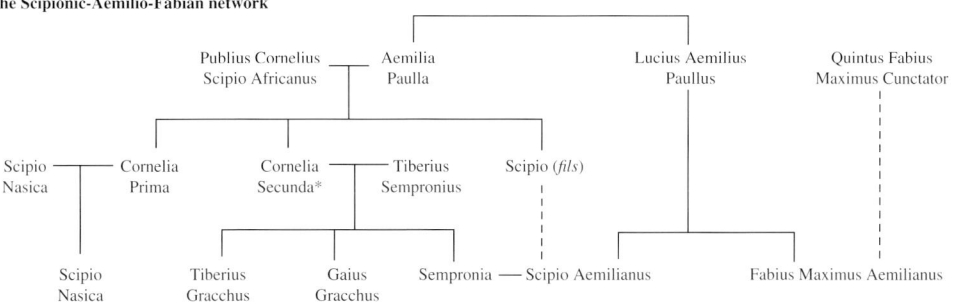

*Allegedly received a marriage offer from Ptolemy VIII in 155 BCE. Dotted lines indicate adult adoption

Figure 10.1 (a) Family connections among Hellenistic dynasts. The underscored were present in Rome at some point in the 170s through the 150s; parentheses and dotted lines indictate "pretenders" to the throne. (b) Family connections among Roman political and military leaders. Dotted lines indicate adult adoptions.

(although the categories were becoming indistinguishable). In the course of the 160s, a remarkable cluster of powerful, well-connected cousins with roots among Hellenistic royalty were present together in Rome (see Figure 10.1a). We have already seen how Demetrius Soter became a hostage for Seleucus IV (Chapter 9). His first cousin, Ariarathes V, heir to Cappadocia, came to Rome at the same time, but as a student. The same was true for Nicomedes II of Bithynia – Nicomedes's uncle Perseus, of the Antigonids, had been married to Demetrius

Soter's sister. Ptolemy VI, also a first cousin of Demetrius Soter and Ariarathes V, arrived in Rome in 164, but as a refugee, having been driven from the throne, probably by a faction supporting his younger brother, Ptolemy VIII. All of these royals must have encountered each other in the city, as well as rubbed elbows with the historian Polybius and the playwright Terence, both detainees of different kinds (Chapter 9).

Increasingly, this loose coterie of leaders and thinkers either used Rome or was used by Rome, or more likely both, in forging ties that helped them stake claims to power and prestige, regardless of their "national" borders. In 163, Ariarathes V inherited his crown and departed Rome for Cappadocia. In the same year, Roman legions escorted Ptolemy VI back to Alexandria. The latter case constituted an unprecedented level of king-making for the Romans: they had certainly supported kings and queens in the past but had not, to date, used direct military muscle to place them on a throne. Helping matters in Egypt was Ptolemy VIII's unpopularity in Alexandria. He was lucky that Rome found a use for him in governing adjacent Cyrene, and no doubt serving as a counterweight to the brother Rome had just propped up. Once Roman suzerainty was clear, Ptolemy VIII took to it with aplomb: when he conceived an interest in seizing Cyprus from Ptolemy VI, he knew to start with an application to the Roman senate. That body agreed that he could have it, but offered no help, and the matter came to nothing when Ptolemy VI mounted a successful defense. In 155, Ptolemy VIII expressed clearly what was becoming obvious to all – that Rome was dictating their fates. A public decree survives whereby he declared that if he were to die intestate, he would leave his kingdom, at the time just Cyrene, to the Roman people as a bequest (see Primary Source 10.1). The decree is usually interpreted as a response to an assassination attempt by agents of his brother: if Ptolemy VI could be made to gain nothing from killing Ptolemy VIII, presumably they could abide by a form of détente.

Primary Source 10.1

Testament of Ptolemy VIII

In this decree of 155, Ptolemy VIII seems to use Roman support as a trump card against his brother, Ptolemy VI, who apparently was a behind a plot to oust him from the throne in Cyrene. Ptolemy VIII promised to leave his kingdom to Rome should he die prematurely, provisions which were never carried out as Ptolemy VIII came to bear many heirs and was eventually able to return to Alexandria when his brother died in 145.

> "This is the testament of Ptolemy (VIII), *basileus*, the younger son of Ptolemy (V), *basileus*, and of Cleopatra (I), *basilissa*, gods manifest. A copy of this has been conveyed to Rome. May it be (possible) for me with the blessings of the gods to take justifiable revenge on those who formed a despicable plot against me and endeavored to take not only my kingdom but also my life. But if any mortal end should befall me before I have left successors (*diadochoi*) for my kingdom, I leave to the Romans the kingdom belonging to me, for whom friendship and willing alliance have been undertaken by me from the start. To them I transfer my property, beseeching them by all the gods and by their good name that if anyone were to come against my cities or my land, may they assist with all their strength, in keeping with the friendship and alliance that we rightly hold for one another. I call as witness the Zeus of the Capitoline and the great gods and Helios and Apollo Archegetes ("founder"), to whom these words are also consecrated. With good fortune (*tyche*)."

If one were to identify a trouble spot for Rome at this time, it would be the Seleucids. In 162, two years into the reign of the regent Lysias and boy-king Antiochus V (Chapter 9), the senate dispatched an inspector to look into stories of the Seleucids' rearmament. The envoy, Gnaeus Octavius, indeed found more warships and more battle elephants than permissible and ordered their destruction. The man was rash, we are told, and a protester assassinated him, which would surely bring retribution. Moreover, in 162, Demetrius Soter took it upon himself to escape from his captivity in Rome. He had petitioned the senate for his release for years with the argument that with both his father, Seleucus IV, and uncle, Antiochus IV, now dead, he was serving as hostage for no one, but the senate still found it more useful to keep him in Italy. In gripping detail (see Primary Source 10.2), Polybius describes how he himself helped the young prince fabricate an alibi of a hunting expedition outside Rome so that his overseers would not notice that anything was amiss for the first two or three days after

---

Primary Source 10.2

Polybius, *Histories*

In this passage, the historian Polybius recounts how he (referring to himself by name and in the third person) helped Demetrius Soter, hostage in Rome for the Seleucid court, escape from captivity. It is interesting to find that the historian, who owed much to Scipio Aemilianus as his patron, was willing to describe actions that seemingly undermined Roman authority. Note also the role that easy, everyday connections with both Carthage and Ptolemy played in the plot.

31.11.4–5; 12.6–11; 13.4–5; 14.11–13: "Demetrius, excited at the announcement [that the senate treated the sitting king of the Seleucids in a cold manner] called upon Polybius and indicated his uncertainty about whether he should appeal [his status as a hostage] with the senate. Polybius entreated him not to trip on the same stone, but to have faith in himself and to dare some action worthy of a king, for many opportunities were evident. [… Nevertheless, against Polybius's advice, Demetrius did appeal to the senate and asked to be released, but the senate refused …] Demetrius, having sung his swan's song, realized what Polybius meant by not tripping on the same stone … All he had to do was find a way out from Rome undetected, with no-one discerning his plan. Having made up his mind, he sent for Polybius, asking for his help and calling upon him to help him plot his escape. It happened that a certain Menyllus of Alabanda was present as an ambassador for king Ptolemy (VI) in order to confront and debate the younger Ptolemy (VIII) (see the disputes between the brothers, above). This decided it, for Polybius knew Menyllus well and trusted him. Thinking he was well suited for the task at hand, Polybius introduced him to Demetrius with much care and admiration. Menyllus agreed to participate in the plan and promised to find a ship and prepare everything else for the voyage. He found anchored in the harbor of the Tiber a Carthaginian vessel for sacred offerings and rented it out. … With the day for the voyage drawing near, it was necessary to plan a gathering at the house of one of Demetrius's friends, in order to justify Demetrius going out, for he could not have a banquet at home since he always invited everyone in his retinue. [… Demetrius led others to believe that he was going on a hunting excursion outside the city …] Demetrius and his attendants arrived (at the ship) at the end of the third watch. There were eight slaves in all – five grown and three boys. After Menyllus conferred with them and showed them the supplies, and introduced them to the captain of the ship and his crew, they boarded and the pilot pulled up the anchor and set sail as dawn began to rise, having no idea what was going on, but thinking he was carrying some soldiers from Menyllus to Ptolemy."

Demetrius had fled. Polybius also reports that he was the one who found secret passage for Demetrius on a ship bound for Egypt, and heartened the prince when he seemed to be wavering. In many ways the episode reads as a statement of the historian's own independence, in the form of his willingness to betray, dupe, and thwart the very Romans who were housing him, and to abet one of their enemies. This resistance to Rome seems to be at odds with other parts of Polybius's famous text, where his admiration for Roman institutions is paramount, such as his praise of the Roman constitution: perhaps the historian, a former anti-Roman statesman (Chapter 9), wanted to show to his Greek readership back home that he was hardly a Roman stooge.

10.3 Royal Pretenders

The Romans had placed Ariarathes V and Ptolemy VI on their thrones, and with the help of Attalus II, who would succeed his brother Eumenes II as king of Pergamon in 159, would eventually do the same for Nicomedes II in Bithynia (in the late 150s), but Demetrius Soter, as a fugitive and a renegade and not a deliberate plant, was viewed as a usurper from the Roman point of view. In 161 Rome formally recognized the Maccabaean regime in Jerusalem as a way of gaining an ally arrayed on Soter's southern border. In the 150s, the Romans plotted further to replace Soter; their candidate was a conveniently discovered long-lost son of Antiochus IV, who took the name Alexander Balas (see Figure 10.2). Ptolemy VI and Ariarathes V lent assistance, making Balas's bid a thoroughly corporate affair. It would still be years before they were successful: Demetrius Soter stormed into Jerusalem, and Judas Maccabaeus was himself killed and replaced by his brother, Jonathan. Finally in 150, Soter was trapped and fell in battle and Alexander Balas had the crown. Now with an army to back his dynastic pretensions, Balas was legitimized even further by marriage to Cleopatra Thea, a daughter of Ptolemy VI and Cleopatra II.

The mechanism of the "found heir," which Rome used to its advantage with Alexander Balas, came to bedevil them soon after. A shadowy figure named Andriscus claimed to be a son of Perseus and quickly threw together a strong army in Thrace, inaugurating what moderns call the Fourth Macedonian War. His speed in conquering the four republics set up by Rome in Macedonia is another case of an imperial tactic backfiring on its perpetrators: so thoroughly had the senate weakened the new Macedonia that Rome's rivals had an easy time of advancing there. Attalus II once managed to capture Andriscus and planned to send him to Rome, but Andriscus managed to escape. It took until 148 for the Roman consul Quintus Caecilius Metellus to defeat him. This time the Romans did away with the four republics and organized Macedonia into a formal province of the Roman empire, its fifth after Sicily, Sardinia, and the two Spains; Metellus then took on the epithet Macedonicus.

When Rome was dealing with monarchies, it gained entrée to their affairs through members of a royal family; when it was dealing with other forms of government – oligarchies, or, federations of cities – it meddled in different ways, making use of the politics available to them. Polybius, for example, returned from hostageship to his hometown of Megalopolis in the Achaean League in 150 and assumed a position of authority as a kind of representative of Rome. He retained close ties to Scipio Aemilianus and conducted himself, at least outwardly, in "pro-Roman" ways. His writings, however, still left room for the subversion of Roman overlordship, as seen in his story of Demetrius's escape, and, to be discussed, his account of the origins of a new war against Carthage.

Figure 10.2 A comparison of coins from the Seleucid dynasty, including the "pretender" Alexander Balas, alleged son of Antiochus IV, who used his likeness on coins to assert a relationship to the dynasty. (a) Silver tetradrachm with Antiochus IV (obv.) and Zeus enthroned holding Nike (rev.), 175–165 BCE. (b) Silver tetradrachm with Alexander Balas (obv.) and an eagle in front of a palm branch (rev.), 150/149 BCE. (c) Silver tetradrachm of Alexander Balas and Cleopatra Thea (obv.) and Zeus enthroned holding Nike (rev.), 150–145 BCE.

10.4 The Morality of Empire

Two separate but related themes are worthy of comment in sorting through the typical confusion of Mediterranean geopolitics in the mid-second century. First, a growing sense of cosmopolitanism, noted in several of the preceding chapters, was continuing apace, to the point of a reconceptualization of ethnicity itself. One's identity became as flexible and free as physical movement had become among the various realms of the Mediterranean: from the level of intellectual conversation among elite philosophers to the practice of religion on a more quotidian plane, evidence exists for cross-ethnic cooperation, albeit still under terms set by prevailing Hellenism. Within the context of a broadening *oikoumene*, a second trend of the second-century may be explained: a growing sense of morality in imperial management led the Romans to enact laws curbing the abusive practices of their generals and troops in the provinces. Both Romans and those in their orbit began to expect (although also continuously debated the nature of, and not always abided by) a code of right and wrong in international relations.

Some examples of both trends exist in Rome's conduct with Athens and the Achaean League. Just as both Ptolemy VI and Ptolemy VIII claimed to be friends of Rome in their civil war (see above), so too did Athens and the Achaean League in a dispute over the small but religiously significant community of Oropus in northern Attica. Oropus was rejecting Athenian authority and appealed to Rome to pronounce its autonomy. Rome instead looked beyond Attica and appointed Sicyon, an Achaean power, to adjudicate the matter as a regional expert. When Sicyon fined Athens a hefty sum for skipping the tribunal, Athens objected to *Rome*. Athens petitioned Rome to lower the fine, and the debate in the senate took on a global, multiethnic dimension. Appearing before the senate in 155, Athens's delegation was led by the heads of its three major philosophical schools – Carneades of the Academy, Critolaus of the Peripatetics, and Diogenes of the Stoics. As Christian Habicht has pointed out, all three hailed from elsewhere than Athens – Cyrene, Lycia, and Babylon, respectively. In presenting their case against Sicyon, the philosophers were essentially arguing against the Achaean League, of which Sicyon was a leading member and whose thousand detainees, discussed above, would have still been prominent in Rome, perhaps even milling about the senate itself. Polybius, himself an Achaean present in Rome, exhibits a negative opinion of the philosophers. The debate achieved a compromise: Athens would still have to pay the fine, but it would be substantially reduced.

It may be that a Carthaginian, remade as a Greek, was also present at this remarkable synod: a certain Hasdrubal (different from the many like-named generals throughout this book) is known to have moved to Athens in the course of the 150s. He joined the Academy and changed his name to Cleitomachus, thoroughly Hellenic, and achieved sufficient notoriety that he headed the school when Carneades died in 129. Despite his name change, he still thought of himself as Punic, such that when Carthage fell in 146 (discussed below), from his safe perch in Athens he drafted a consolation for his brethren that was still famous in Cicero's day.

Delos, in particular, is a good spot for finding several inscriptions that bespeak the negotiations inherent in cosmopolitanism, as brokered by Rome. In 152 a Roman was dabbling in the Phoenician iteration of a Greek cult on Delos: an inscription records how a banker named Marcus Minatius gave an interest-free loan, plus a free grant of initial seed money, for a guild of Poseidon worshippers from Berytus (modern Beirut) to foster a sanctuary for their cult. Minatius was accordingly honored by the group with both a statue and a painted portrait. Similarly, in the same year and also in Delos, worshippers of the Phoenician god Melqart, transplanted to the island from Tyre, asked for permission from Athens to build a shrine that would effectively syncretize their hero-deity with the Hellenic Heracles, and permission was so granted. Delos is also the locus for a statue of Masinissa and his son that was put up by

Nicomedes II at this time, thus effecting the unlikely pairing of Numidians of North Africa, newcomers to this world, with a hyper-Hellenic Bithynian.

Perhaps influenced by a new fluidity to ethnicity, this period also saw greater adherence to geopolitical decorum in diplomacy and international relations. Rome abided by a sense of reciprocity in its foreign policy, to the extent that it was consonant with their needs. When Gnaeus Octavius was assassinated while on his harsh diplomatic mission to Antioch (see above), his assailant dared to demand a day in court in Rome to justify his actions. He was dismissed (and executed) as a criminal outside the law, but the very fact of his petition suggests that the relationship between the powers was not that of an omnipotent hegemon and a subject, but rather was characterized by an expectation of a rule of law. The Romans put such reciprocity into effect in Spain around the same time. Action had picked up once again in the Spanish provinces after the settlements of Sempronius Gracchus (Chapter 9) had deteriorated under more rapacious governors. From 155 to 152, various Roman praetors in Spain had prosecuted ambitious wars that took them into Lusitania (modern Portugal) and even across the Straits of Gibraltar into Africa. In 150, Sergius Sulpicius Galba defeated a particularly thorny tribe in Lusitania through a ruse: he promised them territory of their own should they surrender, but then reneged and slaughtered them when their weapons were down. A faction of senators judged his actions to be incompatible with a kind of battlefield chivalry and brought Galba up on charges. He was ultimately acquitted, but the case gave rise to the implementation of a special court for cases of provincial corruption, established by the *Lex Calpurnia de repetundis* in 149. Even so, the court's juries were to be staffed by fellow senators, so its effectiveness and objectivity could be seen as compromised.

The Iberian campaigns also saw changes in the effect that empire and imperial campaigns had on Rome's own soldiers. The Spanish theater was unusually harsh, with lesser rewards than the East and more by way of hardship, given not only the conditions but also the distances to travel. It was believed that the soldiers and officers who had political connections were managing to dodge the assignment in favor of richer prizes. The nonelite soldiers balked and the tribunes were driven to imprison the consuls in 151 until systems were put in place whereby overseas assignments were determined by lot. With many senators refusing to participate in Spain owing to its challenges, Scipio Aemilianus, the son of Aemilius Paullus who had been adopted out to the Scipiones, volunteered for the service and thus began his political rise.

10.5 The Carthage-Corinth Coincidence

Just because institutions and practices for geopolitical negotiation and provincial administration were developing in Rome did not mean that bald displays of power were in the past. Two great Hellenistic cities, Carthage and Corinth, were destroyed by Rome in the same year, 146, in ways that would be questioned almost immediately as unjust acts.

Cato the Elder, in particular, nursed a suspicion of Carthage. In the years since the settlement of 201 that ended the Second Punic War, Carthage had returned to prosperity, and had even offered to pay off the entire balance of the war indemnity decades ahead of schedule, in 191 – a petition that the senate denied. The Carthaginians poured resources into building a state-of-the-art, two-stage harbor, whose entrance was protected by a massive, manmade mole and whose utility was extended by means of a platform constructed over the water (see Figure 10.3). Ships could pass through the first artificial harbor into a second, which was round and lined with docks, with an island in the middle topped by an observation tower from which all activity could be monitored and managed. Cato the Elder viewed such developments with alarm and

Figure 10.3 Artist's reconstruction of the harbor of Carthage on the eve of the Third Punic War.

began preparing a case against Carthage well before the treaty was due to expire in 151. He began to circulate a slogan, *Carthago delenda est*, or, Carthage must be destroyed (or, "deleted"). Students of Latin grammar will know that the verb form *delenda* – a future passive participle, used to express absolute necessity, or, something that *will be done* – implied that there would be no time or space for niceties like diplomacy, arbitration, or even conversation. Perhaps not coincidentally, around this time Cato also published the *Origines*, a glorification of Rome's past rather like Ennius's *Annales* but wholly different for being composed in steely prose rather than Hellenic dactylic hexameter.

According to Polybius, the eventual Third Punic War, a far briefer and more lopsided affair than the First and Second, was precipitated by perfidious and greedy actions on the part of the Romans. Throughout the period of the Zama treaty, Carthage had consistently yielded to the demands of Rome's regional allies: in the course of the 150s, the Romans twice supported their vassal Masinissa when he requisitioned Carthaginian lands, and in both cases, Carthage acquiesced. Once the terms of the treaty had been met in 151, however, a faction of anti-Romanists in Carthage felt confident enough to propose policies of self-preservation. When the Numidians claimed ownership of yet another parcel of land in 151, these new statesmen challenged Masinissa, and when Masinissa's sons were sent to discuss terms, they drove them from the city in an ignominious way.

The Roman response came with disproportionate vigor. An embassy arrived to Carthage and issued harsh demands. What is more, according to Polybius, the demands were released not at once but in a piecemeal sequence, such that the next debilitating requirement was not known until the one before it had been achieved. The Romans first asked for hostages, and Carthage complied. The Romans then asked for all Carthaginian armor and weaponry; so sacred was the hostage-based agreement that Polybius suggests that such a demand was a breach of trust, but even so the Carthaginians complied. We are told that it was only when Rome issued a third order – that the city be abandoned, its buildings be razed, and the residents be relocated inland to any position so long as it was 10 miles from the sea – that the demand was refused. It was, after all, unthinkable: not only was one's attachment to home sentimental and irremediable, to give the city up would be tantamount to nonexistence. Niceties removed, the Roman fleet settled into a siege of Carthage in 149.

Around the same time, Rome also confronted a challenge in the new province of Macedonia. Metellus, now called Macedonicus (Chapter 9), was worried about his south. Signs of a civil war had been brewing there as Sparta again pondered independence from the Achaean League. Macedonicus issued an abrupt message to both sides to cease and desist. It might have been read as another Day of Eleusis except that this time it did not work. Callicrates, who had managed Achaean affairs for years with Rome's wishes in mind (Chapter 9), had died, and the League was in the hands of Critolaus, a less demurring leader. He spoke out against the Romans and used the device of populism – relief from debt and access to land – to win over adherents. In 147, the senate, as punishment for questioning Roman orders, declared Sparta, Corinth, Argos, Heraclea, and Orchomenus all to be free from the Achaean League, which was rather like its call for Carthage to move inland: it essentially marked the end of a historic power. To the Achaeans, war became an absolute necessity.

Back in Carthage, the siegeworks outside the city were growing in strength as the Roman generals picked off the nearby towns that still professed loyalty to Carthage. Masinissa died and Scipio Aemilianus dictated the division of power among three of his heirs, Micipsa, Gulussa, and Mastarnabal. Scipio also received ships from Mithridates V, the new king of Pontus. Desperate, the Carthaginian Hasdrubal (yet another personage with the popular name) emancipated slaves for service in his army and engineered round-the-clock rearmament methods, since the city had surrendered all its artillery previously. Nevertheless, Scipio Aemilianus took the city. Polybius, who had exposed the anti-Punic maneuvers of 151 as amoral, now attributed to Scipio, his patron, a heroic contemplation of the burning city: in his account, Scipio's reaction to the sack was to weep because, as he is said to have explained to Polybius, he knew that one day the same fate would befall Rome – an ironic lesson, veiled and discursive, from the historian to his readership in Greece that Roman power had its limits.

Carthage's territory was turned into the province of Africa, and the city itself was left to ruin. Among Rome's greatest advantages from the war were its deepening ties to Numidia. Micipsa, one of the kings, eventually sent one of his sons, Jugurtha, to be a kind of hostage-cum-apprentice to Scipio Aemilianus when he was on campaign in nearby Spain some years later.

Not far to the northeast, in Greece, the new consul Lucius Mummius, who had cut his teeth in complex operations against the Lusitanians in 155, swept down from Macedonicus's province against Corinth. According to reports, the Romans, assisted as they were by Attalus II, greatly outnumbered the Achaean League. The Achaeans let themselves be cajoled into battle in spite of the long odds against them, and were summarily crushed. Like Carthage, Corinth was destroyed and not allowed to be resettled.

10.6   The Roman Reorganization of Egypt, 145–139

Following the annihilation of Carthage and Corinth in 146, a third major battle came in 145. Alexander Balas, it will be remembered, had risen to the top of the Seleucid realm with a likely falsified pedigree, a host of allies, and a new powerful spouse, Cleopatra Thea. In the few intervening years, a son of Demetrius Soter, who came to be known as Demetrius II, grew restless on Crete, where he had been raised for safekeeping, and launched a bid to take his father's throne. For some reason, Ptolemy VI, once a Roman ally, chose to switch to his side and had his daughter Cleopatra Thea divorce Balas. Demetrius II, now joined by Egyptian armies and his new Ptolemaic/Seleucid wife Cleopatra Thea, defeated Balas at the Battle of the Oinoparas River in 145. Alexander Balas was killed while in flight, but Ptolemy VI also died shortly after as a result of wounds; it is suggested that one of his final sights was of Balas's decapitated head.

The victory of a rather weak king, Demetrius II, created yet more opportunities for Romans to dabble in regional politics, in measure with their level of interest. A Roman officer, Lucius Minucius Thermus, quickly played a role in promoting Ptolemy VIII to the vacant throne of Egypt. The promotion took not just Roman support but that of several players in Egypt, such as the military elite, represented by Boethus of Caria; the dynastic remnants, most notably Cleopatra II, Ptolemy VI's widow and sister to Ptolemy VIII; and the indigenous Egyptians, whose priests constituted their most powerful class. One group that Ptolemy VIII did not see fit to assuage was the Greek intellectuals and members of the Jewish diaspora that had voiced strong support for his now dead older brother. Many of the immigrant populations are known to have abandoned the Library by the late 140s and resettled in the "old" Greek world. One of the displaced, Galaistes, an Epirote prince who had fled to Egypt after the Battle of Pydna in 168, tried to mount a campaign to return to Alexandria in 141, carting behind him an alleged son of Ptolemy VI (a third "pretender" in this chapter after Alexander Balas and Andriscus), but was defeated.

The device of the marriage alliance was put through ever more torturous paces: Ptolemy VIII now married his sister Cleopatra II and had a son by her, Ptolemy Memphites, only to take as another wife Cleopatra's daughter by Ptolemy VI, called Cleopatra III, in 142. The façade of a new, peaceful, tripartite throne was thus on display – Ptolemy VIII with a sister and with a niece, both named Cleopatra and both now his wives. Scipio Aemilianus arrived on the scene in 139 to evaluate their reigning status. Polybius revels in recounting the contrast between the strong and vigorous Scipio Aemilianus and the fat, sweaty Ptolemy VIII, dressed in silk that clung to his wet skin as he struggled to keep up in walks through the heat of Alexandria. Thermus had set this reorganization in motion in 145, and now Scipio Aemilianus saw to its resolution six years later.

In the meantime, Cleopatra Thea, the older sister of Cleopatra III, was trying to hold on to power among the Seleucids. She and Demetrius II were very soon on the run from Antioch, as a redoubtable general, Diodotus, deployed an alleged son of Alexander Balas, a fourth "pretender," to justify *his* own power. Two competing courts squared off, one in Antioch, where Diodotus advised the now-named Antiochus VI, and the other in Seleuceia-in-Pieria, Demetrius II and Cleopatra Thea's refuge. In 142, Demetrius II was taken prisoner in an engagement with the Parthians in his East. Cleopatra Thea, undeterred, contacted his brother Antiochus VII Sidetes, who arrived from his base on Rhodes. By 138, a year after Scipio Aemilianus had acknowledged the new Ptolemaic regime in Egypt, Cleopatra Thea and Antiochus VII swept back into Antioch, having toppled Diodotus, who himself had already had Antiochus VI killed. For the next decade or so, the Seleucids seemed to have finally retained a ruling pair worthy of the throne's responsibility, and Cleopatra Thea and Antiochus VII Sidetes reasserted themselves against the Judaean and Parthian regimes on their borders.

The year 138 also saw a regime-change in Pergamon. Attalus II had likely surprised everyone in lasting 20 years from his accession in 158 at the age of 60. During his time in power, he rebuilt his kingdom's relationship with Rome, coming to their aid on numerous occasions – in bringing Alexander Balas to power over the Seleucids; in sending a navy to help against Andriscus; in establishing the Roman student Nicomedes II in Bithynia; and in providing troops to the siege of Corinth. He died of natural causes and power passed to his nephew, Attalus III, who was the son of Eumenes II. Not much is known of Attalus III's brief reign. His biggest claim to fame was his decision to leave the kingdom of Pergamon to the people of Rome when he died, which was in 133. The will was unorthodox but not quite unprecedented, given Ptolemy VIII's similar gambit of 155 whereby he published an *intent* to leave Cyrene to the Roman people upon his death (above). Attalus III's bequest of wealthy Pergamon rocked the city of Rome, not just for the amount of wealth and prestige that it represented, but also for its timing, which was utterly convenient in assisting an up-and-coming reformer in radically altering the Roman economy and the political and military systems.

10.7 Economic Crisis and the Rise of the Tribunate

The chain reaction of failed practices in Rome's political economy in the mid-second century is famous and was articulated even in antiquity. The legions had long been manned by recruits who met a minimum property qualification. In most cases, as in any ancient economy, livelihoods were to be had through agriculture, and one would not be far off the mark to visualize Roman legions as assemblages of small-time farmers. Such a system worked adequately when Rome's interests were bound by the Italian coastline, or when overseas campaigning was part of emergency measures that dispersed at the end of the summer fighting season. The system also held for a time after Rome's ambitions abroad had first become permanent, in the 180s and thereafter with the foundation of provinces in Sicily, Spain, Greece, and Africa. But, in the space of a generation or two, the small family farms that sponsored the soldiers began to fold in the absence of hands to work the land. Those dispossessed of their plots tended to move to cities, where state-funded distributions of grain and greater economic opportunity were concentrated. Two vestiges of these trends reveal the dramatic nature of change in the second century. First, the population of Rome grew rapidly, and in a haphazard way unfamiliar to residents of the highly planned metropolises of the Hellenistic East. Second, the property qualifications necessary to be a Roman soldier were lowered. In 202, a net worth of 11 000 *aes* (a basic bronze coin) had been required of soldiers, but by 151, it had been reduced to 4000. This downward shift of standards reflects a more restricted supply coupled with a greater demand.

Exacerbating the problem was a widening gap between the very wealthy and the ordinary citizen. Statistics of the kind that describe modern economic trends are not available for ancient Rome, but a number of signs point to the gross enrichment of aristocratic families, especially if they had *imperium*-bearing praetors, consuls, propraetors, and proconsuls in their ranks. Those tasked with governing a territory could skim off the top of the peacetime revenues they collected in the form of taxes, in spite of the founding of extortion courts in 149. Those who hoarded the new wealth had no shortage of places to spend it. For one, the land being vacated by the displaced farmer-soldiers described above could be had at reasonable rates. A relatively small number of elites thus built up massive estates. Included in their portfolio was not just land that they owned outright but also parcels of *ager publicus*, or public fields, which had initially been won from defeated Italian neighbors and were now leased from the Republic. Such large estates demanded a substantial workforce, and here again, affordable solutions were in the offing: slaves were more plentiful than ever in the form of prisoners of war, a byproduct of the same imperialist process that had created the new wealth. Large-scale slave revolts from this period, not only in Italy and Sicily but also in Athens, Pergamon, and even Delos, whose steep rise in fortunes was owed to the burgeoning slave trade, reveal an obvious problem to an economy so based.

The discontent of slaves need not only come from their physical condition, but could also have an ethnic dimension. The most extensive rebellion at this time was that led by a slave named Eunus, in central Sicily. He came from Apamea-on-Orontes in the heart of the

Seleucid corner of the Mediterranean and is said to have worshiped the Syrian Atargatis as his native goddess. Upon freeing large gangs of slaves in 135, sacking the nearby city of Enna and inspiring slaves around Agrigentum to do the same, Eunus is said to have claimed to be an heir to the Antiochus name and even declared himself a *basileus*. Such pronouncements are often written off as coming from a mad man, or of a propagandist appealing to either the gullible or the irreverent, but there is no reason not to envision a sincere, would-be dynast, calling upon Greek-speaking prisoners of war to seize what had historically been a Greek-speaking realm – Sicily. In the days of Alexander Balas of the Seleucids, Andriscus of Macedonia, and so-called sons of Balas and Ptolemy VI, a "king" Eunus/Antiochus, a fifth such pretender in this chapter, deserved to be taken seriously. The Roman senate certainly felt that way: in 134 they assigned a full consular army to the problem, and it took three seasons – just as long as the Second Macedonian and Third Punic Wars – before the revolt was put down, in 132.

The twin problems of the shrinking of the soldier stock and the risk of rebellions led by slaves called for a political solution. Just as new forms and levels of wealth were to be had, so too were new forms and levels of political power. The urban core of Rome had grown in population and, consequently, also in influence. Since the days of the Struggle of the Orders (Chapter 2), the tribunes of the plebs had held important functions in the legislative and electoral processes, but in practice, the Roman senate, by virtue of its wealth and its virtually lifetime appointment held much de facto sway. In this period tribunes became more assertive, and as new precedents were won, others accrued. In 145, the tribune Gaius Licinius Crassus found the space where his audience had assembled to hear him – between the speaker's platform, or rostra, and the senate house – to be too confining, and so did an about-face and moved the crowd to the wide central piazza of the Forum itself. This "pirouette," as Robert Morstein-Marx memorably called it, altered the topography of the city for centuries to come and evoked in physical space new political realities. Tribunes followed on, in 139, 137, and 131, with laws calling for secret ballots in, respectively, elections, jury decisions, and legislative initiatives. With the new reforms, no longer could a powerful senator monitor the choices of those among his clients who depended upon him. Tribunes went so far as imprisoning consuls, in 151 (as we have seen) and in 138, when they were judged to be abusing recruitment practices for the legions, giving prestigious assignments to friends, and sending others to less lucrative campaigns. Just as tribunes might hinder a consul, they could also act to appoint one: in 148, Scipio Aemilianus was both too young for a consulship and had not yet held the prerequisite office of praetor, but he was able to convince a tribune to propose a law, ad hominem, granting him special eligibility. The measure passed, upon which Scipio went on to command legions in the Third Punic War, a task that was also assigned to him through the popular vote rather than by lot, another unprecedented reform that was wrought by a tribune.

Tribunes were not only acting on behalf of populist, nonelite agendas, but could also be deployed in feuds between aristocratic factions. Note that in the case of Scipio Aemilianus the tribune was working at the behest of one of the most influential senatorial clans. Another vivid example of the trend came in 143: a consul, Appius Claudius Pulcher, was denied a triumph by the senate for a victory over a Celtic tribe. In brazen defiance, Pulcher marched through the city anyway, in full triumphal accoutrement. A tribune who must have been acting on behalf of the senate tried to veto him, but Pulcher trumped him with yet another unprecedented device of political authority: his daughter, Claudia, who was a Vestal Virgin and thus as inviolable as a tribune, forbade any interference. Either this bold Claudia, it should be noted, or a sister of the same name (see Chapter 2 for the problems that arise from the limited naming practices for Roman women) would go on to marry the tribune Tiberius Gracchus.

10.8 The Reforms of Tiberius Gracchus

The rising tide of the office of the tribune and the need to resolve Rome's agrarian crisis intersected in the career of Tiberius Gracchus. He was a son of the consul Tiberius Sempronius Gracchus, who had triumphed over Spain, and of Cornelia, the daughter of Scipio Africanus. He was also linked to Scipio Aemilianus, both through marriage, as Scipio married Sempronia, Tiberius's sister, and through adoption, since Scipio was an adult adoptee of Cornelia's brother, making them cousins after a fashion (see above). In spite of this filial link (or potentially because of it) Scipio and Tiberius became rivals. They clashed openly over the question of a treaty in Spain in 137, which Tiberius, who had served in the theater, had a role in negotiating, but which Scipio had quashed for being too lenient with the enemy. In the same year that Scipio won a spectacular victory over the Spanish town of Numantia, Tiberius Gracchus stood for tribune of the plebs and was elected.

In office, Tiberius took up the issue of land reform with a view to alleviating the host of problems outlined above. His principal gambit, it turned out, was simply to enforce laws that had long been "on the books" but which had been in abeyance for centuries, so as to be effectively defunct. Namely, the Licinio-Sextian Laws of 367, it seems (the sources are problematic), had long restricted the leasing of the *ager publicus* to 500 *iugera* per person, about 325 acres (Chapter 2). In Tiberius Gracchus's plan of 133, the 500 *iugera* limit would be returned to practice, but not without some compromises to counteract its unpopularity with the powerful leaseholders. Keeping inheritance in mind, for example, the law would allow leaseholders to keep an additional 250 *iugera* per son, up to two sons, thus making it theoretically possible for one to use 1000 *iugera* of *ager publicus*. A provision also made allowances for land that had been substantially improved at the leaseholder's expense: if an estate had been cleared of stumps and boulders, for example, the person responsible for the investment could make a case for continuing at that plot. Beyond these provisions, any excess *ager publicus* would revert to the state and would, to Gracchus's argument, redound to the strength and health of Rome in the form of thousands of small parcels of land to be distributed to families who would, in turn, "produce" soldiers just as much as they would crops.

However respectful of leaseholders Tiberius's proposals may seem, the law still spelled limits where there had been none before and so inspired angry opposition. The ire of wealthy senators was further stoked by Tiberius's methods in seeing his law through, which were staggering in their level of provocation. First, anticipating resistance, Tiberius skipped the step of presenting his ideas before the senate, and instead took his bill straight to the popular assembly. It was not illegal for Tiberius to bypass senatorial review, but it was unconventional. Bristling at their exclusion, the senate at first embarked on parliamentary procedures to block him: they convinced (bribed?) Marcus Octavius, one of Tiberius's colleagues in the tribunate, to exercise his legal right to veto the legislation. Tiberius countered with a new law removing Octavius from office. Technically Tiberius's maneuver complied with the letter of the law, but in practice it clearly set up a paradox as Octavius could presumably veto the law against him and then draft one against Tiberius: what should prevent the tribunes from being locked in an eternal cycle of counter-vetoes? It was the force of the crowd, in the end, that won the day for Gracchus, and Octavius was forced from office.

Tiberius's resolve continued: with the law passed, a commission was drawn up to oversee the distribution of land, and the three principal staffers would be none other than Tiberius himself, his younger brother Gaius, and Tiberius's father-in-law, Appius Claudius Pulcher, who with his powerful daughter had defied convention themselves in putting on his illegal triumph a decade earlier. The senate tried to eviscerate the commission's agenda by not allocating any funds to it, such that they would not be able to carry out the expensive bureaucratic and engineering tasks associated with surveying land. It was at this moment that word came of the death of Attalus III and the bequest of Pergamon to the Roman people. Gracchus lost no time in introducing a new law, namely that Pergamene resources should be diverted to the land commission, essentially never even entering the treasury and thus never falling under the senate's purview. Once again, an irresistible force clashed with an immoveable object: the letter of the law had imbued the tribunate with powers that could, in the right (or wrong) hands, contradict the very existence of another "branch" of government, the Roman senate.

With an eye on the calendar, the anti-Gracchan faction in the senate could see that the year was coming to a close. Once Tiberius's term as tribune was up, he would no longer have his precious veto, nor could he set the agenda for public meetings, nor would he be shielded by his office's *sacrosanctitas*. The senate, with its lifetime membership, was prepared to wait out the year before undoing Gracchus's reforms, but again, they were thwarted by the unexpected: Tiberius announced that he would run for tribune again, expecting to stay in power for a second year. Reelection to a consecutive term, along with removing one's rival tribunes, stacking a commission, and redirecting revenues to one's whim, was another gray area in terms of the law.

Tiberius's ambition was undeniable, and to some in the senate, it was dangerous. One of the consuls, Publius Mucius Scaevola, acquiesced to Tiberius's unorthodox reelection; other senators cried nepotism since Scaevola's brother was an in-law of Tiberius. Just as Hellenistic monarchs were often undone by rival relatives, Gracchus was finally confronted by his own cousin, Publius Cornelius Scipio Nasica, the pontifex maximus (their mothers were sisters). Nasica gathered likeminded senators and their henchmen at the Temple of Fides, or Loyalty, a small building just off the open space in front of the Temple of Jupiter Capitolinus where Gracchus's crowd was assembled. A melee ensued in which Gracchus was killed. A tribune had thus been assailed in spite of his sacrosanctity, at once a violation of both religious and political precedent. Tensions were thus at a fever pitch, even as Rome's power overseas was tracing an ever upward trajectory.

10.9 Conclusions

For centuries Roman historians labeled the two political camps at work in the controversy surrounding Tiberius Gracchus as the *populares* – those who pursued initiatives by appealing to the people – and the *optimates* – those who, by contrast, preferred senatorial avenues to power. The terms are largely a modern invention with little grounding in the ancient sources, but they will be applied occasionally in subsequent chapters as a convenient shorthand. Even so, the reader should take care not to associate the *optimates* with the rich and the *populares* with the poor. Tiberius Gracchus, a *popularis* hero, was fantastically wealthy, as were many of his supporters. And the *optimates* senators who opposed him no doubt deployed clients from among the nonelite. Rather, many have attributed the bloodshed not to greed on both sides for public farms, but to Tiberius's constant manipulation and reinterpretation of laws, practices, and powers that had been the status quo for centuries. The *optimates*, as well, as we shall see in the next chapter, became just as creative in "finding" new powers, prompting more and greater public violence.

The use of newly conjured extralegal (as opposed to strictly il-legal) powers by elected officials in the Republic, whether tribunes, consuls, or senators, is analogous to the phenomenon of the royal pretender – the "found" heir – simultaneously deployed with increasing regularity in Hellenistic contests. Both tactics involved a façade of legitimacy – on the one hand, in the case of royals, an attestation of blood relations and perhaps a physiognomic likeness, either real or, via stylized portraits in sculpture or on coins, imagined; or on the other hand, in the context of the Roman Republic, a stylized interpretation of precedent and the locus of authority. Both cases have radical politics in common.

Further Reading

Astin, Alan (2002). *Scipio Aemilianus.* Oxford: Oxbow Books.
Chrubasik, Boris (2016). *Kings and Usurpers in the Seleucid Empire.* Oxford: Oxford University Press.
Eckstein, Arthur (1995). *Moral Vision in the Histories of Polybius.* Berkeley: University of California Press.
Morstein-Marx, Robert (2004). *Mass Oratory and Political Power in the Late Republic.* Cambridge: Cambridge University Press.
Orlin, Eric (1997). *Temples, Religion, and Politics in Republican Rome.* Leiden: Brill.
Roselaar, Saskia (2010). *Public Land in the Roman Republic: a Social and Economic History of Ager Publicus in Italy, 369-83 BC.* Oxford: Oxford University Press.
Rosenstein, Nathan (1990). *Imperatores Victi: Military Defeat and Aristocratic Competition in the Middle and Late Republic.* Berkeley: University of California Press.

11

To 101: The "New Men" of Rome and the Mediterranean

Timeline

132–130: War between Rome and Aristonicus, alleged son of Eumenes II, for Pergamon
131–124: Civil war among Ptolemaic dynasts, culminating in reign of Ptolemy VIII, Cleopatra II, and Cleopatra III
c. 130: Failed bid by Harsiese for pharaonate in Egypt
127–123: Failed campaign of Alexander Zabinas, alleged son of Antiochus VII, for the throne of the Seleucids
122–121: Tribunate of Gaius Sempronius Gracchus
116: Deaths of Ptolemy VIII and Cleopatra II; shared rule among Cleopatra III, Ptolemy IX, and Ptolemy X
115: Accession of Mithridates VI of Pontus
112–105: War between Rome and Jugurtha of Numidia
107, 104–100: Six consulships of Gaius Marius
104–101: War between Rome and the Celts
102: Campaign of Marcus Antonius against pirates in the Aegean Sea; Mithridatic Monument on Delos
101: Campaign of Manius Aquillius against slave rebellion in Sicily

Principal Themes

- Simultaneous but unconnected populist movements occurred in the 120s in Pergamon, Egypt, and Rome, as existing institutions continued to be challenged by outsiders. Similarly, independent, seemingly rulerless, cooperative societies, for lack of a better term – called "pirates" or "bandits" by their enemies – coalesced in Cilicia, Sicily, and elsewhere.
- Citizenship for Rome's Italian allies became a bone of contention in Rome. Gaius Gracchus's efforts to legislate a solution were met with a new political device created by the senate – the *senatus consultum ultimum*, or, "final decree" of the senate, which could effectively institute martial law.
- Gaius Marius, a *novus homo*, rode to prominence in politics by recruiting legions from the urban poor of Rome for the first time, and by exploiting Roman fears of the Celts of the north: he held the consulship in 107 and for five years in a row from 104 to 100.
- Egypt achieved some stability under the shared rule of the brothers Ptolemy IX and Ptolemy X once they agreed, in effect, to a division of power between Cyprus and Alexandria.

The Roman Republic and the Hellenistic Mediterranean: From Alexander to Caesar, First Edition. Joel Allen.
© 2020 John Wiley & Sons, Inc. Published 2020 by John Wiley & Sons, Inc.

- With the end of the Pergamene dynasty, Asia Minor fell under the sway of Mithridates VI of Pontus, a cosmopolitan *basileus* with ancestors among both Macedonians and Persians and with a firm economic foundation in the Black Sea basin.

11.1 Introduction

The last third of the second century witnessed social movements across the Mediterranean as the overlordship of the Roman senate was challenged both in Italy and in Rome's newest provinces. Just as "the people" gathered behind outsiders to political processes in the Roman Republic – newly empowered tribunes following in lockstep with Tiberius Gracchus – in the Successor kingdoms, additional "pretenders" joined with indigenous, non-Macedonian elites to exercise power in their own right, either in parallel with or in contradiction of the royal aristocracies. A Roman war in Numidia generated the rise of political novices on both sides, as the allegedly illegitimate Jugurtha seized power, and in Rome a *novus homo*, Gaius Marius, won an unlikely election to consul. Marius would go on to introduce major military reforms by enrolling unpropertied citizens into Rome's ranks, which in turn spawned yet more social and political change. He capitalized on the innate Roman dread of the Celts to secure election to five additional terms in the span covered by this chapter (he will be elected once more in Chapter 12, for a total of seven consulships). As the Seleucid dynasty collapsed in on itself under numerous competing heirs and under Ptolemaic influence through its queens, a new power rose in Asia Minor, Mithridates VI of Pontus. The consummate Hellenistic monarch forged a super-cosmopolitan identity, combining heritages and alliances that were as Persian and Parthian as they were Greek.

11.2 Aristonicus and the People of Pergamon

Rome's annexation of Pergamon was not as easy as simply enacting the terms of Attalus III's will (Chapter 10). Two factors militated against takeover and transition. First, the leadership in Rome was riven over the question of what to do with the windfall, as we have seen, and their disagreements led to inconsistent policies and failed military campaigns on Pergamene soil. Second, those living in Pergamene territory evidently had not been consulted and were far from sanguine about Roman suzerainty: a significant segment of the population, largely hailing from the agricultural hinterland (while the city of Pergamon itself was friendly to Rome) backed an alleged son of the Attalid dynasty named Aristonicus. Quickly assuming the royal name of Eumenes III and the title *basileus*, the pretender attempted to drive off the profusion of Roman generals who arrived looking to consolidate.

The Pergamenes could be forgiven for not only rejecting Roman control but also for failing to understand it. In 132, senators from an anti-Gracchan faction were sent by their newly elected, allied consul, Publius Popilius Laenas, to organize "Asia," as the new province was to be called, but in 131, a *pro*-Gracchan group held sway and, desirous of resources to support Gracchus's land reform scheme, no doubt approached the assignment in different ways. The anti-Gracchans were first led by Scipio Nasica, who had engineered the lynching of Tiberius Gracchus to begin with (Chapter 10); he died in Pergamon shortly after arriving there. In 131, the Roman electorate gave the consulship to Publius Licinius Crassus Mucianus, the father-in-law of Tiberius Gracchus's surviving brother Gaius and the replacement of Tiberius on the land commission upon his assassination. Mucianus would likely have had his mind on the funding of the commission as he crossed to Asia Minor to secure its revenues.

There is reason to believe that Aristonicus based his support among the inland dwellers of Pergamene territory, most likely agriculturalists. He had been defeated at sea early in his rebellion at Ephesus and from that point he avoided the coast. An inscription in Pergamon, set up by Aristonicus's rivals, offered citizenship to "Macedonians, Mysians, and Masdyenians" if they assisted their cause; whether the offer was accepted or not, the text, by revealing the targets of a campaign to win "hearts and minds," may identify the demographics and ethnicities of Aristonicus's principal followers. If Strabo's later account is to be believed, Aristonicus and his troops were surrounded by a hostile coalition of the urbanized populations of Pergamon, Sardis, and Ephesus, who had further allies in Bithynia and Cappadocia; Delos also seems to have lent assistance. It would seem from all of this that it was tenant farmers of some kind who were dissatisfied with their new status in the Romano-Pergamene system. In 131, Mucianus was defeated by Aristonicus and was either killed or committed suicide in its aftermath. Ariarathes V, the king of Cappadocia and a long-time friend of Rome, was killed in battle against him, as well. It took until 130 for a new Roman consul, Marcus Perperna, to capture Aristonicus, but he, too, did not make it out alive, succumbing to an illness at Pergamon. The consul of 129, Manius Aquillius, was the first to succeed in consolidating the new province; he was assisted by Mithridates V, king of Pontus, a regional ally who had helped Rome against Carthage in 146. Aristonicus was eventually executed in Rome following Aquillius's triumphal procession.

11.3 Paos, Harsiese, and the People of Egypt

As disorder reigned in and around Pergamon, simultaneous upheaval characterized Egypt, the Levant, and Syria, at least at the level of the political elite. A single nuclear family was now largely in control of both major dynasties. As seen in Chapter 10, Egypt was governed by Ptolemy VIII and his sister-wife Cleopatra II, grandchildren of both Antiochus III through their mother and Ptolemy IV through their father. Cleopatra II's daughter, Cleopatra III, made up the final part of the tripartite monarchy as a second, and soon to be primary, wife of Ptolemy VIII (her uncle). Among the Seleucids, Cleopatra III's older sister, Cleopatra Thea, was still queen – perhaps the only element of stability in that fractious dynasty, as she married, in succession, the pretender Alexander Balas, then the brothers Demetrius II and Antiochus VII Sidetes, as they had come in and out of power (Chapter 10). Demetrius II had been in captivity in Parthia since 142, and in 130 he was released; in the same year, Antiochus VII died on the battlefield, conveniently making Cleopatra Thea available again for a second marriage to Demetrius II.

Though Ptolemy VIII and these three Cleopatras were of close relation – a brother and a sister of one generation, and two sisters in the next – their quarrels were frequent and intense, with hasty alliances and abrupt betrayals. In 131, Cleopatra II and her daughter Cleopatra Thea worked in concert across their two realms against Ptolemy VIII and Cleopatra III, who were forced to flee Alexandria for Cyprus. In 130 Cleopatra II held the palace and sent troops to help Cleopatra Thea and Demetrius II enter the Delta, but Ptolemy VIII still had regional allies in Egypt, and the Seleucids were turned back at Pelusion. In the end it was Cleopatra II who had to retreat when her brother/husband and her daughter/sister-in-law came roaring back to Alexandria in 127. Playing the now familiar game of the "found heir," Ptolemy VIII pressed his momentary advantage by sending one Alexander Zabinas, allegedly an adopted son of the dead Antiochus VII, against Cleopatra II and Cleopatra Thea. Zabinas did manage to corner Demetrius II, who died at Damascus in 126, but he made little headway beyond that, for Cleopatra Thea was ready for him, now with her son Antiochus VIII Grypus as rightful heir. She and Grypus appear in the sources as corulers, mother and son, up through 121. By 124, for some reason we do not know, the Egyptian branch of the clan was reconciled: Cleopatra II reentered the former tryarchy with her brother and younger daughter in Egypt. Cleopatra III's daughter Cleopatra Tryphaena married Grypus, apparently sealing a kind of truce. At least by propaganda and circumstance, the three generations were a happy family once more. Zabinas, a leftover pawn, was no longer necessary to anyone; he was hunted down by Grypus in 123.

In 118, the three Egyptian monarchs participated in an amnesty decree, conferring benefits and a degree of autonomy on the indigenous population (see Primary Source 11.1). In 116, both Ptolemy VIII and Cleopatra II died, bringing an end to their generation's long rule of Egypt, in place for some 50 years, and Cleopatra III dictated a new shared throne between herself and two of her sons, Ptolemy IX who ruled with her as *basileus* in Alexandria (and also married his sister, Cleopatra IV), and Ptolemy X who governed Cyprus with a lesser title. The Romans seem to have been involved in the new agreement, as the oldest Latin inscriptions in Egypt date to this year. A chance papyrus find dating to 112 discusses what seems to be pure tourism on the part of a Roman senator, Lucius Memmius, otherwise unknown, who was taking in animal displays and some kind of labyrinth tour in Arsinoe, Egypt.

Primary Source 11.1

Amnesty Decree of Ptolemy VIII

This so-called amnesty decree was preserved on papyrus; the monarchs mentioned are Ptolemy VIII, his sister Cleopatra II (who was once his wife) and Cleopatra III, his niece to whom he was now married. In 118 the tripartite throne was tested by inner strife. The reference to Egyptians making use of public land beyond the allowable limit is similar to contemporaneous issues with the *ager publicus* in Italy, as tackled by Tiberius and Gaius Gracchus.

"[King] Ptolemy and Queen Cleopatra, the sister, [and Queen] Cleopatra, the wife, proclaim an amnesty to all their subjects for errors, crimes, accusations, condemnations, and offences of all kinds up to the 9th of Pharmouthi of the 52nd year (April 28, 118 BCE) except to persons guilty of willful murder or sacrilege. They have decreed that persons who have gone into hiding because they were guilty of robbery or other offences shall return to their homes and resume their former occupations and shall [recover] the property which is still unsold out of (that which had been seized as security). … They have decreed that all recipients of grants of land and all holders of temple land and other liberated land, both those who have encroached on crown land and all others who hold more than their proper portion, shall, on giving up all the excess and declaring themselves and paying a year's rent, be released from responsibility for the period up to the 51st year and have legal possession of the land from the 52nd year …"

(trans. A.S. Hunt and C.C. Edgar, *Select Papryi*, volume 2, Cambridge, MA: Harvard University Press, 1977, 59–61.)

Just as the local communities of Pergamon under Aristonicus were asserting themselves against higher powers of elite politics, the indigenous Egyptians seem to have capitalized on the chaos within the old Macedonian dynasty to claim privileges for themselves. As Ptolemy VIII tried to navigate the land mines laid by his sister in 130–127, his strongest bulwark was a native-born general, Paos, who commanded key operations for him from Thebes. Around the same time, a native Egyptian dared to make a bid for the title of pharaoh, which had belonged almost exclusively to the Ptolemies since 305. Named Harsiese, he failed, although his legacy endured in the so-called "Oracle of the Potter," a text that promised that Egypt would gain salvation from an apocalypse by a native born pharaoh (see Primary Source 11.2), which Günther Hölbl believes could be referring to a Harsiese-like figure. After Ptolemy VIII returned to power, his loyal Paos was given the title

> **Primary Source 11.2**
>
> *Oracle of the Potter*
>
> Like the *Book of Daniel* (Chapter 9) the *Oracle of the Potter* is a story that is set in the distant past – in this case, the 18th Dynasty of 1575–1308 BCE – which "predicts" a series of events that are current to around 130, when it initially circulated. The potter makes reference to the invasion of Egypt by Antiochus IV (again, compare the *Book of Daniel*, Chapter 9), and, seemingly, the uprising by Harsiese (though the sense is difficult to recover from the fragments). The text is a Greek translation of an Egyptian original.
>
> "In the time of the Typhonians, foreigners [likely meaning the Macedonians] [will say] 'Wretched Egypt, [you have been] maltreated by the [terrible] malefactors who have committed evil against you.' And the sun will darken as it will not be willing to observe the evils in Egypt. The earth will not respond to seeds. These will be part of its blight. … A king will come from Syria, he who will be hateful to all men [Antiochus IV and the Sixth Syrian War], [….] and from Ethiopia there will come … He (together with some) of the unholy ones (will come) to Egypt, and he will settle [in the city which] later will be deserted. [Two fragmentary lines may refer to the two-year reign of Harsiese] … But he will not be our king. The fifty-five year king (Ptolemy VIII, ruled 170–116) who will be ours, however, will bring upon the Greeks the evils which the lamb prophesied to Bacharis (a later pharaoh). Good fortune will be taken away from this race. … Their children will be made weak and the country will be in confusion and many of the inhabitants of Egypt will abandon their homes (and) travel to foreign places. … Then Agathos Daimon (a god of Alexandria) will abandon the city that had been founded and enter Memphis, and the city of foreigners (Alexandria), which had been founded, will be deserted. This will happen at the end of the evils (of the time) when there came to Egypt a crowd of foreigners. The city of the girdle-wearers (Alexandria) will be abandoned like my kiln because of the crimes which they committed against Egypt. The cult images which had been transported there will be brought back again to Egypt; and the city by the sea will become a refuge for fishermen …"
>
> (trans. Stanley M. Burstein, *The Hellenistic Age from the battle of Ipsos to the death of Kleopatra VII*, Cambridge: Cambridge University Press, 1985.)

syngenes, meaning that he held the same status in the dynasty as "one of the family": blood relations were still the prime legitimator of authority in this world, as seen with the many pretenders elsewhere, and here it was effected by decree. Furthermore, in 122, after the reconciliation and momentary restabilization of the Ptolemies and Seleucids, an Egyptian priest, Psenptah II, was married to a Berenike, as Gunther Hölbl has shown. We do not know of this Berenike from any other source, but the name was popular among the ruling dynasty: it may be that we have yet more evidence of the elevation of the indigenous to the camp of the royals, engineered, as the argument goes, in order to keep the peace. Repeated amnesty decrees from the Ptolemies in the last third of the second century in any case contribute to the sense of a trend shared with Pergamon: the power elite had to acknowledge the influence of their subjects on their capacity to rule.

11.4 Gaius Gracchus and the People of Italy

Soon Rome would confront in like measure the displeasure of hinterland subjects throughout Italy, who sought their own influence in decision-making at the metropole. The elite among these Italian allies had reason to complain: the redistribution of the *ager publicus* by Tiberius Gracchus's commission had affected them as much as it did citizen leaseholders.

Their complaints were serious enough that Scipio Aemilianus succeeded in passing legislation in 129 that removed all land cases involving Italians from the Gracchan commission and put them under consular jurisdiction. He was reportedly on the verge of proposing new initiatives regarding formal citizenship for Italians when he died at home, presumably of natural causes, at the age of 56. The matter lingered in importance, and the consul of 125, Marcus Fulvius Flaccus, a fellow ideologue of the Gracchi brothers and a member of the land commission since 130, also was preparing a case for granting citizenship to Italians when he was pulled away by a Celtic war in the north. In 124 a praetor, Lucius Opimius, was ordered to march south to quell a major rebellion at Fregellae, a town that was seeking a break from the Roman system, likely also a grievance regarding citizenship issues; it was an uprising that Opimius suppressed with brute force.

In the next year, 123, Gaius Gracchus ran for the tribunate and was elected for 122. Citizenship for the Italian allies was one part of his multifaceted agenda, which was in many respects more radical and far-reaching than that of his older brother a decade before. Gaius put forward a host of policies that had the interests of farmers of all types at heart, citizen or not, in essence seeking to cohere Italy into a unified whole with less pyramidal social structures. In the short term he reduced the content of silver in Roman currency, so that rent and various other debts became instantly – but only temporarily – more manageable. With longer term objectives in mind, he compelled the Roman state to purchase grain overseas and sell it in the city at fixed prices and ordered new networks of roads between villages in Italy to facilitate the movement of goods to market. The military, a function of Italian agriculture as we have seen, also drew his attention: Gaius commissioned colonies at Capua, Tarentum, and Carthage, to be settled by new veteran soldier-farmers with even larger plots than those meted out by his brother's reforms, and he assigned the cost of a soldier's weaponry and panoply to the Roman treasury. Gaius also sought to correct an obvious conflict of interest in the Lex Calpurnia governing corruption trials (Chapter 9): a law of Gaius's colleague transferred the juries from the senatorial peers of the very generals accused of extortion in the first place to the equestrian class. Equestrians also won lucrative contracts to collect taxes in the new province of Asia during Gaius's tribunate. A tribune in their camp sought to defeat a bill that would have given part of Phrygia to Mithridates V for his assistance against Aristonicus; his aim presumably was to keep the tax revenues for Rome.

The senatorial elite (see Figure 11.1), as the creditor class by-and-large, were on the losing end of Gaius's reforms. In the course of the following year, for which Gaius had been reelected as tribune, a faction of senators noticed that in the process of broadening his power base to all of Italy, Gaius was alienating the core urban constituencies at Rome, which could now be receptive to other tribunes. While Gaius was away in North Africa overseeing the settlement the new colony at Carthage, a rival tribune, Marcus Livius Drusus, working in the interests of senators, portrayed the project in a xenophobic light, as a scandalous revival of a hated foe. Livius Drusus also painted the work of Fulvius Flaccus, a tribune in 122, with a similar brush: as Flaccus planned to extend citizenship in Italy, Livius Drusus argued in opposition that soon the strong vote of the city of Rome would be diluted by rural voting blocks. If anything, Livius Drusus proposed tightening Rome's grip on Italy. He made promises for the creation of a dozen new colonies, but at desirable locations in Italy rather than on foreign soil. Such a measure, if enacted, would surely have triggered a serious civil war, given the displacement that such a land grab would entail, but Livius Drusus did not have to worry about the details since he dropped it once his rival was done away with. Gaius tried to run for a third term as tribune in 121, but Drusus's electoral strategy worked and Gaius no longer had the votes.

Some of Gaius's supporters rioted, and the consul of 121, Lucius Opimius, who had annihilated the Latin resistance at Fregellae four years prior, responded with a new and deadly procedural device, the *senatus consultum ultimum*, or, the final decree of the senate. The "*ultimum*"

Figure 11.1 The Arringatore Bronze, a portrait of Aulus Metellus (Aule Metele in the Etruscan script), wearing the toga and boots of the senatorial elite and in the pose of one addressing a crowd, late second, early-first century BCE.

meant that this decree was, somehow, uniquely immune to a tribune's veto: it declared a state of emergency and effectively enacted martial law. Though it possessed a cold veneer of bureaucracy, the decree was, in fact, unprecedented, and thus retaliated in kind against the Gracchi brothers' plots to augment the authority of the tribunate beyond tradition. Fulvius Flaccus and Gaius Gracchus were declared enemies of the state; the former was murdered in the streets and the latter committed suicide with the assistance of a slave. The violence extended even to the Vestal Virgins: years after Gaius Gracchus's death, three of them were brought up on charges of unchastity. One of them, Licinia, appears to have had ties to the Gracchan clan; she and one other of her colleagues were acquitted but then soon retried and found guilty and were accordingly executed. Scholars have seen in Licinia's death possible political motivations, or the settling of a vendetta, though the sources are equivocal. In any case, few could deny that the ruling elite of Rome were becoming as bloody as the dynasties of the Hellenistic East.

11.5 Adherbal vs. Jurgurtha, in Numidia and in the Roman Senate

While Gaius Gracchus had been in Africa organizing a colony (which was quashed after his death), it is likely that he had contacts with Rome's staunch Numidian ally, Micipsa, the son of Masinissa and, thanks to Roman support, the most powerful leader in the region (Chapter 10).

Micipsa died in 118, leaving multiple heirs: his two sons, Hiempsal and Adherbal, were to share power with a nephew, Jugurtha, who, we have seen, had won much admiration from Scipio Aemilianus and other Romans as an apprentice of sorts at the siege of Numantia in Spain (Chapter 10). The princes were soon plunged into civil war: Hiempsal was killed in short order (allegedly by Jugurtha who had forged copies of the keys to his chambers to facilitate assassins), and Adherbal and Jugurtha faced each other.

In a monograph written in the 40s, the Roman proconsul and historian Sallust described how the Numidian cousins maneuvered themselves in the domestic politics of Rome to win vital backing for their respective bids, and how the senators in question used the Numidians in their own factional disputes at home. Sallust's account presents Jugurtha as a villain and a conniver, relying on bribery to win over allies, but such a picture, first, forgets the favor that Jugurtha enjoyed, apparently by merit, as a youth in Roman service, and second, ignores the likelihood that Adherbal was making promises of his own to *his* backers, most notably Marcus Aemilius Scaurus, the *princeps*, or, "first man" in the senate. According to Sallust, in 116 a senatorial faction led by Lucius Opimius among others carried the cause in Jugurtha's favor and organized a better parcel of agricultural land for his portion of the kingdom. Adherbal repaired to a more urban and commercial realm, and détente held for some four years. The Roman economy appears to have benefited from the settlement, as a later episode reveals, however tragically as we shall see, that a large community of Italian tradesmen set up businesses in Cirta, Adherbal's largest city.

The line between domestic and foreign, between political and geopolitical, continued to blur. When Jugurtha began to experience one success after another against the Romans in Africa in the coming years, prominent tribunes placed blame on recalcitrant or corrupt members of a senatorial faction who looked the other way. In 112 Jugurtha felt confident enough in Roman apathy that he went on the offensive and laid siege to Adherbal in Cirta. When Jugurtha finally breached the walls, the Italian merchants and tradesmen inside were slaughtered alongside Adherbal and his Numidian forces. Even after this affront, as Sallust construes it, a declaration of war by Rome was not forthcoming, as a pro-Jugurtha faction in the senate was arguing that Adherbal had been the aggressor. Nevertheless, the tribune Gaius Memmius called for action. Jugurtha sent his son to argue on his behalf, or, according to Sallust's predetermined account, to bribe as many senators as he could. On the surface it must have looked like Micipsa's sending Jugurtha to join Roman senators in a previous generation, or like any other Hellenistic monarch sending a son to Rome – a common enough practice, as we have seen – but the embassy was rebuffed. Bowing to Memmius's pressure, the senate announced that a war in Numidia would be one of the consular assignments for 111, and it went to Lucius Calpurnius Bestia.

Again, ancient commentators correlated the two sides of the war in Numidia for the first couple of years with factional divisions in Roman politics. Bestia's campaign was, at best, only one of intimidation: there was scarcely any engagement with Jugurtha, and instead the two sides tried to arrange a settlement. Memmius once again attributed the lack of action to a corrupt aristocracy and called upon Jugurtha himself to testify before a jury of equestrians in Rome about his connections with powerful senators. Just as some Romans supported Jugurtha and thus sought peace, others were now backing yet another cousin resident in Rome, named Massiva, and intended to put him on the throne through warfare. Jugurtha dealt with this threat by having Massiva assassinated, barely managing, we are told by Sallust, to smuggle his hitman out of Rome, citing a kind of diplomatic immunity. The African campaign of 110, led by Spurius Postumius Albinus, was more active in the field, but still, Jugurtha capitalized on some tactical errors by Rome and once humiliated a defeated troop by forcing them to pass beneath the yoke, reminiscent of the Romans beaten by the Samnites at the Caudine Forks in 321

(Chapter 3). Another tribune, Gaius Mamilius, followed Memmius's pattern and argued that the failure resulted from intentional passivity by bribed officials. The Roman people agreed: Albinus, Bestia, and Opimius were all censured and exiled.

Finally in 109 and in the years following, the Romans began to make inroads against Jugurtha. The consul for that year, and then proconsul with *imperium* in 108, was Quintus Caecilius Metellus, a member of a powerful clan whose members had led Rome to recent victories in the Balkans. Active both as a general and a diplomat, he took back Cirta as well as made a critical alliance with Bocchus, king of the Mauretanians on Jugurtha's western flank. One of Metellus's lieutenants, Gaius Marius, also distinguished himself on the battlefield. After a year of service and, according to Sallust, a productive working relationship with the consul, Marius asked Metellus to support him in a run for the consulship. Metellus reportedly suggested Marius be more patient and perhaps wait until Marius could run with Metellus's own son, which was an insult since this meant a delay of over a decade. It was thus on his own initiative that Marius went to Rome to run for consul.

11.6 Marius and the People of Rome

Gaius Marius's candidacy for the consulship was partly run of the mill and partly unorthodox. Like any aspirant to power, he had strong ties to prominent Roman families: in addition to serving under Metellus he had married Julia, of an old patrician clan (her nephew would be the Julius Caesar of this book's title). He had also made a name for himself in a course of offices, including a tribunate in 119 and a praetorship in 115. Like other politicians involved in Numidian affairs, he appealed to voters by claiming to wield influence over a would-be vassal housed among them: Adherbal and Massiva had both been tested and lost, but now Marius deployed Gauda, a half-brother of Jugurtha and also, more crucially, a grandson of the beloved Masinissa. In these ways Marius was a typical candidate, but in one crucial regard he was not: as the first in his family to advance thus far in politics, he was a *novus homo*. He hailed from Arpinum, a town in Latium that had only received the full franchise in 188. He lacked the ancestral prowess that characterized most successful candidates, but he was elected nonetheless. The campaign speech that Sallust attributes to Marius is surely a piece of dramatic fiction, but his emphasis on deeds, not words, and on battle scars, not great family portraits, captures Marius's revolutionary quality.

As consul in the next Numidian campaign, Marius pursued a strategy of the surge, seeking to overwhelm Jugurtha with a far larger army than had been in play before. His methods to achieve greater numbers have been identified by historians both ancient and modern as another turning point in Roman politics: not content with the roster afforded by recruitment from landed families, he turned to the *proletarii* of Rome and offered to kit them out at state expense with armor and weaponry and all else needed for a soldier's career. The result was a new troop of urban soldiers who, while untrained and perhaps even surprised to find themselves across a sea and staring down a hostile enemy, were numerous and, if all went well, potentially grateful to Marius. The tales of derring-do of the new legions are grippingly told by Sallust and Appian: a bold move on a desert stronghold; a rock-climbing expedition to infiltrate a citadel under siege; the ever popular feigned retreat followed by surging advance. In the end, what finally got Jugurtha was not the valor of Marius's neophyte roughs but a delicate, risky maneuver by one of his lieutenants, Lucius Cornelius Sulla. In what Sallust describes as a tense standoff at the court of Bocchus, Sulla gambled all on the shaky loyalty of that Mauretanian king, who was also being courted by Jugurtha and his ready bribes. Bocchus chose Sulla, and Rome at last had its prisoner, who was marched in triumph in 104 and executed in the Tullianum. From this Sulla we shall hear much more. For the time being, Numidia was divided between an augmented Roman province of Africa and the loyal Bocchus, who received land shaved off from the Numidian West.

11.7 A Celtic Resurgence

As Metellus, Marius, and Sulla were performing well in Numidia from 109 to 105, their counterparts in the North – also a combination of an aristocrat and a *novus homo* – were faring poorly. The Celtic tribes of the Cimbri, Teutones, and Tigurini, in and out of alliances with each other, were triggering various skirmishes due to occasional migrations in search of better land. Consuls in 112 and 109 were defeated by divisions of them, and in 107, a consul was even killed in battle and Roman troops were made to pass beneath the yoke. The consul of 106, Quintus Servilius Caepio, managed some measure of revenge, but not outright victory. The next year's consul for the project, Gnaeus Mallius Maximus, was, like Marius, a *novus homo*, and also like Marius, he is said to have suffered a measure of ill will from his peers in the command as a result of his lower social status. Uncertainty about who had the supreme authority to lead developed between him and Caepio, who was still on the scene as a proconsul. Our sources blame at least part of their massive defeat at Arausio in Gaul (modern Orange) on disagreements between them, rather like the disputes between the generals at Cannae in 216 (Chapter 7).

Once again, Marius was in the right place at the right time: the disaster at Arausio coincided with his return from Africa, and the people elected him consul for a second time with the assignment of stabilizing the far Alps. The Celtic tribes had, in fact, scattered after Arausio and seem not to have constituted a serious threat until 102, yet Marius was reelected consul and appointed to the region every year up to that point. It was an unprecedented string of consecutive offices, and illegal, as well, given that, in view of the growing power of generals in the Second Punic War and the wars against Macedonia and the Seleucids, limits had been placed on repeated consulships by legislation, the Lex Villia of 180. In 102, Marius defeated the Teutones at Aquae Sextiae, and in 101, he and his fellow consul annihilated the Cimbri at the Battle of Vercellae. Simultaneously that year, his old colleague Sulla faced down the Tigurini in the region of modern Slovenia, but their retreat meant that he did not have the opportunity to win the same glory as Marius.

Marius's army of *proletarii* had by now followed him through two difficult theaters of war, and it became of prime political importance that they be compensated. Not as adept with words as in the field, Marius relied in no small measure on an allied tribune, Lucius Appuleius Saturninus. Though comfortable in the Forum, Saturninus was no less ham-handed, it turned out, than Marius. Among Saturninus's political outrages are threats to fellow tribunes, a riot against the censor Metellus Numidicus, Marius's former superior officer in Numidia, and even the assassination of a rival for office. A later source says that Saturninus produced a "pretender" in the Hellenistic vein, claiming to have with him an illegitimate son of Tiberius Gracchus, but Gracchus's sister Sempronia refused to acknowledge him.

11.8 Shifts Among the Ptolemo-Seleucids

Among the Ptolemies, by 114 Cleopatra III was the elder matriarch of a still-powerful dynasty. Two of her daughters and two of her sons were active in politics. As we have seen, one of her daughters, Cleopatra Tryphaena, was married to Antiochus VIII Grypus and was thus ruling over the Seleucids. The other three children ruled in traditional Ptolemaic domains, with Cleopatra IV and Ptolemy IX governing Alexandria in a sibling marriage and Ptolemy X governing in Cyprus, and by 114, also holding the title of *basileus*. Cleopatra IV made a bid for power in her own right in 113, when she left her brother-husband and moved north to the Levant to strike an alliance with Antiochus IX Cyzicenus, brother of Antiochus VIII Grypus. Tryphaena apprehended her in 112 and did away with her before the marriage could take place, but Tryphaena had her comeuppance the next year, 111, when Cyzicenus defeated her and her husband, and Tryphaena was herself executed, though Grypus continued to rule in his shrinking section of Syria. Cleopatra Selene, the last daughter of Cleopatra III, moved to Grypus's court and replaced her older sister as queen.

In Egypt an equilibrium in this confusing saga held for a time among Cleopatra III and her two sons. But in 107, as Marius was embarking on his career in Numidia, the Ptolemies again disintegrated, when Cleopatra III for some reason turned on Ptolemy IX. As Ptolemy X sailed to Alexandria in her support, Ptolemy IX had to fight his way out and sought refuge in Cyprus, whence his younger brother had just departed. The brothers had essentially switched places, and both would stay put in these respective realms for at least 20 years. Cleopatra III remained bold and defiant into her 60s: she organized a successful campaign against Judaea in 103. Realizing that her realm was a toxic environment for young princes, she sent three of her grandsons (two sons of Ptolemy IX and one of Ptolemy X) to the island of Cos for safekeeping. It was good timing, for she died in 101; one rumor alleged she was murdered by Ptolemy X. In spite of all this sparring, and perhaps because of the stability achieved in 107 by the brothers' balance, the Ptolemies remained a major power. Syria, to summarize, was still divided between the brothers Antiochus VIII Grypus and Antiochus IX Cyzicenus, the former with a Ptolemaic wife.

11.9 Mithridates VI

In Asia Minor, a new power was on the rise after the removal of Aristonicus in 129, in many ways exhibiting the same amalgamated, incestuous, and murderous political tendencies that characterized the Ptolemies and Seleucids. It will be remembered that one of the regional allies enlisted by Rome both against Carthage in 146 and in outflanking Aristonicus in 129 was Mithridates V of Pontus. His father's line had predominantly Persian roots, while his mother was a granddaughter of Antiochus III (and thus a cousin of Ptolemies VI and VIII and Cleopatra II). His wife was Laodike, who is also described in our texts as a member of the Seleucid dynasty, though her place in the family tree is uncertain. His daughter, also named Laodike, was married to Ariarathes VI, the Cappadocian king, whose ancestors had close ties to Rome (Chapter 10). The Mithridatic family was thus fully entrenched in the pan-Mediterranean overclass (note the Hellenic features of Mithridates's portraiture in Figure 11.2). When Mithridates V died in 120, a Ptolemaic-style tripartite monarchy was established by the widowed queen with her two sons, but by 115, mother and younger son were dead, with Mithridates VI assuming sole power at the age of 20. The nature of his rise is hard to ascertain in our questionable, novelistic Roman accounts, but to imagine a civil war of some kind would not be farfetched. Fanciful tales of Mithridates's childhood are surely later inventions: he allegedly roamed the forest, a near-wild urchin, learning about animals, hunting techniques, and natural poisons.

Mithridates VI went on to have a long and successful reign, and given the internecine conflicts among the Seleucids and Ptolemies, could be ranked as the most powerful Hellenistic monarch of his generation. The foundation of his economy was the Black Sea, which he consolidated nearly in its entirety shortly after taking the throne. In part, he was invited in: Hellenic cities in Crimea were being harried by Celtic tribes in ways similar to the Romans and Macedonians, and

Figure 11.2 Roman copy of a portrait of Mithridates VI wearing a lion-skin in the style of Hercules and Alexander the Great.

they sought Mithridates's aid in keeping them at bay. Once Mithridates had Crimea to hand, he did not relinquish it but annexed it for himself. He likewise badgered his way into direct control of Colchis to his East. In both land grabs, Mithridates was a particularly adept builder of citadels, a network of which was quickly cast over his new domain like a net. These victories enabled him to cut an imposing figure when he asked for alliances from other Black Sea players, like Thrace, the Celts, and eventually, the rich and well- connected Bithynians, as now led by Nicomedes III. Around 105, Mithridates and Nicomedes III marched as allies on Paphlagonia and Galatia. The Roman senate sent envoys to object, but the aggressors seem to have been aware of Rome's troubles in Numidia and Gaul at that time, and the Romans received no satisfaction. Laodike, Mithridates's sister and queen of Cappadocia, soon got into the act, allegedly poisoning her husband Ariarathes VI in favor of her invading brother. She became the regent over the child-heir, Ariarathes VII, a clear gain for Mithridates's growing sphere of influence.

Historians have made much of the romantic tale of Mithridates's subsequent tour of Asia Minor, which he allegedly conducted in disguise, the better to gather intelligence in secretive ways. In truth, given his family connections and the tight economy of Asia Minor, he probably already knew many of the listed destinations: Pergamon, Ephesus, Rhodes, Cilicia. An inscription from Chios attesting to his participation in horse races demonstrates that he easily garnered attention, thus obviating the claims that he could travel *incognito*. Rather, the anecdotes hinge on Mithridates's negative reputation of being deceitful and cunning, propagated after the fact by Roman sources. Roman sources also alleged that Mithridates relied heavily on poison to manage his inner court, but we should read this with caution as poison was viewed in antiquity as the province of women, and such allegations served to depict one's enemy as an aberration of nature. Mithridates's part-Persian background also opened him up to suspicions of unmanliness. It can be a challenge to view Mithridates objectively; in truth, he was in pursuit of the same regional influence that the Romans, too, were seeking, and no less bloodily.

A remarkable monument on Delos, dating to 102/101, demonstrates Mithridates's lofty goals at this point in his career, as well as his cosmopolitan pretensions. The so-called Mithridates Monument lined up 12 members of the Pontic king's inner circle, three portrait busts on each of the side walls of a portico and six along the back. An accompanying inscription proclaimed a local priest of Poseidon as its commissioner and asserted its approval by both Athens and Rome. As with Alexander the Great, and with Achilles before him, a boyhood friend was accentuated – Dorylaus, playing the same role as Hephaestaeon and Patroclus. Also like Alexander, Mithridates's prestige was heightened by his association with intellectuals, such as his physician, his historian/secretary, and a priest, all of whom were included in the monument. Since Delos was a crossroads, both sacred and commercial, of all the Mediterranean and not just the Aegean Sea, Mithridates also had depicted Antiochus VIII Grypus, the barely lingering Seleucid monarch, and Ariarathes VII, his nephew whom he and Laodike had only recently promoted to his throne. One innovation for Mithridates in the monument was the inclusion of two Parthian figures of the ruling dynasty of the Arsacids. Again, a comparison with Alexander is appropriate in terms of his interest in cultural mélange.

Mithridates had thus emerged by 101 as an unusually stable, well-founded king, with an economic terrain – the Black Sea – that was almost as unassailable as the Ptolemies' cherished Nile, and with an knack for administration that would rival the Romans. With Gaius Marius and the other consulars staving off emergencies to their north, Rome was less interested in checking Mithridates's rise.

11.10 So-called Pirates and Bandits

The Romans' only substantial campaign in the East at this time targeted a regime of so-called pirates based on the southern Cilician coast of Asia Minor. In 102, Marcus Antonius attempted to lead a fleet against a corps of ships that menaced trade on Delos. An inscription from Corinth suggests that he experienced navigational difficulty after pulling the fleet across the Isthmus. Though not much seems to have come from Antonius's campaign, he and his Roman navy enjoyed the support of local regimes, enthusiastically declared in inscriptions at Athens, Rhodes, Byzantium, and the Lycian League, which immediately abutted the coastline sheltering the marauders. An inscription from Athens reveals that the class of ephebes made sacrifices on behalf of the Romans at this time.

But calling the group "pirates" has been challenged of late: if they had been led by some renegade Seleucid, some Ptolemy, or some other storied dynastic aristocrat with no other change to the nature of their collective, would not historians have spoken of them as legitimate states? The independence of the seafaring settlements (we are avoiding the loaded term of "pirate" deliberately) might rather be viewed in kind with a contemporaneous slave revolt in Sicily, which broke out in 101, led by a ringleader who, like Eunus/Antiochus (Chapter 10), was a displaced Hellene who assumed the title *basileus*. Manius Aquillius, the son of the first governor of Asia (see above), was sent to Sicily to quell the uprising. However, as these movements of pirates, bandits, and rebels were well organized and dealt in the vocabulary of Hellenistic politics it would not be a stretch to refer to them as quasi-states.

11.11 Conclusions

Uncertainty characterized the eastern Mediterranean in the final decades of the second century. Historians in antiquity tended to dwell on aristocracies and brilliant personalities, but several episodes of challenges to long-time institutions, strikingly similar from realm to realm, suggest a trend of populism and a distaste for the residue of Alexander the Great's successors. Outsiders like Aristonicus, Harsiese, and Gaius Gracchus led movements in Pergamon, Egypt, and Italy, respectively. However nationalistic such factions may have been, the presence of Rome could not be denied, and political rivals in non-Roman territories on the periphery came to fight their battles through analogs in Rome's own senate. The internationalization of politics meant that when Rome finally descended into formal civil war, and not just disorganized rioting, as will happen in the next chapter, the rest of the world went with it.

Gaius Marius had achieved an unlikely rise on the backs of landless soldiers. The fact that they did not want to remain landless meant that he had a potential crisis on his hands when his campaigning was complete. Attempts at settling veterans would become further cause for wars among tribunes.

Further Reading

Hölbl, Gunther (2001). *A History of the Ptolemaic Empire*. New York: Routledge.
Kallet-Marx, Robert (1996). *Hegemony to Empire: the Development of the Roman Imperium in the East from 148 to 62 BC*. Berkeley: University of California Press.
Mayor, Adrienne (2011). *The Poison King: The Life and Legend of Mithridates, Rome's Deadliest Enemy*. Princeton: Princeton University Press.
Robb, Mike A (2010). *Beyond Optimates and Populares: Political Language in the Late Republic*. Stuttgard: Franz Steiner Verlag.
de Souza, Philip (2000). *Piracy in the Graeco-Roman World*. Cambridge: Cambridge University Press.
Steel, Catherine and van der Blom, Henriette (eds.) (2013). *Community and Communication: Oratory and Politics in Republican Rome*. Oxford: Oxford University Press.

12

To 79: Boundless Violence

Timeline

100: Assassination of the tribune Saturninus in Rome; Mithridates controls Cappadocia behind Ariarathes IX
99: Departure of Marius for the East
96: Sulla escorts Ariobarzanes to the throne of Cappadocia; death of Antiochus VIII Grypus; alliance of Mithridates with Tigranes II of Armenia
93: Mithridates ousts Ariobarzanes of Cappadocia and Nicomedes IV of Bithynia
91: Tribunate of Livius Drusus, son of the tribune of 122 of the same name
91–89: The Social War between Rome and its Italian allies
90: Roman mission to reinstall Ariobarzanes and Nicomedes IV
88: Violence against Romans in Asia Minor, as ordered by Mithridates
86: Sack of Athens by Sulla
87–84: Consecutive consulships of Cinna
83: Splinter movement in Spain led by Sertorius, on the run from Sulla
81: First full year of Sulla's dictatorship
80: Ptolemy of Cyprus and Ptolemy XII Auletes in Alexandria installed by Mithridates

Principal Themes

- Mithridates took advantage of coincident vacancies on several thrones to consolidate his power in Asia Minor and beyond.
- The evidence is patchy, but the Roman senate appears to have pursued efforts at rebuilding its authority and prestige in the 90s, following the challenges put to it in preceding decades by the Gracchi brothers, Marius, and Saturninus.
- Roman abuses of their power overseas prompted violent reprisals as, first, the Italians and, second, the subjects of Mithridates targeted Romans for extermination based on their national and ethnic identity.
- Civil war erupted in Rome as Marius and Sulla turned on each other in quests to command legions in response to crises, especially in the East.
- Athens, which had betrayed Romans to Mithridates's general Archelaus, was sacked by Sulla after a brief siege.
- By early 81, Sulla had revived the office of the dictatorship, dormant for over a century, in order to pass sweeping reforms to the Roman political system, including curbing the power of the tribunate.

The Roman Republic and the Hellenistic Mediterranean: From Alexander to Caesar, First Edition. Joel Allen.
© 2020 John Wiley & Sons, Inc. Published 2020 by John Wiley & Sons, Inc.

12.1 Introduction

For the 22 years span covered by this chapter, the reader will encounter multiple episodes of destruction and violence on a massive scale, as the buildup of both military power and the resentment of the subjugated reached a tipping point in geopolitics, and new, radical forms of political power eschewed negotiation and compromise in favor of brute force, provoking chain reactions of recriminations. Senatorial factions in Rome perpetrated (yet another) large-scale riot and lynching of a tribune and his allies, and twice reigns of terror were carried out against the supporters of Sulla, each time prompting Sulla himself to march on Rome to retaliate in kind (also twice). In addition to these examples of violence in the city, foreign leaders in southern Italy and again in Asia Minor carried out what might be classified as genocides of Romans in the sense that the victims were targeted for their national identity as opposed to any direct affronts against the perpetrators. Sulla's march East to deal with the rise of Mithridates required a sack of Athens, another case of devastation. It seemed that all involved were now playing for higher stakes.

12.2 Marius and Saturninus, Cornered by/in the Senate

After his victory at Vercellae in 101 (Chapter 11), Marius ran for the consulship yet again, and although the emergency, whose Celtic nature terrified Romans considerably, had now been neutralized, he still carried the vote and began the year 100 in his sixth term as consul. The political allies that had proven useful to him in the past were still around: Saturninus, who as tribune in 102 and 101 had helped Marius's veterans into plots of land, now held the same office for a third time. Such a political alliance was critical to Marius, for it would seem that the new realities ushered in by his empowerment of the nonelite through military careers were not yet appreciated: the senate still expected a degree of deference in the conduct of government, whose limits Saturninus enjoyed testing. Saturninus's populist agenda would have been business as usual – land redistribution, primarily, in keeping with the work of the Gracchi brothers – had it not been for, first, his inclusion of lands in *Gaul* for redistribution (and not just in Italy), recently recovered or seized in Marius's campaigns, and second, the provocative requirement that all senators swear an oath to abide by it. Even if a senator were sympathetic to the policy, the new stipulation inherently questioned one's integrity in insulting ways, and Metellus Numidicus, Marius's former superior officer against Jugurtha, could not bring himself to participate and accepted exile instead. Moreover, Saturninus put forward a new grain law, familiar as an idea, but here again pushed to an extreme as the new price of subsidized grain was to be a mere quarter of what Gaius Gracchus had proposed decades before. Reactions were swift as the senate issued another *senatus consultum ultimum*, similar to its condemnation of Gaius Gracchus in 121.

Marius once again found himself out of his depth: the senate was calling upon him as consul to purge a menace, even as he needed Saturninus's legislation to continue as a viable leader to his land-hungry troops. He arrested Saturninus rather than attack him with deadly force, and moved him to impromptu detention in the senate house while he pondered his next actions. The question went moot as an angry mob surmounted the roof, broke it open, and managed somehow to kill Saturninus with blunt missiles from above. Whether Marius had contributed to its success or not, the *senatus consultum ultimum* had had its desired effect. Marius left the city in due prudence the next year, out of consulships and suddenly unpopular; he conveniently recalled that he had sworn a vow to visit Cybele/Magna Mater at Pessinus in Asia Minor (compare Chapter 7), at a convenient remove of hundreds of miles.

In some ways, the scene of Saturninus's death by stoning in the senate house functions as an apt metaphor for the plight of reformer tribunes like him. Hemmed in on all sides by centuries-old structures built by and for the senate, one could not move far before hitting a wall. Espied from on high by untouchable enemies, he suffered in his lower position with no chance to parry. In spite of having to face sporadic outbursts of radical activism, the senate banked on an inertia that was in part borne of the fearful attitudes of underlings. Saturninus may have come from the wealthy nobility, and was as much the victimizer as its opposite, but the total mastery of the senate, at least as of 100 BCE, may conjure some amount of sympathy for his cause. The senate's perch would seem less unassailable within a decade.

The next couple of years are not well told in our sources, but hints here and there imply that the senate moved to reaffirm its authority in the absence of Marius. A new law was passed in 98 that required a waiting period between the time when a law could be proposed and when it could be voted on. The lag would apparently give the assembly time to follow their heads and not their hearts; in other words, aristocratic opponents of radical reform would have over two weeks to organize counter arguments. In 97, another new law was passed outlawing human sacrifice – a peculiar prohibition on its own, but in the context of the purges of the Vestal Virgins discussed in the previous chapter, where three women died as possible scapegoats in political controversies, the move seemed to forestall the kind of fiery passions characteristic of mob decisions.

12.3 The Cappadocian Throne: Mithridates VI vs. Rome

Marius's eastern sojourn has been described by some historians as a forward-looking mission to uncover his next great military opportunity – his natural comfort zone – now that Numidia and Gaul had been subdued and his own city was in turmoil. But it is also possible that Marius expected to find only, or at least mostly, allies in the East. Nicomedes III of Bithynia was friendly enough that Marius conceived of asking him for aid against the Celts back in 104. The kingdom of Cappadocia, at the time of Marius's departure from Italy, was likely expected to be in the hands of Ariarathes VII, whose family had a long history of aiding Rome. As we have seen, a monument to Mithridates stood on Delos (Chapter 11), through which Marius is likely to have passed (though this is speculation) owing to its large Roman population, active trade, and location at the hub of all spokes of Aegean travel. An inscription of 95, carved shortly after Marius would have visited, declared that a priest of Serapis on Delos was the sincere friend of "Athens, Rome, and Mithridates," a sentiment whose bedfellows would read as strange within a few years.

The date and veracity of a colorful story of Mithridates's betrayal of Ariarathes VII are uncertain, and so we cannot fully know its relevance to Marius's excursion. Some time after 101, the date of Mithridates's monument on Delos where Mithridates and the Ariarathes VII were shown as friends, Ariarathes began to come of age and assert his independence. Mithridates plotted his removal, proposing a meeting on neutral ground. Ariarathes asked him to submit to a search, but it was not thorough enough for Mithridates concealed a dagger with which he slew Ariarathes unaware. Mithridates then set up his own son, now called Ariarathes IX (with the change of name, another kind of "pretender"), although the power lay with Gordius, Mithridates's legate and now regent over Cappadocia.

Some years later the senate would seek revenge for the ousting of the true Ariarathean line, which had long been their friends. In 96, they ordered Gordius to step down in favor of a new king named Ariobarzanes. The timing was right for Sulla, Marius's lieutenant in Numidia and part-hero of Jugurtha's defeat (Chapter 11), who was about to set out for a praetorship in Cilicia and could escort Ariobarzanes to the throne. Sulla's demands of Mithridates and his dabbling in Cappadocia may have struck the East as presumptuous, especially given the distance of these kingdoms from Rome and how long it had been since Roman legions had shown their muscle in the region. Indeed, animosity toward Rome was building, though Sulla and the senate failed to detect it. The province had been bled dry since Gaius Gracchus's law empowering equestrian tax-collecting agencies to exercise jurisdiction in Asia Minor (Chapter 11). Moreover, Roman businessmen and their families were using their connections to dominate trade and money lending, and new usurious interest rates were crippling the indigenous population.

Marius, Sulla, and other Roman representatives in the East also missed a slight tilt in the balance of power in the region at this time. A minor king in Cyrene died in 96 and may have left the territory to the Roman people in his will, as Attalus III had done with Pergamon, but in truth, he left a vacuum, as Rome did nothing to pursue an administrative presence there. Antiochus VIII Grypus was assassinated in a *coup d'état* in the same year. His brother, Antiochus IX Cyzicenus, was left to contend with no fewer than five of Grypus's surviving sons as legitimate heirs to the throne. Cleopatra Selene, Grypus's widow (and Ptolemaic heiress), immediately married Cyzicenus, giving him a Ptolemaic edge in the competition. No matter, for he was killed by a son of Grypus the following year; Selene then married Cyzicenus's son, Eusebius, who became Antiochus X. To summarize her history of marriages, Cleopatra Selene had moved from Antiochus VII Grypus to his brother Antiochus IX Cyzicenus to his son Antiochus X Eusebius and was still holding on to power by 90. Though she thus held sway in Syria, and though her brothers, Ptolemy IX and Ptolemy X, were still kings in Cyprus and Alexandria, respectively, there is no denying that a void was inviting ambitious outsiders to try something.

Yet another event of 96, seemingly minor, tickled Mithridates's antennae. On the throne of Armenia the old king Tigranes I died that year and his son, Tigranes II, inherited the crown. Tigranes II, now in his mid-forties, had been living in Parthia since the age of 16 as a diplomatic hostage in the Parthian court; it was with Parthia's help that he assumed the throne. It should be remembered that the Mithridates Monument on Delos included officials from the Arsacid court and, with as much Persian blood as Greek, Mithridates was perhaps more open to working with Tigranes II than the Greeks and Romans had been. Tigranes agreed to accept one of Mithridates's daughters as his queen, and an alliance was struck. In essence, Mithridates benefited in 96 in some way from simultaneous shifts in Cappadocia (new king), Cyrene (no king), Syria (many kings), and Armenia (allied king). In 93, Mithridates and Tigranes II put their alliance into action and collectively drove Ariobarzanes from Cappadocia in favor of old Gordius and Ariarathes IX again. They also toppled Nicomedes IV, the son of Nicomedes III, who had ascended to the throne of Bithynia. Asia Minor was largely theirs.

12.4 The Origins of the Social War

The second half of the 90s in Rome is as poorly attested in our sources as the first half, yet still, the political trends of earlier in the decade toward a reempowerment of the senate can be discerned. In 95, the consuls Quintus Mucius Scaevola and Lucius Licinius Crassus set up special courts tasked with exposing false claims of Roman citizenship by Italians, and with expelling such perpetrators. Here we have evidence of how serious the question of citizenship was becoming to both sides – the Italians, desperate enough to take the step of counterfeiting credentials, and the Romans, passionate enough about their exclusivity to legislate against them. Perhaps it was as early as this moment that Italian tribes began to prepare for war. Appian says that they began to exchange hostages – a sure sign of alliance formation – shortly before 91.

In 91, Marcus Livius Drusus assumed the tribunate and in many ways pursued the same initiatives as his same-named father who had opposed Gaius Gracchus 30 years earlier (Chapter 11). Once again, poor sources prevent us from a perfect sequence of events but a number of events are reasonably attested. As with many of his predecessors in the office, Drusus sought more land for veterans, in Italy and Sicily, and also fixed the price of grain, with subsidies from the state to make it so. More provocative was his attempt to return senatorial influence to the juries for the extortion court. To maintain the support of the equestrians, whose voices would thus be diluted, he proposed elevating some 300 of them into the senate, presumably overnight. His effort to grant concessions to both sides ended up infuriating both: one of the consuls spoke out against him, and riots ensued once again.

Another of Drusus's proposals, whose timing in the year is frustratingly uncertain, was to call for broad Italian citizenship once again. Was this part of the platform that had incensed the outspoken consul, or was it floated by Drusus later in the year in retaliation against that opposition? In either case sources imply that he was viewed as something of a hero by the Italians for speaking up in such a way; an anecdote in Plutarch suggests he even fraternized with Poppaedius Silo, who would shortly become the most charismatic leader of an Italian revolution. In any case, reaction in Rome was swift: Drusus was assassinated, and another tribune set up a special court to root out collaborators for the movement for Italian citizenship, which was now construed as tantamount to treason. Many of Drusus's close associates were charged.

Late in the year, the Italians had had enough, and at Asculum a murderous putsch was carried out against all Romans in the town, apparently regardless of their activity for or against the Italians. The ethnic quality of the terror might be construed as "genocidal." Many tribes, mainly in the Apennines and along the Adriatic coast, joined immediately and the so-called Social War, from the Latin word *socius* meaning ally, was underway.

Fighting began in earnest in 90, and the Romans may have been surprised at the extent and the level of organization of the effort against them. The Italians had chosen as their capital city, Corfinium, now renamed Italica, and had devised a federal system of representation not unlike the Aetolian, Achaean, Thessalian, and Lycian Leagues of the Hellenistic world. Dues would be paid to a common treasury, from which a shared coinage would be minted. Delegates to an Italian assembly would represent their own constituencies; it probably fell to them to elect the dual executives that we know of for the coming year, a system seemingly modeled on the Roman consulship. The war was fought on multiple fronts and was ineffably bloody: many historians then and now compare the level of carnage to Hannibal's tear through the peninsula in the Second Punic War. The Italian army was massive, skilled, and fresh, owing to its involvement in recent wars in Africa and Gaul (which, of course, was a principal reason for the rebellion).

The Romans countered by calling upon other, extra-Italian allies, and they put to field Numidians, Spaniards, and Gauls, in addition to loyalist Italian troops, rather like the Carthaginians when they fought their own mercenaries in the 230s (Chapter 6). Both consuls stayed in Italy to fight; one was killed in battle against Poppaedius Silo that summer, and his replacement came to the same fate shortly thereafter, caught in an ambush. The persistent vacancy led the senate to call old Marius out of retirement, and to good effect, with Sulla again serving under him. The surviving consul, Lucius Julius Caesar (an elder cousin to the more famous Gaius Julius Caesar), fought on a different front against Gaius Papius Mutilus and managed to protect Capua, as important now as it was in the war with Hannibal, but many of the towns inland from the Bay of Naples fell to Mutilus, or opened their gates to his troops, and perhaps their minds to his ideas. It is telling how quickly the violence of the affair changed Roman minds: Lucius Julius Caesar promulgated a law granting citizenship to the Etruscans and the Latins – the very phenomenon he was struggling to deny to the southern and middle regions of Italy.

12.5 Attempts to Recover Asia Minor

The year 90 began much more fruitfully for Rome in Asia. In the course of 91, no doubt before the revolt at Asculum demonstrated that Rome would have other emergencies to face, the senate plotted to send a delegation to Asia to reinstall Nicomedes IV as king of Bithynia and Ariobarzanes as king of Cappadocia. Early in 90, Manius Aquillius accordingly arrived to support the Roman governor at Pergamon, Gaius Cassius Longinus, and the two prepared for an invasion. Aquillius was a natural choice for the hardliners in Rome who sought to bring Asia to heel: he had celebrated a triumph for crushing the Hellenistic-style slave rebellion in Sicily in 101, and his father of the same name had been the first governor of Asia, from 129 to 126, when the exploitation of Asia first took shape (Chapter 11). Aquillius likely passed through Athens on his way, where he would have drawn confidence from the supremacy of Medeius of Piraeus, who was at the head of a Roman-friendly faction controlling the city. Coins from this year in Athens depict the personification of Roma next to Athena's customary owl (see Figure 12.1). In Asia Aquillius was swift in his success, and both kings had back their thrones that year. He endeavored to push on and this time to take the war directly to Mithridates in Pontus; perhaps by now he had in mind the expenses of the Social War back home, which had to be paid with revenues other than Italian taxation. Nicomedes IV owed Rome a great debt, and so Aquillius called on him to lead the way: Bithynia sent a fleet into the Black Sea, the heart of Mithridates's economic foundation, and dispatched his land forces to Sinope. Mithridates naturally objected and prepared a counter invasion.

12.6 The Conclusion of the Social War

In 89 both consuls once again remained in Italy and once again, one of them would not see the end of the year: Lucius Porcius Cato died in battle against the Marsi, though the tribe was ultimately defeated. The surviving consul Gnaeus Pompeius Strabo completed a siege of Asculum that had been laid the previous autumn, and moved on to take Cofinium/Italica, whence the Italian capital was displaced to Bovianum, which itself was soon to fall. The Roman victories belie the carnage that continued: a former consul of 98 was killed in battle, and a former consul

Figure 12.1 Silver tetradrachm depicting Athena (obv.) and her owl perched on an amphora (rev.), 90/89 BCE. Some scholars have argued that the seated woman in the background on the reverse is Roma, a possible reference to the archon Medeius's support of Rome just before the city shifted to Mithridates.

of 99 was undermined when his troops mutinied. Sulla was acquitting himself well on the southern front, laying siege to Nola late in the year. The fact that the Social War was demanding a full six legions reveals that the conflict was far from over.

Desperate concessions of citizenship continued apace. Lucius Julius Caesar, who had proposed the franchise for Etruscans and Latins the year before, held the censorship for 89, surely elected to the post to carry out the promised enlistment. Cicero later blithely noted that, in fact, he did little of the sort that year; whether one should attribute Lucius Caesar's delaying to the chaos in Italy or to a willful recalcitrance is uncertain. Pompeius Strabo carried a new law to extend the old Latin Rights to Cisalpine Gaul. This was not at all citizenship but perhaps it would be enough to keep them out of the war. Tribunes proposed a compromise that would give the citizenship to all free born Italians, but would incorporate them into just eight of the 35 voting tribes, thus keeping them from constituting a majority in decision-making. The Italians were not tricked by such gerrymandering and the question of their allocation in voting tribes soon became a second phase in the conflict, for which violence would shift from the battlefield to the senate house. Late in 89, the Romans finally succeeded in eliminating Poppaedius Silo, a ringleader and figurehead of the rebellion. Cities like Nola were still holding out under siege, but they were contained and the active fronts were disintegrating.

12.7 The Resurgence of Mithridates

Rome could not call the end of the Social War a victory, and the mood in the city would be depressed even further as reports of what was transpiring in Asia trickled in throughout the year. Fortified by a just cause, Mithridates turned the tide and made swift inroads against the Romans and Roman-friendly troops in Asia Minor. By the end of the year he possessed almost all of the landmass, as well as the large coastal islands and the powerful Ionian cities. His rampaging success can be attributed to a mixture of clemency, generosity, and technical innovation. As he moved into Bithynia and sent Nicomedes IV packing in flight back to Rome (again), he forgave the region and its armies for their invasions of the previous year. As he entered into territories not previously familiar to his reign, he lavished gifts upon them, along with promises of a tax amnesty for five years, such that many opened their gates willingly. He set an example of his policies by proffering a significant donation to Apamea following damages wrought by an earthquake. No doubt he was reminding his Greek audience that his great grandfather Mithridates II had done the same for Rhodes after its famous tremor of 227 (Chapter 7). Mithridates's credentials as a Hellene were sound: his forces were led by Neoptolemus ("New Ptolemy"), a Greek, though he was also joined by Nemanes, an Armenian on loan from Tigranes.

As with many episodes in Italy at this time, an absolute chronology of events in Asia is not to hand, but either in this year or the next, Mithridates managed to capture two Roman commanders. One, Quintus Oppius, who headed the armies of central Asia Minor, was put on display as Mithridates's menial servant. The other, Manius Aquillius himself, was captured at Lesbos trying to escape and occupied center stage, literally, in a gruesome spectacle. As Appian tells us, he was dragged into the theater at Pergamon by a giant Celt, and after some amount of humiliation, his mouth was prized open and molten gold poured down his throat, a metaphor for the dangers of Roman greed. In the background of the stage, built as it was on a dizzying cliffside, the spectators could gaze out upon some of the most fertile land of Asia Minor – the real wealth in antiquity – now fully their own if Mithridates was to be taken at his word. Cassius Longinus, the sitting proconsul, was the only one to make it to safety, at Rhodes, which remained loyal. Delos, too, did not switch sides, and archeologists sensibly date the destruction of the Mithridates Monument to this context.

Mithridates was successfully cutting a figure both Alexanderesque and Alexandrian, befitting the new power of Asia Minor. On the island of Cos, he discovered a cache of treasure and the retinue of dynastic heirs that had been stashed there by Cleopatra III for safekeeping (Chapter 11). By now likely to be in their late adolescence or young adulthood, two were sons of Ptolemy IX on Cyprus and one was the son of Ptolemy X, who still held Alexandria. Questions were raised in antiquity as to the lineage of these heirs and whether they had full royal legitimacy, but in any case Mithridates sent them back to his court. As these youths were both Ptolemaic and Seleucid in descent (purportedly), they added a cosmopolitan dimension to Mithridates's regal character and would come in handy in service to his imperial aspirations, just as the Romans and Parthians and others had deployed hostages and students. Reaching back further in time than just the Ptolemies, Mithridates's embrace of Alexander's imagery was also carefully calculated. Portraits from the time show him decked in a lion skin, very much staking a claim to Alexander's personage. Whereas the quintessential Hellenistic hero rallied his support against Persia as a shared enemy, Mithridates was making similar use of Rome and the Romans.

12.8 Sulla Seizes Command

The new consuls of 88 were Sulla and Quintus Papirius Rufus. They may have had reason, if only for a brief time, to feel optimistic about the year in front of them: though something would have to be done about Asia Minor – and Sulla had the command assigned to him – the emergency of the Social War was passed, with only some mopping up operations in the far south of Bruttium and around Nola under a prolonged siege. Many of the major responsibilities for the year were held by Sulla's in-laws. His coconsul was the father of his daughter's husband, and he himself was married to Caecilia Metella, the cousin of Quintus Caecilius Metellus Pius who was pursuing the remnants of the Samnites.

These foundations, however, were almost immediately undermined by the tribune Publius Sulpicius Rufus. Sulpicius Rufus called for the new Italian citizens to be distributed across all 35 tribes and thus not confined to an electoral ghetto that would have neutralized their numbers. He also passed a law that limited the amount of debt that a senator could hold, which must have resulted in some expulsions from the body. But the true throwing down of the gauntlet was when Sulpicius Rufus shifted the Asian command against Mithridates from Sulla to, of all people, Marius. Marius was no doubt hoping to remind Rome of his heroics against the Numidians and the Gauls in times of emergency, and he could add now that he had accomplished much in the Social War and that he had been to Asia Minor before. But, as Sulla would have replied, the Marian miracle was over 10 years ago, and Sulla, too, had both achieved victories against the Italians and dealt with Mithridates on his home turf. What is more, it was he who had been elected consul and had been first assigned to command. Sulla tried to block Rufus's legislation with a woefully transparent claim that the gods did not approve. This only led to riots in which the other consul's son, who was also Sulla's son-in-law, was killed.

Sulla and Quintus Pompeius Rufus scattered to raise troops and fight back. Pompeius Rufus went north to take over the legions from Pompeius Strabo but his troops mutinied and he was killed. Sulla, however, had a personal connection to the troops he was aiming for: the soldiers laying siege to Nola had served under him on the other side of the winter that had just passed. One legion was left behind to maintain the siege while the other five followed Sulla against Rome and took the city by storm. More riots, more deaths; Sulla called for the heads of both

Sulpicius Rufus and Marius, his old commanding officer. Marius escaped and fled to his veterans in Africa, but Sulpicius Rufus was apprehended and executed.

12.9 Genocide, of a Form, in Asia Minor

The thuggery that was unleashed on the streets of Rome, both against Sulla and then at his own agency, would pale in comparison to, once again, dire rumors of horrors unfolding in Asia Minor. As the story goes, Mithridates secretively dispatched orders throughout the region that on an appointed day and time, his loyalists should rise up and kill all Romans in their communities. Scholars have again used the term genocide to describe the plot; they are assisted in this grim analysis by an inscription surviving from Nysa in which the local Chaeremo is exposed as a friend of the Romans, who have the appositive, "the common enemy of all mankind" (see Primary Source 12.1). Generalizing an entire variegated population as a single, monolithic constant – a *genos* – is the first step in perpetrating a geno-cide and by many accounts, the label fits this bill. Ancient estimates were that some 80 000 Romans and Italians were killed. Even if this is an exaggeration the figures reveal both the scope of Mithridates's mission and the extent to which Romans had infiltrated the region since the creation of the province.

Mithridates followed the bloodbath by sending a flotilla to take Rhodes, which was sheltering the fugitive proconsul Cassius Longinus but he was defeated. Rhodes thus survived intact, but Delos was not so lucky. Either in 88 or early in 87, Mithridates's general Archelaus, the brother of Neoptolemus, delivered revenge to the island, ransacking its treasury and extending the "genocide" to the approximately 20 000 Romans living there. Delos's treasury was packed off to Athens, which had joined the major cities of the Ionian coast in switching to Mithridates's side. Mithridates's navy supplanted that of Rome in Athens in 87, and another rash of executions added to the devastation in the East. Mithridates was also gaining an edge in Egypt: in 88, Ptolemy X was ousted from Alexandria and died in a desperate bid to retake Cyprus. He allegedly left his kingdom to Rome in a will, though this was questioned even at the time. In any case Ptolemy IX took his place; suddenly Mithridates's possession of the Ptolemaic heirs he found on Cos raised his stock in that corner of the Mediterranean, too.

Primary Source 12.1

Letter of Mithridates to Leonippus of Ephesus

This decree from Mithridates was set up in Ephesus and seems to refer to the famous purge of Romans and Roman sympathizers by the Pontic king. The reference to Romans as "the common enemy of all mankind" suggests they were targeted for their origins and not for any specific crime – or, a genocide. Note that Mithridates's hostility was not universally felt, if it is true that Chaeremo helped some Romans to escape.

> "King Mithridates to Leonippus, greetings. Chaeremo, son of Pythodorus, before this got the fugitive Romans away with his sons to Rhodes, and now, learning of my arrival, he has taken refuge in the sanctuary of Ephesian Artemis, and from there he sends communications to the Romans, the common enemy of all mankind. His impunity for the offenses he has committed is a stimulus for the actions against us. Think how you may, preferably, bring him to us, or how he may be kept under guard in confinement until I am rid of the enemy."

(trans. Naphtali Lewis and Meyer Reinhold (eds.), *Roman Civilization, Selected Readings, Volume 1*, third edition, New York: Columbia University Press, 1990.)

Sulla was finally able to embark for the East at the start of the campaigning season of 87. He enacted a few makeshift reforms in Rome in order to keep the homefront quiet in his absence; these included making the *comitia centuriata*, where the wealthy had a famous edge in procedural voting, the main legislative body, taking that role away from the assembly and the *concilium plebis*. He asked the new consuls, Lucius Cornelius Cinna and Gnaeus Octavius, to swear an oath to abide by the new system – what else could he do? – and then sailed away. Not surprisingly Sulla could not halt the movement just with some administrative turns, and Cinna felt confident enough to shred his oath early in the year. His coconsul Octavius chased him from the city, but Cinna found a receptive army among the Samnites of the south. What is more, Marius saw his opening with Sulla's departure and himself sailed from Africa, landing in Etruria. Marius and Cinna marched on Rome in a pincer movement from two directions and took Rome later in the year. They pursued a heinous reign of terror against their enemies; the dead included the other consul Octavius, plus Lucius Julius Caesar, the former consul and censor, and Publius Licinius Crassus.

12.10   The Sack of Athens

Sulla was not far from the tumult, but he elected to press on with his original mission to Asia and to deal with Italy later, where he was now officially an outlaw. The gates of Athens were closed to him and so he encircled the city and Piraeus with his five legions and bivouacked in Eleusis with his wife Caecilia Metella who had fled Cinna's Rome. Completely bereft of a navy, Sulla could only watch as ships sailed in and out of the harbor with fresh supplies. He dispatched a lieutenant, Lucius Licinius Lucullus, to seek out ships at Crete, Cyrene, and Alexandria, but it came to nothing as Lucullus was compelled by Mithridates's navy to shelter in Alexandria for the winter. In the meantime, another Mithridatic army gathered in northern Macedonia to relieve the siege of Athens the following year, if need be.

The year 86 began with Cinna entering his second consulship and Marius his record-setting seventh. Much of what transpired that year, however, was attributable to Cinna alone, as Marius died of natural causes within a month. With free rein to pursue his initiatives, Cinna finally enrolled the new Italian citizens across all 35 tribes as they desired, maximizing their electoral impact. Many efforts at debt relief had been attempted in previous regimes to no avail, but here Cinna was unopposed, and under the policy of an allied tribune, fully 75% of all principal on loans was wiped from the books. He also sent Lucius Valerius Flaccus east to take command of the legions now illegally led by Sulla. Flaccus soon realized that Sulla was coasting with such great momentum that tangling with him would have been a fool's errand; instead, he overshot Greece and made directly for Pergamon. For reasons unknown, Flaccus was assassinated in a mutiny by Gaius Fulvius Fimbria; it does not seem to be factionally motivated, as Fimbria remained as antagonistic toward Sulla as his predecessor had been. At Pergamon Fimbria encountered a welcome reception by the locals. Mithridates, it turned out, had reneged on his promise not to tax Asia in the short term. He successfully stormed the city and put Mithridates in flight back to Pontus.

Mithridates's forces were also suffering against Sulla in 86. Early in the year, Roman troops had finally breached the walls first of Athens and then of Piraeaus. Reports of indiscriminant plunder and rapine are confirmed by layers of ash and charred ruins in Athenian archeological excavations. It was this melee that Flaccus elected to pass by to the north: Sulla's men would not be stopped (for other disruptions wrought by Sulla in Greece, see Primary Source 12.2). Archelaus sailed free to the northern army and pushed into Boeotia later in the year, but Sulla's army defeated him at Chaeronea and Orchomenos, allegedly thwarting Mithridates's famous

> **Primary Source 12.2**
>
> **Delphic Decree Honoring Polygnota of Thebes**
>
> The war referred to in this decree seems to be Sulla's invasion of Greece during his campaign against Mithridates. Note that the Panhellenic Games at Delphi were suspended but rituals for the god continued nonetheless.
>
> "Since Polygnota of Thebes, daughter of Socrates, a harpist, was living in Delphi when the Pythian Games were to be conducted (but were not conducted because of the state of affairs), she still performed that day and participated throughout the day; and, having been asked by the magistrates and the citizens, she performed for three (more) days and was greatly appreciated as worthy of the god and of the Theban people and of our city, and we honored her with [five hundred drachmas]. With fortune fair, (the city) shall praise Polygnota of Thebes, daughter of Socrates, for her piety toward the god and her purity and for how she conducts herself by her skill and her art. To her and her descendants shall be bestowed by the city the status of *proxenos*, and priority with the oracle, priority in court, inviolability, exemption from taxes, a front seat at the games which the city puts on, and the possession of land and a house, and all other honors such as belong to the other *proxenoi* and benefactors of the city. It shall summon her to the prytaneion to the public table. It shall front her with a sacrificial victim for Apollo …."

scythed chariots by digging long ditches in the battlefield as obstacles before the engagement. Lucullus finally returned to Sulla later in the year, but with no luck in terms of providing a supporting fleet. Ptolemy IX, newly reinstalled at Alexandria, had housed him in style but could apparently do no more, given that Mithridates still possessed his two sons and nephew, and Sulla, he surely knew, had no legitimacy as a commander in the eyes of the Republic.

The following year, Sulla moved toward Pergamon in the face of two potential enemies, Mithridates and Fimbria. Though he possessed money and high morale from the previous year, he still lacked seapower and state authority, which must have been factors in his decision to do the unexpected: he came to terms with Mithridates. Acting through envoys, the two agreed to the so-called Peace of Dardanus, named for a town near Troy. In essence a nonaggression pact, from it Sulla got little out of Mithridates beyond a vow to leave Asia Minor and to allow the Romans to govern their province again as they saw fit. One unexpected boon, it seems, came in the form of one of the Ptolemaic hostages: the one son of Ptolemy X defected to Sulla's side, a future trump card for Egypt. With Sulla holding a powerful hand, Fimbria the mutineer fell to a mutiny himself.

Compared with Sulla's march on Rome and sack of Athens, the year 85 was less challenging for him: he spent it visiting disloyal subjects in Asia Minor and the islands and arranging suitable penalties. In the main, the war indemnities that he assessed amounted to five years' worth of back taxes, to be paid in full, immediately, a sum reportedly totaling 20 000 talents. To meet this obligation, city after city borrowed once again from Roman lenders, who stepped into the breach opened up by the genocide of Italians a few years earlier, and again at crushing rates of interest. By contrast, Sulla rewarded the loyalists, especially Rhodes, which had been deprived of Rome's highest favor since 167; now the mainland tracts of Lycia were awarded back to the island's control.

In 84, Sulla returned to Athens, continuing to take a measure of leisure before the coming reckoning with Rome. His own city had been in the hands of Cinna, who held four straight consulships, from 87 to 84, and Gnaeus Papirius Carbo, who joined him for 85 and 84. Now in Attica, Sulla was initiated into the Eleusinian Mysteries, and he removed some impressive columns from Antiochus IV's unfinished Temple of Zeus in Athens (Chapter 9) and sent them to Rome as bounty, and also bought the libraries of Aristotle and Theophrastus (Chapter 4) cheaply, another package shipped off to Rome. Sulla also reinstated oligarchic elements to the Athenian constitution. The democratic assembly became inoperative, and we know of no substantial decrees from it from Sulla's conquest through the rise of Caesar some 40 years later.

12.11 Sulla's Dictatorship

In 83, Sulla's forces went back on the offensive, in two directions. In Asia Minor, the legate he had left in charge, Lucius Licinius Murena, violated the terms of the Peace of Dardanus and attacked Cappadocia. It is unknown whether his invasion came before or after Tigranes II moved armies into Syria and was welcomed as the new king: did Murena trigger this move by Mithridates's strongest ally, or was he responding to it? In any case, Mithridates formally complained and Murena was recalled, but the fact that he ultimately celebrated a triumph suggests that he was not acting without at least Sulla's sanction, if not the senate's. More important for Rome's history was Sulla's own campaign of that year. He crossed from Greece to Brundisium where he was joined by an army of allies led by some of the sons of now dead friends, who had scattered at the rise of Cinna. Metellus Pius arrived from a haven in Africa; Marcus Licinius Crassus, the son of the consul of 97 who had exposed fraudulent Italian citizens, came in from Spain; and Gnaeus Pompeius, known conventionally with the English transliteration Pompey, arrived with three legions from Picenum, the traditional seat of his clan, where his father Pompeius Strabo, consul of 89, had died of an illness. Cinna had been slain in a mutiny of dissatisfied soldiers in 84 as he was preparing to confront Sulla's return, and many of his armies switched to Sulla. In spite of the tide in Sulla's favor, the fighting was still hard, and the year ended with no resolution, Sulla still outside the walls.

In 82, the new consuls were Carbo, again, and the son of Gaius Marius, who had the same name. Sulla managed to trap Marius *fils* at Praeneste, but Carbo proved more elusive, and the Samnites allied with him remained as fearsome as ever. Eventually Carbo fled to Africa, and Sulla's enemies were consolidated at a last stand at Rome's Colline Gate in late 82. The battle was a rout in Sulla's favor, and Praeneste succumbed shortly thereafter, leading the younger Marius to commit suicide. Sulla again invested Rome, much as he had done in 88, and as Cinna and Marius had done in 87. A city that survived Gallic and Punic incursions thus had been infiltrated three times in six years by its own generals, statistics which set aside the countless riots and political murders occurring in the same span. As Sulla assembled the senators and addressed them before the Temple of Bellona (see Map 12.1), a goddess of war, he reportedly had to raise his voice over the cries of imprisoned Samnites facing execution.

Soon indiscriminant murder gave way to a more macabre, discriminating kind: Sulla began publishing in the Forum new lists of public enemies, Roman citizens alike, who could be killed with impunity. These "proscription lists" had the aura of governmental writs, but they were thin disguises for score-settling not unlike the previous *senatus consulta ultima*, which had been more limited in scope. The numbers offered by Appian are that 90 *senators* and 2600 *equites* fell victim to the scheme. Sulla took on the epithet Felix, meaning happy or fortunate. Was this itself a form of retribution, to make explicit the contrast between his current station and those of his enemies? More likely, it drew upon the powerful personification-goddess of Fortune/Tyche of the Hellenistic East (Chapter 4), as Sulla attained the stature of a monarch (for Hellenistic qualities in Sulla's architectural commissions, see Figure 12.2).

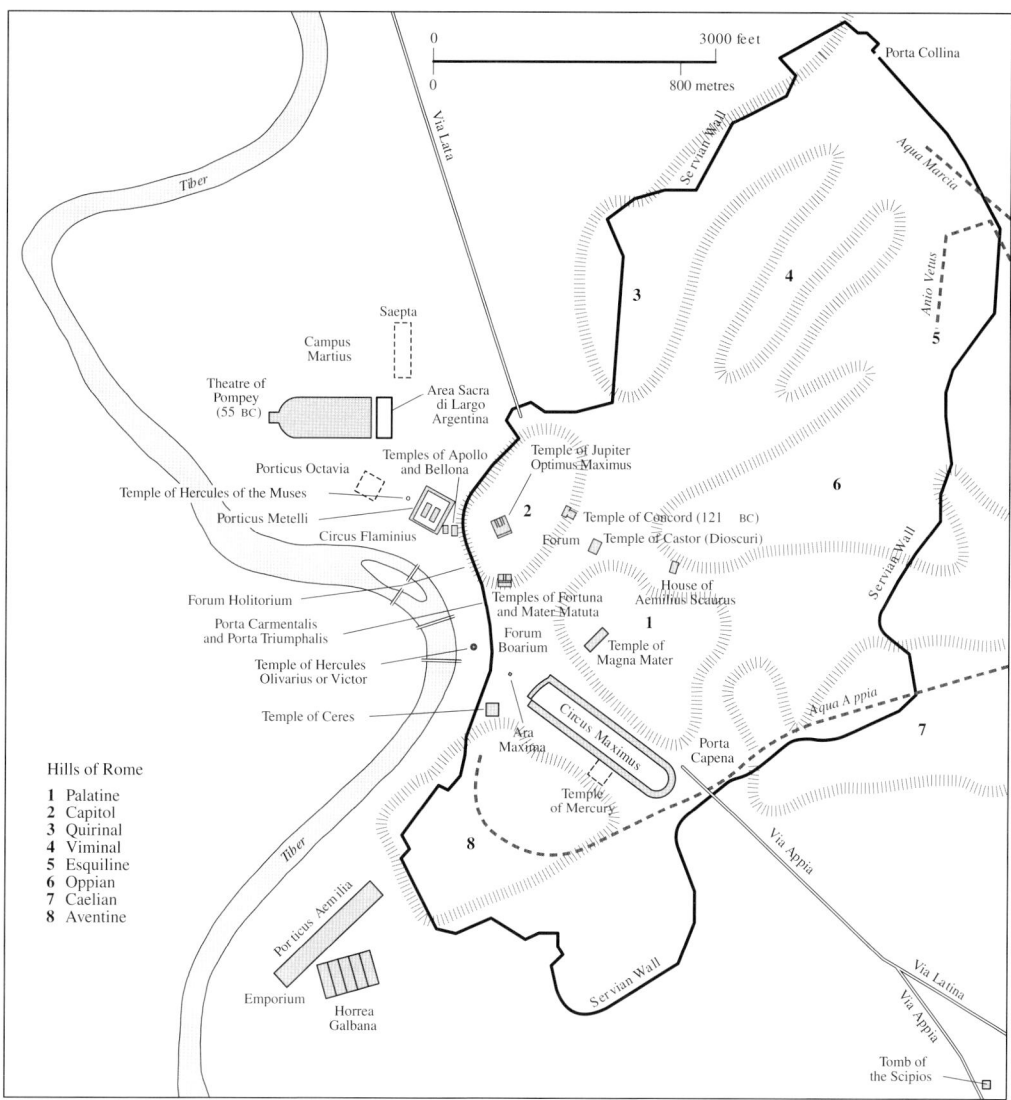

Map 12.1 Rome in the late Republic.

Rome was in chaos. Vague elements of the constitution needed clarifying, for example, the tribunes' *true* rights and privileges, as opposed to the rights and privileges that had been concocted recently by ambitious strivers. To take on this monumental task, and in view of the emergency in which Rome found itself, Sulla dug into the collective knowledge of Roman political history and hit upon the dictatorship. Dictatorship has been a relatively common office in the early Republic, and the last dictator to have been appointed was at the end of the Second Punic War, multiple generations before. Sulla seized the title, or rather received it from an official *interrex* from the senate, surely on his encouragement.

All previous dictators had been charged with a mandate, and Sulla's was to "reestablish the Republic," and he spent the next two years seeking to carry it out. He began with the troublesome (to him) tribunate: he removed their right to initiate legislation, as well as their right to

(a)

(b)

Figure 12.2 (a) Artist's reconstruction of the sanctuary of Athena at Lindos, Rhodes, c. 200 BCE. (b) The sanctuary of Fortuna Primigenia at Praeneste near Rome, c. 120 BCE. (c) The Tabularium on the Capitoline Hill in Rome, 78 BCE. The construction of the Tabularium during Sulla's regime demonstrates aspirations to Hellenistic monumentality in architecture.

(c)

Figure 12.2 (Continued)

veto other magistrates' and assemblies' decrees. He also forbade any former tribunes from advancing to higher office, effectively turning it into a political dead end. The beneficiary of his reforms was, in large part, the senate. Juries for important courts were taken from equestrians and returned to senators: cases involving public crimes such as extortion, bribery, embezzlement, and other forms of corruption would now be tried by the peers of those charged. He also promoted 300 new senators to the body, restoring it to a steady group of around 600 members. Leadership was also curtailed in a way that would enhance the constancy of the senate: the office of *princeps senatus* was eliminated, and the old rule requiring consuls to wait 10 years between repeating the office was reinforced. Since Sulla also established the minimum age of 42 for the office, any one man could not expect to live long enough to serve more than two or at most three consulships, theoretically. Under Sulla's system, consuls would also have to stay close to Rome with only promagistrates leading armies in the provinces, thus giving imperial authority to the senate, which decided provincial assignments, and not the electorate.

New rules for the provinces were also designed to stem the ambitions of a would-be revolutionary and to deprive rivals of Hellenistic-style leadership. Governors were not allowed to leave their province, and could not wage war without senatorial approval. On the reverse, once a successor was named, an outgoing governor had just one month to vacate. Cisalpine Gaul, which had received Latin Rights in 89 by a law of Pompeius Strabo, was organized into Rome's tenth province, joining Sicily, Sardinia-Corsica, Near Spain, Far Spain, Macedonia, Africa, Asia, Transalpine Gaul, and Cilicia. The Spains, however, were now of questionable status, as

Quintus Sertorius, a proconsul and past Marian supporter and surely one of those named on Sulla's proscription lists, had fled there and effected a split from the empire, ruling independently rather than returning to face Sulla. The general Pompey, who had married Sulla's stepdaughter, was an overseas enforcer for Sulla, capturing and executing Carbo in Sicily in 81 and defeating an anti-Sullan holdout in Africa in 80. He demanded a triumph upon his return and was given it once the upraised eyebrows realized that in this day and age, even a 26 year old could make such a case, in spite of Sulla's recent laws on age requirements.

In a final foreign policy move, Sulla sent "his" Ptolemaic heir to Egypt in 81, upon the death of Ptolemy IX. Called by historians Ptolemy XI, he did not last long: he married Ptolemy IX's daughter, Cleopatra Berenike, in good form but had her executed within a few weeks. After spending 15 years on Cos, four years with Mithridates, and four more years with Sulla, in Alexandria he had no idea what he was doing, and the crowd, which had held Berenike dear, lynched him with alacrity. With the throne now vacant, Mithridates, still strong, self-assured, and ambitious, deployed *his* remaining two Ptolemies, the sons of Ptolemy IX, whom he moved to Syria to Egypt. He likely knew the regime more thoroughly, understanding the equilibrium that had held for the past 20 years with Cyprus and Alexandria balanced by two kings: thus, one of his Ptolemies became known as Ptolemy of Cyprus while the other, referred to by moderns as Ptolemy XII Auletes, took Alexandria. Sulla himself expired: he took the unexpected step of abdicating his dictatorship and retired to a quiet life outside the city. Perhaps he realized he was fatally ill, for he soon died of natural causes, just like Marius.

12.12 Conclusions

Many scholars of Roman history have argued that the 90s is the decade for which they most wish more historical information could be recovered. Our knowledge of the domestic politics for those 10 years is scant, and we know fewer details than usual for international relations, as well. And yet, the period that ensued in the 80s was tumultuous across the board, with unprecedented levels of violence, especially for Rome and the Romans. For his part, Sulla identified the radical causes and methods espoused by the tribunes as the culprit, but of course, there were ideological opponents who would object to that, citing the mismanagement of provinces on the part of the elite who governed them. Corruption was at the root of horrific blood-letting in Asia Minor, just as Mithridates pursued his own ambitions.

In either case, the beginning of the first century was the forge in which the worldviews of the subsequent generation of Roman power brokers were cast. Pompey, Julius Caesar, and Cicero are just the marquee names, to be encountered in the next chapter, among statesmen who came of age amid chaos, and who would go on to exploit it even as they tried to fix it to their own tastes. Overseas territories, increasingly falling to Rome's outright possession, and Hellenistic styles of rule within them would play instrumental roles in their plans.

Further Reading

Gruen, Erich (1992). *Culture and National Identity in Republican Rome.* Ithaca: Cornell University Press.

Habicht, Christian (1997). *Athens from Alexander to Antony.* Cambridge, MA: Harvard University Press.

Hojte, Jakob Munk (ed.) (2009). *Mithridates VI and the Pontic Kingdom.* Aarhus University Press.

Keaveney, Arthur (2005). *Sulla: The Last Republican*, 2e. New York: Routledge.

Phang, Sara (2008). *Roman Military Service: Ideologies of Discipline in the Late Republic and Early Principate.* Cambridge: Cambridge University Press.

Steel, Catherine (2013). *The End of the Republic, 146 to 44 BC: Conflict and Crisis.* Edinburgh: Edinburgh University Press.

13

To 63: Extraordinary Commands

Timeline

78: The radical consulship of Marcus Aemilius Lepidus
76: Links between Sertorius in Spain and Mithridates in Asia Minor
74–71: Marcus Antonius's failed campaign against the so-called pirates
74: Roman annexation of Bithynia
73–71: Rebellion of Spartacus
73: Invasion of Asia Minor by Lucullus
71: Assassination of Sertorius in Spain
70: Consulship of Crassus and Pompey; restoration of the tribunate
69: Sack of Delos by the pirates
69–65: War between Rome and Mithridates in Asia Minor
67: The Lex Gabinia gives Pompey command against the pirates
66: The Lex Manilia gives Pompey command against Mithridates
63: Consulship of Cicero
62: The death of Catiline

Principal Themes

- Sulla's unexpected death made the conservative reforms of his dictatorship susceptible to revision, and the tribunate, most notably, was restored to its full, radical authority.
- Diplomatic and military ties can be found in our sources to link six disparate powers in the 70s – Sertorius in Spain, Mithridates VI in Pontus, Tigranes II in Armenia, Ptolemy XII in Egypt, Spartacus in Italy, and the so-called pirates. Whether these acted cooperatively or not, similarities among them suggest a trend in the resistance of locals against larger imperial powers, especially Rome.
- Gaius Julius Caesar and Marcus Tullius Cicero, both young, ambitious climbers, made their debuts in politics, the former as an heir to Marius's political ideology, the latter as an orator taking on, first, corruption in the provinces.
- Pompey received special commands, first against the pirates and then against Mithridates, which enabled him to establish de facto Roman influence over the entire eastern Mediterranean, but which also opened new, extralegal paths to power for himself.
- Having reached the consulship, Cicero joined the camp of Pompey and claimed to have exposed a conspiracy by a political rival, Catiline, though the evidence for Catiline's guilt is sketchy.

The Roman Republic and the Hellenistic Mediterranean: From Alexander to Caesar, First Edition. Joel Allen.
© 2020 John Wiley & Sons, Inc. Published 2020 by John Wiley & Sons, Inc.

13.1 Introduction

This chapter proposes a somewhat novel interpretation of the activities of states, and state-like groups, surrounding Rome's Italian peninsula. In the course of the 70s, Rome dealt with a number of breakaway territories and resistance movements, in regions as far flung as Spain and Asia Minor, as well as "in their own backyard" in Italy. These are often treated as separate phenomena, but a comparison of their timing, their interstate connections, and most importantly, the nature of their assertions of independence may give substance to brief literary accounts of contacts among them all – a kind of daisy chain where Sertorius was linked to Mithridates in one source, and Mithridates to the "pirates" in another, and the pirates to Spartacus, and Spartacus to the Celts, and so on. If indeed a level of cooperation existed among them – and even if it did not – Rome faced conflicts on multiple fronts. Solutions both military and political were in the offing, but both required departures from past practices. Pompey and Cicero, in particular, rose to prominence with their proposals for change, but not without triggering new unrest in the city. The controversies surrounding an alleged conspiracy against Cicero during his consulship also attest to beguiling uncertainties.

13.2 Sertorius, Mithridates, and the "Pirates"

Sulla's reconstitution of the state, effected during his dictatorship (Chapter 12), faced a serious challenge almost immediately. In 78, one of the consuls for the year, Marcus Aemilius Lepidus, though likely an adherent of Sulla's during his struggles against the Marians, performed an ideological about-face. He had been sent north to deal with a disturbance concerning land tenure at Faesulae, near modern Florence, but at some point abruptly assumed the outlook of a *popularis*. Nothing about his plans, according to our meager sources, was lukewarm: he supported a full restoration of the tribunate to its former powers and stature, and a return to subsidized grain prices. Those Italians who had been displaced by Sulla's veteran colonies were to receive some kind of compensation, and those who had fled the proscriptions or were formally exiled for their politics were invited to return. These included Cinna's son-in-law, Gaius Julius Caesar, now age 22, about whom we will soon hear much. So complete was Lepidus's reversal that he even opposed staging an official funeral for Sulla upon his death. The political capital to be gained from such radical positions must have been obvious, as Lepidus was soon joined by another prominent patrician, Marcus Junius Brutus.

Violence was renewed surprisingly soon. Lepidus and Brutus had the means to march on Rome, Sulla-style, and were expected to do so. From a military camp, Lepidus issued a demand that he be eligible for a repeat consulship in 77, endeavoring to remove the prohibition of consecutive years in office (Chapter 12) to join the others of Sulla's reforms that were being discontinued. In early 77, Lepidus's former coconsul Quintus Lutatius Catulus gathered an army in opposition. He was joined by the ubiquitous Pompey, Sulla's capable lieutenant who had skipped from Sicily to Africa and back to Italy in chasing down Sulla's last enemies (Chapter 12). Still never having held elected office, Pompey was nonetheless imbued by the senate with the *imperium* of a propraetor to lead his own contingent of soldiers. This separation of the authorities of an office from the office itself was a neat, supralegal trick that would increasingly come in handy to ambitious statesmen; as we shall see, it both made the Republic better equipped to handle emergencies, and also ruined its institutions and formed the nucleus of a revolutionary political system. In any case, the device was effective: Pompey defeated Brutus at Mutina and had him executed, and Catulus put Lepidus to flight from a battle near the Mulvian Bridge north of Rome.

Lepidus and a significant body of his soldiers headed westward, aiming to join their ideological confrere Quintus Sertorius, the Marian who had been roaming the Iberian peninsula since 83 (Chapter 12). Sertorius was an obvious destination for Lepidus not only because of his politics but also because of his security. He had effectively carved out a separate state within Rome's sketchily drawn provinces, governing not only by the trappings of Roman power, but also by alliances with local leaders who were being incorporated into his own private, quasi-imperial system. By means of acculturating hostage-taking practices, Sertorius is said to have trained the next generation of indigenous Spanish chieftains in Roman ways, a display of respect that engendered solidarity and strengthened ties. Sertorius is also said to have been fomenting rebellion in the province of Transalpine Gaul, and had made it possible for the pirates, formerly concentrated in the East, to move into western theaters. From this unified foundation, Sertorius confined Metellus Pius, the Roman originally dispatched against him by Sulla, to southern Spain and himself began expanding his influence into Lusitania and points north.

Pompey was eager to give chase, and before the end of the campaign of 77 against the Lepidans, he demanded that the senate extend and amplify his command for another season. Pompey confronted many detractors: why fight for Sulla's program if it meant ignoring its central tenets forbidding unusual terms of power? But his supporters overcame their opposition and Pompey's *imperium* was elevated from propraetorian to proconsular. Lepidus was killed in Sardinia en route to Spain but many of his fugitive troops made it to Sertorius safely.

Around 76, following on continual victories over Metellus in the field and soon over Pompey, too, Sertorius is said to have massively outflanked Italy by entering into a treaty with none other than Mithridates in Pontus. It is said that Mithridates sent 40 ships and 3000 talents for Sertorius's use in Spain, and Sertorius sent some of Marius's old allies to Mithridates to help train his army. Whether Mithridates wanted to employ Roman techniques or simply to get a better understanding of their tactics, he now had access to valuable advisors. Presumably those serving under Marius had learned a thing or two about imparting complex military practices to those who had never experienced them before, as they had already done for Marius's *proletarii*. Sertorius still had Roman interests at heart: Plutarch says that he explicitly barred Mithridates from taking the Roman province of Asia, in spite of their new bond.

The alliance of Sertorius and Mithridates brought many corners of the Mediterranean into a network of allies, or if not a formal network, then an assemblage whose degrees of separation were few. Both leaders had found uses for the so-called pirates. As seen previously (Chapter 12), the term "pirate" robs the participants of any organizational traits or sense of a mission, on par with a state, and yet their navy, it has been estimated, was 1000 ships strong at this time and included scores of fortified bases on thousands of miles of coastline. Many among their numbers were fugitives of one kind or another from more established regimes and had begun their careers with thorough training and exposure to military rigor. In addition to them, Sertorius and Mithridates could also count on Tigranes II of Armenia whose alliance with Pontus was still strong. What is more, the two Ptolemaic kings now ruling in Cyprus and Alexandria owed their positions to Mithridates. Though Ptolemy of Cyprus and Ptolemy XII Auletes are not known to have engaged in the efforts of Sertorius and Mithridates, the circumstantial evidence is strong that they brought a third corner of the Mediterranean to a potential diplomatic cooperative. Indeed, the coalition of these powers against Rome, complete with a spectrum of allies ranging from the active to the lethargic, reminds one of earlier Hellenistic monarchs, who banded together when any one held the upper hand, such as when Antipater, Ptolemy I, and Craterus rallied against Perdiccas in 321 (Chapter 3), and Ptolemy I, Seleucus I, and Lysimachus collected against Antigonus in 301 (Chapter 4), and Ptolemy Ceraunus and Seleucus I moved on Lysimachus in 281 (Chapter 5), and so on.

The evidence for the Ptolemies in this period seems to bear a direct correlation to the stability of the regime: as kings and queens became more and more transient, we hear less and less about their policies. One exception is Ptolemy XII's promotion of the son of the priest of Ptah in Memphis, which took place in 76 around the time when Sertorius and Mithridates were coming together. The previous priest of the god had died and in his place Ptolemy XII appointed the priest's adolescent son, who would come to be called Psenptah III. A political relationship was born, whereby Psenptah III lent Ptolemy XII, a potentially illegitimate member of the dynasty, it should be remembered (Chapter 12), some credibility with the indigenous population: he crowned Ptolemy XII pharaoh in the same year. Likewise, Ptolemy intermingled with the indigenous elite, marrying one of their number in the mid-70s. Günther Hölbl has suggested that this, and not Ptolemy's marriage to his sister, may have been the union that produced at least some of his heirs, including the famous Cleopatra VII and her siblings, Arsinoe IV, Ptolemy XIII, and Ptolemy XIV. In any case, the attention paid by this Ptolemy to the interests of the non-Hellenic population of his realm may be consonant with what leaders like Sertorius in Spain and Mithridates in Asia Minor and the pirates were about.

The Romans were not idle while their enemies seemed to form a circle of sorts around them. As early as 78, before the Lepidan uprising had done its damage, the senate empowered yet another consular to deal with the pirates. For some three seasons, Publius Servilius Vatia cruised the coasts of Lycia, Pamphylia, and Cilicia in southern Asia Minor and dealt with what he believed to be key pirate strongholds. Piecemeal in fashion, however, the campaign could not stem the reach of a force that was elusive, flexible, and, somehow, superbly managed. In 75, the senate also empowered Gaius Scribonius Curio, governor of Macedonia, to march north and east, up to the banks of Danube River, perhaps motivated by knowledge of a Sertorian-Mithridatic "axis" (though this is speculation).

Tensions came to a head in 74, when the death of Nicomedes IV of Bithynia removed a buffer from among them all. Bithynia's location on the Bosporus, controlling shipping lanes between the Black and Aegean Seas, could form a hub at the middle of a new wheel if its throne fell to the control of another power. In his will Nicomedes left his kingdom to Rome, following the pattern set by Pergamon in 133 and Cyrene in 96. While the Romans had felt no urgency in capitalizing on the bequest of Cyrene when it occurred (perhaps smarting from the expenses of doing so in Pergamon), now in 74 they leapt at these opportunities. The senate consolidated Cyrene as a province; this may have functioned as a check on Ptolemy XII, if we are to see in him sympathy with Mithridates. A base at Cyrene would also be useful for the ongoing effort against the pirates. In 74, Marcus Antonius, son of the man of the same name who fought the pirates in 102 (Chapter 11), was charged with the same task.

Rome also readily annexed Bithynia as a province in 74. Both of the consuls were assigned to the region: Lucius Licinius Lucullus had command in Cilicia, and Marcus Aurelius Cotta in Bithynia, both of them likely training their attention on Mithridates. Meanwhile, Metellus Pius and Pompey kept up their struggles against the formidable Sertorius in Spain, and one may consider the Roman world of 74 to be one of many fronts. Indeed, the year ended bleakly for Rome: Cotta's fleet, based at Chalcedon across the Bosporus from Byzantium, was stolen right from under him by Mithridates, who then bolted across the Sea of Marmara and laid siege to the major city of Cyzicus on its southern horizon. Lucullus shifted over to establish his own siege, stationing his soldiers, and ships in an outer ring around Mithridates. The stand-off continued as the campaign season passed into winter.

13.3 Spartacus

The following year opened with little cause for hope for Rome. A gladiator-slave named Spartacus, of Thracian origins near where Curio and Cotta were fighting Mithridates, broke from captivity near Capua and quickly acquired a following of fellow fugitive slaves. Celts and Germans are said to have been particularly attracted to his movement, as well as compatriot Thracians. They ranged about Italy in the course of 73 and 72, defeating two consuls and the governor of Cisalpine Gaul. As with the slave rebellions of 135 and 102 (Chapters 10 and 11), and as with the stories of the pirates, it would be a mistake to write off Spartacus and his supporters as anarchic roughs whose extinction was simply a matter of time. Appian reports that Spartacus entered into an alliance with, once again, the pirates, for the purpose of acquiring supplies and, if need be, transportation out of Italy. He nearly crossed the Alps into his Thrace, but turned back, perhaps because of the advance successes of Curio in the Balkans since 75 (see above).

Spartacus's story has long inspired drama because of the salacious nature of gladiatorial combat and the romance of a fight for freedom. Stanley Kubrick's film of 1960 was criticized by ancient historians for its greater interest in the social movements of the United States at the time, such as the struggles surrounding the promotion of a Civil Rights Act, than in historical accuracy, but given Spartacus's extra-Italian alliances with the pirates and others, who had made connections with marginal groups, perhaps Kubrick was not far off the mark. Whether it was Mithridates extirpating predatory Roman moneylenders, or Sertorius backing Marius's enlistment of the proletariat and cultivating noncitizen Spaniards, or Ptolemy XII's radical intermingling with his subjects outside Alexandria, or the pirates' very existence and prosperity without the guidance of an aristocratic elite, it is tempting to see an ideology on Spartacus's part, mirrored in contemporary Mediterranean leaders (compare Figure 13.1). To call the arrangement a partnership or an axis or a network, with multiple poles and a shared ideology counter to Rome, would be pushing the evidence beyond what it allows, but the coincidence of the various campaigns bears notice.

Figure 13.1 Bronze figure of a workman or artisan with a wax tablet tucked in his belt, first century BCE. Nonelite, manual activity seems to be ennobled in this fine work.

13.4 Rome Steadily Consolidates

Though still in opposition to all of the above, the Romans themselves, even those of *optimates* leanings, were bending to social trends: Gaius Aurelius Cotta, brother of the failed consul of 74, removed the law making a tribunate the last office in a political career (Chapter 12). Tribunes, for the moment, still lacked the teeth of the veto, but the office itself was no longer a dead end. The senate also took the desperate step in 73 of pardoning Lepidus's associates, now serving with Sertorius; clearly a tactic to undermine their adversary, it also constituted a political concession to those with an opposing point of view. Moreover, in 73, as Roman supply lines were compromised by Spartacus and the pirates, a food shortage crippled the city, and the consuls had to commandeer grain surpluses from Sicily, now governed by the newly arrived Gaius Verres, and send them to Rome at subsidized prices.

In the second half of 73, the Romans in the city finally had some reason for optimism. Lucullus had successfully relieved Mithridates's siege of Cyzicus. After that success, he sailed to nearby Lemnos and defeated another Mithridatic fleet, under the command of the mysterious and intriguingly named Marcus Marius, almost certainly one of the Italians lent by Sertorius in the previous year. With the wind at his back, so to speak, Lucullus stormed into Galatia on the mainland and broke through even to Pontus, on Mithridates's home turf. The Romans also had the luck of nature on their side, as a storm simultaneously wrecked much of Mithridates's Black Sea fleet. Mithridates, who had held fast through two Roman wars, was now fleeing for his life, seeking refuge with his daughter and her husband in Armenia. Even Mithridates's son, Machares, turned on him from his territory on the northern shore of the Black Sea.

In the following several years, Rome's remaining enemies fell one by one. In 72, Sertorius was taken unawares and assassinated by his own lieutenant, Marcus Perperna. Perperna was a lesser figure, and Pompey and Metellus Pius finally had their break and won some major victories against him. Later that summer, Perperna himself was trapped by Pompey and killed, while Sertorius's followers, perhaps in keeping with Cotta's decree of 73, were treated with clemency. Spartacus and the pirates, however, had not been defeated. That changed in 71, when Marcus Licinius Crassus, another Sullan who had helped him march on Rome in 83 (Chapter 12), was given six legions to deal with the fugitives, a force he reputedly augmented by hiring recruits with his own fortune. Crassus cornered Spartacus's army in Bruttium and nearly destroyed them all, including their leader. He famously lined the Appian Way with some 6000 crucifixes of the slowly dying prisoners of war. But a smaller detachment of Spartacus's forces had escaped northward, and these were apprehended by Pompey as he was landing from Spain. He overwhelmed them with numbers and it was an easy victory. Mithridates in 73, Sertorius in 72, Spartacus in 71: this left just the pirates as an enduring threat (setting aside the inactive Ptolemies): in 72 and 71, hardly cowed, they had crushed Marcus Antonius's navy off the coast of Crete and still seemed indomitable.

Lucullus was active, for his part, in the years from 72 to 71, but in civil, not military ventures. With Mithridates's forces dispersed and the legendary Pontic fortresses compromised one by one, he turned to the administration of the Asian provinces, specifically tackling their economic difficulties. The 20 000 talents that had been levied by Sulla as a punishment for the genocide of 88 (Chapter 12) had mushroomed to 120 000 talents of outstanding debt thanks to usurious rates of interest. If not forgiven in some form, the problem would go on compounding beyond any possible resolution (for an example of a debt problem, see Primary Source 13.1). The situation was tenuous even for Rome: in a later speech of 66, Cicero spoke of complex financial derivatives in Rome that were based on the Asian debt. If debt that was, in fact, unpayable was being counted as an asset in Rome, the diseased Asian economy could easily infect Italy via defaults. Lucullus took steps to provide a realistic plan for repayment: he immediately forgave two-thirds of the outstanding obligation and set up plans for the remaining 40 000

> **Primary Source 13.1**
>
> **The City of Gytheion Honors Numerius and Marcus Cloatius**
>
> This decree comes from Gytheion, the main harbor town of Sparta. Dated to 71, the decree honors Numerius and Marcus Cloatius for helping the city renegotiate its debt and for intervening to relieve the city of other demands that were put on it by Romans. Note the reference to Gaius Julius Caesar, whose career at this point would be just beginning with service overseas in Greece. The inscription goes on to mention a loan to the city from the honorees to help them meet required contributions to a Roman campaign against the pirates. The benefactors graciously charged half of the prevailing interest rate, lowering it from 48 to 24%!
>
> "Since Numerius and Marcus Cloatius, sons of Numerius, Romans, *proxenoi*, and benefactors of our city, from the very beginning have continued to act justly both toward our city and, privately, toward those of the citizens who approached them (with a request), omitting nothing of zeal and ardor, because of which at appropriate times the city gratefully made public mention and voted suitable honors for them. In the year of Lachares's magistracy, when they were negotiating our release from the obligation of the first loan, and in the year of Phleinos's magistracy, when concerning the second loan of 3,965 drachmas which the city had borrowed [previously], they accepted the people of Athens as arbiters in the time of Marcilius and (then) after being implored by the citizens, they permitted the payment of what the citizens persuaded them; and in the year of Biadas's magistracy, when, asking for (it as) a personal favor from Publius Autronius (Paetus) and Lucius Marcilius, who were their guests whom they had put up at their own expense, they successfully pleaded for (the city) to be spared the soldiers and other considerable burdens imposed by (the legates), through which action they brought relief to the city. … And they have brought into good will and support for the city many of the (Roman) leaders, the legate Gaius Julius (Caesar) and the legate Publius Autronius (Paetus) and the legate Fulvius, doing all these things out of goodwill toward the city and its citizens.
>
> (trans. Robert Sherk, *Rome and the Greek East to the death of Augustus*, Cambridge: Cambridge University Press, 1984.)

talents to be paid at reasonable interest rates in a workable timeframe. The effect on the Roman creditors must have been staggering, as a full 80 000 talents of "paper" was vaporized in an instant. In Asia Lucullus was cheered, but in Rome he was performing radical politics, and he would come to face far trickier adversaries than Mithridates back home for it.

13.5 The Consulship of Crassus and Pompey

A populist agenda was the ironic hallmark of the consular year 70, under the leadership of Crassus and Pompey. Their beginning may have been inauspicious to many, as they followed their unbalanced victories over Spartacus by camping near the walls of Rome in late 71, from which position of strength they demanded to be considered eligible to run for election. Pompey, however, had yet to hold any elected office, even though his experience of holding *imperium* of different ranks was by now vast. Their campaign of intimidation bore fruit and they were elected. If the *optimates* senators were expecting sympathetic ears, however, they would be disappointed. Prime among Crassus and Pompey's reforms was the full restoration of the tribunate: veto power, sacrosanctity, and legislative powers. They also diluted the senatorial influence on juries by returning an equestrian presence. If there was any doubt as to their political proclivities, all was made clear when they organized an election of censors, whose ensuing work resulted in the expulsion from the senate of some 64 members, likely newcomers from Sulla's stacking of the body. In some ways, Crassus and Pompey were not all that different from Lepidus, right down to their veritable march on Rome, only *they* had not been criminalized. Their intimate knowledge of the plight of provincials and of the hinterland, from their campaigns in Italy and Spain, may have contributed to their outlook.

The consulship of Crassus and Pompey was also witness to the political debut of Gaius Julius Caesar, who boldly asserted his former association to Gaius Marius. Either late in 70 or early in 69, he delivered funeral orations for his aunt Julia and his wife Cornelia. Plutarch says that he celebrated their lives through the men of their families; given that Julia was the widow of Marius and Cornelia was the daughter of Cinna, such funerals were politically provocative. Julius Caesar had remained on the periphery of major events up to this point: having narrowly survived the proscriptions in 83; having served on a mission to king Nicomedes IV of Bithynia in 80; having been kidnapped by pirates and ransomed from them in 75, after which he reportedly got violent revenge; and having served in Spain in 70, a witness to the settlement of the erstwhile Sertorian forces. His mother Aurelia was the sister of the consul who took steps toward reempowering the tribunate around 73 by making it no longer a dead end (Chapter 12). Caesar's public speeches were thus additional signs of an ambitious political career among the *populares*.

Caesar was joined in his debut around this time by the unlikely ascendance of Marcus Tullius Cicero, which, too, had a populist context. In 70, Cicero led the prosecution of Gaius Verres, the governor of Sicily who had carried out the orders to seize grain and pack it off to the metropole in 73. After a couple of more years in office, Verres had earned a reputation for excess that outpaced this initial, emergency writ, and he was charged with extortion. The juries had not yet undergone Crassus and Pompey's reconstitution with equestrian members, and so Verres was to be judged by peer senators with similar interests. Since Verres's defense was taken up by Quintus Hortensius, a renowned orator of the day, he must have had confidence in a positive outcome. His prosecutor Cicero was a *novus homo*, hailing from Arpinum just like Marius; unlike Marius, Cicero had completed a thorough education that had taken him to tutors in Athens, Asia Minor, and Rhodes. Cicero had been quaestor in Sicily in 75, so he had had access to relevant witnesses that had suffered under Verres, and his evidence was incontrovertible in its clarity. His dismantling of Verres was so withering that the great Hortensius shriveled before mounting the podium, and Verres skipped town for a comfortable retirement-cum-exile in Massilia. The unified front put forth by a senatorial faction under Sulla's dictatorship, and institutionally enshrined by his reforms, had cracked and was swiftly crumbling by the fall of 70.

13.6 Lucullus and the Origins of the Third Mithridatic War

Mithridates had been neutralized, but he was still alive, and his son-in-law Tigranes II still held sway over the rickety machine of Seleucid Syria; both of them stood to gain from the as-yet unscathed pirates. In 69 the pirates had continued their bold maneuvers, sacking Delos for good and bringing to an end its super-century of commercial prominence. In the following year, they sailed right up to Rome's harbor at Ostia, within 16 miles of the city, where they cut out a fleet of the consul Marcius Rex.

In 69, Lucullus saw an opportunity to strike Mithridates from Cilicia, intending to do damage to the pirates, as well, in a single blow. Another thoroughgoing success, Lucullus beat Tigranes at Tigranocerta, the passage through the Taurus Mountains into the Armenian heartland, in spite of inferior numbers. On the diplomatic side, he negotiated with the Parthians to ensure their neutrality, and placed a bona fide Seleucid, meager though he was, back on the Syrian throne. Antiochus XIII Asiaticus, born to Antiochus X Eusebius and Cleopatra Selene, obscure dynastic players from the previous chapter, had been in Rome from 75 to 71, and however ineffectual he would turn out to be, Lucullus could be sure he would be more malleable than the alternatives. In 68, Lucullus pushed even deeper into Armenia, perhaps drawing confidence from the arrival of a senatorial fleet led by Quintus Caecilius Metellus, soon to be called Creticus, against pirate strongholds in Crete that year. But as with his raid into Pontus in 73, Lucullus went too far, too fast, only this time those that nearly undid him were on his own side: his troops bristled at his excessive discipline and mutinied. Lucullus was forced to pull back for the winter, to Nisibis, further from settled Roman lands or friends than any camp had wintered before, trusting in Parthian neutrality, Armenian defeat, and Seleucid poverty.

13.7 Tribunes and Imperial Commands

In 67, activist tribunes continued their assault on senatorial power and privilege. Various loopholes that the senators had created for themselves were tied shut: owing to tribunate legislation of this year, much of it from one Gaius Cornelius, about whom we know little, senators could no longer exempt members of their body from the laws unless a quorum of 200 were present at the decision. The prohibition implies the existence of a practice that is otherwise poorly attested in our cursory sources. Further, anyone convicted of bribery in pursuit of an election was barred from seeking office in the future; without this rule, given the massive amount of wealth in the city, little could stop a wealthy senator from eventually gaining power simply on that basis.

The tribunes also pursued policies that effectively internationalized Roman government at the expense of a senatorial role. One new law, for example, sponsored by a tribune, required that the senate put the reception of foreign embassies at the top of their docket for a year's activities. The result was that the concerns of provincials, allies, and even of enemies were not delayed interminably. More aggressive along these lines, the tribune Aulus Gabinius put forward his own plan for dealing with the pirates, which delivered a form of rebuke for the repeated failures of the senatorial initiatives. A special command, held by a single overseer, would be created, to which a large number of ships, infantry, senatorial staffers, and funds would be allocated, with jurisdiction over all coastlines, whether mainland or islands, regardless of province, to a distance of 50 miles inland. Even though the law would pass massive power onto the general (unnamed for now) contrary to Republican practice, Gabinius and his allies saw the plan as one of good government, systematic and rooted in fundamental goals having to do with the quality of life. Tribunes thus did not simply begrudge senators their power; they were rejecting the body as inefficient and in the dark about their surrounding Mediterranean. The kind of destructive extortion perpetrated by Aquillius, Verres, and multiple other governors was being addressed in advance this time, rather than after the fact. A bitter standoff between Gabinius and other tribunes backed by his senatorial opponents was on the verge of escalating into familiar violence, until the most outspoken anti-Gabinian tribune was intimidated to silence and the measure passed.

Surprising no one, Pompey was selected for the post by the assembly, and the extent of resources at his disposal increased, as well, to a total, it is said, of 500 ships, 120 000 soldiers, 5000 cavalry, 24 praetorian staffers, and 6000 talents. The crowd of infantry and cavalry, both land-based resources, may read as odd for what was to be a maritime engagement but the use for such numbers was revealed in the execution. Moving west to east, Pompey methodically swept the seas clear, and when the pirates made for harbor, in many cases they faced land armies with which they were wholly unacquainted, at least of late, and were trapped and defeated. Pompey had divided the Mediterranean into 13 divisions to clarify the focus for the staff of each, and in the course of the campaign received hostages from Crete and organized it as a province, exercising his *imperium* to do so over the objections of Metellus Creticus, still holding his own *imperium* in the region. Within three months Pompey had corralled the corsairs into their traditional strongholds on the Cilician coast. Again, land-based siegeworks were in the offing, and the threat was finally pushed to the point of elimination. As he had with his enemies in Spain in 73, Pompey dealt with a significant number of the so-called pirates with clemency, and placed them on plots of land in Asia Minor and elsewhere. Such an idea, of course, would never have occurred to him if the defeated had had no history of agriculture, and his settlement of them in this way contributes to theories of the identity of these ancient "pirates" beyond notions of Blackbeard and Barbarossa. The pirates of this time were as much a sociological phenomenon as the Marian recruits, the escaped slaves (really, prisoners of other wars), and the tax-burdened residents of the provinces.

By the end of the year, Pompey was a hero in Rome, for fixing a problem whose greatest symptom, as far as the city was concerned, was higher food prices. By contrast, from Asia the Romans gathered only bad news. Two of Lucullus's legions, under the command of a legate, had been butchered in an ill-advised confrontation with a resurgent Mithridates at Zela. Thus, just as the pirates were on their way out, another rival was on a comeback, and again the tribunate proposed a solution that bypassed the senate's traditional domain over foreign policy. Gaius Manilius drafted legislation for the entire Asian theater to fall under the direction of Pompey, this time explicitly naming the commander at the start, who would have an *imperium* that superseded all other governors. Cicero's speech in support of the law survives and is a *tour de force* of persuasion based on fear (see Primary Source 13.2): he conjured up, before the audience's eyes, visions of the genocide of 88, as well as horrors of deprivation that awaited Rome without the elimination of their national foe.

Primary Source 13.2

Cicero, on the Imperium of Pompey

In 66, Cicero delivered arguments in support of granting unusual powers to Pompey for the purpose of prosecuting a war against Mithridates in Asia Minor. His rationale included expected references to the "genocide" of 88 (Chapter 12) and to the Roman sense of pride. More striking, perhaps, is his detailed exposition of the financial instruments in Rome that hinged on Asian debt: according to Cicero, investments in the region were, simply put, too big to fail.

> 7.17:
> "[Among the tax collectors in the region] are diligent, industrious men, some of whom are themselves doing business in Asia (whose interests you should consider in their absence), while others have much money invested in the province. It would be a feature of your humanity to save a great number of them from ruin, and a feature of your wisdom to realize that the ruin of so many fellow citizens cannot be disjoined from (the ruin of) the Republic ... We ought to retain in our memory that which this same region of Asia taught us, and which that foul Mithridates taught us at the start of the war there – lessons in the nature of certain ruin. For at the time when a great many men lost their fortunes in Asia, we know that with the payments on loans suspended, the system of credit at Rome collapsed. For many men in a single state cannot lose their fortunes without dragging still more into the same ruin. Guard the Republic from such a danger and trust me – something you yourselves also observe – this system of credit and finance which operates at Rome in the Forum is all wrapped up in the money in Asia and hinges upon it. That [which happens in Asia] cannot fail without that [which happens in Rome] also failing in the same destabilizing blow."

13.8 Pompey Becomes "Great"

Plutarch took the opportunity of the shift of power over Asia to imagine the hand-off of armies from Lucullus to Pompey: the former called the latter a vulture, for swooping in to scavenge upon the beasts that other predators had felled. Having arguably done just that, in Spain and against Spartacus, Pompey indeed intended to capitalize on the work of his forebears. He negotiated with the Parthians and both they and he moved on Tigranes, respectively in succession, and the Armenian king quickly came to terms, trading 6000 talents and his son as a hostage for the right to stay on his throne. Mithridates was again put to flight, and with Armenia no longer a refuge, retreated to his territories in Crimea, displacing his disloyal son Machares in the process. Against all odds Mithridates was once again safe, and would remain so for several more years. Pompey spent the year 65 ranging around northwest Asia Minor, toying with crossing the Caucasus Mountains and skirting the Caspian Sea in pursuit of Mithridates, only to give up the hunt and return to Asia Minor, satisfied that his adversary understood a new reality.

In 64, Pompey acted in a power vacuum in Syria and the Levant in what he thought were Rome's interests. He removed Antiochus XIII from the throne once and for all and planned a province in his stead. He could not finalize the arrangement, however, for it would require senatorial approval. The Seleucid dynasty was officially at an end, an ignoble conclusion for the once grand royal family; as Peter Green put it, they had "fizzled obscurely." Ptolemy XII, perhaps hoping to stave off a similar end to his own regime, sent Pompey a gold crown. It may have been upon this occasion that Pompey took on the epithet *Magnus*, or Great, in acknowledgement of Alexander-like accomplishments. Pompey continued southward in the following year, perhaps given assurance of Asian security by news that Mithridates was finally dead: he committed suicide in the face of a *coup* by another son, Pharnaces II. Pharnaces pledged allegiance to Rome, or effectively to Pompey himself since it was he who received Pharnaces's diplomatic hostages and, as prisoners, the Pontics who had allegedly poured the molten gold down Manius Aquillius's throat in 87 (Chapter 12). At Jerusalem Pompey intervened in a civil war and by force of his own legions and by cavalry provided by the increasingly obsequious Ptolemy XII, put John Hyrcanus in charge as High Priest, over his more skilled and by measures more dangerous brother Aristobulus. Ptolemy XII invited Pompey into his own realm, to help him put down a revolt, but Pompey declined.

Taking stock of four years of activity, Pompey, on his own initiative and as empowered in unusual ways by tribunes, had organized the heartland of Asia Minor and the Levant, a region that had been the prize that the great Hellenistic contenders of the third century had striven for in the six Syrian wars (Chapters 5–9). It included the new provinces of Syria and Crete, plus new territories that had been added to preexisting provinces, as Bithynia got part of Pontus and Cilicia received part of Lycia (see Map 13.1). Pompey's so-called client kings who had pledged allegiance to him or to Rome in one way or another included Tigranes, Pharnaces, and Hyrcanus, already discussed, plus the Galatian Deiotarus, the Nabataean Arab Aretas, who was in possession of Damascus, and an Antiochus in Commagene, apparently not a Seleucid but borrowing the name for the sake of legitimacy.

A monument left by this Antiochus of Commagene demonstrates the cultural strategies of a regional *basileus* at this time (see Figure 13.2 and the cover illustration of this book). The extensive and rather well-preserved ruins of his tomb survive today: it was located atop a high mountain, today called Mt. Nemrut, which was made even taller by a deposit of loose rock stacked into a massive cone, likely burying the chamber (which has not been excavated). The deceased was depicted in colossal portraits, some five times life size, guarded by lions, eagles, and gods. The representations of the gods were deliberately syncretistic as inscriptions labeled them with the names that were used for them by Greeks and Armenians, both local to

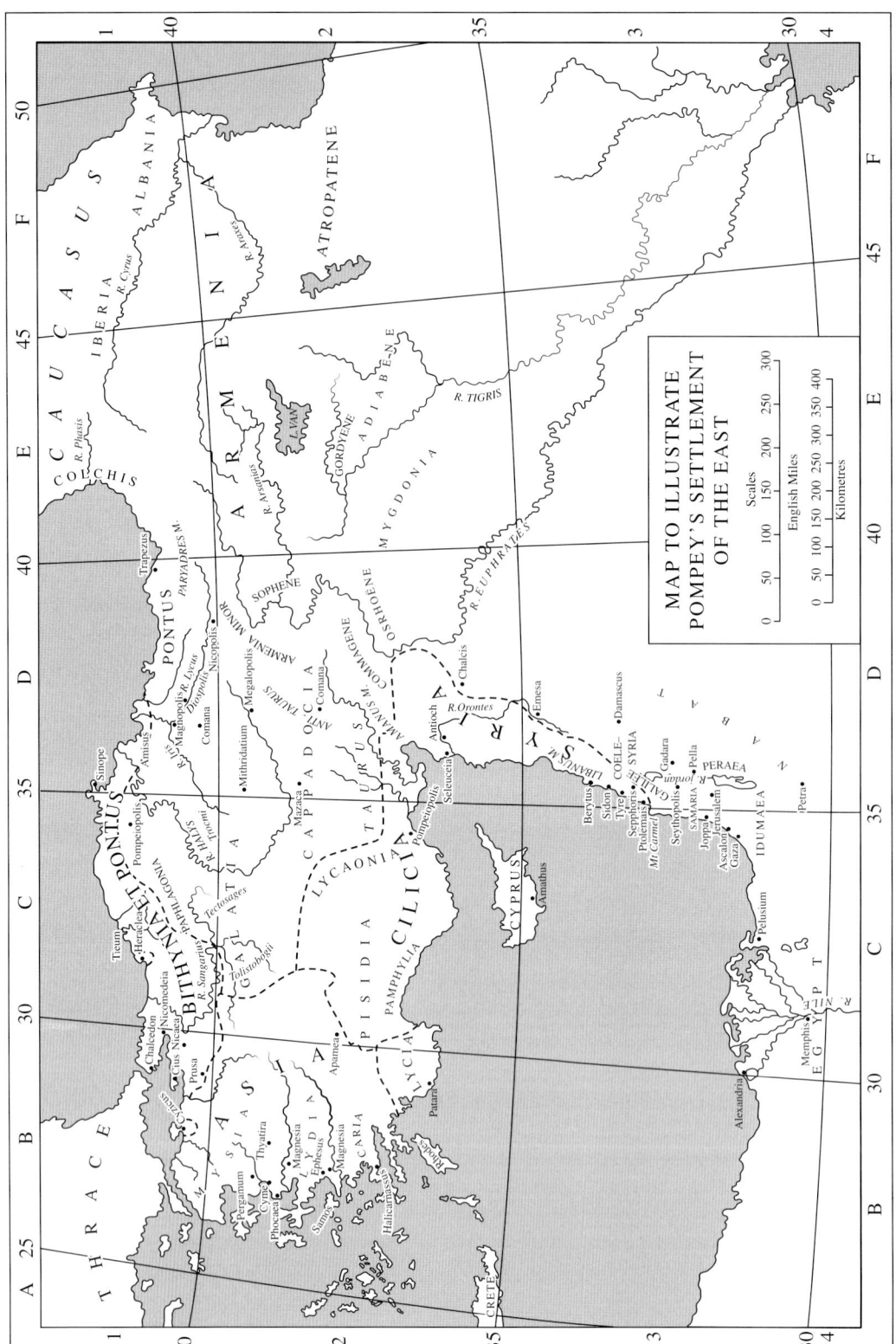

Map 13.1 The distribution of Roman provinces and allied kingdoms in the East following Pompey's settlement.

Figure 13.2 The east terrace of the tomb complex of Antiochus, a lesser *basileus* in Commagene in central Asia Minor, located at the peak of Mt. Nemrut, 62 BCE. Colossal statues of the king and flanking deities from both eastern and western pantheons demonstrate the cosmopolitanism of the region. Astronomical notations on reliefs from the complex (not pictured) are in keeping with Hellenistic interests in scientific inquiry.

Antiochus's realm – Zeus/Aramazd (or, Ahura Mazda), Apollo/Mirh/Mithras, and Hercules/Vahagn, to name a few. The sculpture groups were repeated on two platforms, which flanked the tomb facing east and west, ideal for witnessing the rising and setting of the sun and perhaps denoting eternity. Stelai below Antiochus and the gods depicted the king's ancestors, Persian on his father's side and Macedonian on his mother's, both equally celebrated. Another stele presents the position of stars and planets on a specific date, July 7, 62, likely marking the monument's dedication. Religion, ethnicity, and even astronomy came together at Mt. Nemrut and undoubtedly played a role in the king's political status. It is conceivable, though conceptual, that Pompey witnessed this remarkable complex shortly before it was consecrated, and that Julius Caesar passed by in 47 (Chapter 15). Given their experiments in royalist politics and public architecture, their reactions to Mt. Nemrut would be nice to know.

13.9 Rome in the Absence of Pompey

In spite of, or perhaps because of, his unimpeachable success, Pompey was not without rivals back in Rome. Foremost among these was his former consular colleague, Crassus, elected censor for 65. Behind the screen of allied tribunes, he seems to have maneuvered for lucrative commands for his political allies, to balance Pompey's Asian authority. The sources are vague but one of

Crassus's ideas may have been to make Egypt into a province, essentially ignoring the weak presence of Ptolemy XII. The law was thwarted by Cicero, whose speech *On the Alexandrian King* unfortunately exists only in fragments. In the meantime, Caesar, as aedile, was making a name for himself with funds borrowed from Crassus. By now a known acolyte of Crassus, Caesar brought charges against a certain Gaius Rabirius, now around 70 years old, for crimes committed during the assassination of Saturninus, the henchman of Caesar's uncle Marius, who was reimagined as a champion of the people rather than the public enemy of Sulla's characterization (Chapter 12). Again, Cicero defeated the prosecution through oratory; his *On Behalf of Rabirius* survives. Lucullus, too, is said to have attempted an anti-Pompeian slight by organizing a tribune into prosecuting Manilius, the tribune who had proposed Pompey's mega-*imperium*. Again, Cicero took up the defense, still operating on Pompey's behalf.

Crassus and his associates next turned to the matter of land allotments, surely to be necessary as Pompey's soldiers returned. Crassus enlisted the tribune Publius Servilius Rullus to propose a land commission to identify parcels for distribution, both in Italy and overseas: if the board were in place before Pompey's triumph, Crassus could wield some influence over the process. Cicero, finally elected consul as a *novus homo* in 63, fought the measure, and a comparison of his two speeches on the matter, one before the senate and one before the people, demonstrates how he crafted arguments differently depending on audience (see Primary Source 13.3). Addressing the senate, Cicero cultivated an "us vs. them" argument: senators were under assault by rabble-rousing tribunes who effectively pushed through new policies at large, informal gatherings of crowds called *contiones* (singular, *contio*), often just in the streets. Then, apparently in the same week, or perhaps on the same day, Cicero spoke on the same issue of Rullus's land reform before a *contio* of the Roman people that he himself organized. Whereas before the senate, Cicero decried the degradation of lofty concepts like trust and dignity, at the *contio*, he emphasized potential material losses for the people. Rullus's measure was thus defeated. In defense of Rabirius and Manilius; in opposition to Rullus and to the plot to provincialize Egypt – by and large Cicero was holding the line against Pompey's adversaries.

> **Primary Source 13.3**
>
> **Cicero, *On the Farm Bill*, Before the Senate and Before the People**
>
> At the start of his consulship in 63, Cicero took up the matter of a bill proposed by the tribune Rullus to distribute land in small allotments to the people. One of the stipulations of the bill was that a board of 10 men, the decemviri (to be distinguished from the Decemviri of the Laws of the 12 Tables, Chapter 2), would be tasked with dividing the land around the rich town of Capua for the settlement of new colonies. We have two of Cicero's speeches in opposition, one delivered before the senate and one delivered before the people. Read together, they demonstrate the versatility of Cicero as a politician, crafting a message of political chaos for the senators and a message of economic destitution for the people.
>
> *On the farm bill* (before the senate), 20–22: "Now all the cities that are around Capua will be occupied by colonies per the terms of the decemviri, for the law itself allows them to take whatever towns they wish and put colonists in them, whomever they wish. And it orders for the fields in Campania and the land around Stella to be divided among these colonists. Now I'm not complaining of the reduction of our resources, nor of the shame of this seizure and loss … I'm talking rather about the danger to our safety and our liberty. For what do you suppose will remain intact for you in maintaining your liberty and dignity when Rullus and his henchmen, whom you fear

much more than Rullus, with their band of the damnable and the dispossessed, with all their forces, with all that silver and gold, occupy Capua and the cities around Capua?"

On the farm bill (before the people), 76–79: "Campanian farmland is to be divided up under the terms of this law, the most beautiful (land) in the world, and a colony will be established at Capua, the richest and most splendid city. What can we say about this? … Rullus orders that 5,000 colonists will be registered for Capua, and to get to this number, each (of the decemviri) will choose 500 on their own. Please, do not think that you will be among them; think about it, seriously. You don't think that there will be room in this number for you, do you, you who alike are upright, peaceful, calm men? … For they themselves – the decemviri – have been eyeing Campania, which they are dangling before you. They will lead their own men, by whose names they themselves will hold and profit from (the land) … I see that nothing is lacking to these men in terms of money, except plots of land of this type, with whose produce they'll be able to support the lavish luxury of their own country estates at Cumae and Puteoli."

13.10 The Conspiracies of Catiline and Cicero

The year 63 was thus an important one for Cicero's career in its multivalent defense of Pompey's interests, but his most notorious feat would fall in the waning months when he might otherwise be considered a lame duck. With memories of Sulla's brutal return from the East still fresh, and mindful of Crassus's, Caesar's, and others' various affronts against Pompey in 65 and 64, the political elite in Rome of all stripes had reason to feel tension as 63 came to a close and the return of Pompey the *Magnus* was imminent. In October, Cicero began announcing his suspicions that another radical and potentially violent movement was afoot. At the center of his declarations was Lucius Sergius Catilina, commonly Anglicized as Catiline. A known partisan of the *populares* faction, he had led a political career that was conventional in its sequence of offices, yet punctuated with episodes of controversy. When he returned from a praetorship in Africa in 66 he was brought up on charges of corruption; this, in and of itself, was not wholly unusual and the fact that Cicero, the anticorruption hawk who took on Verres, considered arguing in his *defense* at the time (Att. 1.2.1) may be grounds for doubting any egregious crimes. Catiline was acquitted but the proceedings still kept him out of the running for the consulship of 64, which we are told he ardently desired.

At this point, assessments of Catiline's career are clouded by Cicero's four speeches of invective against him, and by those of subsequent generations who inherited his account. Sallust, the historian who wrote about Jugurtha (Chapter 11), also produced a history of the controversies swirling around Catiline, but various of Sallust's asides present inconsistencies in the narrative, as we shall see.

The stories told by Cicero unfold as a detective yarn starring himself. As he tells it, he cleverly and doggedly uncovered secret deals, working against the odds and the clock. His version of events might be encapsulated as follows: ever since Catiline's bid for the consulship was cut short in 65, he has been plotting revolution. He tried to murder the new consuls of 64 out of bitterness for his exclusion but the plot failed. After missing out on the consulship a second time in the election of late 64, which Cicero ultimately won, his machinations accelerated. He organized crews of likeminded reprobates (as Cicero would tell it) and plotted simultaneous eruptions of activism in the Italian hinterland surrounding Rome, with a view toward marching on the city and removing his rivals by force. He even solicited aid from a delegation of Celts, the Allobroges, a tribe north of the Alps, inviting them to help his invasion. All the while Cicero conducted investigations and interviewed satellites in the know, such as a conspirator's courtesan,

Fulvia (different from the woman of the same name married to Clodius Pulcher and Mark Antony, below).

Cicero delivered two speeches in November against Catiline, but lacked the proof that would have generated a legal response. Nevertheless, Catiline felt the pressure and left the city, though not charged. Finally, when some conspirators' letters to the Allobroges, still sealed with wax and embossed by the relevant signet rings, fell into Cicero's hands, he presented them to his peers in the senate and had guards immediately incarcerate some of those named directly. He moved quickly and persuaded the senate and people to authorize the execution of the "conspirators" at that very moment without a trial, and his motion carried. After five conspirators were hanged in the Tullianum, Cicero uttered the single, loaded word, *vixerunt*, meaning, "They have lived" (past tense intended). An army was dispatched to hunt down Catiline and he died in battle in Etruria early in 62.

At almost every turn, it is possible to cast doubt on Cicero's version of the plot. Sallust gives enough hints in his narrative to allow an understanding of entrapment followed by false testimony. The historian suggests that one of the more fantastical claims about Catiline – that he compelled his comrades to swear an oath of loyalty marked by a draught of human blood – was propagated by Cicero after the fact, when he was in political jeopardy for ordering the hasty executions. Moreover, Sallust says that one of the key witnesses against Catiline, Tarquinius, was seen by many at the time as a perjurer and an opportunist. He also recounts how Cicero offered freedom to slaves who would testify against Catiline, which would obviously not guarantee objectivity. In Sallust's account, the guileless Allobroges arrive in Rome for wholly different, run-of-the-mill provincial business, and Cicero encourages them to be receptive to offers from Catiline's henchmen. Dithering this way and that, they ended up in possession of incriminating letters and were arrested outside the city: as Sallust tells it, they hardly knew what was going on. In Sallust's account Catiline at times seems mystified by what is happening to him; in a letter quoted by the historian, he says he is departing for the north but that he is innocent. According to Sallust, Catiline died fighting valiantly with wounds in the front, not the back, which would be out of keeping with the characteristics of scoundrels, as Cicero would have it.

Sallust also presents speeches in the senate on two sides of the debate regarding the fate of the "conspirators." In the end, his tone is decidedly anti-Catiline: in his account of just how Catiline hoped to overthrow the state, he used the word "simultaneous" (*simul*) three times in three sentences (Sallust, *Catiline* 43). The idea of simultaneity would have touched a nerve in the audience of 63: Mithridates's genocide of 88 was said to be perpetrated "on the same day" in scores of cities; and the simultaneous struggles of 73, against Sertorius, Mithridates, Spartacus, and the pirates, had led to deprivation and famine, as well as fear. The notion of multiple fronts is one that had frightened Romans for a long time, and so Sallust's culminating depiction of Catiline is not flattering, but his Catiline is also not the only villain. Both factions were guilty of nefarious activity. As with his treatise on the war with Jugurtha (Chapter 11), the true emphasis of Sallust's history of the controversy is on the faults of the Roman system, in general, where corruption was seemingly easy and pervasive.

13.11 Conclusions

Opposition against Cicero was pronounced before the bodies of the conspirators were cold. A tribune vetoed Cicero from giving the customary end-of-the-year speech in which outgoing magistrates typically summarized their accomplishments. As we shall see in the next chapter, Cicero took great heat for the extraordinary capital punishment of senators; he was ultimately convicted of treason and exiled, in spite of his own voluminous exhortations of his greatness and status as a savior of the Republic. Was it Catiline who exercised a conspiracy, or Cicero? Or perhaps both? Whatever the truth, we see plainly how Rome's performance and experience of warfare and diplomacy in the East were outstripping the capacity of the city to be governed by its usual institutions. All were on edge about how Pompey would act upon returning with his armies.

Pompey had settled dozens of new political arrangements in the eastern Mediterranean, from new provinces to new client kings (see Map 13.1). Upon returning to Rome he would make sure the people of the city understood the breadth of this accomplishment, not only through a triumphal procession but also by a monumental new "museum" (see the next chapter). After all, he needed senatorial approval to legitimize his eastern settlements … or did he? Powerful individuals were increasingly governing by dint of their own personal authority, circumventing traditional institutions.

Further Reading

Hölbl, Gunther (2001). *A History of the Ptolemaic Empire*. New York: Routledge.
Rawson, Elizabeth (1994). *Cicero: A Portrait*. Bristol: Bristol Classical Press.
Russell, Amy (2015). *The Politics of Public Space in Republican Rome*. Cambridge: Cambridge University Press.
Seager, Robin (2002). *Pompey the Great: A Political Biography*, 2e. Medford: Wiley-Blackwell.
Steel, Catherine (2013). *The End of the Roman Republic, 146 to 44 BC: Conquest and Crisis*. Edinburgh: Edinburgh University Press.
Tempest, Katherine (2011). *Cicero: Politics and Persuasion in Ancient Rome*. New York: Continuum Books.

14

To 52: The World According to Pompey

Timeline

62: The Bona Dea Scandal disgraces Publius Clodius Pulcher and the wife of Julius Caesar
61: Triumph of Pompey with detainees from the Seleucids, Pontus, Armenia, and Judaea
60: The so-called First Triumvirate of Crassus, Pompey, and Caesar, joined together extralegally in pursuit of shared interests
59: The consulship of Caesar
59–50: Caesar's conquest of Gaul
58: Tribunate of Clodius Pulcher; annexation of Cyprus
58–57: Exile of Cicero from Rome; displacement of Ptolemy XII from Egypt
57: Assassination of Alexandrian envoys in Italy; the poet Catullus in Bithynia
55: The second consulship of Crassus and Pompey; reinstallation of Ptolemy XII on the throne in Alexandria; Pompey's stone theater
52: Sole consulship of Pompey

Principal Themes

- Pompey and Caesar struck a political alliance in securing legislation favorable for their various initiatives; the alleged involvement of Crassus as a third player has led analysts to view them as a "triumvirate," governing as a parallel state alongside the regular government and only partially beholden to existing offices and political traditions.
- Pompey's manipulation of the East was celebrated by the dedication of his new stone theater, a massive complex that put eastern animals, plants, and works of art on display, as well as staging performances in a Hellenic vein.
- Julius Caesar claimed similar mastery over Gaul in the West, which he conquered for Rome and described for audiences in Rome by means of his *Commentaries*, a serial dispatch of his deeds that accentuated the cultures of Gauls, Germans, and Britons as well as news of battles and campaigns.
- Ptolemy XII, limping along through familiar internal conflicts, was shored up, both on his throne and while in flight, by Pompey's support, which seems to have come in exchange for financial backing from Egypt.
- New poets like Catullus operated in political and provincial circles, but often focused on erotic or quotidian themes following Hellenistic Alexandrian precedents.

The Roman Republic and the Hellenistic Mediterranean: From Alexander to Caesar, First Edition. Joel Allen.
© 2020 John Wiley & Sons, Inc. Published 2020 by John Wiley & Sons, Inc.

14.1 Introduction

As a result of his special, extralegal commands in 67 and 66, Pompey seems to have developed an affinity for working athwart the traditional institutions of the Republic. His maintenance of a kind of shadow state reached an apogee in the formation of a political alliance with Julius Caesar, to which Marcus Licinius Crassus made a tangential third addition, in 60. Together, they helped each other achieve objectives for their various supporters, mainly soldiers who had fought for them in both East and West. Pompey's ties to Ptolemy XII, also informal and private, were a source of much controversy in the city; tensions reached a fever pitch when an anti-Pompeian embassy from Alexandria was shockingly killed under mysterious circumstances outside Rome before it could address the senate. Pompey's near mastery of the *oikoumene* itself was revealed in glorious fashion by his stone theater, unveiled in 55, which housed exotic plants and works of art, in addition to a shrine to Venus Victrix, Venus the Conqueror.

14.2 Pompey's *Pompa*

In 62, Cicero declared a new era of *concordia ordinum*, or peace among the orders (meaning patrician and plebeian), following the turmoil of 63. It may be a case of protesting too much since the trappings of a *concordia* were hardly in evidence. Granted, Pompey did not sack the city when he finally returned from the East, though he had both the physical wherewithal to do so and understandable motivations to heed – land for his veterans, plus senatorial ratification of his new provinces, boundaries, and diplomatic agreements – as well as the Marian and Sullan precedents to follow. But only an inveterate optimist could view the absence of a massacre as a species of peace, as Pompey's detractors were numerous and emboldened. Lucullus had already celebrated a triumph for victories in Asia, in 63; his campaign had been eclipsed and usurped by Pompey some five years prior, and they were not on friendly terms. Crassus was still questionable, and even Cicero, Pompey's legislative champion in 63 (Chapter 13), was more engaged in self-laudatory exhalations for his quelling of Catiline than concerned with Pompey's deeds. Pompey also divorced his politically connected wife Mucia; whether it was for her infidelity during his military mission as was alleged, or to distance himself from a political camp – Mucia was related to powerful consulars – is uncertain. In any case it was another step in Pompey's political isolation. In the course of 61, he tried to enlist sympathetic, or bribe-receptive, tribunes to his causes, but made little headway.

The discrepancy between Pompey's political failures and his popular success was thrown into stark relief when he celebrated his triumph in late September of 61, proximate to his birthday. *Pompa* is a Latin word for parade, and it would be easy to make a pun relating the scope and scale of Pompey's celebration to his very identity at this moment in his career. According to Plutarch, he conquered 15 lands – Pontus, Armenia, Cappadocia, Paphlagonia, Media, Colchis, Iberia (of Asia Minor), Albania (also of Asia Minor), Syria, Cilicia, Mesopotamia, Phoenicia, Judaea, and Arabia, with the stateless pirates thrown in for good measure, unable to be identified with geography (see Figure 14.1). Plutarch adds that Pompey was unique in having won triumphs over all three continents, not just Asia as now, but also Africa, in service to Sulla as a young man, and Europe, from his Spanish campaign against Sertorius. Pompey also reportedly made available figures of the revenues that were coming to Rome as a result of his victories, and gave pride of place in the procession to distinguished hostages, like the sons of Pharnaces and Tigranes. Aristobulus, detained since Jerusalem, was marched in disgrace.

The crowd may have enjoyed the show and the largesse that came with it, but in terms of the political elite the spectacle backfired for Pompey. The conquests had been carried out in Rome's

Figure 14.1 Portrait of Pompey, c. 50 BCE. The arrangement of the locks of hair in this portrait has famously been compared with that of Alexander the Great, whose epithet Pompey was adopting as Magnus.

name, yet it was clear that Pompey had personally attained riches on a level that dwarfed even wealthy Crassus's estate. One of the controversies swirling around Pompey was his relationship to Ptolemy XII, the erstwhile hostage of Mithridates who had been stationed on the throne by the Pontic king in 80. We have already seen how Ptolemy XII conspicuously switched sides to Pompey once Mithridates was out of the picture (Chapter 13), and now he continued his campaign to win him over, with a view toward Roman ratification of his right to the throne. Papyri indicate that he was facing a rebellion of farmers on his estates near Heracleapolis in 61, and anecdotes in Diodorus speak of tensions stemming from cultural and religious misunderstandings between the indigenous Egyptians and a growing population of Italians. Ptolemy is thought to have offered 6000 talents to Pompey for his support, and borrowing from Romans to raise the funds – an enormous figure that normally pertained to state budgets, not to an individual's pockets. Thus, Ptolemy XII was certainly, and Pompey was potentially, willing to view power in the Mediterranean theater as the province of an overclass coalition that could take precedence over national identity. The future of the Egyptian throne became a major bone of contention in Rome.

As 61 wore on into 60, a hostile consul, Quintus Caecilius Metellus Celer, cousin of Mucia, was elected to office and garnered the support of Lucullus, still envious of Pompey's success, and Cato the Younger, a great-grandson of Cato the Elder, who had a reputation for following closely the propriety and power-sharing traditions of the Republic. When it came time to vote upon Pompey's settlements, these three argued for piecemeal consideration of each region by itself, which they expected to take months and years. A tribune in Pompey's camp tried to interpose his own body – a sacred relic per the rules of the tribunate – between Celer and the exit from his house, in order to keep him effectively under arrest, but Celer simply broke through his own back wall to rejoin the political fray. As 60 came to an end, Pompey was no closer to satisfaction than he had been when he returned over two years earlier.

In the background of the brinkmanship of 62 to 60, the senate was further ensnared in the fallout of the so-called Bona Dea Scandal. In 62, a wealthy patrician from one of the most storied clans of the Republic, Publius Claudius Pulcher, had been caught attending a women-only religious observance at the Regia in the middle of the Forum, the symbolic "house" of the *pontifex maximus*, Julius Caesar. Dressed as a woman, he had infiltrated the inner sanctum allegedly in pursuit of an affair with Caesar's wife, Pompeia. Turning a comic plot into a tragic one, Cicero promulgated a special law making Pulcher's actions into a crime. There were no convictions thanks in part to bribery on the part of Crassus, but Pompeia was divorced by Caesar – even a whiff of sordid behavior, he said, was beneath him – and what is more, Claudius Pulcher was humiliated. From this point forward he incubated a powerful contempt for Cicero and his invective.

When Caesar was seeking a triumph in 60 in recognition of his work as a propraetor in Spain the previous year, he, too, found Cato the Younger standing in the way. Somewhat as he had argued against Pompey but on a smaller scale, Cato cited rules stating that Caesar could not both hold a triumph and run for a consulship in 59, as he had wanted, for the latter required that he appear in person to announce his candidacy, while the former meant that he could not cross the city limits unless he relinquished his command (and with it any prospects for the triumph). Caesar released the bird in the hand and went for the two in the bush, dropping his *imperium*, losing out on a career-boosting triumph (for the time being), and choosing to run for consul. Cato continued to thwart his progress: he led the charge in defining the consular tasks for 59 as the maintenance of the forests of southern Italy, sure discouragement of any candidate seeking the glory of an overseas command. Cato also backed his own brother-in-law, Marcus Calpurninus Bibulus, as a rival candidate. In what must have been a split electorate (we cannot know balloting tallies), Caesar and Bibulus were both elected to office.

14.3 The so-called "First" Triumvirate

At the start of 59, Caesar, now consul, embarked on an ambitious legislative agenda that was so oriented around Pompey's success that our ancient sources concluded that they had entered into an unofficial alliance, making use of each other's strengths with a view toward effecting legislation that helped each other. With Crassus added to the mix as a wealthy power broker in their camp (though one whose benefits from the arrangement would not materialize in any clear way for several years), historians have referred to them as a Triumvirate, or a board of three men, such as existed in Roman administration from time to time. It should be emphasized that this "First" Triumvirate was never institutionally defined, unlike the equally famous "Second" Triumvirate of 43 (see Epilogue), which was enshrined by the senate. Conveniently timed marriages in 59 – Caesar to Calpurnia, the daughter of a Pompeian ally, and Pompey to Julia, Caesar's own daughter, a generation younger than her husband – contribute to the theory of their cooperation, rather like the network of sons-in-law that Antipater had assembled after the death of Alexander the Great (Chapter 4).

Noting that his political capital was greatest at the start of his term as consul, Caesar began with agrarian legislation seeking parcels of land, at last, for Pompey's veterans. The senate was opposed, and their arguments found articulation in Caesar's colleague Bibulus and the indomitable Cato the Younger. Blocked in the senate, Caesar took it to the assembly; Bibulus countered by declaring that every single day of the year that was not already a religious holiday would have festal significance, thus forestalling all public business. The move was an absurd response to an equally silly stunt, when excrement was poured over Bibulus's head on the steps of the Temple of Castor and Pollux in the Forum. Some of Pompey's troops now showed up in the city, obviously timed to intimidate Bibulus and his followers. Humiliated first, but even more so outclassed, Bibulus was in over his head, and he shied away to his house for the rest of 59. With Bibulus's silence and Pompey's clout, Caesar became practically unstoppable.

With the help of the tribune Publius Vatinius, Caesar next tackled the ratification of Pompey's settlement of the East. Cato's and others' calls for disentangling the block were dismissed and the whole sprawling program passed intact. Throughout the year, Caesar kept a prudent eye on the East in other ways. He set the region on a more Roman-friendly path by forgiving one-third of all the tax collection contracts, which were proving to be impossible to meet (rather like Lucullus's forgiveness of huge amounts of debt in 71, Chapter 13). He created new rules for provincial management in a similar spirit of good government: governors were required to maintain archives of their correspondence, acts, and other administrative documents (a provision that Caesar also put in place for the senate and assemblies in Rome itself); the restrictions against governors leaving their provinces were reinforced (Chapter 12); and provincial staff were forbidden from accepting gifts from local grandees. This last was especially ironic, as it was also under Caesar's consulship that rumors were swirling about Ptolemy XII's alleged bribe. Ptolemy XII was finally recognized as king of Egypt, and his realm was spared inclusion in Caesar's Mediterranean-wide land redistribution scheme for veterans.

After these enormous strides had been made on behalf of Pompey, Caesar also set out to acquire a fortune of his own. He secured the command of Cisalpine Gaul with the vision of invading Illyricum, perhaps planning to follow Curio's lead in reaching the Danube (Chapter 13). His mission was redefined and enhanced when Metellus Celer, Pompey's old adversary, died unexpectedly. Celer's command of Transalpine Gaul was appended to Caesar's upon Pompey's recommendation to the senate. As we shall see, events and opportunities soon pulled Caesar in this more northwesterly direction toward the heart of Gaul. Finally, Caesar oversaw the elections for 58 and seems to have done more than simply administer them. His new father-in-law, Lucius Calpurnius Piso Caesoninus (see Figure 14.2), was elected consul, along with Aulus Gabinius, who as tribune had won Pompey the command against the pirates, which had launched his rise to begin with. Although Crassus was associated with Pompey's and Caesar's alliance as a third man in the room, his contributions and gains in 59 were not obvious. Some historians have attributed the benefits that were afforded to equestrian tax collectors to his agency, owing to his involvement in the world of finance, but the evidence is not explicit in this regard. What he offered in intangible support, however, was clear – a past associate of Pompey's, once estranged but now returned.

Another election for 58 surpassed the others in its drama. Claudius Pulcher, disgraced by the Bona Dea Scandal, had set his sights on the powerful and versatile tribunate but was ineligible owing to his patrician birth. So determined was he that he underwent formal, adult adoption to a plebeian father to shift his status and thus enable him to declare his candidacy. With his change of order, Pulcher's *nomen* switched from Claudius to Clodius, and he became the next in the line of radical tribunes of the late Republic. He reinstated the *collegia*, or guilds based on neighborhoods and professions that helped the nonelite to organize political efforts; because of their tendency toward violence, they had been outlawed since 64. In this sense, Clodius may have been inspired by the so-called triumvirs: with existing governing institutions too unwieldy or inefficient, Clodius would do better with coalitions of smaller, more concentrated, "nongovernmental organizations," of a type. Clodius also won subsidies for grain sufficient not simply to lower the price but to make it completely free of charge, a disastrous bill that soon led to black markets and famine.

Clodius's most trenchant case was an assault on Cicero. He promulgated a law by which anyone who had executed a Roman citizen without a trial should suffer exile, obviously with Cicero's treatment of the alleged Catilinarian conspirators in mind. Cicero's old allies, most

Figure 14.2 The Getty Museum in Malibu, California, modeled on the Villa of the Papyri in Herculaneum, which was perhaps owned by Lucius Calpurnius Piso, Julius Caesar's father-in-law.

notably Pompey, deserted him, perhaps a testament to the gross illegality of Cicero's actions. Cicero fled to Thrace, and his house on the Palatine was confiscated and demolished (compare the potential parody of Cicero at Figure 14.3). In its place Clodius commissioned a shrine to personified *Libertas*, or, Freedom. Cicero's letters to his wife, Terentia, reveal both the financial straits into which the family was plunged, and Terentia's expertise as a money manager, making deals and using her own estates to keep futures alive for their daughter and son (see Primary Source 14.1).

14.4 Clodius's Imperial Tribunate

One characteristic of Clodius's tribunate that sets him apart from his forebears was his intense interest in the government of the eastern Mediterranean, beyond the urban borders that were a tribune's usual focus. Past tribunes had proposed that certain commands go to certain of their political allies, but Clodius surpassed them in directly expanding provinces, manipulating diplomatic hostages on his own, and appointing client kings. He passed a law annexing Cyprus, still under the rule of the brother of Ptolemy XII; the island was to be grafted onto the administrative writ of the governor of Cilicia. What is more, Clodius carried a provision that Cato, the senator who was in every way his opposite, was to carry out the task. We are told that Cato did not want the post but accepted it out of a sense of duty to the Republic. Working from Rhodes,

Figure 14.3 Relief from the Basilica Aemilia in the Roman Forum depicting Romans rebuilding the walls of the city with a matron, likely a personification of Roma, looking on, late first century BCE. Some scholars have likened the central figure with portraits of Cicero, suggesting the relief was either a tribute to, or a parody of, Cicero's claims to have rescued the city from destruction.

Primary Source 14.1

Letter From Cicero to Terentia

Cicero wrote the following letter to his wife Terentia from exile in Greece. Dated November 25, 58, it demonstrates the precarious position of Cicero's family following his conviction and their attempts to keep funds in place for their children's future.

Ad Fam. 14.1: "Tullius, sending greetings to his Terentia, little Tullia, and (young) Cicero. It is brought to my attention through many letters and conversations with everyone that your courage and strength are not to be believed, and that you never tire from labors of the mind or the body. How miserable I am to think that you, of such courage, faithfulness, honor, and humanity have tumbled to such depths because of me. And to think that our little Tullia who once took such joy from her father now receives the same amount of sorrow on his account. And what can I say about our (young) Cicero? Since he first began to understand (the world), he has beheld the bitterest grief and misery … My Terentia, you wrote to me that you are going to sell (your) collection of houses. How miserable I am! What, I ask you, what is going to happen? If this same bad luck continues to beleaguer us, what will become of our poor little boy? I cannot write more, so great is the flow of my tears, and I shall not drag you into the same torrent. I write only this: if I have any friends in truth, money will not be lacking; if I do not, then you will not be able to make it right with your own money (in any case). Even with our miserable misfortune, see to it that we do not lose our son amidst the loss. If we have anything to keep him from poverty, it's possible for him to achieve the rest with a modicum of courage and of luck. Make sure you keep up your strength and send me notes so that I know what's happening and what you all are doing. I'll be waiting with baited breath. Say hello to little Tullia and our Cicero. Best wishes to you all."

Cato opened negotiations with the Cypriot Ptolemy, offering him a prominent priesthood in exchange for a peaceful abdication, but feeling dishonored, Ptolemy instead committed suicide, and Cyprus was duly joined to Cilicia.

Back in Rome Clodius also sought to detain aristocratic hostages by which Pompey and others had enhanced their prestige. He pried away Tigranes, the son of the king of Armenia, who was resident with a Pompeian client. The accounts are spotty, but Tigranes was next known to have been driven by a storm to Antium, near the Bay of Naples. Was Clodius releasing him outright, or, dispatching him somehow to the Armenian throne? In any case, representatives of Pompey cared enough to race to Antium to win back possession of Tigranes, and a scuffle ensued between them and Clodius's men, resulting in the death of a Pompeian. Finally, Clodius seems to have been behind the elevation of Brigitarus to the throne of Galatia, which he was sharing with his father-in-law Deiotarus. This, at least, is what Cicero alleges in accusing Clodius of taking bribes. In the same speech, Cicero says Clodius also removed a priest of Magna Mater at Pessinus, evidently through tribune legislation. It was a new age for Rome when its most domestic of political offices – the tribunate of the plebs – joined the consuls, praetors, and senators in playing games with foreign territories, as if the entire Mediterranean were becoming their "state."

14.5 Poets and Politicians

Gaius Memmius, a praetor of 58, combined an active career in politics with an interest in the poetry of his day, in ways that illustrate the literary sidelines that were typical among senators and other members of the elite. Though later writers referred to Memmius's compositions, none have survived; rather, his contributions to literature survive in the works of others. He was a patron of some kind to the poets Gaius Valerius Catullus and Gaius Helvius Cinna. Both came from northern Italy (Cisalpine Gaul), and both served on Memmius's staff when he was propraetor in Bithynia in 57. As with Memmius, very little of Cinna's poetry survives; Catullus, however, has left a rich and varied oeuvre. They were all part of a trend in avant-garde poetry that Cicero dubbed the *poetae novae*, or "new poets," which is referred to in scholarship as the "neoterics," from the Greek *neoteroi*. The neoterics embraced the literary values of Callimachus, the Alexandrian poet who disdained long and ponderous epic in favor of short, jewel-like observations of daily life and relationships (Chapter 6). Catullus experimented with different projects, including a Latin version of a poem by Sappho from the sixth century, in which he even hewed to the same meter, and a Latin version of Callimachus's *Lock of Berenike* (Chapter 6). His themes departed from the patriotic interests of Ennius (Chapter 9), sometimes in a controversial way, such as his poem about a priest of Cybele/Magna Mater (Chapter 7), who castrated himself in order to serve her. For his beloved, to whom he dedicated numerous erotic verses, Catullus used the pseudonym Lesbia, in reference to the meter used by Sappho who hailed from Lesbos. It is believed that she was Clodia, the sister of Publius Clodius Pulcher, whose chastity Cicero would come to question in memorable fashion (see below).

Catullus's work seems utterly apolitical, and yet he served on a provincial staff and mixed with powerful senators in their milieu. Poems written during his time in Bithynia may not reveal anything of the matters that typically draw historical inquiry – administration, economy, politics, military – but they do demonstrate the kinds of internal, emotional journeys that Roman functionaries could experience. An example is Catullus's dedication to his brother who died in Bithynia, probably on the same kind of mission as Catullus, and was buried near Troy. The opening line is "through many nations and across many seas I have been carried" [to the tomb], and goes on to contrast the distance traveled with the ancient funeral ritual of their hoary Italian ancestors. As Catullus saw it, Rome may have spread its power far and wide, while always honoring its rustic roots, but all Catullus really cared about was his brother and what he lost. But at the same time, Catullus could write about trifles that might make the reader laugh. In another poem, after he returned to Rome, he complains in ways either playful or embittered, perhaps both, of how he failed to make a fortune overseas; in colorful terms, to say the least, he berates poor Memmius for abetting his poverty (see Primary Source 14.2).

Primary Source 14.2

Catullus, Poems about Service in Bithynia

The poet Catullus spent time in the province of Bithynia on a praetor's staff. The following two poems reveal his less than enthusiastic opinion of his service overseas, displaying an eagerness to return home and a degree of disillusionment with what he gained (or did not) in the process.

Poem #46: "Now spring brings back its thawing warmth; now the fury of the equinox's weather grows calm with the pleasant western breezes. Phrygian fields are abandoned, Catullus, and the fertile land of boiling Nicaea (both in the province of Bithynia). Let us fly to the famous cities of (the province of) Asia. Now my trembling thoughts turn to travel, now my feet grow strong and fast with zeal. Farewell my sweet band of companions, who set out together far from home and whom different roads are bringing back in different ways."

Poem #10: "My (friend) Varus took me to visit his girlfriends, out of the Forum where I was lounging around. One seemed to me right away to be a bit of a strumpet, but not entirely disagreeable or inelegant. As we arrived various topics came up in discussion, including how things were in Bithynia, what was going on there, and did I make any money. I replied the truth, that there was nothing for the praetors themselves nor for their staff, and no one comes back richer, especially when they had a rapist for a praetor (Memmius) who didn't lift a finger for his staff. "But surely," she said, "nevertheless you brought back men to carry your litter, since it's said that they are bred over there." So that I could appear more impressive to the girl, I said, "It was not so unfortunate for me that I could not bring back eight stout men, however bad the province happened to be." But I had none, neither here nor over there, who could put on his back even the broken beam of an old cot. Then she said, like any little wench, "Oh, please, my Catullus, lend them to me for a little bit! For I want to be carried to the Temple of Serapis." "Hold on," I said to the girl, "well darn it – what I said just now that I had – I wasn't thinking – my friend Cinna, yes, Gaius Cinna – he's the one who brought back (the slaves). But whether they're his or mine, what's it to me? I use them as if I had brought them. But damn are you annoying, little trifle, you who won't let someone misspeak."

Memmius receives a more respectful dedication from another experimental poet of the 50s, Titus Lucretius Carus. Not one of the neoterics who favored brevity and wit, Lucretius wrote a long and complex poem using the dactylic hexameter of Homeric epic, called the *De Rerum Natura*, "On the Nature of Things." In it, he "sang" of the precepts of Epicureanism, the philosophy born in Athens in the late-fourth century (Chapter 4). All things, he claimed, were made of small, irreducible particles, invisible to the eye and in a constant state of motion; his prescience of atomic theory, borrowed in part from certain earlier Greek philosophers, is striking today. The repercussions of his worldview were radical – anything can be explained; religion is an invention of man; the soul perishes along with the body; everything disintegrates. For these reasons, Lucretius lived for *ataraxia*, "freedom from care," an ethic first spelled out by Epicurus (Chapter 4).

14.6 The Scandal of the Alexandrian Embassy

New opportunities were opening up in the East with a major regime-change in Egypt in 58. The power brokers of Alexandria had had their fill of the Romanophile king when he acquiesced without a fight in Clodius's and Cato's seizure of Cyprus, a solidly Ptolemaic domain for over 200 years. Put to flight, Ptolemy XII sought refuge with Cato, still on Rhodes, and from there made his way to Pompey in Italy and was housed at his estate in the Alban Hills. Ptolemy's daughter, Berenike IV, then ruled in Egypt in her own right. Efforts were afoot at court to find her a husband. Various heirs to the now disempowered Seleucid line came forward, but one died prematurely and another was blocked by Aulus Gabinius, who had moved to the governorship of Syria as proconsul in 57. A pretender, uncreatively calling himself Seleucus, was wed to Berenike but was killed within days when he was revealed to be unsuitable in some way. Finally, Berenike IV was approached by Archelaus, the son of the general of the same name who had fought effectively under Mithridates at the height of his power (Chapter 11). In all probability, this Archelaus had known Berenike's father, the now exiled Ptolemy XII, since both spent part of their childhoods at the Pontic court.

What to do with Egypt became a vexing and ultimately destabilizing question in Roman politics. Word soon arrived in Alexandria that Pompey was arguing in the senate for a mission to reinstall Ptolemy XII. The Alexandrians accordingly dispatched an embassy of some 100 members to plead their case in Rome. What transpired upon the arrival of the embassy in Italy revealed, like Gabinius's disruption of old Seleucid marrying habits, the price paid by Hellenistics for relying on Roman protection with no muscle of their own to shape their destiny. Many of the Alexandrian delegation died under mysterious circumstances at the harbor town of Puteoli, and those that managed to survive were intimidated into silence. The lead envoy managed to make it to the protection of a senator in Rome, but he was evidently poisoned at a meal there.

Pompey, the champion of the Ptolemy XII, stood to gain much from the erasure of this embassy, but its outright annihilation was almost certainly beyond him; nevertheless he fell under suspicion. A lightning strike on a statue of Jupiter Latiaris near Pompey's estate prompted a consultation of the Sibylline books, which were interpreted as forbidding any effort to back a king in Egypt. A number of investigations in the coming years would lead to accusations and trials of Pompey's acolytes in an effort to root out the conspiracy. Ptolemy XII, meanwhile, moved, or was moved, to Ephesus to await developments. The murder of the Alexandrians thus ignited a crisis in Roman politics, as it spelled an assertion of pan-Mediterranean power devoid of the niceties of diplomacy, and whoever perpetrated it stood to be propelled far higher than his senate.

14.7 Caesar in Gaul

While Pompey's domain – the entire East – seemed chaotic in the course of 58 and 57, Caesar was regularly sending dispatches from the field in Gaul that demonstrated a mastery of tactics and administration, as well as a knack for storytelling. His planned mission to Illyricum had been reoriented at the start of 58 when one Gallic tribe, the Helvetii, in the vicinity of modern Switzerland, was threatening to overrun another, the Aedui, the northern neighbors of Rome's Transalpine province who had first opened diplomatic relations with Rome as long ago as 120. Caesar marched to "protect" the Aeduans and wrote missives to Rome to explain his methods and motivations.

Caesar's *Commentaries* are models of what one scholar called "artful reporting" – a deliberate presentation of events in such a way to promote Caesar not just in terms of his Gallic adventures but also in relation to what was happening in Rome and elsewhere. Caesar managed to hold off the Helvetii at Lake Geneva, but this only delayed a longer campaign as they attempted to march around the Roman position. At the root of the upheaval was the Germanic chieftain Ariovistus, of the Suebi, who had settled in Alsace, a prize in a tug of war between Gaul and Germany long before the famous contests for it in the twentieth century. Caesar had to pull more legions across the Alps and raise fresh recruits quickly, and he was happy to tell his readers that he succeeded: at Bibracte, he defeated the Helvetii and pushed them back to their traditional homeland for good. Caesar reports further that he compelled the Helvetii to surrender hostages, always a measure, in Roman eyes, of a multifaceted victory. His commentaries on this episode were evidently popular in the city: an otherwise poorly known poet, Varro Atacinus, was inspired by them to pen an entire epic poem titled *Bellum Sequanicum*.

In 57, Caesar pressed westward against the Belgae. He reported that they had initially formed a kind of united federation that was worrisome for its combined strength, but that the leaders fell to bickering among themselves. As their collective effort disintegrated, Caesar had a less-challenging time in dealing with them one by one. In this way his account may be read as a cautionary tale for Rome, especially given the factious nature of Clodius's tribunate the year before. All such weakness could be avoided if the cooperative model set forth by Caesar, Pompey, and Crassus was sensibly heeded, and order brought to the Republic. Added to Caesar's Belgian victory was the proactive advance work of Publius Crassus, the triumviral son, in the regions of Normandy, where he accepted the submission of native tribes without any serious engagement. Caesar was rewarded with a 15-day *supplicatio*, a ceremony of public thanksgiving to the gods.

14.8 The Return of Cicero

The senate's surprise at Clodius's industriousness in 58 had hardened into antipathy toward him by 57, and his adversaries began to organize more effectively. It was perhaps at this point that Clodius's radicalism became unsavory to Caesar and especially to Pompey, who was barricaded for a time in his house by Clodius's hostile *collegiae*. Pompey turned to Titus Annius Milo in response, a supporter who organized thuggish groups of his own. An effort to reverse Cicero's exile had been afoot since 58 but was constantly disrupted by violence. Now, in 57, Cicero's advocates combined Milo's muscle with the parliamentary device of shifting the vote for his recall from the assembly to the *comitia centuriata*, a conservative institution, where it passed.

Upon his return Cicero wasted no time in getting revenge on Clodius. In a collection of speeches from 57 and 56, he kept up a withering and mocking barrage on Clodius's character, parrying Clodius's own recent rhetorical jabs at him as well as recalling the Bona Dea disgrace at many turns. In a speech titled *On His House*, Cicero purported to explain how Clodius's destruction of his home on the Palatine was unjustified, but the lion's share of the speech was about Cicero's political conduct as consul, such that the "house" of the title might be construed as Rome itself. He also rebuilt his political status by hitching back to Pompey, as he had in 66. In 56, he promulgated a bill to give Pompey *imperium* to deal with the grain shortage sparked by Clodius's law demanding that food be provided for free. Clodius responded by interpreting a convenient omen – a thunderclap on a clear day – as the gods' displeasure at a number of affronts, including the assassination of ambassadors (an allusion to the murder of the Alexandrians) and the desecration of a holy site (an allusion to Cicero's reclaiming his house and knocking down the shrine to *Libertas* to do so). Cicero artfully thought up other episodes which, while obscure, implicated *Clodius* as the target of the omen. As Cicero described it in the speech, *On the responses to the haruspices* (the seer-priests who interpreted the will of the gods), the omen was not referring to the deaths of the Alexandrians – clearly still a sensitive issue – but to the deaths of a certain Theodosius, whom he alleged was killed by Clodius. Cicero had already dealt with the question of his house and the phony shrine to *Libertas*, and so he argued that the problem of the desecrated holy site, which the haruspices warned against, in fact referred to Clodius's occupation of a house and family shrines whose owner he had killed. The speech effectively neutralized an attack based on divine interpretation by exposing its subjectivity and, thus, its unreliability for a court of law.

Clodius kept up his attack by proxy. He was either directly involved in or associated with a charge in 56 against Marcus Caelius Rufus concerning, once again, the assassination of the Alexandrian embassy. One of the charges of the prosecutors was that Caelius attempted to poison his lover Clodia, the sister of Clodius, at the same time as the Alexandrians. Cicero's speech in defense of Caelius survives (see Primary Source 14.3). Cicero fixated on the presence of Clodia in the case, and used her as a way of turning the tables on her brother, alleging they engaged in an incestuous affair. Cicero's flair for the dramatic was on display: he conjured up the spirit of the family's great ancestor, Appius Claudius Caecus (Chapter 4), as if in a séance, and in a feigned voice did an impression of Caecus expressing disgust at the decadence of his descendants.

> **Primary Source 14.3**
>
> **Cicero, *In Defense of Caelius***
>
> In 56 Cicero used a defense speech on behalf of Publius Caelius Rufus as an opportunity to insult Clodius's reputation. Seizing upon a part of the case that involved Clodia, the sister of Clodius (and likely the beloved of Catullus, see above), he alleged an incestuous affair between brother and sister, irrelevant though it was to the court case at hand, and sarcastically contrasted them with the storied clan of the Claudii of old.
>
> 13–14: "Every angle in this case, gentlemen of the jury, deals with Clodia, a woman not only noble but notorious, too, about whom I shall say nothing except that which may dispel the charges (against my client) … I would make the case rather strenuously, but what hinders me are the altercations I've had with her husband – oops, I meant brother; I always make that mistake. I shall proceed with modesty … Should I deal with (Clodia) in an old-fashioned, serious, and severe manner, or in the softer, more sophisticated vein? If by means of the former austere style, then someone should be conjured by me from among the bearded men we see in statues and *imagines* – not the little trendy beards by which she likes to be tickled, but those long grey beards. Therefore let someone from her own family come forth (from the past) … there's none better than Appius Claudius Caecus (Chapter 4), for he would suffer the least by virtue of not being able to look at her. If he *came* forth, he would *hold* forth and speak as follows: 'Woman, what are you doing with Caelius? Why are you involved with such a young man, with someone not in your family? Why did your brother's vices influence you more than your father's and your grandfather's virtues which have been repeated (through the centuries) up to our own age, not only among the men but also the women? Did I build that aqueduct (the Aqua Appia) so you could use its waters unchastely? Did I built that road (the Via Appia) so you could walk such streets accompanied by other women's husbands?'"

Just as Clodius was dabbling in the eastern provinces, so too was Cicero. His *De Provinciis Consularibus*, "On the consular provinces," of 56, discussed Macedonia, Syria, and Gaul. In it Cicero criticized failed governors, as he saw them, such as Aulus Gabinius and Calpurnius Piso, not coincidentally senators who had favored his exile, and praised successful ones, like Caesar (though he was son-in-law to the same Piso). Caesar's *Commenatries* were contemporaneous with the speech and their popularity may have influenced Cicero's point of view. Cicero's speech, *In Pisonem*, "Against Piso," of 55, returned to an attack against the governor of Macedonia, the same year as Pompey's theater was to open (see below).

14.9 Displaying the "Exotic"

In early 56, Caesar, still in northern Italy, would have had knowledge of the cases being bandied about in Rome. Both Clodius's and Cicero's interest in how the provinces were being managed, however much in counterpoint, would have caught his attention as it spelled growing dissatisfaction, at least among some, of the triumvirate's eclipse of Rome's traditions of power-sharing and of the importance of the electorate. Caesar summoned Pompey and Crassus to Luca, a town on the very edge of his imperial province, and plotted a renewal and extension of their cooperation. Pompey and Crassus pooled their resources and contacts to help each other to the consulship of 55, repeating their partnership of 70 (Chapter 13). Caesar's *imperium* in Gaul would be extended for another five years. It was probably also worked out at this time that Pompey and Crassus would each receive commands of their own, in Spain and Syria, respectively.

In spite of this organized effort at Luca, the continuation of the triumvirate was not a *fait accompli*. A massive revolt among the Veneti in Gaul drew Caesar's attention as it threatened to undo all his gains from the previous years. Not only did he have to return to the region, but he also had to figure out a way to navigate the Atlantic coast, on which the Veneti were situated, and to fight their ships in spite of heavy surf and tides whose violence was not familiar to someone from the Mediterranean Sea. Caesar's *Commentaries* for 56 have a different tone from those of previous years: he eked out victory with the usual pluck, devising a tool for cutting the ropes on the Venetian sailing ships from afar – essentially knives on poles – but his response was not as clement as before. He reports on mass executions and martial law to subdue the enemy. Readers in Rome could not have missed Caesar's new propensity toward violence as they made their own political decisions and went to the polls and found Pompey and Crassus on the slate.

The new world order and Pompey's role in it were unmistakable in the course of 55. In short order, Crassus got the Syrian command that he was anticipating. He would take over from Gabinius in the following year who was now tasked with finally shifting Ptolemy XII from his refuge in Ephesus back to his Egyptian throne. Gabinius moved swiftly, aided by a lieutenant, Marcus Antonius, the grandson and son of the generals who fought the pirates in 102 and 71 (Chapters 11 and 13), and who would enter Anglicized history as Mark Antony. They defeated Archelaus and Berenike IV, who were quickly executed. Even so, Ptolemy XII's position was precarious enough that Gabinius left him with a troop of bodyguards, partly of Gallic and Germanic descent, who would linger in service to the throne. They are later called the Gabiniani by Caesar, when he himself faced them in 47 (Chapter 15). A Roman financier, Rabirius Postumus, also stayed on and was appointed Ptolemy's *dioikistes*, or financial minister, surely intended to follow up on Ptolemy's debts to Pompey.

Pompey's Ptolemaic candidate was now back in place, and Pompey himself had a command in Spain coming up, which would have connoted an all-encompassing influence – "from east to west" – with Rome in the middle of it all. The year 55 not coincidentally saw the opening in Rome of a huge new entertainment complex, built by Pompey, which articulated in stone his primacy over the world. The Theater of Pompey, as it was called, towered over the Campus Martius. Though the building has left no ruins, the curvature of its *cavea*, or semicircular rows of seats, is still present in the street plan of modern Rome. Atop the seats was a shrine to Venus

Victrix, Venus the Conqueror, foremother of the Roman race through her son, Aeneas, and now in the guise of a champion of empire.

Much more than just a theater, Pompey's building was fronted by a massive portico, 300 m long by 150 m wide (or, three football fields, to use a common conceptualization of space), which appears to have been the main attraction, not the bleachers and the stage. Inside it were gathered sculpture groups of famous figures from mythology, history, and the dynasties of the East, including the nine Muses (thereby superseding the nearby Temple of Hercules and the Muses, Chapter 8), the 14 *nationes* (nations) that Pompey had conquered (depicted as female personifications), and famous poets and scholars, likely from the institutions at Alexandria, Pergamon, and Athens. Tapestries hung on the walls; water flowed through fountains. Spectators enjoyed the curious and the strange: one portrait honored a woman who had given birth 30 times, and there were sculptures of exotic animals, rather like the dioramas of a modern museum of natural history. Gardens were also a popular draw, featuring trees that had been transplanted from Pompey's conquests or from territories nearby, including balsams from Judaea, palm trees from Ethiopia, and plane trees from Asia Minor. The exhibits betrayed a certain level of optimism and even glee that set them apart from the eastern centers of cosmopolitanism. Whereas the various Attalid monuments (Chapters 7, 8, and 9) depicted dead or dying enemies, Pompey's specimens were alive and, as plants, not constitutionally hostile. In short, the East was on display, in Rome, contained within stone walls, controlled and making tangible for the Roman visitor a world beyond their reach (but not beyond Pompey's), like a triumphal procession made permanent.

As the Romans were experiencing this new showpiece of Pompey's, they would have also encountered new sorts of missives from Caesar, who was doing his own part to push the borders outward. In 55, he had made a daring crossing of the Rhine, his engineers erecting a spectacular bridge across an impossible current. Later in the year, he broached an even wider body of water, the English Channel, as for the first time Roman legions set foot in Britain and skirmished with local chieftains. Caesar's stated goal in so doing was to deprive the rebellious Veneti of their allied Britons, but one should note that Caesar also stood to gain politically in presenting his ethnographic explorations at precisely the same time as the opening of Pompey's theater. Caesar's fourth book put Germans in a kind of zoo of the mind, where readers learned what they looked like; what they ate and drank; the clothes they wore; how they raised their children; their conceptions of gender roles; and the ways in which they practiced both agriculture and warfare. Soon his *Commentaries* reported on the Britons and on the Druids and their kin, another batch of (defeated) exotics to titillate the Roman audience. Both "monuments" – Pompey's museum and Caesar's "encyclopedia" of sorts (see Primary Source 14.4) – cemented their places as universal leaders, and their power came closer and closer to resembling that of the *basileis* of the Hellenistic East.

Primary Source 14.4

Julius Caesar, *Commentaries on the Gallic War*

With his *Commentaries* on the war, Julius Caesar did more than just report on troop movements and the outcomes of battles. He also included ethnographies of the Gauls, Germans, and Britons, partly to describe the enemy but also to compete with contemporary rivals in Rome, such as Pompey, who derived much prestige from spectacles and the display of the exotic. In many places, these ethnographic digressions are clearly sensational and exaggerated.

On the Germans, *Comm.* 4.1: "They survive not so much on grain as on milk and meat and they are often occupied with hunting. These characteristics – the nature of their food, their daily exertions, and the freedom of their lives (for because of a lack of duty and discipline from boyhood they do nothing at all that is against their will) – feed their strength and generate a race of massive bodies. And they're made stronger by their custom that even in the coldest climates they wear nothing but animal skins, on account of whose skimpiness the greater part of their body is exposed. And they wash in rivers.

On the Britons, *Comm.* 5.13–14: About these islands some have written that night lasts for thirty continuous days in the winter. We could not confirm this through thorough observation, except that by means of a precise water clock we saw that their nights are indeed longer than on the mainland … All the Britons dye themselves with *vitrum*, which generates a cerulean color and so in battle they are rather terrifying in appearance. Their hair is shaggy, with every part of the body shaved except their heads and their upper lips. Men by the tens and twelves hold their wives in common among themselves, especially among brothers and between fathers and sons."

On the Gauls, *Comm.* 6.16: "The entire nation of Gauls is given over to religious beliefs and on account of this, those who are afflicted with a rather grievous illness and who are engaged in battles and (other) dangers, either practice human sacrifice or vow that they will do so, enlisting the Druids to conduct the rituals. They believe that the will of the immortal gods cannot be assuaged with regard to the life of one man unless the life of another is given over, and so they stage official rituals of such a kind in public. Others create effigies of massive size, filling the limbs, which are made of wicker sticks, with living humans. When these are lit on fire, the victims perish entirely wrapped in flame."

14.10 Challenges to the Triumvirate

In 54, events were militating against Pompey, and so he decided to remain near Rome even though he was technically the governor of Spain. By then Calpurnius Piso had been recalled from his province in Macedonia, owing to the speech by Cicero. Rabirius Postumus, the financial minister to Ptolemy XII, had overstepped his bounds in Alexandria and had been put under arrest by the Egyptians but managed to escape to Rome. In Rome Rabirius was brought up on charges of extortion and was defended by Cicero in a speech that survives. Another friend of Pompey's and lieutenant in the East, Gabinius, was also charged at the end of 54 with extortion; in his case, the charge was joined with treason for leaving Syria to support Ptolemy XII. Gabinius's mission to Egypt may have been blessed by Pompey, but he did not have senatorial approval, which was not only customary but legally required. On the latter charge, he was acquitted but on the former he was convicted and departed to exile. All the while, Pompey sat outside the city, in possession of *imperium* but rather ineffectual for one with his own army. Caesar was in Gaul and Crassus departed to campaign against Parthia. Pandemonium characterized the elections in 54 for 53, with riots led by Clodius and Milo.

In 53, Crassus attempted a full-scale invasion of Parthia. He crossed the Euphrates with some 35 000 men, expecting additional cavalry support from Artavasdes, the successor of Tigranes in Armenia. But the Armenian horses never materialized, and so Crassus was at a significant disadvantage at the Battle of Carrhae, where the Parthian cavalry surrounded his troops. Adroit with bow and arrow even on horseback the Parthians freely picked off the Romans, never coming within a pike's reach. Arab allies assisted the Parthians logistically by refreshing their quivers from camel trains near the battlefield. Both Crassus and his son were killed. More damaging to the Roman psyche than the defeat was the humiliation. Orodes, the Parthian king, put on display the standards of the defeated legions as trophies and even used Crassus's decapitated head as a prop in a staging of Euripides's *Bacchae*, in the "role" of Pentheus, the hubristic mortal who was torn to pieces (by his mother, among others) for daring to attend sacred rites of Dionysus. The very staging of the play in Parthia bespeaks the enduring influence of Hellenic culture in the region, refined in Orodes's deployment of an allegory in which the Parthians are represented by the East–West hybrid Dionysus, and the Romans as sacrilegious, Pentheus-esque interlopers.

Caesar also suffered uncharacteristic setbacks in 53. His time in Britain may have lent him a propaganda *coup*, but he paid for his absence from Gaul with the emboldenment of a local tribe, the Sugambri. He lost over a legion's worth of men in his skirmishes with them, making the most of it by reporting on the panic that gripped his troops until he himself could personally calm them down and steel them for counter-resistance. He had been able to recross the Rhine, but had little to show for it apart from new ethnographies. A new kind of Gallic chieftain was coming to the fore: Vercingetorix possessed remarkable skills in organizing alliances and fielding new, larger armies. The situation was dire enough that Caesar asked to borrow a legion from Pompey's force in Spain, and Pompey consented.

The bad news flowing into Rome in 53 added elements of fear to the residual uncertainties of the failed, postponed, and, as yet, still unresolved elections of the previous year. Electoral campaigns were under way for the consulships of 52 before the two victors for 53 had even taken office. Milo was one of the candidates, and Clodius, his nemesis, was running for praetor, which would have given Clodius *imperium* for the first time. Outside the city, Milo's and Clodius's entourages engaged in their most heated confrontation yet, and ex-gladiators, we are told, chased down a wounded Clodius and ran him through. A large segment of the population had never wavered in its support of Clodius, and his funeral devolved into a raucous affair in which flames of his pyre were cast upon the senate house that Clodius so loathed. With this arson, Rome was teetering on the edge of dissolution. Some were calling for a dictatorship, with Pompey in mind to hold it. Calpurnius Bibulus, who was on the losing end of the triumvirate during his failed coconsulship with Caesar, proposed instead that Pompey be made sole consul for the start of 52. Such a position should have been a contradiction in terms – the consulship was by definition a dual phenomenon – but the compromise was accepted by Pompey's opponents as better than the powers afforded dictators, and Pompey was duly appointed.

14.11 Conclusions

Most of the dynasties that followed Alexander – the Antigonids, Seleucids, Attalids, and Mithridatics – were long since gone, politically speaking, by the point of this chapter, and the sole remaining one, the Ptolemies, was nearly entirely a creation of Rome. Yet the cultural forms of their realms endured, as now interpreted by Romans like Catullus and Lucretius and unnamed sculptors and artists. Their political forms, namely the monarchy, were also gaining currency, only partially for now but very soon on a greater scale by ever more powerful Roman generals.

Appian, in his account of Pompey's triumph in 61, said that Pompey allegedly wore a cloak of Alexander the Great, but he expressed doubts whether that was true. The anecdote, complete with the historian's skepticism, serves as a metaphor for Pompey's stature at the point of his zenith. With his conquest of nearly all the East and his urban munificence at royal dimensions, he would seem to be worthy of his new epithet *Magnus*. But as Plutarch also cynically pointed out in his account of the triumph, whereas Alexander was only in his early 30s upon his "world domination," Pompey was pushing 40, and whereas Alexander's early death ensured a form of heroic immortality, Pompey would lose it all and be dragged down from his heights. It is a bit of foreshadowing, which Plutarch and Appian were able to construct because they knew of the rise of Caesar, which would seem to be a bolt out of the blue when he made his move in winter, 49.

Further Reading

Gruen, Erich (1974). *The Last Generation of the Roman Republic*. Berkeley: University of California Press.

Millar, Fergus (2002). *The Crowd in the Roman Republic*. Ann Arbor: University of Michigan Press.

Morstein-Marx, Robert (2008). *Mass Oratory and Political Power in the Late Roman Republic*. Cambridge: Cambridge University Press.

Mouritsen, Henrik (2001). *Plebs and Politics in the Late Roman Republic*. Cambridge: Cambridge University Press.

Riggsby, Andrew (2006). *Caesar in Gaul and Rome: War in Words*. Austin: University of Texas Press.

Welch, Kathryn and Powell, Anton (eds.) (1998). *Julius Caesar as Artful Reporter: the War Commentaries as Political Instruments*. Classical Press of Wales.

15

To 44: Roman Alexanders

Timeline

52: The Battle of Alesia: Caesar defeats Vercengetorix. Pompey's sole consulship ends before the year is out with the election of his father-in-law as colleague.
51: Cicero as governor in Cilicia; death of Ptolemy XII
49: Caesar crosses the Rubicon, initiating civil war with Pompey
48: Battle of Pharsalus: Caesar defeats Pompey; death of Pompey in Alexandria
48–47: Caesar's sojourn in Alexandria with Cleopatra VII, followed by campaigning in Pontus and Numidia; birth of Caesarion
46: The quadruple triumph of Caesar, lasting on and off for a month; construction of the Forum of Caesar and Temple of Venus Genetrix; 10-year dictatorship awarded to Caesar by the senate, along with the powers of a censor for three years
45: Caesar campaigns in Spain
January, 44: The "perpetual" dictatorship of Caesar
March, 44: The assassination of Caesar at the Theater of Pompey

Principal Themes

- Pompey's and Caesar's alliance imploded, and efforts at reconciliation between them failed, in large part due to politics beyond their control. Caesar swiftly gained an edge in an armed conflict.
- Pompey's Egyptian contacts deserted him, and Caesar entered the game of the Ptolemaic dynasty with an opportunistic alliance with Cleopatra VII.
- Following the death of Pompey, Caesar crossed to theaters of warfare in all corners of the Mediterranean, from Asia Minor to North Africa to Spain, to eradicate most of his remaining opponents.
- Consolidating his power quickly, Caesar embarked on major reforms in Rome, covering every aspect of life from politics to culture; all of these betrayed the influences of, and thus perhaps aspirations for, Hellenistic-style kingship.

The Roman Republic and the Hellenistic Mediterranean: From Alexander to Caesar, First Edition. Joel Allen.
© 2020 John Wiley & Sons, Inc. Published 2020 by John Wiley & Sons, Inc.

15.1 Introduction

The institutions of the Republic finally buckled under the enormous power that individuals were able to amass through wealth and military prowess, both mutually dependent. The surest sign of the efficacy of provincial achievements for political success was the attempted involvement of unsuitable participants in this sphere, such as Cicero. Tribunes and senators tried to use their age-old methods to return their system to normal, but Caesar saw the clearer path and marched on Rome. Tracing a roughly counterclockwise tour through the ever important realm of the East, he defeated Pompey in Greece, picked up valuable resources in Egypt, and appointed loyalists as new governors in the Levant and Asia Minor.

Returning to Rome, Caesar demonstrated remarkable industry in thinking through every facet of public life – politics, military, economy, religion, entertainment, and even the keeping of time. The Republic, however, entrenched by nearly 500 years of existence, was not done yet, and a group of senators killed Caesar on the Ides of March. Ironically, their political ethic – broad, oligarchic power-sharing inimical to monarchy – would also gasp a dying breath.

15.2 Pompey's Sole Consulship

With his appointment as sole consul in 52, Pompey may seem to have reached the height of prestige and influence. Acknowledging his preternatural abilities as an organizer, the senate trusted him with restoring order, but hewing to their respect for old institutions it forewent the dictatorship that Sulla inhabited and instead put Pompey in an office still subject to veto and auditing. Pompey seems to have divided his tasks between short-term problems and those concerned with major systemic failures. In pursuit of the former, he prosecuted the associates of both Clodius and Milo, in spite of his previous relationship with Milo, on charges of bribery and violence. Cicero endeavored to defend Milo but thought better of it, and Milo ended up in exile in Massilia.

Turning to the Republic's long-term future, Pompey rightly saw provincial management as a source of destabilization. He was not the first to realize this: in 53 the senate had proposed requiring a five-year waiting period between a magistracy with *imperium* and prorogation to a province, but it had gone nowhere. Now Pompey saw to the necessary legislation to make it so. He also put obstacles in place to slow movement in the opposite direction, from province to high office, as he reinforced a law requiring candidates to be present in Rome, in person, in order to be eligible for election, which would require them to be without *imperium* for a time. Julius Caesar, with his current command in Gaul and his well-known ambitions to repeat as consul, was so obviously in contradiction of Pompey's new laws that Pompey had to make allowances for him lest he only spark new upheavals in the process of trying to curb them. Caesar was granted a special exemption, upon his request, such that he could run for consul in absentia. Pompey also did not forget himself: his own command in Spain, which would be awkward if not illegal under his own new rules, was nevertheless extended. The two remaining "triumvirs" continued thus to operate above the law. Even Crassus was not forgotten: Pompey now married the widow of Crassus's son, another Cornelia, and contributed to her prestige by working to see that her father, Quintus Caecilius Metellus Scipio, was elected as his coconsul for the last few months of 52.

The need for Pompey to placate Caesar had become increasingly apparent in the course of the year, as news of Caesar's suppression of Vercingetorix's revolt in Gaul arrived in the usual serial dispatches. Coming out of winter fortifications in 52 both with his own legions and still with the one lent from Spain by Pompey (Chapter 14), Caesar had suffered a military setback at Gergovia, and then a diplomatic one, as the Aedui, long Rome's most reliable ally in the region, switched to Vercingetorix. Matters came to a head when Caesar trapped the Gallic federation's principal army at Alesia and settled into a careful siege. As he tells it, Caesar put into practice the best of Roman engineering, building a ditch and wall circumvallation in great haste. When significant Gallic reinforcements were said to be on their way to relieve Vercingetorix, he built yet another wall, defending his siegeworks, creating a kind of doughnut of Romans with Gauls inside the ring and out. Into the no-man's land between the central citadel and the Roman position, Vercingetorix ejected the sick and starving, in order to save resources for his soldiers, and so the concentric circles of Alesia became even more bizarre. A relieving force of Romans, led by Mark Antony and Gaius Trebonius, arrived and forced the outer Gauls to regroup. Vercingetorix had no choice but to stake everything on forcing his way out, but Caesar's defenses were unassailable and many Gauls were killed or captured in the course of Vercingetorix's escape. Titus Labienus, among Caesar's best officers for the entire Gallic project, distinguished himself. In September, the Gallic chieftain was surrendered by his own troops to Caesar along with much war prize. The senate ordered a 20-day *supplicatio* for Caesar's success.

Obeying his writ to maintain order in Rome after the chaos of 53 and prior, Pompey was scrupulous in managing the elections for 51, and the results suggest at least the opening of a factional cleavage between Pompey and Caesar. One of the new consuls was Marcus Claudius Marcellus, who came to pursue a virulent agenda against Caesar's interests. Marcellus made clear his intention to bring Caesar's *imperium* to a close at the start of the year in 51, but his law got nowhere. Later in the year with the matter of the expiry still unresolved, Marcellus tried another tack, including Gaul in the package of commands for the consuls of 50, which would not include Caesar, but tribunes managed to veto him.

Meanwhile, Cicero was absent from Rome for the year 51. The law delaying provincial commands by five years for office-holders had the likely unintended effect of creating a dearth of eligible proconsuls, forcing the senate to scrape the bottom of the military barrel where Cicero abided; it had been 12 years since his consulship in 63 and so he could legally be pressed into service. Cicero was made governor of Cilicia and he set off for the East. Not entirely averse to the assignment, he enjoyed lectures and cultural pursuits at Ephesus along the way, even hiring a philosopher, Cratippus of Pergamon, for the eventual education of his son. Once in his province, he seemed to take sudden interest in military endeavors, Alexander-style, now that he was in the region of the legendary Battle of Issus. Some of his letters adopted a Caesarian flair, including reports of his role in battling bandits. The Parthians had made an assault on Syria, the province next door, but Cicero focused his military efforts on mountain tribes, to which he laid siege at one point. His reports were drafted in the same kind of clipped, no-nonsense prose that had characterized Caesar's Gallic *Commentaries*, and were not at all in keeping with Cicero's usual discursive style (see Primary Source 15.1). Even Cicero, the creature of law-court oratory, was thus now joining in the game of ascending to political heights through the provinces, endeavoring to reacquire his previous prestige, which had been on the wane under the monopolization of power by the "triumvirs."

Primary Source 15.1

Letter from Cicero to Cato the Younger

This letter from Cicero to Cato the Younger, dated December, 51 and dispatched from Asia Minor, demonstrates Cicero's adoption of Caesarian styles of prose in describing his performance in a military maneuver, not normally his forte. A comparison with his speeches (Chapters 13 and 14) reveals that he chose his writing style depending on audience and objective. Some comparison with Demosthenes's *On the Crown* (Chapter 3), in listing the ways Cicero built up a variety of defense measures, may show further his interest in that orator as a model.

> *Ad Fam.* 15.4.10: "I surrounded the town with a wall and ditch; I enclosed it with six forts and substantial fortifications; I attacked with earthworks, mantlets, and towers; using many catapults and arches and at great personal toil; without any damage to or expense from our allies I finished the task on the 57th day, so that, with every part of the city in ruins or burned, they were driven to surrender to my authority and fearlessness; once Pindenissus was captured, however, I received hostages from them. I then dispatched the army to its winter camp."

15.3 A Planned Eastern Mission, Divisive and Unrealized

Ptolemy XII died in March 51 leaving behind two daughters and two sons who would contend for power in typical Ptolemaic fashion for the next decade. The oldest daughter and the oldest son were matched in a sister–brother marriage, and the dead king's will called upon Rome to protect their rights to the throne. Cleopatra VII was around 18 years old, and Ptolemy XIII, around 10. By late summer, documents were created from which Ptolemy's name is absent, implying some kind of power play by Cleopatra. If that was the case, it was over by 50, when Ptolemy XIII returned, and in precedence to his older sister. A severe drought could have been the catalyst for the dissension, as the Nile had failed to flood to expected levels for over two years, leading to a decree whereby food was ordered from the hinterland to Alexandria to alleviate famine.

The Parthian Empire was becoming emboldened in this period, whether owing to confidence following their destruction of Crassus's army (Chapter 14) or to the political and economic weaknesses of the once great Seleucids and Ptolemies. We have already seen their attempted assault on Syria in 51 when Cicero was governor nearby; in 50, the new governor of the province, Calpurnius Bibulus, Caesar's old ineffectual consular colleague, sought to strengthen his position by recalling from Egypt the Gabiniani, the Roman bodyguard that had been assigned to the Ptolemaic throne by Pompey (Chapter 14). He sent his sons to collect them but they were both killed; Cleopatra sent the perpetrators to Bibulus in chains for punishment. Back in Rome, an alarm was sounded: if the Romans were taking over for the Hellenistic project in the East, then the Parthians were assuming the role formerly played by the Persians as the Great Eastern Threat. The senate sought to collect reinforcements for a war, and to spread the redeployment around, it called on Caesar and Pompey each to contribute one legion. Both complied, but in such a way as to lay bare the irreconcilable nature of their competing ambitions. Caesar sent a Gallic legion to Rome, while Pompey chose not one of the legions currently in Spain, but the very legion he had loaned to Caesar in 53 to fight Vercingetorix. Caesar thus effectively felt the loss of two legions, and Pompey, none. What is more, when both legions arrived in Italy, rather than sending them on their stated mission, Pompey stationed them at Capua.

The debacle of the legions for the Parthian campaign gave Caesar more than enough cause for concern. Pompey, both in charge in Spain and commanding allegiance from great powers in the East, now had two fresh legions in striking distance of Rome. One of the new consuls of 50, Gaius Claudius Marcellus, cousin of the previous year's Marcus who had tried to take Caesar down, was also untrustworthy. One of the new tribunes, Gaius Scribonius Curio, tried to play peacemaker. He had spent the year pursuing a *popularis* agenda, arguing for debt relief and road construction. Now sensing that his constituency of nonelites was also in imminent danger of a triumviral clash, Curio proposed that Caesar and Pompey both relinquish their commands simultaneously. The senate agreed, we are told, by a vote of 370 to 22: Romans of all stripes seemed eager to divest the "triumvirate" of its powers and return to their old Republic. Instead matters came to a head. The proconsul Caesar refused to comply; the senate issued a *senatus consultum ultimum* against him; the tribune Curio vetoed it; but the consul Marcellus ordered Pompey to march north to face Caesar. Some of the tribunes-elect for 49, including Mark Antony, who had decamped from Gaul to Rome to protect Caesar's interests, felt obliged to flee for their lives. Two years of dithering among the various stakeholders over how power should be practiced in Rome ended in a rapid denouement.

15.4 The Start of a New Civil War

Given the political tension at the end of 50 and the heightened stakes of success, Romans in the city were likely expecting Caesar to march against them, and so the only thing surprising about his decision to do so may have been that it came in the dead of winter. On January 10, Caesar headed from Ravenna to Ariminium, along the way crossing the Rubicon, the stream marking the limits of his legitimate power in Cisalpine Gaul. Holding *imperium* outside his province, he was breaking the law, but then so, too, he would have said, were his adversaries when they ignored the sacrosanctity of tribunes like Mark Antony who were seeking to veto measures against him. All of this was a weak façade covering the contest for power between Caesar and Pompey. Caesar's winter surprise – the first of many unseasonal moves for the coming years – caught Pompey and the others off guard, with their recruits unmustered. Caesar had faced no obstacles when his force was quadrupled by additional legions arriving from Transalpine Gaul, with which he arranged a rendezvous in Etruria. Pompey fell back to his legions at Capua, and thence to Brundisium. He was joined by a host of recent former consuls and prominent senators, including Marcus Marcellus and Sergius Sulpicius Rufus, the coconsuls of 51 who had beleaguered Caesar; Faustus, a son of Sulla; Cato the Younger; Metellus Scipio, Pompey's father-in-law; Bibulus, who had returned from Syria; and after some delay, Cicero, against whom Caesar had argued at the time of the Catilinarian conspiracy (Chapter 13). Even Titus Labienus, who had accomplished great things with Caesar in Gaul, defected to Pompey's side. Caesar had taken charge of the Capuan legions, which in fact constituted a reunion just one year after he had sent them to Rome. The one thing Caesar lacked was an effective navy, and so he could not give chase as Pompey and his lofty adherents slipped away to Greece. Caesar thus occupied Rome, though with hardly any bloodshed. He ordered his troops to act with clemency and restraint, and his orders were heeded – no mean feat considering he now had an unwieldy 10 legions beneath him, not one of which he lawfully commanded. The remnants of the senate still in the city had remained defiant and refused to legitimize his status in any conventional way.

Occupying the center of empire, with thousands of men and the nearly unlimited resources of the Roman treasury, Caesar dispatched troops in four different directions. One contingent went to Illyricum, north of Pompey's landing in Epirus, to stall him should he attempt to retake Italy by land. Another went to Massilia, on the Gallic coast, where Lucius Domitius Ahenobarbus, consul of 54 and now a Pompeian ally, held the port as a base for Pompey's navy. To Sicily, and from there to Africa, he sent Gaius Scribonius Curio, promoted from tribune to commander in the space of months – perhaps not an unusual promotion given that Curio's father had been the consul of 75 who was the first Roman to march to the Danube (Chapter 13). Caesar himself marched on Spain, the biggest threat by virtue of Pompey's command there since 56 (though the soldiers there had likely never seen their absent commander in the flesh). Almost all met with success. At Massilia, Caesar's lieutenants Decimus Junius Brutus and Gaius Trebonius took the town by siege. In Spain, Caesar put Pompey's legions to retreat at Ilerda and later confined them to a hilltop where they surrendered, adding more legions to his total. The Illyrian legion saw no action at all. Curio's African campaign was the exception: perhaps trying to mimic Caesar's lightning swiftness in January, he lurched deep into the African hinterland beyond Utica with two legions, only to be caught and killed by Juba I of Numidia, a descendant of Masinissa who was working in alliance with the Pompeian governor. Still, Curio had at least won the capitulation of Sicily along the way, securing a critical grain supply for the city as Caesar planned his next move.

As Caesar was pushing troops out to secure the fringes of the West, Pompey was pulling troops in, to join him at Dyrrhachium in northwest Greece. His son Gnaeus sailed to Alexandria and brought back 500 additional cavalry of the Gabiniani, plus 50 ships. Around this time, Cleopatra VII had been forced from power and fled with her sister Arsinoe IV to Upper Egypt. It is not known whether this is related to any Pompeian alliance with Ptolemy XIII. Still more legions came to Pompey from Syria, after he negotiated a peace with Parthia to relieve pressure on that border. Eventually Pompey would hold 11 legions, as well as control of the seas. His senators were numerous enough to convene a makeshift quorum at Thessalonica, and to pass decrees that would later be contested as coming from an illegitimate venue.

The senators still in Rome lacked the luster of famous names, but their location made their legitimacy unquestionable. Now amenable to Caesar's right to rule, following on his success and his clemency both, the senate appointed him dictator at the end of 49 for the purpose of carrying out the election for 48, in which he himself was returned for the consulship. One of Caesar's laws from late 49 or very early 48 was to award a blanket grant of citizenship to Cisalpine Gaul, the province that had contributed many of his legions over the previous decade. The law was also timed to create a northern bulwark for his side as he planned to pursue Pompey, who might try to elude him by coming around the Adriatic.

Caesar's second winter surprise came at the start of 48, when he set sail for Dyrrhachium. His paucity of ships, relative to the number of legions that he wanted to transport, meant that he would have to make multiple crossings, there and back. Against him were weather and Bibulus, and as Caesar rightly calculated, the former kept the latter from the sea, such that Caesar's first installment of troops passed safely, but many of his ships were captured when they made the return trip. Caesar thus had to make do with fewer troops than he wished: against Pompey's 11 legions he could field only seven. A vain attempt at besieging Pompey's camp failed because of these fewer numbers and because Pompey was able to revictualize easily by sea. Caesar was beaten and had to flee, and the only path open to him was deeper into Macedonia. He sent a detachment under Quintus Fufius Calenus to southern Greece, who easily took Delphi, Thebes, Orchomenos, and Piraeus – a boon, as Caesar would soon be in need of supplies – but Athens closed its gates and declared for Pompey. Pompey gave chase but was reportedly not eager to engage. As seen in his campaigns against Spartacus and Mithridates, Pompey's preference was not to take the field unless his position was vastly superior and odds heavily in his favor. Though Caesar was outnumbered and very nearly surrounded he still possessed a sterling reputation as a tactician. It was the senators who forced Pompey's hand and encouraged him to line up his troops at Pharsalus; with some 40 000 men to Caesar's approximately 20 000, he was not entirely wrong to acquiesce.

Nothing went Pompey's way. His cavalry turned in flight in the middle of an attempt to encircle Caesar, and the infantry followed suit. Many legionnaires surrendered, and Pompey and his consulars scattered in multiple directions. Marcus Marcellus and Sergius Sulpicius Rufus, the anti-Caesarian consuls of 51, fled to Lesbos and Samos, respectively. Labienus, Cato, and Metellus Scipio went to the province of Africa. A number of senators were pardoned by Caesar and made their way back to Rome; these included Cicero, who was leisurely enough in his pace to stop in Athens to visit his son who was studying there. Pompey himself, with Lucius Cornelius Lentulus Crus, a former consul of 49, sailed for Alexandria with a remnant force of around half a legion. The situation Pompey found there was not very different from what his son had encountered the year before. Cleopatra VII and Arsinoe IV, still out of power, were at the head of troops at Pelusium, facing down their brother Ptolemy XIII. Still only 13 years old, he was ruled by a committee of advisors, led by Achillas and Pothinus. Most of the Gabiniani, Pompey's old troops, were still with Ptolemy XIII, which must have given him confidence as he sought refuge there, but it was not to be: Achillas ordered Pompey's execution as he landed. Some of Pompey's ships managed to escape but many were captured, including that of Lentulus Crus, who was also shortly executed.

15.5 Siege and Sojourn in Alexandria

After Pharsalus, Caesar's men once again headed in multiple directions, in pursuit of the various paths of flight of the Pompeians. Aulus Gabinius, the close associate of Pompey's for most of his career who had switched to Caesar rather like a reverse Labienus, was sent into Dalmatia; again, we see Caesar interested in this Balkan passage. Gnaeus Domitius Calvinus was sent to Asia Minor to confront, or at least to monitor, Pompey's loyal client kings, such as Pharnaces II in Pontus and Deiotarus in Galatia. Calenus moved from Piraeus to a siege of Athens where some Pompeians held out. The city fell, prompting Athens to make up for lost time with fresh statues of Caesar both on the Acropolis and on Delos. Caesar must also have received updates from his representatives still in Rome, most notably his lieutenant Mark Antony and the urban praetor, Marcus Aemilius Lepidus. They had had their own momentous year, as Milo had returned from Massilia, and he and Caelius Rufus, a praetor now (whom Cicero had defended against Clodius, Chapter 14), were agitating for the usual *populares* causes. Caesar's Italian troops put them to flight and they both died fighting in southern Italy. Once the senate heard about Pharsalus, they appointed Caesar dictator, with Mark Antony as his *magister equitum*, or, second in command. Given this state of war, no other officials, save tribunes, were elected for 47. Caesar himself sailed for Alexandria, evidently behind Pompey by just a matter of days.

Affairs were unfolding so quickly that it is possible that Ptolemy XIII and his advisors were unaware of Caesar's approach as they killed Pompey. That is, while some historians have argued that Ptolemy XIII and others were trying to appease Caesar, it could just as easily have been the case that they were asserting their independence from Rome, full stop. We have already seen how forces in Egypt had pushed out Ptolemy XII for his sycophancy toward Rome; how the Alexandrians instead backed their own Berenike IV, provocatively married to a son of Mithridates's general, hated in Rome; how Rabirius Postumus was arrested for abusing Roman power (all Chapter 14); and how Bibulus's request for the Gabiniani was answered with violence (above). Egypt's anti-Roman stand would gather even more momentum with Caesar's arrival. At first, his force of some 3000 men could not be denied, and he organized a meeting with Ptolemy XIII and Cleopatra VII, who famously was alleged to have been secreted into his chambers rolled up in a carpet. Caesar reinstated Cleopatra and thus was complying with Ptolemy XII's will to ensure the siblings' corule. Caesar was shown the tomb of Alexander, an interesting choice of tourist attraction: could it be that Caesar was looking for inspiration, or, that the Alexandrians who had him in their charge were seeking to demonstrate their own mettle and their resolve to be self-determinant?

Whatever the case, Caesar soon found himself locked in the palace, as riots of Alexandrians, assisted by the ever fearsome Gabiniani, kept him at bay. In one of the melees, a large part of the famous library burned to the ground. In the confusion, Arsinoe IV made her own move: she joined up with Achillas outside the city, only to replace him with her own servant, Ganymedes. Caesar's situation became ever more dire. Ganymedes found a way to pump salt water into the palace's plumbing, such that new wells had to be dug for survival. Relief came in late March of 47 when a navy led by Mithridates of Pergamon, a mysterious pretender who claimed to be the son of the genocidal Mithridates, yet, strangely, was a friend to Rome, broke into the harbor. Additional troops were provided to Caesar by Antipater, a minister from Judaea, and Malchos, an Arabian king. Once again, we see the liquid nature of Mediterranean diplomacy, with multiple former enemies now finding common cause. Ptolemy XIII was ejected from the palace and drowned in the Nile in the ensuing battle. Caesar quickly gained control, and Cleopatra traded her 14-year old brother-husband for a 12-year old one, as Ptolemy XIV was elevated to her consort-king. Arsinoe IV was detained and sent back to Rome as a prisoner. Caesar spent the next couple of months sailing down the Nile. Often represented as a pleasure cruise with a decadent queen 30 years his junior, the expedition in fact made sense, as a victorious general who aimed even higher took stock of Egyptian resources firsthand, and took time to gauge the worth of 23-year old ally.

Readers have likely already discerned that this is the Cleopatra, of all the ones encountered thus far, who entered the pantheon of famous global historical figures. The myths surrounding her exist on a spectrum between the outrageous (drinking pearls dissolved in vinegar) to the reasonable (her associations with the goddess Isis, in keeping with previous queens). Somewhere in the middle one might place the story of her preternatural facility with languages. According to Plutarch, she could speak seven of them, and was the only Ptolemaic monarch to learn the tongue of indigenous Egyptians. This is possible, and it is assisted by an understanding of her filial background, as her father was occasionally challenged as an illegitimate member of the dynasty, as we have seen. She had been born, after all, just as Ptolemy XII was making extensive ties with the indigenous community, including through marriage, such that her mother may well have not come from the usual Macedonian stock. Alexandria was as cosmopolitan as ever, and plentiful opportunities existed for polyglotism.

Shortly after Caesar's departure, Cleopatra VII gave birth to a son whom she claimed to be his. His official name would have typically been rendered by modern historians as Ptolemy XV Caesar, but the moniker Caesarion, or "Little Caesar," has achieved inertia (Figure 15.1). Caesar, of course, must have known that Cleopatra was pregnant as he traveled the country with her. Still, he did not acknowledge paternity until much later. After all, given that the birthdate was June 23, the child would have to have been a month premature in order for it to be biologically his.

15.6 Caesar in Asia, Then Africa

Caesar set off from Alexandria in the early summer of 47 to deal with Pompey's remaining allies around the Mediterranean. His eight-month interlude in Egypt had given them time to regroup and become entrenched in their current positions in Asia, Africa, and Spain; as much on another fact-finding tour as a military march, Caesar took the overland route through the East. In Syria, he stationed Sextus Julius Caesar, a cousin of some kind, as the new governor. On through Cilicia and Commagene, Caesar surely passed by Mt. Nemrut and the brand new mountain of a tomb of the *basileus* Antiochus (Chapter 14); perhaps he made note of its universalist, syncretizing qualities and pondered on them for his own model of the Mediterranean, though this is speculation. Finally he reached his lieutenant Domitius Calvinus near Zela, who had contained, but had not managed to entice to battle, Pompey's old ally Pharnaces II. Caesar swiftly won a major battle in his stead: the brevity of his famous slogan from the victory, *veni,*

Figure 15.1 Relief from the Temple of Hathor in Dendera, Egypt depicting Cleopatra and Caesarion.

vidi, vici ("I came, I saw, I conquered"), may have been an ironic commentary on the two years for which Calvinus had roamed around Asia Minor to little effect, contrasted with Caesar's quicksilver efficiency. The Pompeian king Deiotarus was also reduced, with much of his territory being carved off and assigned to the loyal Mithridates of Pergamon. By September Caesar had made it all the way back to Rome, perhaps passing through Athens on the way where he saw to the construction of a new walled marketplace next to the Classical one, today called the Roman Agora.

Advance missives would have alerted Caesar to the havoc that had erupted in Rome in his absence in 47. Another patrician, Publius Cornelius Dolabella, had taken the drastic step of undergoing plebeian adoption in order to run for tribune and had thus begun whipping up opposition to Caesar, calling for the cancelation of debts. Caesar's most cherished legion, the 10th, perhaps in response to this popular affront, had become violent and oppressive. They were abetted by Mark Antony, who was proving to be much less of a political leader than a military one. Caesar shouted down the mutinous legion and replaced Antony as his second-in-command with Lepidus, the former urban praetor. The same Lepidus then ran for the consulship of 46 alongside Caesar, and not surprisingly, both were elected.

Time was still of the essence: Caesar spent less than three months in Rome before embarking on yet another winter surprise. In December he made the treacherous crossing from Sicily to North Africa to confront the greatest remaining asylum for Pompeians. Unlike in 49 and 48, Caesar's winter opponents of early 46 were ready for him. A host of talented generals had spent the past year-and-a-half building up a formidable army around Utica. Pompey's two sons,

Gnaeus and Sextus, along with Cato, Metellus Scipio, Faustus, and Labienus shared 10 legions among them, and their local ally Juba I had the equivalent of another four. Against this massive force, Caesar loaded eight legions onto transport ships. Upon landing he was joined by Publius Sittius, an exile from 57 who brought his own indigenous ally, Bocchus II, the king of Mauretania and son of the king who had surrendered Jugurtha some 60 years before (Chapter 11). In April, Caesar found himself surrounded near Thapsus, but he benefited from an overconfident enemy. Facing Metellus Scipio, he feigned retreat, drew him in, and then wheeled around to reverse the momentum. Unlike in Caesar's previous engagements against Romans in Italy and Pharsalus, clemency was abandoned. Faustus, Metellus Scipio, and others were killed; Cato committed suicide; Labienus and the Brothers Pompey escaped to Spain. The senate in Rome ordered a 40-day *supplicatio*. Before he left, Caesar appointed one of his lieutenants as praetor – Gaius Sallustius Crispus, the historian Sallust referred to in Chapters 11 and 13.

15.7 A Month-Long Triumph

By the time Caesar returned to Rome in the early summer of 46, it had been three years since he had invested Italy and skipped around the Mediterranean, from Spain, to Greece, to Egypt, to Asia Minor, and to Africa, with intermediate stops in Italy – four peninsulas and a delta. With huge victories and massive stores, he took the time to stage a triumphal celebration to outdo all others, most notably Pompey's of 61. With indefatigable energy, he designed celebrations that were as taxing as his battles. Whereas Pompey had marked three victories at once (Chapter 13), Caesar would have four, against Gaul, Egypt, Pontus (the Battle of Zela), and Numidia (emphasizing Juba I and not his fellow Romans). Whereas Pompey's triumph lasted for as many days as victories (three), Caesar would stage his on and off for the space of an entire month. There would be, of course, food, wine, games, and shows, including a mock naval battle on a purpose-built artificial lake. Always helpful in illustrating total mastery, Caesar put his living and breathing captives at center stage, including Vercingetorix, who was executed publicly. Ptolemy XIII and Juba I were already dead, and Pharnaces II still on his throne in Asia, but Caesar had ready Arsinoe IV, Cleopatra's sister, and Juba II, the toddler heir of Numidia, as foreign representatives.

The celebration started off well, but Caesar encountered some unexpected and unwelcome surprises in the reactions of the crowd. Arsinoe IV elicited sympathy rather than its opposite, and he soon allowed her to leave for Ephesus, probably to quiet these newfound friends. The crowd returned to cheering for the Zela narrative against Pharnaces II, but cries of woe returned when Caesar turned to Numidia. The audience knew full well what had become of Cato the Younger and the others at Thapsus; the effort to suppress bad memories of fallen Romans had failed. Indeed, Cato would go on to become something of a martyr for the cause of the old Republic, with appreciations written by several senators including Cicero. The "history" of Cato was important enough to Caesar for him to compose his own treatise, singling out by contrast Cato's faults and lost cause.

Part and parcel of Caesar's intellectual rejection of Cato and all he represented was a political settlement that he reached with the senate in the course of 46. Outmoded and inefficient trappings of the Republic were jettisoned in favor of a 10-year dictatorship for Caesar along with the powers of a censor for three years. Critically, it should be emphasized that it was the *powers* of a censor that Caesar held, and not the office itself – a separation of rights and privileges from the mess of election that had been pioneered by Pompey and would be exploited by successive political leaders after them. Later Caesar would also be afforded the *sacrosanctitas* of a tribune, but not the office, for which he was ineligible anyway as a patrician. With one foot in, or on, the tribunate, he did the same with that office's frequent adversary, the senate: he loaded the body with his political allies, increasing its size by half and thereby diluting, but not silencing, his opposition. With a view to the provinces, as troublesome as they were lucrative, he limited propraetorships to one year, and proconsulships to two. In any case, this area of politics was neutralized by virtue of Caesar's publication of his plans for who should hold the provinces for the next several years; naturally, his choices were mostly his allies, especially in the more militarized provinces. When he himself departed for Spain, he protected his rear by appointing a special prefect to govern in his absence and in his name.

A surprising, and ultimately fatal, plank in Caesar's platform was the clemency he offered to former antagonists, even the ones who had fought him at Pharsalus. Marcus Claudius Marcellus, the former consul who had fled to Lesbos, was officially forgiven. It did not end well for Marcellus, however, and Cicero's collected letters from his associates around the Mediterranean supply us with the details. In one of the letters, Marcellus himself wrote to Cicero to thank him for his advocacy, even at a time when, he said, he had few friends. But in another letter, a friend of Cicero's reported to him how Marcellus had been murdered in Athens on his way back to Italy. Stabbed in the stomach and behind the ear, but still alive, Marcellus dispatched couriers with a request for physicians, but a following note revealed that it was too late and he had expired. Suspicion fell on Caesar: had he or his associates ordered some kind of "hit," in spite of the official reprieve? Cicero believed not, suggesting there was a different, private motive, but the rumors reveal what was possible. Many may have at least expected that Caesar's vaunted clemency was a sham.

Two characteristics are prominent in Caesar's new worldview. First, following on a complete circumnavigation of the Mediterranean he sought to deemphasize the role of the city of Rome as the locus of political, social, and cultural authority in the far-flung territories. Caesar founded new cities, empowered existing ones, and spread citizenship to worthy recipients, broadly defined. The list of his veteran colonies is long – Seville and Tarragona in Spain; Arles, Lyons, and Geneva in Gaul; Cirta in Africa; Sinope and Heraclea in Asia Minor. He also reversed the twinned destructions of Carthage and Corinth of 146 (Chapter 10) by reestablishing both as colonies nearly simultaneously, and almost exactly a century after they had fallen. The new settlements had the effect of siphoning off large numbers of the urban population in Rome, and with those numbers in decline, so too did the demand for grain become more manageable, with a concomitant easing on prices. Still more of the urban population was expecting to receive prime Italian plots once Caesar could carry out planned drainage projects in the Pomptine Marshes and at the Fucine Lake, which would have created arable land out of nothing. Caesar died before the idea could be realized, and the Fucine Lake would not be emptied until the emperor Claudius, and the Pomptine Marshes not drained until Mussolini.

To existing cities that already had their own long histories, Caesar gave reason to feel invested in a Roman project. He ended the practice of tax farming in Asia, for example, and relied instead on local governments to collect and deliver their obligations to Rome. An inscription from Heraclea in Italy demonstrates that he had plans to establish municipal governments based on the Roman model, writ small. A *cursus honorum* of sorts would regularize political careers and expectations, and the executive power would be dualized, just like the Roman consuls (this reform was also not put into place until after his death). Caesar was also liberal with grants of citizenship. One of his legions, recruited from Gaul, was rewarded with the franchise, as were prominent philosophers and scholars. Cratippus of Pergamon, whom Cicero had engaged as an instructor for his son, received such a grant on Cicero's instigation. We have already seen Caesar's blanket grant to Cisalpine Gaul; similar mass enrollments were carried out at the Iberian cities of Cadiz and Lisbon. The former was home to Gaius Cornelius Balbus, who became an important advisor to Caesar and would continue on in that role to Caesar's heirs. Other cities received Latin status, such as Avignon and Toulouse in Gaul, as well as all of Sicily. After Caesar, more and more people who had never been to Rome or even to Italy would live their lives from birth to death as "Romans."

Second, even as Roman identity was thus being dispersed and diffused, political power was to be concentrated in Caesar, a single individual. We have already seen his assumption of the dictatorship, of the powers of a censor, and of the sacrosanctity of a tribune. There were also numerous suggestions of an interest, at least, in Hellenistic-style ruler worship. A bronze statue of Caesar was slated to be added to the Temple of Jupiter, obviously the *basileus* of the gods. What is more, Caesar boldly allowed his own profile to appear on a new series of gold coins, the first time a living person was so honored in the city of Rome. The senate would eventually decree a new temple to Clementia Caesaris, "the clemency of Caesar"; while not dedicated to the man himself, it displayed a fine line. At a religious festival, the Lupercalia, Mark Antony tried to place a crown on Caesar's head, twice, and both times Caesar squirmed free. Here Caesar was publicly renouncing enthronement, but his statues were reportedly crowned, even so. Caesar would not accept the title of *rex*, and certainly not *basileus*, but he later would acquiesce when the senate offered him *dictator perpetuo*, in January of 44.

15.8 Caesar's Hellenistic Capital

Holding many powers at once, Caesar tackled a host of domestic initiatives from 46 to 44. His first summer, in 46, turned out to be an unusually long one, literally. As early as 50, Scribonius Curio, when still a tribune, had been engaged in a debate about inserting a new intercalary month into the year; with all the rioting and conflicts, adjustments to the lunar calendar had been overlooked, such that festivals meant for the autumn were falling in the peak of summer heat. In the end Caesar, with help from the Alexandrian mathematician Sosigenes, extended the year by an extra 90 days in order to bring the months back into synchronicity with their respective seasons. Since the timing of the seasons was early by 49, one wonders if Caesar's "winter" actions in 49, 48, and early 46, may in fact have been warm weather exercises.

Caesar set out to make his mark on the fabric of the city, sponsoring two major building programs. First, he commissioned a long new basilica, the Basilica Julia, which would effectively form the southern boundary of the old Roman Forum. Second, he laid out plans for an entirely new forum nearby, the Forum Julium. Like Pompey's theater, it was made of stone, was principally defined by a rectangular portico, and included a temple to Venus. Unlike Pompey's theater with its Venus Victrix, Caesar's Venus shrine was dedicated to her in her role as *Genetrix*, or foremother/ancestress. The epithet could have been construed as a reference to Venus's motherhood of Aeneas, a mythical founder of the entire Roman race, but just as easily, it could also have been interpreted as an allusion to the Julian clan's descendance from "Julus," a son of Aeneas and therefore a grandson of the goddess. In this way, the forum may be considered alongside the other evidence, above, for an interest in divinity on Caesar's part.

Neither the basilica nor the forum was completed in Caesar's lifetime, and a host of other projects were planned but not even started. These included a new theater, though one without a portico like Pompey's, and a new temple to Mars. Not only would a dedication to the war god be appropriate for Caesar's prodigious military career, the god was also paired with Venus in mythological episodes, again redounding to Caesar's prestige. Lest all of Caesar's thinly veiled self-reverence be unpalatable to his audience, Caesar also planned to balance the personal projects with buildings that emphasized republican institutions. He planned a massive new enclosure, the Saepta Julia, to be used as a venue for voting, as well as a new senate house. In these ways – new facilities both for elections and for those with lifetime tenure – he would be appealing to the so-called *populares* and *optimates* alike. Finally, he hoped to add a grand library, in keeping with Hellenistic culture that was all the rage in some circles at the time.

In the fall of 46, an entourage that knew something about libraries and harbors arrived in Rome as Caesar's guests – Cleopatra VII, her husband/brother Ptolemy XIV, and Caesarion, aged 24, 13, and 1, respectively (compare Figure 15.2). The motivation for Cleopatra's trip at this moment is not clear. Perhaps she heard of the popular feelings for her dangerous sister Arsinoe IV and sought to compete with her in the flesh. Perhaps Caesar brought her in the spirit of his quadruple triumph, just as Pompey derived prestige from Aristobulus, Tigranes, and many others. She was entertained at Caesar's villa across the Tiber, and Caesar is said to have put a gilded image of her in the Temple of Venus. One wonders if Caesar was drawing inspiration from Pompey's shrine of Venus Victrix in his theater. As we have seen (Chapter 14), that complex was known as a repository and showcase of all things exotic and under Roman control, and Caesar may have wanted Cleopatra to be perceived in a similar vein.

Before the end of this long, momentous year, Caesar was back on the march, this time for Spain in yet another winter surprise. With eight legions and, again, help from Bocchus II of Mauretania, he defeated the Pompeian remnants at the Battle of Munda in early 45. Labienus died on the field; Gnaeus Pompey was loose for a few weeks before being apprehended and executed; Sextus Pompey eluded capture and would live to compete for Hellenistic-style power in the next generation. It is now that Caesar probably established the colonies at Seville and Tarragona and gave citizenship to Cadiz and Lisbon.

Figure 15.2 Boy in eastern dress characteristic of Armenia in northeast Asia Minor, mid-first century BCE. The findspot in Egypt has led scholars to suggest it represents Alexander Helios, the son of Antony and Cleopatra (see Epilogue), though the identification is not secure.

Caesar seems like the type of figure that must keep moving forward in order to survive. By now the Mediterranean was effectively encircled by Caesar's forces. West was the ocean; what remained, therefore, was the world farther East, not coincidentally a famous trophy for Alexander the Great. Even apart from the personal ambitions of their leader, the Romans had an incentive to make a move on Parthia. The Parthians still possessed the standards of Crassus's legions, which were won at the Battle of Carrhae and displayed in humiliating ways. In 46, Parthia had also helped a renegade Roman, Caecilius Bassus, overthrow Sextus Julius Caesar, governor of Syria; Bassus remained in control until after Caesar's death. Caesar's choice of route was to set out from Macedonia, march beyond the Balkans, pass north of the Black Sea, and descend through the Caucasus Mountains. To the Parthians, such an overland attack would have been unexpected and destabilizing: perhaps Caesar had Hannibal in mind, and his surprise land-march to Italy from Spain (Chapter 7). To those living around the Black Sea, such a move meant that Rome would control their shores: perhaps Caesar had Mithridates in mind, and how he founded his economy on that region (Chapter 11). In preparation, Caesar amassed legions in Macedonia, but the campaign would become another unfulfilled project.

15.9 Conclusion: Caesar Exits a World

The senate had boldly mounted campaigns of resistance in the face of overbearing Romans before, and it was no different now. A large conglomeration of conspirators plotted Caesar's murder. There were strange bedfellows among them. The ringleaders were former Pompeians whom Caesar had pardoned: Gaius Cassius and Marcus Junius Brutus, who was the nephew and son-in-law of Cato, had both fought at Pharsalus on Pompey's side and had received clemency. Another thing that Cassius and Brutus had in common was their age: as both were about 15 years younger than Caesar, Cicero, and Pompey, which meant that in 44 they were approaching their early 40s, the traditional age for first-time consuls, which may have contributed to the timing of their bold plan. Probably surprising many, they were joined by longtime adherents of Caesar's, like Decimus Brutus and Trebonius, who had won Massilia for Caesar in 49.

The timing and location for the assassination were both strategic and symbolic. The Ides of March – March 15 – was just three days before Caesar was due to depart, Alexander-style, for his campaign against Parthia. The choice of venue was also deliberate: the senators cornered Caesar in a room of some kind in the theater complex of Pompey. As the premier gift to Rome from Caesar's former friend, then rival, the theater figuratively staged the killing as the settlement of a vendetta. Also, as the most state of the art building in Rome, designed along Hellenistic lines, it garnered attention and oriented the act toward an idealized future. As a museum of the East – the region made famous by Alexander's campaigns, which Pompey alleged to inherit – the theater was a microcosm of the world. Caesar began his eternity, in a way, where he had always hoped to end.

Further Reading

Gurval, Robert Alan (1999). *Actium and Augustus: The Politics and Emotion of Civil War*. Ann Arbor: University of Michigan Press.
Osgood, Josiah (2006). *Caesar's Legacy: Civil War and the Emergence of the Roman Empire*. Cambridge: Cambridge University Press.
Roller, Duane (2011). *Cleopatra: A Biography*. Oxford: Oxford University Press.
Seager, Robin (2002). *Pompey the Great: A Political Biography*, 2e. Chichester: Wiley-Blackwell.
Yavetz, Zvi (1983). *Julius Caesar and his Public Image*. Ithaca: Cornell University Press.

Epilogue: Not the End

Ep.1. New "Funeral Games"

The week following the death of Caesar was a bizarre period of détente, slowly driven awry by confusion and fear – not dissimilar from how Alexander's command dissolved among his acolytes following *his* death. Mark Antony went into hiding for 24 hours until Lepidus, Caesar's other legate in town, led some of his fresh recruits into the city. Lepidus happened to be mustering outside the gates before a planned departure to Spain, which contributes to the theory that the conspirators had not thought things through. Caesar's soldiers laid siege to many of the conspirators on the Capitoline Hill, but the appetite for civil war, at least among the political elite, was not strong. A meeting of the senate was called for March 17 in which both sides hammered out an unlikely compromise that allowed them, ironically, to follow along the path that Caesar had recently plotted for the state. To do so, they had a paradox to solve: exonerating the conspirators outright – tantamount to claiming they had murdered the dictator justly – would tarnish Caesar as a criminal, which would require jettisoning all his productive work of the past several years, and yet, calling for the punishment of the conspirators – saying they committed a crime – would also destabilize the state. Cicero is credited with the way out: Caesar should not be villainized, and thus the conspirators would bear some guilt, but they should be granted an amnesty (different from an acquittal), essentially for the sake of practicality and peace. In theory, important conspirators could continue on to the provinces to which they had been assigned as if nothing had happened, such as Caesar's own treacherous lieutenants, Decimus Brutus and Trebonius, to Gaul and Asia, respectively. A new coconsul would be elected to fill Caesar's vacancy and to finish out the term with Mark Antony. Dolabella was returned by the electorate, and together the coconsuls passed symbolic acts of solidarity, such as abolishing the controversial office of the dictatorship and appointing Arsinoe IV as queen in Cyprus, countering the power of the unpopular Cleopatra VII in her Alexandria and returning the Ptolemaic realm to its traditional bifurcated nature. Antony also staged a public funeral for Caesar with the consent of the senate.

After their negotiations, Antony and the conspirators went their separate ways, but each sought out strong redoubts for the next steps. On March 20, at Caesar's funeral, the grumblings of the crowd had implied a rough road for the "amnesty." Their love for Caesar would only grow upon the publication of his will, as each Roman citizen would receive 300 sesterces, and all would be welcome in Caesar's private gardens, now opened as a kind of park. As the messenger and eulogist who got to read out the testament, Antony garnered some amount of reflected credit for its benefactions. As consuls, Dolabella would have the lucrative command in Syria for 43, and Antony would have Macedonia, where, not coincidentally, Caesar had stationed his best armies for the planned march to the Black Sea and beyond (Chapter 15). Brutus and Cassius, ringleaders of the conspiracy, would have Crete and Cyrene, respectively – not insignificant for any senatorial career, unless, that is, they harbored greater ambitions.

Everyone seems to have realized that a race for power was due to start in the next year, and so each began to inch in front of the starting line, as it were. In the summer, Antony traded his Macedonian command, but not his legions, for a five-year stint in Gaul. His troops were ordered to march in that direction; it could not have been a more baldly Caesarian move. In the early fall, Brutus and Cassius responded by shoring up their position in the East well beyond their Crete and Cyrene. Cassius skipped ahead to Syria to seize the province before Dolabella could get there, while Brutus operated out of Athens and managed to commandeer the armies of Illyria. In Rome Cicero also joined a growing resistance, skylarking in his chosen realm of oratory with a series of giddy speeches attacking Antony for his apparent disregard of the Republic. The speeches were styled as the *Philippics*, modeled on Demosthenes's jeremiads against Philip II that had been delivered in Athens from the context of a democracy against a monarchy (Chapter 1). In November, Antony advanced the timetable for his command in Gaul by declaring it to have begun then and there, displacing the conspirator Decimus Brutus forthwith and not waiting for the traditional winter hand-off. Decimus Brutus objected and Antony settled into a siege of his forces at Mutina.

A new contender for power came out of nowhere later in 44. Gaius Octavius, the grandson of Caesar's sister (of all things), began to pursue independent ambitions. Still in his teens and with many factors against him, any rise would be against the odds for him. He had been far off in Macedonia on the Ides of March, likely preparing to participate in Caesar's planned megacampaign. Though he had been present with Caesar at Thapsus and Munda, he had remained obscure, not joining in battles usually owing to illness or tardiness to the action. He had been elevated to patrician status by Caesar (unlike Caesar, Octavius's father was plebeian), and was mentioned in Caesar's will, but then so were other relatives and associates. Moreover, Octavius's seeming ace – that he was not only mentioned in the will, but was formally adopted as Caesar's son by its terms – was procedurally unprecedented as a posthumous act, and could easily be argued down by the requisite political and religious bodies. While Octavius took to using his new adoptive name anyway, Gaius Julius Caesar – modern historians append the adjective Octavianus to distinguish him – principal players like Cicero whose correspondence survives did not call him that. It was not until the fall of 44, when increasing numbers of senators were turning on Antony, that Octavian finally proved his mettle. He convinced two of Antony's Macedonian legions, on march to Gaul, to follow him instead, and raised additional troops among Caesarian loyalists in Campania.

The aftermath of Caesar's assassination was a low point for Cleopatra. She fled quickly back to Alexandria to consider her options from a place of safety. No doubt in an effort to remove distractions, she rid herself of her little brother-husband and by April was ruling as the sole monarch. She must, of course, have been aware of her sister's promotion to Cyprus. To make matters worse, the Egyptian economy suffered as the Nile inundation once again fell short of normal levels and would continue to do so for the next couple of years. At the start of 43, she cast her lot with the Caesarians, which may be understandable given her son's name. She tried to send Dolabella, the incoming governor of Syria, the four legions that Caesar had left in Egypt, but Cassius managed to seize Syria first and not only absconded with Cleopatra's "gift," but also received ships from Cyprus. Our sources do not say if these to him came by order of Arsinoe IV in her new role, even as she remained in Ephesus, but that would make sense given how alignments were taking shape. Trapped, Dolabella committed suicide at Laodicea. Cleopatra endeavored to send another fleet to Antony, but it was wrecked in a storm. Nothing was going right for her.

Cassius was not the only successful conspirator in early 43. Brutus was organizing a strong force across the entire eastern empire, collecting sympathizers in Athens such as Cicero's son, and forging strategic alliances such as with Sextus Pompey who had a large fleet. Cicero argued for an unusual retroactive proconsulship for Brutus, backdated to 44, in order to justify his requisition of the Illyrian troops against Antony's interests. Cicero probably made use of his notes on justifying illegal powers from the speech of 67 for Pompey's eastern command (Chapter 13); constitutional experiments, which had undone the Republic to begin with, were thus continuing furiously. The senate also ordered the new consuls of 43, Aulus Hirtius and Gaius Vibius Pansa, to march north to contest what they viewed as Antony's illegal seizure of Gaul from Decimus Brutus. Octavian's army was in the north, too, and Antony, now realizing his opponents in Italy were too numerous, lifted the unsuccessful siege at Mutina and retreated over the Alps. It was a victory for the republicans, but it came at the expense of Hirtius and Pansa, who both died as a result of the relieving battle. Safely in Caesarian territory, Antony received the defections of the governors of Spain and Gaul, including Lepidus, to his side, and thus compiled a massive army in his own right.

Ep.2. The Second Triumvirate

As powerful as Antony's army became, it was a whim of Octavian that gave him the greatest advantage for his political future. Refusing to make common cause with Decimus Brutus who, after all, had been one of the group that killed his "father," Octavian made a bold move in support of Antony and turned his armies on Rome itself. In July he marched into the city unopposed, demanded that he and a cousin, who was also named in Caesar's will, should hold the consulships left vacant by the deaths of Hirtius and Pansa, and declared for Antony's side. Decimus Brutus was killed by a Celtic chieftain as he tried to march out of Italy to join Marcus Brutus in Greece. The conspirators thus had no army in Italy, and Octavian quickly laid out his cards: his peculiar adoption by Caesar was ratified; the amnesty against the assassins was revoked; and Antony was exonerated for his resistance of the consular armies. Later in the fall, Antony, Lepidus, and others made their way down from Gaul and met with Octavian at Bononia, modern Bologna, to make plans. On an island in the middle of the river, they devised new political offices for themselves that were modeled on Sulla's dictatorship of 82. Whereas Sulla was the dictator for the sake of "restoring the Republic," they would be the *tresviri*, or, board of three, charged with the same task. This group, Octavian, Antony, and Lepidus, are conventionally referred to as the *Second* Triumvirate by modern historians, but it should be remembered that Caesar, Pompey, and Crassus, the so-called First Triumvirate, never ratified their cooperation with such formal labels.

If the titles seemed ominous to some, given Sulla's drastic actions in pursuing his purpose, their fears were soon realized. After the Triumvirate was established by law on November 27, the trio began to release proscription lists, both to eliminate their rivals and, perhaps more importantly, to confiscate their estates. Antony made sure that Cicero, author of the vicious *Philippics*, was on the list. He briefly attempted an escape to the coast, probably aiming to seek refuge in Greece, but was apprehended and killed on December 7. Over a hundred other senators fell victim to the purge, as well as thousands of *equites*; still more fled Italy and resurfaced in later years. A remarkable funeral epitaph, in which a man mourns the wife who predeceased him, tells of her heroism and ingenuity as she pawned jewels to fund her husband's escape and suffered torture, but still stood firm before the triumvirs to petition for his acquittal. Scholars believe the monument is for the woman Turia who is mentioned in a similar vein in later literary accounts – the coincidence would otherwise be incredible – and the epitaph has taken on the name, the *Laudatio Turiae*, or "in praise of Turia."

Beyond the proscription lists, other stipulations of the triumvirate included three 5-year commands for the signators. Antony was to continue on in Transalpine and Cisalpine Gaul; Lepidus would have both Spains and coastal Gaul, called Narbonensis; and Octavian, the youngest and least tested militarily, would have Sicily, Sardinia, and Africa. Marriage alliances sealed the deals and articulated Antony's central role, as his daughter was betrothed to Lepidus's son, while his stepdaughter Clodia married Octavian. Finally, Julius Caesar was to be deified, complete with his own priests and a temple, which would go up in the heart of the Forum. The political implications of Caesar's deification included increased prestige for Antony, his chief priest; for Octavian, his adoptive son; and perhaps residually, for Cleopatra, who now had a god's son of her own. The cultural implications are that the Roman world took another major stride in its transformation into a fundamentally Hellenistic power.

In 42, Antony and Octavian made the difficult crossing to Greece in pursuit of the conspirators. Brutus and Cassius meanwhile reunited with their various forces, and the two sides met at Philippi in the early fall. Founded by Philip II, the town, like Cicero's *Philippics*, provides another apt resonance between the monarchical Triumvirate and the Macedonian Ur-king. Cassius's side was essentially defeated by Antony, while Brutus's made inroads against Octavian. Fearing prematurely that Brutus had been defeated too, Cassius committed suicide. Antony moved his troops over to take on Brutus days later, with much the same result – the suicide of the leader conspirator. The third triumvir Lepidus had fallen under suspicion of having worked with Sextus Pompey, prompting a reconsideration of their three provincial assignments, such that Lepidus was moved to Africa and Octavian received the Spains. Antony again proved the strongest as he continued to hold the Gauls, but now also took on the task, Caesar-esque, Pompey-esque, Sulla-esque, and perhaps more than all of these, Alexander-esque, of mopping up the eastern Mediterranean. He finished out the year 42 in Athens, absorbing Hellenic culture – religion, athletics, philosophy. In early 41, he sailed on to Ephesus, and by late 41 had progressed to Tarsus in Cilicia.

The route to power still lay in the East, while Italy presented a bumpy road. Octavian was tasked with finding land for the returning soldiers, who were seeking remuneration in like measure to the extent of their many victories going back to Caesar's days in Gaul over a decade previously. Antony stood to gain should Octavian's luster fade, and so he deployed his brother, Lucius, and his wife, Fulvia, to complicate Octavian's affairs. They whipped up anti-Octavian sentiments among disgruntled veterans and would have marched directly on Rome had not Marcus Vipsanius Agrippa, Octavian's boyhood friend and close military aide, waylaid them into a trap at Perusia. Agrippa ringed the walls and forced them into submission after a prolonged siege. Some of the stone missiles that Agrippa's catapults hurled against the Perusines have been found by archeologists. They were inscribed with bawdy, taunting slogans, which were obviously unreadable as they whistled through the air and crushed into the other side, but which demonstrate a morbid sense of humor in the midst of warfare. The aristocracy of Perusia was executed *en masse*; their land, confiscated. Deep divisions among Italians thus plagued Octavian's attempts to govern.

Ep.3. The Return of Cleopatra and the Ptolemies

At about the same time as the siege of Perusia in Italy, Antony, still in Cilicia, received a visit from Cleopatra. According to Plutarch, she had fitted out her vessel with the trappings of divinity and wealth, with a golden keel and a crew of "nymphs." If the story is true – and with Cleopatra one must always be on the alert for overactive imaginations inspired by her later legend – then such ostentation came in spite of Egypt's economic distress at the time. In any case, whether it was through spectacular promises of riches or, as is more likely, a result of close geopolitical plotting, an alliance was formed between them. Antony spent the ensuing winter in Alexandria and departed in the spring of 40 for Cyprus and then back to Athens. For the moment, Cleopatra's most significant gain was the elimination of Arsinoe IV, whom Antony ordered executed in Ephesus at the age of 19. Cleopatra was now the last of her siblings. She would soon give birth to twins, a daughter and son, allegedly Antony's, who, with Caesarion, represented a potent new future for the long Ptolemaic line.

Many readers will know already that Octavian would go on to become Augustus, the first of what we call the "emperors" of Rome (though no equivalent title existed in Roman politics at the time). Given that he would have a long reign and that Rome would undergo a total reorientation in politics, society, and culture under him, one may be tempted to view historical events as marching steadily toward his conclusion. But as of 40, the Mediterranean was still a mess of competing warlords, all with legitimate chances at winning it all. Sextus Pompey was still a major factor, with his control of the seas; the nature of his power was much the same as the so-called pirates of the previous century, though he is rarely called that in our sources. Moreover, a son of Titus Labienus, Quintus, had fled to Parthia, where he was given charge of an army. He and Pacorus, a son of the king, invaded the province of Syria and the kingdom of Judaea and would hold them both for over two years. Open hostility among Antony, Octavian, and Lepidus had to be repaired through makeshift pacts on several occasions. Royalistic marriage alliances came and went in the Roman sphere, as Octavian, whom we saw was married to Antony's stepdaughter, divorced her in favor of a kinswoman of Sextus Pompey, only to divorce *her* in short order (and after his only child, Julia, was born) to marry Livia, the daughter of a senator whom he had once proscribed. Antony's Fulvia died in Greece in 40, and in the same year, he married Octavian's sister Octavia, a relationship famously complicated by his alleged paternity of Cleopatra's new twins, whom he did not acknowledge as his own for years.

Antony and Octavian still acted in collaboration, but only so long as it helped them both. By 34, they were each strong enough to move on the other. Antony had installed the Roman-friendly Herod on the throne (as a *basileus*) in Jerusalem in 37; had driven Labienus and Pacorus from Syria in 36, making inroads against Armenia, even detaining king Artavasdes, the son of Tigranes II; and had captured and executed Sextus Pompey in 35. In one of the summers he almost lost everything in an ill-fated invasion of Parthia, but recovered with help from the funds of Cleopatra. By 34, Octavian had made his own advances. He had recovered military standards that had been lost to the Illyrians by Gabinius in 48; had put Sextus Pompey to flight, which culminated in capture by Antony; had confined Lepidus to house arrest in Rome following a failed coup; and had managed to hold Italy together in an uneasy peace. The relationship between the two men was ever on the brink of total disintegration. Octavian once deliberately withheld troops that he had promised to Antony, and Antony repudiated Octavia, in spite of having two daughters with her.

A remarkable event in Alexandria in 34 might be viewed as the point of no return for the triumvirs' total estrangement, and for Rome's inexorable embrace of the Hellenistic. In a ceremony where Antony fancied himself a New Dionysus (the same title used by Ptolemaic kings before him), he divided up the eastern Mediterranean – the heartland of the Ptolemies, Seleucids, Antigonids, and Attalids – among Cleopatra and the children. Cleopatra and "Ptolemy XV Caesar" (Caesarion, age 13) were crowned queen of kings and king of kings. The twins by Antony were christened Alexander Helios and Cleopatra Selene – "Sun" and "Moon" – imbuing their mother with cosmic stature as well as linking her in a direct expression to Alexander the Great himself. Helios, age 5, was "given" Parthia, as yet unconquered, and other regions mainly associated with the Seleucids; Selene, same age, of course, would rule Crete and Cyrene, even though these were technically still Roman provinces. A third child by

Antony and Cleopatra, called Ptolemy Philadelphos, would rule parts of Asia Minor when he came of age. Antony, for his part, would supply Rome. The effect of these so-called "Donations of Alexandria" was to resurrect, at least in the audience's minds, all of Hellenistic history in a single assemblage. Helios was dressed as an Achaemenid upon his coronation (see Figure 15.2), and the younger, infant son, as a Macedonian; Antony was probably in a toga and Cleopatra, in Egyptian dress. The claims to power of this hyper-ambitious family read as so egregiously contrary to Roman identity that historians have assailed the story as a sham of anti-Antonian propaganda commissioned by Octavian (compare Figure Ep.1). Even if they are false, the formulation of the attack in such a way bespeaks what was thought to be possible for the Mediterranean, and for Rome's assumption of Hellenistic characteristics. After all, even as Octavian was pummeling Antony with allegations of eastern pretensions, even breaking the seal on his will in Rome and publicizing the contents, which scandalously revealed Cleopatra as his heir, nevertheless he himself would link his mansion on the Palatine Hill with a new temple to Apollo, as if they shared the same house.

Ep.4. The End of the Roman Republic, but Not of the Hellenistic Mediterranean

Foreign monarchs continued to serve as proxies for internecine conflict. When Octavian finally declared war in 32, it was against Cleopatra, not Antony, and when he celebrated a triumph after his victory, it was over the obscure Adiatorix of Galatia and Alexander of Syrian Emesa, minor allies on Antony's side. The naval battle that won the war for Octavian took place at Actium in 31, not far from where Alexander of Epirus launched his invasion of Italy in 334 (Chapter 3), and where Pyrrhus began his in 280 (Chapter 5). On the site, Octavian founded Nikopolis, "Victory City," which was crowned with a large square altar with a commanding view, not unlike the great Altar of Zeus at Pergamon (Chapter 9; see Figure Ep.2). Just over the

Figure Ep.1 Bowl depicting Hercules and Omphale, based on a myth of gendered role reversal with a domineering queen and submissive hero. Scholars have interpreted the images as a satirical commentary on Antony and Cleopatra.

Figure Ep.2 Altar to victory at Nikopolis overlooking the site of the battle of Actium and modeled according to Hellenistic styles of symmetrical, terraced architecture (compare Figures 9.1 and 12.2a–c).

mountains were Pydna (Chapters 4 and 9), Pharsalus (Chapter 15), and Philippi (above). Antony and Cleopatra managed to escape from Actium, and Octavian took much of the following year, 30, to make his way to Alexandria where first Antony and then Cleopatra committed suicide.

Modern historians often mark Cleopatra as the famous final Ptolemaic monarch, and so, the last ruler of the Hellenistic Age, yet this is not at all the case. Octavian spared the lives of the young twins (though not of the adolescent Caesarion); brought them back to Rome; and gave them to his sister Octavia to raise alongside her two daughters, their half-sisters since they had Antony in common as a father. In 25, just five years after her mother's suicide, Selene, age 15, was married to Juba II, age 25, and they were made queen and king of Mauretania, roughly conterminous with the coast of modern Algeria and Morocco. In Hellenistic fashion, they grew up to build several showpiece cities with impressive harborworks, temples, palaces, and theaters, and they left behind familiar coinages. Juba II also wrote works of science and of local African history in Greek, presumably as much for a universal readership as for a Roman one. Selene would rule there until her death around 6 BCE; when Juba II died in 23 CE, the throne passed to their son, named, as one might guess, Ptolemy. This grandson of Cleopatra VII was finally toppled in 40 CE, a victim of the brief and tumultuous reign of the Roman emperor Caligula.

The idea of Cleopatra as the final Hellenistic monarch is flawed not just for reasons of her ongoing family line, but also for the fundamentally Hellenistic quality of the Roman regimes that followed her. An examination of examples could fill another book, ranging from the banal, such as the Alexander-esque haircut featured by Octavian/Augustus in his public portraiture, to the weighty and complex, such as political, economic, urban, cultural, religious, and social trends. Augustus sponsored a walk-in mural map of the world at the Porticus Vipsania, which charted out the locations of both the familiar Mediterranean cities and the more far-flung territories of India and China, still alive in public imaginations from the legends of Alexander and his Seleucid successors. Augustus's Altar of Peace (Ara Pacis) featured royal foreign youth from both directions of the compass, a western Gaul and an eastern prince, in the context of a procession. Dynastic intrigues and Roman meddling did not abate: the management of Judaean, Armenian, and Thracian kings and queens are well documented for the Principate, as are the efforts of five different emperors to infiltrate the Parthian court with former hostages as vassals. Caligula's procession over connected barges on the Bay of Naples, galloping atop the waves like Neptune, has Hellenistic features, as does Nero's later participation in the Olympic Games and his initiation into the Eleusinian Mysteries. The father and son emperors Vespasian and Titus's sack of Jerusalem, followed by the detention of the enemy general-turned-writer Josephus, bears similarities to the relationship between Scipio Aemilianus and Polybius (Chapter 9). The emperor Trajan's basilica in Rome, or "*basileus* hall," included twin libraries which, as they elevated Latin literature to an equal status with Greek, paid compliments to the latter. His successor Hadrian brought "Egypt" to his Italian villa, recreating stone crocodiles and river gods along an ersatz Nile; he also deified his "father" (by adoption, the preceding emperor Trajan) and circumnavigated the Mediterranean to universalize his reign. Hadrian's Panhellenion, a network of predominantly Greek-speaking cities to which membership was exclusive and competitive, guarded and celebrated the Hellenic – but really, what we would call by now, Hellenistic – heritage of Greece, Asia Minor, North Africa, and the Levant. Local aristocrats, like Herodes Atticus of Athens, left behind commissions that showed that they, too, like emperors and kings, could aspire to Hellenistic globalism: Herodes staffed a philosophical school filled with students from all over the world, including Ethiopia, and also recreated his own version of the Nile at his villa in Marathon. Septimius Severus and Julia Domna, who ruled the empire from 193 to 211 CE, brought their birthplaces, Cyrene and Syrian Emesa, to the halls of Roman power.

Roman religion in the subsequent era also advanced preexisting trends. The ruler cult that was developed in the Hellenistic crucible was pushed to greater heights through the resources and objectives of the emperors. Mystery cults, such as those of Demeter, Isis, and Mithras, melded Greco-Roman, Egyptian, and Mesopotamian elements. Many scholars have shown that Christianity, a kind of Greek-speaking cult of Jesus, is a Hellenistic religion in its essential elements of baptism, salvation, and an afterlife. Literature, art, architecture – again, it would be impossible to enumerate the many valences. The plots of Menander's comedies, for example, with their pirate abductions and mistaken identities in far-flung places, inform the relatively new literary genre of the prose novel for the Principate. In architecture, Hadrian's Pantheon and Julia Domna's Septizodium, among others, exhibit the same spirit of experimentation and dramatic surprise seen at Alexandria and Pergamon.

Almost all of our sources for Alexander the Great – Plutarch, Arrian, Curtius, Justin – come from this later period of the Roman Principate. By the time they were writing, they knew full well about the parade of heroes and villains from the Republic and the Hellenistic Mediterranean – all the Antiochuses, Scipios, Ptolemies, Metelluses, Cleopatras, and Cornelias – but even so, their greatest fixation was upon the military demigod with family problems and cosmopolitan pretensions who started it all. In writing about the Great One as they did, they were as much writing about their own expansive world.

Index

Note: Page numbers in italics reflect a relevant image or quoted text of the entry.

a

Abdalonymus (satrap of Sidon)   41, *42*, 49
Achaean League   90, 95–97, 104, 114, 121, 123, 128, 135, 142, 156
   war with Rome   159
Acrotatus of Sparta   60
Ada (satrap of Caria)   40
Adherbal (Carthaginian admiral)   95
Adherbal (Numidian king)   174–175
adoption, of adults in Rome   32, 150–151, 163, 221, 243
Aemilius Lepidus, Marcus (consul of 78)   200–201
Aemilius Lepidus, Marcus (consul of 46)   241, 243, 249, 251
Aemilius Paullus, Lucius   140, 142–143, 145–146
Aemilius Scaurus, Marcus   174
Aeneas   33, 102, 116, 146, 230
Aeschylus   13–14
Aetolian League   16, 72, 78, 90, 97–98, 103–104, 106, 113
   war with Rome   123, 127–129
Agathocles of Syracuse   59–61, 65, 71, 79
Agis IV of Sparta   97, 106
Agrigentum   79, 81, 93, 114, 162
   siege of, by Rome   88–89
Ai-Khanoum   46–47
Alexander III ("the Great")   16
   accession of   36–37
   campaign in Asia Minor   37–41
   campaign in Central Asia   45–47
   image of, used as propaganda by others   178, 188, 209, *219*
   paranoia of   47
   propaganda of divinity   37, 44, 47–48
   siege of Tyre   43–44
   theories of cultural policy   49–50
Alexander Balas   154, *155*, 159–160
Alexander Helios   *247*, 253
Alexander Zabinas   169–170
Alexander of Epirus (brother of Olympias)   16, 53
   campaigns in Italy   41–43
Alexandria (Egypt)
   foundation of   44
   locus of culture   62–63, 94, 95, 102–103
Annius Milo, Titus   227, 231–232, 236, 241
Antigonus I Monophthalmus (the "One-Eyed")   44, 53, 54–56, 60–62, 64–65
Antigonus II Gonatas (the "Knock-Kneed")   72–74, 78, 79–80, 81–82, 90, 91–92, 94, 96–98
Antigonus III Doson   106
Antioch, city of   *64*, 65, 80, 143–144
Antiochus I Soter   71, 79–80, 82–83
Antiochus II   91–92, 94, 96
Antiochus III   106, 110, 117–118, 124–126
Antiochus IV   138, *155*
   campaign against Egypt   140–141
   depiction in the *Book of Daniel*   144–145
   hostageship in Rome   128–129, 137, 143–144
Antiochus VII Sidetes   160
Antiochus VIII Grypus   169–170, 176–177, 179, 184
Antiochus IX Cyzicenus   177, 184
Antiochus X Eusebius   184, 207
Antiochus XIII Asiaticus   207, 209

The Roman Republic and the Hellenistic Mediterranean: From Alexander to Caesar, First Edition. Joel Allen.
© 2020 John Wiley & Sons, Inc. Published 2020 by John Wiley & Sons, Inc.

Antiochus Hierax   96, 106
Antiochus of Commagene   209–211, *211*, 242
Antipater   38, 44, 53–55
Antonius, Marcus (commander against pirates in 102)   179
Antonius, Marcus (commander against pirates in 74–71)   202, 204
Antonius, Marcus (triumvir)   229, 237, 238, 241, 243, 246, 249–254
Apollonius of Rhodes   102–103
Appii Claudii, see "Claudius [+ *cognomen*], Appius"
Appuleius Saturninus, Lucius   176, 182–183, 212
Aquillius, Manius (consul of 129)   169
Aquillius, Manius (consul of 101)   179, 186–187
Aratus   94, 96–97, 98
Archimedes   112
Ariarathes IV   128
Ariarathes V   151, 152, 169
Ariarathes VI   177–178
Ariarathes VII   178–179, 183
Ariarathes IX   183, 184
Aristonicus   168–169
Aristophanes   13, 15, 58
Aristotle   16, 55, 59, 60, 192
Arsinoe II   55, 65, 73, *78*, 80, 83, 90, 95
Arsinoe IV   240, 241–242, 244
Ashoka, and edicts   91–92, *92*
Athens
 arbiter of diplomacy   114, 123, 128, 135, 140, 142, 156, 205
 and Demetrius Poliorketes   61, 63, 65, 71–72
 locus of culture   57–59, 63, 241
 resistance to Macedonia   37, 41, 53–54
 sack of, by Sulla   190–191
 war against Antigonus Gonatas   90–91
Atilius Regulus, Gaius   90, 94–95
Atilius Regulus, Marcus   93–94
Attalid Monument, Greater   105–106, *105*
Attalid Monument, Lesser   121, *122*, 137
Attalus I   105–106, 116–117, 121, 123
Attalus II   154, 159, 160–161
Attalus III   160–161, 163

b

Babylon   40, 44, 53, 61, 106
Bacchanalia, controversy of   131

Barsine   41, 53, 56
basileus, title of   61–62, 65, 67, 90–91, 161, 242, 246, 253
Behistun, inscription at   10
Berenike I   55, 71, 72
Berenike II   94, 95, 103
Berenike IV   226, 229
Berenike Syra   94, 96
Bocchus I of Mauretania   175–176
Bocchus II   244, 247
Book of Daniel   144–145
Buddhism   91–92

c

Caecilia Metella   188, 190
Caecilius Metellus Celer, Quintus   219, 221
Caecilius Metellus Creticus, Quintus   207, 208
Caecilius Metellus Macedonicus, Quintus   154, 158–159
Caecilius Metellus Numidicus, Quintus   175, 176, 182
Caecilius Metellus Pius, Quintus   188, 192, 201–202
Caecilius Statius   146
Caelius Rufus, Marcus   228–229, 241
Caesar, "see Julius Caesar, Gaius"
Calas (satrap of Phrygia)   39
Callicrates   135, 142, 158, 159
Callimachus   80, 94, 95, 110, 224
Callisthenes (historian of Alexander III)   47
Calpurnius Bestia, Lucius   174–175
Calpurnius Bibulus, Marcus   220–221, 232, 238–240
Cannae, Battle of   109–110
Capua   31, 56, 110, 112, 172, 185, 212–213
Carthage
 foundation of   8
 mercenaries of   16, 79, 97, 117
 rivalries in Sicily, Classical era   12, 15, 16
 struggles in Sicily, before the Punic Wars   59–60, 78–79
 treaties with Rome, before the Punic Wars   29, 31, 77, 79
Carthago Nova   107, 114
Cassander   54–56, 60–62, 70–71
Cassius, Gaius (conspirator)   250–252
Cassius Longinus, Gaius   186, 187, 189
Cato, see "Porcius Cato, Marcus"

Catullus, see "Valerius Catullus, Gaius"
Caudine Forks, Battle of   48
Celts
    ethnic stereotypes of   80, 93, 95, 103, 121, 142
    migration into Asia Minor   80, 91
    wars with Pergamon   105–106
    war with Ptolemy Ceraunus   77–78
    wars with Rome   29–30, 31, 66, 76, 104, 123–124, 176
Chandragupta   61–62, 91
Chremonidean War   90–91
Cicero, see "Tullius Cicero, Marcus"
citizenship, Roman, for Italians   184–185, 188–189, 240, 245, 247
city foundation
    by or in honor of Alexander   46–47, 92
    by or in honor of *Diadochoi*   62, 71
Claudia (Vestal Virgin)   162
Claudius Caecus, Appius   56–57, 66, 77, 228
Claudius Caudex, Appius   88–89
Claudius Decemvir, Appius   26–27
Claudius Marcellus, Marcus (consul of 222, et al.)   102, 105, 111–112, 114–115
Claudius Marcellus, Marcus (consul of 51)   237, 239–240, 245
Claudius Nero, Gaius   115
Claudius Pulcher, Appius (consul of 143)   162
Claudius Pulcher, Publius (admiral in First Punic War)   95
Cleomenes III of Sparta   106
Cleonymus of Sparta   65–66, 81
Cleopatra (sister of Alexander III)   53, 55–56
Cleopatra I (daughter of Antiochus III, mother of Ptolemy VI)   137–138
Cleopatra II (sister of Ptolemies VI and VIII)   137, 159–160, 169–170
Cleopatra III   160, 169, 170, 176–177
Cleopatra IV   176–177
Cleopatra VII
    alliance with Julius Caesar   241–242, *243*, 247
    alliance with Mark Antony   249–255, *254*
    early career of   238, 240–241
Cleopatra Selene (daughter of Cleopatra III)   177, 184, 207
Cleopatra Selene (daughter of Cleopatra VII)   254–255
Cleopatra Thea   154, *155*, 158, 169
Cleopatra Tryphaena   170, 176–177

Clodia   224, 228
Clodius Pulcher, Publius   221–222, 223–224, 227–229, 231–232, 236, 241
collegiae   221, 227
colonization, Roman   29, 74, 82, 104
    by Gaius Gracchus   172
    by Julius Caesar   245, 247
    and the Samnite Wars   48–49, 65–66
    by Scipio Africanus, in Spain   115
    by Sulla   200
comedy, see "Aristophanes", "Menander", "Plautus", "Terence".
comitia centuriata   25, 121, 124, 190, 227
consulship
    origins of   26
    prorogation of   48, 57, 111
Corcyra   65, 71, 104
Corinth   65, 90, 66, 106, 120–121
    sack of, by Rome   159
Cornelia, mother of the Gracchi   150
Cornelii Scipiones, Gnaeus and Publius (brother-generals in Spain)   113
Cornelius Cinna, Lucius   190–192
Cornelius Scipio Aemilianus, Publius   154, 160
    adoption of   32, 150, 162
    in Spain   157, 162
    in the Third Punic War   159
Cornelius Scipio Africanus, Publius   138
    campaign in Africa   117
    campaign in Asia   127–128
    campaign in Spain   114, 115
Cornelius Scipio Asiaticus, Lucius   127–128
Cornelius Scipio Barbatus, Lucius   66, *67*
Cornelius Scipio, Gnaeus   89
Cornelius Scipo Nasica, Publius (consul of 138)   164, 168
Cornelius Sulla, Lucius
    and civil war   188–189
    dictatorship of   192, 196, 204, 251
    in Numidia   175–176
    war against Mithridates VI   184, 190–192
Crassus, see "Licinius Crassus, Marcus"
Craterus   47, 53–54, 59
Cyrene   8, 44, 60, 82, 95, 152, 160, 202
Cyrus the Great   9, 25

d

Darius I   9, *10*, 25
Darius III   37, 38, 40–41, 45–46

'Day of Eleusis'   140–141
Decius Magius   110
Decius Mus, Publius   66
Deidameia (sister of Pyrrhus)   63, 71
Deiotarus of Galatia   209, 224, 241, 243
Delos   12, 142–143, 145–146, 156–157, 189, 205
Delphi, Oracle at   8, 16, 72, 78, 90, 111, 116, 139–140, 191
Demetrias (modern Volos)   71–72, 120, 121, 127
Demetrius II (son of Antigonus Gonatas)   106
Demetrius II (son of Demetrius Soter)   159–160, 169
Demetrius of Macedonia (son of Philip V)   129, 135, 137
Demetrius of Phaleron   57–58, 61–63
Demetrius Poliorketes   54–55, 61–65, 70–73
Demetrius Soter   137, 151, 153–154
Demosthenes   16, 36–37, 44–45, 54, *73*, 238, 250
dictatorship, Roman   26, 28, 109, 193–195, 240, 241, 244
Duilius, Gaius   89
Duris of Samos   71–72

e

Ebro River   107
Ennius, Quintus   130, 146–147
Epicureanism   61, 63, 225
epimeletes ("protector")   53, 54–55, 145
ethnicity
   and Alexander's conquests   46–47, 49
   on Delos   156–157
   ethnographies of Julius Caesar   230–231
Etruscans   12, 15, 20–21, 29, *30*, 57, 66, 76
Euclid   80
Euhemerus   63
Eumenes I (*basileus* of Pergamon)   91, 105
Eumenes II   123, 127, 134, 136, 139–140
Eumenes (general of Alexander III)   53–54
Eunus, rebellion of, in Sicily   161–162
Eurydice (daughter of Antipater)   53, 72–73
Euthydice (descendant of Miltiades)   60, 61, 63

f

Fabius Maximus Cunctator, Quintus   109, 114, 150
Fabius Maximus Rullianus, Quintus   57, 66

Fabius Pictor, Quintus   111, 129–130
Fasti Triumphales   30, 77, 88, 90
Flaminius, Gaius   104, 105, 109
Fortuna, see "Tyche"
Fregellae   48, 56, 172
Fulvius Fimbria, Gaius   190–191
Fulvius Flaccus, Marcus   172–173
Fulvius Nobilior, Marcus   128, 130
funeral, Roman customs of   32–33, 147

g

Gabiniani   229, 238, 240–241
Gabinius, Aulus   207, 221, 226, 228–229, 231, 241
gladiatorial combat   98–99, 202–204
Glaucias   70–72
Gracchi Brothers, see "Sempronius Gracchus, [*praenomen*]"

h

Hamilcar (Carthaginian general of 480)   11–12
Hamilcar Barca   96, 97–98, 107
Hannibal (admiral of First Punic War)   89–90
Hannibal (general of Second Punic War)   107, 134
   campaign in Italy   109–110, 111–113, 114–115
   crossing of the Alps   109
   defense at Zama   117
   refuge with Antiochus III   127
   refuge with Prusias I   128, 134
Hanno (Carthaginian general at Messina)   88
Harsiese of Egypt   169–170, 171
Hasdrubal (brother of Hannibal)   115
Hasdrubal (brother-in-law of Hannibal)   107
Hasdrubal, renamed Cleitomachus in Athens   156
Hephaestion   37, 48
Heracles
   and Mark Antony   *254*
   in Rome   130
   syncretized as Melqart   156
   syncretized as Vahagn   211
   worship of, alongside Titus Quinctius Flamininus   123
Herod   253
Herophilus   80

Hiero II of Syracuse 87, 106, 110
Hieronymus of Cardia 52, 70, 71
Homeric epic, Roman engagement with 29, 33, 99

i

imperium 26, 48, 57, 66, 97, 114, 200–201, 220, 227, 229, 231–232, 236–237, 239
Issus, Battle of 40–41

j

Jason (priest in Jerusalem) 138
Jerusalem 44, 125, 138, 140, 143, 153, 209, 253
Juba I 240, 244
Juba II 244, 255
Jugurtha 159, 174–175
Julius Caesar, Gaius
    and civil war 236, 238–241, 242–244
    Commentaries on the Gallic War 226, 229–231, 237
    deification of 252
    early career 200, 205, 206, 212
    and the "First Triumvirate" 220–222
    proconsulship in Gaul 226–227, 236–237
    triumph of 244–246
Julius Caesar, Lucius (consul of 90) 185–186, 187, 190
Junius Brutus, Lucius (co-founder of Roman Republic) 26
Junius Brutus, Marcus (conspirator) 249–252

l

Labienus, Titus 237, 239, 240, 243, 244
Lanassa, daughter of Agathocles 71, 73, 79
Laodike (wife of Antiochus III) 94, 96–97
Laodike (sister of Mithridates VI) 178–179
Latin League 20–21, 29, 31, 41
Laws of the Twelve Tables 26, 27
Lex Calpurnia de repetundis 157
Lex Hortensia 76
Lex Manilia 208–209
Lex Oppia 111, 124
Licinio-Sextian legislation 28, 30–31, 163
Licinius Crassus, Marcus, triumvir 204, 205–206, 211–212
    invasion of Parthia 231
    and the "First Triumvirate" 220–221
Licinius Lucullus, Lucius 190–191, 202, 204–205, 206–208, 218–219
Lilybaeum 79, 94–95, 97
Livius Andronicus 82, 99, 146
Livius Drusus, Marcus (tribune of 122) 172
Livius Drusus, Marcus (tribune of 91) 185
Lucretius Carus, Titus 225
Lutatius Catulus, Gaius 97
Lycophron 80
Lysicrates Monument 58
Lysimachus 53–55, 64–65, 71–74

m

Macedonian Wars
  First 113, 114
  Second 120–121
  Third 140
Maccabaeus, Jonathan 154
Maccabaeus, Judas 144, 154
Maccius Plautus, Titus 129–130
Magas of Cyrene 82, 90–91, 92, 95
Magna Mater, cult of *116*, 182–183, 224
Mago, brother of Hannibal 115, 117
Mamertines 81, 87–89
Manilius, Gaius 208
Manlius Vulso, Lucius 93–94, 95
Marcellus, see Claudius Marcellus, [*praenomen*]
Marius, Gaius 206
    and civil war 182–183, 188–189
    in Numidia 175–176
    war against the Celts 175
Mark Antony, see "Antonius, Marcus (triumvir)"
marriage
    and Alexander's soldiers 47–48
    ius conubii and the Latin League 29, 49
    Roman legislation concerning 28
Masinissa of Numidia 115, 117, 140, 156–157, 158
medicine 74, 80
Memmius, Gaius 224–225
Memnon of Rhodes 38–40, 41
Menander 58–59, 99, 129, 146
Menelaus (priest in Jerusalem) 141
Micipsa of Numidia 159, 173–174
Mithridates I 91
Mithridates II (*basileus* of Pontus) 107
Mithridates V 159, 169, 172, 177

Mithridates VI   *178*, 196
   monument on Delos   179, 183
   rise of   177–179, 183–184
   wars against Rome   189–192, 200–202, 208–209
Mithridates of Pergamon   242–243
Mottones   114
Mucius Scaevola, Publius (consul of 133)   164
Mucius Scaevola, Quintus (consul of 95)   184–185
Mummius, Lucius   159
Muses
   Musaion in Alexandria   62–63, 80
   Temple of Heracles and, in Rome   130

n

Nabis of Sparta   123, 126
Naevius, Gnaeus   102–103, *103*, 105
navy, Roman   55, 89
   shipwrecks   93, 96
Nicaea (daughter of Antipater)   53–54, 64–65
Nicomedes I   80, 91
Nicomedes II   151–152, 154, 156–157
Nicomedes III   178, 183
Nicomedes IV   184, 186–187, 202
novus homo   89, 175, 176, 206
Numantia, siege of   163

o

Octavia   253, 255
Octavius, Gaius (triumvir)   250–256
Octavius, Gnaeus   153, 157
Octavius, Marcus   163
Olympias   36, 44, 53–54, 70
Ophellas   60
Opimius, Lucius   172, 174–175
Oracle of the Potter   170–171

p

Pacuvius   146
Paestum   82, *98*
Papirius Carbo, Gnaeus   192
Papirius Cursor, Lucius   56–57
Parmenio   37, 40, 47
Parthenon   *13*, 105
Perdiccas   53–54
Pergamon   73, 105–106
   alliances with Rome   113, 115, 120–121, 127–128, 133–135
   Altar of Zeus   136–137
   bequeathed to Rome   160, 163, 168–171
   independence from the Seleucids   91
   province of Asia   186, 188, 190–191
Persepolis   40, 45
Perseus (son of Philip V)   135, 137, 138–140, 145
pharaoh   4, 44
Pharnaces I of Pontus   135
Pharnaces II   209, 218, 241–242, 244
Phila (daughter of Antipater)   53–55, 63, 71, 72
Philetairus   73, 91
Philip II   15–16, 48
Philip V   106, 113–114, 117–118, 137
   alliance with Hannibal   111, 115
   expansion following Second Punic War   120–121
piracy   179, 200–202, 203, 206–208, 218
Plautus, see "Maccius Plautus, Titus"
Polybius   28, 135, 153–154
   friendship with Lucius Aemilius Paullus   142, 147
   ties to Scipio Aemilianus   154
Polygnota of Thebes   191
Polyperchon   55–56
Pompeius Magnus, Gnaeus (Pompey)   192
   and civil war   239–241
   commands of   207–211, 218–220
   consulships with Crassus   205–206
   and the "First Triumvirate"   220–222
   sole consulship of   236–238
   theater of   229–230
   war against Sertorius   200–201
   war against Spartacus   204–205
Pompeius Magnus Pius, Sextus   243–244, 247, 251, 252–253
Pompeius Strabo, Gnaeus   187, 192, 196
Popilius Laenas, Gaius   141
Popilius Laenas, Publius   168
Poppaedius Silo   185, 187
Porcius Cato, Marcus (Cato the Elder)   124, 130, 157–158
Porcius Cato, Marcus (Cato the Younger)   219, 220–221, 223–224, 237–238, 240, 244

Porus   46
praetorship   31, 97, 104, 112, 124, 138
proscription lists   193, 200, 251
prostates ("guardian")   53, 59
Prusias I (*basileus* of Bithynia)   114, 120, 128
Prusias II   142
Ptolemais (daughter of Ptolemy I)   72–73, 94
Ptolemy I Soter   61–65, 71, 72–74
Ptolemy II Philadelphus   55, 72, 80, 82, 94
Ptolemy III   94, 95–96, 103, 106
Ptolemy IV   110, 117–118
Ptolemy V   118, 124, 137
Ptolemy VI   137–138, 141, 144, 152, 159–160
Ptolemy VIII   138, 141, 150–151, 159–160, 169–171
   testament to Rome   152
Ptolemy IX   170, 176–177, 189, 191
Ptolemy X   170, 176–177, 189
Ptolemy XII Auletes   188, 196, 201–202
   alleged bribe of Pompey   219, 221, 226, 229
Ptolemy Ceraunus   72–74, 77–78
Ptolemy of Cyprus   188, 196, 222
Publilius Philo, Quintus   48, 112
Punic War, Third   157–159
Pyrrhus   63, 64–65, 70–71
   compared with Alexander III in antiquity   70, 79, 81
   Sicilian campaign   78–79
   war with Rome   76–78, 81

q
Quinctius Flamininus, Titus   121, 122–123

r
Regulus, see Atilius Regulus, [*praenomen*]
road construction, Roman   56–57, 105
Rhodes   53–54, 114, 134–135
   ally of Rome   127
   earthquake in   107
   siege of, by Demetrius Poliorketes   63
Rome, city of
   aqueducts in   57
   basilicae   130, 223, 246
   Circus Flaminius   105
   foundation of   20–24
   Tabularium   *195*
   theater of Pompey   229–230
Romulus   24, 33, *75*
Rosetta Stone   124–125
Roxane   46, 53–55

s
Saguntum   107
Sallustius Crispus, Gaius   3, 174–175, 213–214, 244
Samnite Wars
   First   31
   Second   48, 56–57
   Third   66–67
Sardinia   90, 98
Saturninus, see "Appuleius Saturninus, Lucius"
Scipiones, Cornelii, see "Cornelius Scipio [+ *cognomen*], [*praenomen*]"
Scribonius Curio, Gaius (consul of 76)   202
Scribonius Curio, Gaius (tribune of 50)   238–239, 240, 246
Seleucus I Nikator   54, 61–62, 65, 71, 73–74
Seleucus II   96, 106
Seleucus IV   127, 137–138
Sempronia (sister of the Gracchi Brothers)   150, 162, 176
Sempronius Gracchus, Gaius (tribune of 123–122)   171, 173
Sempronius Gracchus, Tiberius (consul of 177)   130, 138, 156–157
Sempronius Gracchus, Tiberius (tribune of 133)   163–164
senate, Roman   76
   lifetime tenure of members   57
   origins of   24
   senatus consultum ultimum   172–173, 182–183, 193
Sergius Catilina, Lucius   213–214
Sertorius, Quintus   200–202
Servius Tullius   25
shah   40, 47
slave rebellions   161–162, 179, 186
Sosibius   110
Spartacus   202–205
Stoicism   61, 63, 106
Stratonike (daughter of Demetrius Poliorketes and Phila)   71, 73
Sulpicius Rufus, Publius   188, 189
Syphax of Numidia   113, 117

Syracuse
    foundation of   8
    and the origins of the First Punic War   87–88
    sack of, by Rome   112, 113, 116
    struggles with Carthage, before the Punic Wars   56, 59–60, 78–79
    under Agathocles   59–60, 65
Syrian Wars
    First   82, 90–91
    Second   91
    Third   95–97
    Fourth   110
    Fifth   125–126
    Sixth   140–141, 144

t

Tarentum
    enlists aid from Sparta   60, 65–66
    enlists Alexander of Epirus   42
    enlists Pyrrhus   74, 76
    Roman colony at   172
Terentia   222–223
Terentius Afer, Publius (Terence)   146–147
Terentius Varro, Marcus   109, 112
Teuta of Illyria   104
Theocritus   80, 82
Theophrastus   59, 192
Thessalian League   36, 71
Thessalonike (sister of Alexander III)   53, 55–56
Tigranes II of Armenia   184, 187, 192, 201, 209
tribune of the plebs   26, 162, 195–196, 204
triumph, Roman   30, 66, 116, 123–124, 145, 147, 162–163, 196, 218–220, 244–245

Tullius Cicero, Marcus   26, *223*
    consulship of   211–214
    exile and return of   221–223, 227–229
    governor of Cilicia   237–238
    opponent of Second Triumvirate   249–251
    prosecution of Verres   206
    support for Pompey's command   208
Tyche   63–64, *64*, 193
"Tyrannicides"   8, 44, 61

u

Utica   97, 243–244

v

Valerius Catullus, Gaius   224–225
Valerius Laevinus, Marcus   114, 121
Valerius Laevinus, Publius   76–77
Valerius Maximus Messala, Manius   88
Venusia   74, 77
Vercingetorix   236–238, 244
Verginia   27–28
Verres, Gaius   206
Vestal Virgins   32, 111, 116, 162, 173

x

Xanthippus of Sparta   93

z

Zeus, in propaganda
    Alexander III and Zeus Ammon   44
    Antiochus IV and   143–144
    Antiochus of Commagene and   209–211
    Ptolemy II and   82
Zipoites (*basileus* of Bithynia)   67, 80